PENGUIN BOOKS

A WELL-SEASONED APPETITE

Molly O'Neill is the food columnist of *The New York Times Magazine* and a reporter for *The New York Times*. She is also the author of *New York Cookbook*, which won the Julia Child/IACP and James Beard awards. She lives in New York City, where everything is in season all the time.

ALSO BY MOLLY O'NEILL

New York Cookbook

RECIPES TESTED BY LEE ANN COX

ILLUSTRATIONS BY AMY HILL

PENGUIN BOOKS

A WELL-SEASONED APPETITE

RECIPES FOR EATING WITH THE SEASONS,
THE SENSES, AND THE SOUL

Molly O'Neill

PENGUIN BOOKS
Published by the Penguin Group
Penguin Books USA Inc., 375 Hudson Street, New York, New York 10014, U.S.A.
Penguin Books Ltd, 27 Wrights Lane, London W8 5TZ, England
Penguin Books Australia Ltd, Ringwood, Victoria, Australia
Penguin Books Canada Ltd, 10 Alcorn Avenue, Toronto, Ontario, Canada M4V 3B2
Penguin Books (N.Z.) Ltd, 182–190 Wairau Road, Auckland 10, New Zealand

Penguin Books Ltd, Registered Offices: Harmondsworth, Middlesex, England

First published in the United States of America by Viking Penguin, a division of Penguin Books USA Inc. 1995
Published in Penguin Books 1997

10 9 8 7 6 5 4 3 2 1

Several of the selections in this book first appeared in somewhat different form in *The New York Times Magazine.*

Grateful acknowledgment is made for permission to reprint excerpts from the following copyrighted works: "Lemon Tree," words and music by Will Holt. Copyright © 1960 (renewed) by Lemon Tree Music Inc. Administered by Music Sales Corporation (ASCAP) worldwide. International copyright secured. All rights reserved. Reprinted by permission. "A Lemon" from *Selected Poems of Pablo Neruda*, translated by Ben Belitt. English translation copyright © 1961 by Ben Belitt. Used by permission of Grove/Atlantic, Inc. "Cherries" from *Collected Poems 1953–1983* by Lucien Stryk, Ohio University Press/Swallow Press, 1984. Reprinted with permission. "American Pie" words and music by Don McLean. © 1971, 1972 Music Corporation of America, a division of MCA, Inc., and Benny Bird Music. All rights controlled and administered by Music Corporation of America, a division of MCA, Inc. All rights reserved. International copyright secured. Used by permission. "The Happy Wanderer," words by Antonia Ridge, music by Friedrich W. Moller. Copyright © 1954 and 1982 by Bosworth & Co., Ltd. For all countries. All rights for the United States and Canada assigned to Sam Fox Publishing Co., Inc., Santa Barbara, California. All rights reserved. Used by permission. "The Sound of Silence" by Paul Simon. Copyright © 1964/Copyright renewed Paul Simon. By permission of Paul Simon Music. "Paring the Apple" from *Collected Poems 1951–1981* by Charles Tomlinson, Oxford University Press, 1985. By permission of Oxford University Press. "Rice" from *New and Selected Poems* by Mary Oliver. Copyright © 1992 by Mary Oliver. Reprinted by permission of Beacon Press.

THE LIBRARY OF CONGRESS HAS CATALOGUED THE HARDCOVER AS FOLLOWS:
O'Neill, Molly.
A well-seasoned appetite: recipes from an American kitchen/Molly O'Neill.
p. cm.
Includes index.
ISBN 0-670-85574-X (hc.)
ISBN 0 14 02.3782 8 (pbk.)
1. Cookery. I. Title.
TX714.O547 1995
641.5—dc20 94–43961

Printed in the United States of America
Set in Columbus
Design and illustration by Amy Hill

To Virginia Gwinn O'Neill

The author wishes to thank some of the superb editors at *The New York Times*, particularly Eric Asimov, Claudia Payne, and Andy Port, who try to make me look good in print each week, and Dawn Drzal, who edited this book and did her best to keep me from embarrassing myself in perpetuity.

Nancy Harmon Jenkins, Suzanne Hamlin, Faith Willinger, and Paula Wolfert, as well as the dauntless Julia Child, have cooked with me, sipped with me, and laughed with me. They survived test runs, suppressed grimaces, and never stopped cheering.

For that, and much more, I thank them.

CONTENTS

Introduction xiii

SPRING

A Season of Second Chances *3* · A Case of the Vapors *6* · Sauté Reconsidered *14* · Druids with 360-Degree Vision *22* · The Asparagus Also Rises *27* · As Life Unfurls *32* · The Young and Tender *36* · A Favorite Thing *40* · The Hours Betwixt Incarnations *46* · A Loose Net and a Very Sharp Knife *53* · A Will and a Destiny *57* · Floundering Around *63* · Spring Chicken *69* · Innocence and Dinner *75* · Forever Fresh *80* · A World of One's Own *86* · The Bitter and the Sweet *92*

ALMOST SUMMER

Act Now, Eat Later *99* · Recipes to Make One Day Ahead *101* · Recipes to Make a Few Hours Ahead *104*

SUMMER

The Season of Brashness and Languor *111* · A Slow Burn *112* · Rubbing the Belly of the Beast *118* · The Quick Fix: Salsa for Grilled Food *123* · To Flavor a Fine Oil *128* · Distilling the Season: A User's Guide to Deploying Vegetable

Juices *134* · Dressing Lightly *139* · Cold Snap *147* · To Make a Cool and Supple Grain *152* · Considering Tomatoes *157* · Essential Eggplant *164* · An Embarrassment of Riches *169* · Garlic Young and Old *173* · Fresh Shell Beans *179* · Why Corn Won't Go Away *184* · Last Call for the Lean and the Sweet *191* · A Full Moon in June *197* · Those Who Follow *202* · To Capture and Cook a Dinosaur *206* · Tender Monsters *212* · Blue Skies and Berries *219* · A Georgia Peach *225* · A Jolt of Cool *230*

ALMOST AUTUMN

Summer's Last Stand *237* · A Supple Maturity: Oven-Drying *239* · Smoked Foods *249*

AUTUMN

A Bittersweet Season *261* · Soothing an Ambivalent Appetite *263* · Cooking Down to the Bones *268* · Fennel from Bulb to Seed *280* · The Rose Beneath the Thorns *285* · Heavy on the Vine *290* · Witches, Warlocks, and the Great Pumpkin *296* · Before the Breakwater Is Submerged *301* · Sweet Muscle in a Cold Bay *306* · Aiming Toward the Sky *311* · The Unfashionable Cloven Hoof *318* · Eve Was a Libra *323* · A Lexicon of Pears *328* · There Are Nuts Everywhere *333*

ALMOST WINTER

As the Wind Blows *345* · To Bake Without Remorse *346* · To Cook a Fine Shank *352*

WINTER

A Selfish Appetite *361* · The Life and Times of a Fine Puree *363* · Taking Stock *368* · Sweet on Yams *380* · The Square Root *387* · Tough Lettuce *393* · Brussels Sprouts *398* · Let the Game Begin *403* · Home on the Range *407* · Rabbit *414* · Easy as Tarte Tatin *422* · Renewing Vows *428* · Sweet Dissonance *432*

ALMOST SPRING

Never Mind the Wind *441* · The Rice Also Rises *443* · Spring Thaw *448*

Index *453*

INTRODUCTION

*T*his is a book about cooking with the seasons. At the most apparent level, each season presents discrete ingredients that taste best when cooked in a certain way. At another level, individual ingredients are the symptom, not the cause, of why we eat what we eat when we eat it. The slant of the sun is no bit player in the vicissitudes of human appetite. This is a book about the interplay between the ingredients traditionally associated with each season and the yearnings and appetite that accompany them. It is a book that attempts to build a bridge between traditional longing and contemporary feasibility at the table. It is a book about cooking for fun and getting a good meal in the bargain.

Health concerns, techonology, and time constraints have eroded the instincts that once informed dinner. Relative prosperity has, for many, eliminated scarcity and the consequent dependence on the seasonal. But the ability to choose any meal at any time has risen in direct proportion to the decline in knowing what one really wants to eat on any given day. Increasingly, we eat by whim. And eating to satisfy a fleeting burst of individual fancy leaves the human hunger for communion unappeased.

In an attempt to cook less lonely meals, I've spent the past three years parsing a basic fact of life that humans share: the passage of time. *A Well-Seasoned Appetite* considers the moods and the atmosphere, the ingredients and the hankerings that weave through the calendar, and tries, ingredient by ingredient, to define and celebrate desire.

The impressionistic—how an individual ingredient tastes, smells, cooks, what it evokes, how it has played in history—helps clarify the specifics. If, for instance, one spends enough time around soft-shell crabs, one begins to understand not only the crab but also the world around the crab and the world within one's self. Cooking is the sum total of the three, and, after a while, cooking becomes second nature.

One begins to recognize the appetite of spring, for instance, as delicate and careful, at its best a little awed and thus predisposed to savor. Perhaps this is some archaic deference to the ephemeral nature of the season's offerings, or maybe it is just a subclinical anorexia that blooms in the time of impending swimsuits. In either case, appetite and ingredients coalesce to demand specific cooking techniques and suggest certain dishes. The impressionability of a life not yet weathered is the essential charm of spring ingredients: they are fragile, tender, mildly flavored, and easily bruised. Likewise, in the spring, you tend to tread gingerly the line between the raw and the cooked, to sauté lightly, to steam.

Summer's appetite, on the other hand, is like an indecisive lover. Subdued, or perhaps subordinated, by heat and the mixed blessing of long, slow days, warm-weather hunger is laconic and lackadaisical. It is loath to commit to a full meal, looking to be convinced. The season obliges with overabundance, bigger flavors, and the siren call of fresh air. In a macho capitulation to summer's lush charms, cooks rush to the grill and barbecue. In quieter moments, one cooks and cools food to eat later, one reinvents salad, considers soft fruits and berries. As overbearing as summer is, the season has its tender side. Of course, in the dog days, the tenderest berries become an icy sorbet, a shale of violent, glassy crystal. Summer's appetite summons extremes.

Fall brings ambient longing to the table. The anticipation of spring and the adolescent excess of summer turn inward and become bittersweet. One begins to think "this matters," and Nature taunts the contemplative hunger of autumn, throwing down the gauntlet of wild game. It's not yet cold enough to dismiss such meals as mere acts of survival. We try bundling game with the harvest, which was earned, after all. The consequence is stews and one-pot dishes. Baking and simmering make their annual comeback. More than any other season, autumn's appetite seeks reassurance.

Winter allows the appetite to indulge in a fantasy of survivalism. With the exception of a rare storm that might block the way to the local grocery, the man-over-Nature mood of winter is not based on reality. But the appetite abides. Roasting, whether in the oven, the fireplace, or a black iron skillet, is impossible to resist. Meat seems the only way to redeem dowdy root vegetables, bitter cabbages, and greens. Dried fruits and then exotic fresh fruits have their day. The fish from cold waters require more coddling than their warm-water cousins. Most winter ingredients demand more of the cook, which perhaps underscores the survivalist mood. In any case, the season's culinary mandates produce a cozy blanket of steam on the kitchen windows.

There are, of course, the cusps between the seasons, when cooking, ingredients, and appetites waver. And there is, of course, reality.

When was the last time you squished along a riverbank in quest of wild cress or took aim at a quail? The purpose of this book is not to turn frenzied urban dwellers into foragers and farmers. It is merely to outline the emotional and sometimes primitive underpinnings of contemporary appetite and move toward satisfying it.

After a decade in restaurant kitchens and ten years of writing about food, I, like most people I know, really cook only on the weekends. Otherwise, I make dinner and make do. There are recipes in this book that take lots of time. There are also recipes that require very little time. In either case, the aim of the essays that precede the recipes is to allow cooking to be more meditation than it is drudgery.

It is impossible to consider the nature of each season without pondering the nature of modern life. Appetite seems to have evolved more slowly than the biological human organism. We *want* certain foods at certain times, but more often than not, we don't *need* them, at least not nutritionally, or in their traditional manifestations. In reflecting on the nature of ingredients and the nature of appetite, I've tried to develop techniques that deliver the flavors and textures that a season demands—with a little less meat, a little less butter and cream, a little less la-di-da.

It is, for instance, entirely possible to use vegetable juices or meat essences to replace oil both as a cooking medium and as a sauce. It is possible to sauté with little or no added fat. It is possible to reverse the traditional proportions—thick cut of meat and soup spoon of vegetables—and create a wholly satisfying meal. And as a woman with a life quest for thin thighs, such innovations are my constant occupation.

But in the end, cooking should nourish life at more than the cellular level. *A Well-Seasoned Appetite* delves into the nooks and crannies of tastes primarily through the senses, those particular ways of experiencing the world that the world, of late, has admonished us to distrust but that remain, nevertheless, the final arbiter of a satisfying meal.

SPRING

A SEASON OF SECOND CHANCES

Shad still runs when it will on the Hudson. Blue crab requires a spring temperature, salinity, and, apparently, a self-selected hiding place for shedding its shell. Aquaculturists have yet to produce consistent crops of the soft-shell crab that appears in the marsh grass of the northern Chesapeake in mid-May. Morels still confound cultivators and continue to poke through the Michigan underbrush around the same time. Despite wide-scale cultivation, there is still something brave and hopeful about the armies of wild asparagus that push through the dark New England soil like so many miners clawing toward the light of a spring day.

But seasonal cooking has been greeted for the past few years with a growing chorus of "Bah! Humbug!" Farmed salmon is available any month of the year. Chilean asparagus doesn't wait for a thaw, and dried morels can take the place of fresh ones summer, winter, and fall. Soft-shell crabs from the Gulf of Mexico and southern Chesapeake have stretched the season from three to nearly eight months. To modern epicurean rationalists, cooking with the biological clock is a quaint notion. When it comes to ingredients, the clock ticks not.

And, of course, they are right. Sort of. Technology has smoothed the boundaries between seasons. Delicacies like shad roe, fresh morels, and peelers from the Eastern Shore are weird little artifacts of a life where things had a beginning, a middle, and an end. Today, individual desire usually triumphs over the vicissitudes of nature, at least when it comes to dinner. You can celebrate this fact as "convenience" or you can bemoan, as a friend of mine does, "the agribusiness's sameness machine." But if you want asparagus at Christmas, you have it. And to feel the slightest quickening at the sight of coiled fiddlehead ferns in Maine, ramps in the Appalachians, or watercress along a creek bed in Virginia or to experience a rush of sweet optimism at the sap rising in Vermont maples is to risk a sloppy sentimentality.

Well, call me a Hallmark card cook. I don't forage Manhattan's parks for salad makings, stalk the East River for shad or keep yews on my terrace for spring lambing. I eat chicken year round. But I've yet to suppress the racing of my pulse when the fish market around the corner from me tapes a hand-lettered sign in its window that announces the arrival of shad roe. To manifest an imperturbable calm would be, for me, giving up some kind of basic hope. Or excuse for hope.

A few springs ago, I was sitting with a group of hip and extremely cool fashion designers, sipping an *express* in a Paris café. Gaggles of the young-and-in-love stumbled by, all hands and lips and smiles. My companions were unmovable, black-draped sphinxes wearing Ray-Bans. Being so far beyond it all, it seemed to me then, was the surest admission that we were, none of us, spring chickens. Which made me wonder about a world in which the tenderest chicken is no longer limited to spring.

The downside of the seasons-be-damned pantry, it seems, is a demise of anticipation, at least the kind of slow-building cultural anticipation that can erupt in rituals like the National Mushroom Hunting Championship each May in Boyne City, Michigan, or the Shad Derby held in Windsor, Connecticut, during the same month. That there is something determinedly optimistic (and atavistic) about allowing the weather to determine one's fate, or at least one's dinner, is reflected in the banner that was stretched across the path from Windsor's town green to the banks of the Farmington River during the festival several years ago: "The Shad Always Return."

In addition to the handful of plants and fungi and fish whose return tells time, certain cooking urges seem untamable and bear subtle witness to the rustle of the calendar's page. Grilling is summer, baking is fall, and long, slow stewing is a fact of winter. Spring is the season of blanching and steaming, gentle, quick panfrying, and rapidly assembled stews.

"The first gastronomic climax of the year brings foods so fresh and young that sauces and spices must be muted," wrote the late Roy Andries de Groot back in 1966, when years still experienced "gastronomic climax" and he published *Feasts for All Seasons*.

"This is the season for cooking lightly and simply, to make the most of natural flavors," he went on. Is it merely coincidental that wild asparagus require blanching or quick steaming or that small chickens are best coddled, gently stewed or braised? The culinary imperatives of ingredients must be obeyed if they are to continue to appease the particular appetite conjured by a certain slant of the sun, the smell in the air, the ambient friskiness that abides in spring; don't ask why.

When spring is in the air, appetite, like other basic human urges, responds. There is a renewed taste for the naive and unembellished. The most thoroughly modern cooks smother and bake their asparagus in the winter, but give these stalwart citizens of the kitchen daylight saving time and the tall pot for steaming asparagus is back on the front burner. Cool, damp evenings, tinged with hope, bring steamed dishes, sauté dishes, and delicate stews.

Unlike the earthy, hefty porridges of winter, the dishes of spring are sprightly, bold in a quiet key, unreconciled, too young to know any better. The flavors summon more giddiness than introspection. Think of dinner as a kick. Think of it as ephemera. Think of being young and in love.

You will then produce fresh and gentle flavors, ones that are in harmony with the shift from winter's muffled reticence to the frivolous season, when humans, like plants, unwrap and uncoil and stretch toward the light.

Even those who find this sort of anthropomorphism of dinner embarrassing have to admit that steaming, sautéing, and gentle stewing fit the spring mood. The resulting flavors resonate with the season of second chances. A rationalist can call it coincidence. Anyone can enjoy the fresh, innocent food.

A CASE OF THE VAPORS

*T*he harbingers of spring are young and tender, like sweet spring chicken or lamb, in comparison to the flavors of their elders. More often than not spring pickings—the first shoots of wild asparagus and watercress, sprouts of cultivated Chinese pea greens, wild morels, and the first of the season's field spinach—are more winsome and giving than they would be as mature individuals.

Like toddlers, youthful ingredients are painfully malleable. They need a judicious hand. The most precious of the season's offerings, such as fiddlehead ferns and shad roe, aren't even fully gestated. Soft-shell crabs and crawfish are actually between incarnations. An overbearing cook can make them old before their time.

Nevertheless, like the photographer who snaps wildly to capture a particular play of light, the cook needs emphatic methods to capture the winsome flavors of spring. Steaming and blanching, sautéing and flash frying offer a quick bridge from field to table. Steaming and blanching have a particular accord with the appetite of spring. What better for the season of second chances than a moist, pure method of cooking that neither adds to nor detracts from the nature of the thing?

In the case of blanching, ingredients are dropped into boiling (and, to my taste, lightly salted) water where, for a few uncovered moments, they are tossed around and tickled by the bubbles then quickly drained, refreshed under cold running water, drained again, and tossed with olive oil, lemon, a vinaigrette, or a sauce. Blanching, therefore, is tantamount to a falling-hard sort of first love: all consuming, quickly ending, only lightly bruising. Nothing surpasses blanching for readying spring vegetables for light marinades or dressings, or for preparing greens to add later to sauté dishes. Blanching loosens the skin and heightens the color. The method leaves asparagus (which should be blanched in a bundle, stem end to the bottom of the pot, until barely tender), fiddlehead ferns (which require four to five minutes in the pot), as well as pea greens, cress, spinach, and purslane (all of which need only be dipped into boiling water and then refreshed) slightly softened and ready for more. The only thing that differentiates blanching from boiling is duration. Which, in the younger years at least, is everything.

Steaming, on the other hand, is more a sustained flirtation than a headlong immersion. Placing less than an inch of liquid in the bottom of the pan and bringing it to a vigorous boil, the cook arranges the ingredients on a rack, suspends them to be cooked in the steam of the boiling liquid, and covers the pot—which, like closing the door, allows nature to take its course. Bathing in the aura of the liquid is, at least from a cooking point of view, more powerful than submersion. The vaporized water is hotter; it moves around the contents of the pot more furiously. Unlike the liquid for blanching, steaming liquid absorbs almost nothing of what is cooked in it. Rather, it warms ingredients in their own essence, forcing them to become more themselves in the crucible of the moment.

Like blanching, steaming doesn't allow the natural sugars in any ingredient to brown and acquire the caramelized flavors that sate cooler weather appetites. Done properly, cooking in liquid warms an ingredient's inner fibers and tissues but leaves them intact, preserving integrity and, in the case of spring vegetables, safeguarding their audacious, grassy flavors. Ah, to be young again, at least for dinner.

To use water as a medium is to steam most innocently. But in an age when the most simply steamed food can't count on a more complex or richer companion on the dinner plate, exotic steaming liquids become more attractive.

Steaming over an intense broth of lemon grass, chili, and mint or over a bouillon with roasted lemon and garlic can give chicken, fish, rice, or spring vegetables a fresh, subtle taste. Orange, chili, and rosemary hint at summer. Like a good perfume, an exotic steaming liquid enhances but doesn't compete with the ingredient's natural flavor.

Steaming is the mandate of microwave ovens, and the recent proliferation of heavy-duty plastic cookware with steaming baskets makes adapting the following recipes for microwave use a matter of understanding the power and predilections of your own machine. For the most intense flavor, it is crucial to get a tight seal with microwave plastic wrap; otherwise, the results are indistinguishable from recipes prepared on the stove.

In any case, despite the fact that using an intensely flavored liquid yields a vapor of powerful perfume, the flavor that the steam imparts is a subtle one. The vapor leaves a hint that life is more complicated than bucolic moments with young spring things. For now, a hint is enough.

Fiery Lemon Grass and Mint Steam

This mixture imparts a flavor that best flatters shrimp, scallops, chicken, or rice.

3 stalks fresh lemon grass, coarsely chopped
1 large jalapeño, cut across into thin slices
1 cup fresh mint, with stems
3 cups water

Combine the lemon grass, jalapeño, mint, and water in the bottom of the desired steaming equipment. Bring to a boil. Reduce heat and simmer for 1 minute. Add ingredients to be steamed. Top up with water if too much of the liquid evaporates before cooking is complete.

Makes about 3½ cups

Salmon and Shiitakes Wrapped in Lettuce Leaves

1 teaspoon olive oil
1 cup thinly sliced fresh shiitake mushrooms
1 tablespoon water
¼ teaspoon kosher salt, plus more to taste
Freshly ground pepper to taste
8 large romaine lettuce leaves
Fiery Lemon Grass and Mint Steam (page 8)
4 pieces salmon fillet, 4 ounces each, halved

1. Heat the oil in a medium nonstick skillet over medium heat. Add the mushrooms and the water and cook until the mushrooms are wilted, about 5 minutes. Season with the salt and pepper.

2. Steam the lettuce leaves over the steaming liquid for 30 seconds. Remove the liquid from the heat. Cut the center stem out of each lettuce leaf and overlap the lettuce where the stem was. Season the salmon with salt and pepper.

3. Place 1 piece of salmon on the center of each leaf and top with some of the mushrooms. Fold the sides of the leaves in over the salmon and mushrooms, then roll the salmon up in the leaves, making a tight little package.

4. Bring the steaming liquid back to a simmer, place the salmon in the steamer, cover, and steam for 8 minutes. Place 2 packages on each of 4 plates and serve immediately.

Serves four as a main course

Roasted Lemon and Garlic Vapor

This steam gives a fresh, slightly roasted punch to potatoes, leeks, or couscous. It also brings out the best in chicken, shellfish, and white fleshed fish.

2 small heads garlic, smashed
2 lemons, cut across into ⅛-inch slices
2 tablespoons olive oil
1 bay leaf
½ teaspoon black peppercorns
3 cups water

1. Preheat the oven to 375° F.

2. Put the garlic on a large sheet of aluminum foil and surround with the lemon slices. Drizzle with the olive oil. Wrap the foil into a package and roast until the garlic is soft, about 1 hour.

3. Place the garlic, lemon slices, and accumulated juices in the bottom of the desired steaming equipment with the bay leaf, peppercorns, and water. Bring to a boil. Reduce heat and simmer for 1 minute. Add the ingredients to be steamed. Top up with boiling water if too much of the liquid evaporates before cooking is complete.

Makes about 3½ cups

Chicken Rolls with Couscous and Green Olives

20 pitted green olives
1 cup Italian parsley leaves
2 tablespoons fresh lemon juice
6 tablespoons water
2 boneless and skinless chicken breasts, about 8 ounces each, split
Kosher salt and freshly ground pepper to taste
2 cups cooked couscous
Roasted Lemon and Garlic Vapor (page 10)

1. Put the olives, parsley, lemon juice, and water in a food processor. Process until the mixture forms a loose paste, stopping several times to scrape down the sides of the bowl.

2. Pound the chicken to a scant ¼-inch thickness and season with salt and pepper. Press ½ cup couscous over the surface of each piece of chicken. Divide the olive mixture among them and spread it over the couscous. Starting with one of the long sides of the chicken, roll it up tightly, like a jelly roll. Repeat with the remaining chicken.

3. Place the chicken rolls in a steamer, cover, and steam over the liquid for 12 minutes. Trim off the ends and cut across into 1-inch slices. Divide among 4 plates and serve immediately.

Serves 4 as a main course

Orange, Chili, and Rosemary Vapor

This steam is subtly sweet and spicy and complements duck, pork, rice, or full-bodied fish.

1 cup orange juice
¼ teaspoon grated orange zest
5 sprigs fresh rosemary
1 small jalapeño, cut across into thin slices
½ cup white wine
2 cups water

Combine the orange juice, zest, rosemary, jalapeño, white wine, and water in the bottom of the desired steaming equipment. Bring to a boil. Reduce heat and simmer for 1 minute. Add the ingredients to be steamed. Top up with boiling water if too much of the liquid evaporates before cooking is complete.

Makes about 3 ½ cups

Trout with Sticky Rice, Zucchini, and Pine Nuts

1 cup cooked sticky rice (also called sweet or high-gluten rice)
½ cup finely diced zucchini
2 teaspoons grated orange zest
1 tablespoon chopped Italian parsley
2 tablespoons toasted pine nuts, coarsely chopped
1 teaspoon kosher salt, plus more to taste
Freshly ground pepper to taste
4 trout fillets, 4 ounces each
Orange, Chili, and Rosemary Vapor (page 12)

Stir together the rice, zucchini, orange zest, parsley, pine nuts, 1 teaspoon salt, and pepper. Season the trout fillets with salt and pepper. Divide the rice mixture evenly among the fillets, pressing it into a mound running the length of the fish. Place the fillets in a steamer, cover, and steam over the liquid until the trout is just cooked through, about 5 minutes. Divide among 4 plates and serve immediately.

Serves 4 as a main course

SAUTÉ RECONSIDERED

Spring celebrates any signal of the new eclipsing the old. In a settled society, this is always a surprising occurrence, and that's compatible with Brillat-Savarin's take on sautéing. He called the instant transformation of food in a hot skillet, its sizzle, its seizing and browning, "the surprise." The initial violence of the technique is mitigated by its end result: The heat blasted on the surface of the food browns and flavors it, while moving gently inside a paillard of meat, for instance, to barely warm its center.

When I was initially tutored in the fine art of sautéing in professional kitchens, this action was called "sealing." The prevailing philosophy was that by crusting, or browning, the meat, the cook formed a sealed container for the precious (and in the case of young, spring food, the scant) juices inside. This was held as a God-ordained truth, with much citing of Escoffier, who referred to the browned exterior of sautéed food as "armor."

When paillards of meat brown quickly in a hot skillet, a subtle contrast of flavors is created between the cooked and the uncooked; less subtle is the contrast in texture between the meat's crusty exterior and its barely warm, pliant center. The same thing happens to fish, shellfish, and vegetables, only faster: Browning draws the juices from the center to the surface, but with less fat inside to mitigate the flow, a second too long and the succulence becomes cardboard. This is particularly so when sautéing a thin fish fillet or a tiny shrimp with a Spartan amount of fat. You must, therefore, prepare very carefully for those few seconds of sizzle.

First, choose your weapon. According to *Larousse Gastronomique*, sautéing should be done in a shallow copper pan with straight sides. For heavier cuts of meat or fish, there's a logic to this choice—the pan's construction promotes an even and sustained distribution of heat. But for smaller morsels, a slope-sided skillet is a better tool. It's easier to shake.

Vigorous and almost constant shaking prevents the food from sticking and helps brown the surface evenly. This is paramount. More than any other cooking technique, sautéing requires a finely calibrated symmetry between heat and motion.

A copper pan with a tin-lined surface makes it difficult to achieve kiln-high temperatures. Better to use a heavy-gauge stainless steel, aluminum, or nonstick skillet.

Next, choose your medium. When using slimmer cuts of meat or fish, the key is high heat and quick exposure. The longer the food is cooked, the more its juices are pulled into the pan. The cook may eventually recapture these juices by deglazing the pan with water, wine, or broth and creating a sauce. But gravity can't pull the juices back into the food as fast as heat can leach them out. Vegetable oil, including olive oil, which can be heated as high as 450° F., is therefore a better medium for thin cuts than butter, which can only reach about 250° F. before burning.

Next, prepare your subject. By lightly seasoning the surface of food with salt and pepper, you get a head start on pulling the juices to the surface. Seasoning is one of the finer points in the rhythm of sauté. After watching me bend over some shrimp, salt pressed between thumb and index finger, one chef advised, "Season from on high," raising his forearm in a 90° angle above the food to demonstrate. "There's not enough flesh or enough cooking time to even out an erratic parceling," he explained. He was right. Symmetry, again.

After seasoning, heat either a nonstick pan or heat oil in a conventional skillet over high heat until it threatens to smoke. Then, moving fast, tip the skillet (and therefore the oil) away from yourself to avoid a spiteful spatter. Quickly place the ingredients in the pan. There will be a sizzle and a hiss as the cool food collides with the fiery surface, which are your cue to shake the pan.

To shake with alacrity, grasp the handle and, moving from the shoulder not the forearm, begin pulling it back and forth on the burner until the food is cooked evenly on all sides. Unless fish is dusted lightly with flour prior to sautéing, the visual change is subtle, much more so than with meat. Instead, the cook will first notice a change in aroma: the same roasted smell that's separated man from beast since the first neolithic spit.

But do not stop to consider your forebears. At this point, a contemplative moment could cost you your dinner. That first whiff is your signal that a perfect balance has been reached between the food's toasted exterior and the moisture still within it. Seize the moment! Get the food out of the pan and proceed to make the sauce or top with the salad that will add more volume, more contrast, and more flavor to the dish. Expect applause.

Flounder Sauté with Asparagus and Crab Vinaigrette

¾ pound asparagus, ends snapped off, cut into 1-inch pieces
2 teaspoons fresh lime juice
3 teaspoons olive oil
1 cup lump crabmeat, picked over for cartilage and shells
Kosher salt and freshly ground black pepper to taste
2 tablespoons all-purpose flour
4 flounder fillets, 3 to 4 ounces each, or 2 fillets, 8 ounces each,
    split down the center

1. Bring a medium pot of water to a boil. Add the asparagus and blanch until tender, but not soft, about 3 minutes. Drain and place under cold running water until cool. Whisk together the lime juice and 2 teaspoons of the olive oil in a medium bowl. Toss the asparagus and crabmeat in the vinaigrette sauce and season with salt and pepper. Set aside.

2. Place the flour on a plate and season to taste with salt and pepper. Lightly dust the flounder on both sides with the seasoned flour. Heat the remaining teaspoon olive oil in a large heavy nonstick skillet over high heat. Place the flounder in the pan and sauté on one side for about 90 seconds. Turn the fish over and immediately spoon the asparagus and crab mixture over the fillets. Remove from the heat. Cover the pan and let stand for 1 minute. Divide among 4 plates and serve immediately.

Serves 4 as a main course

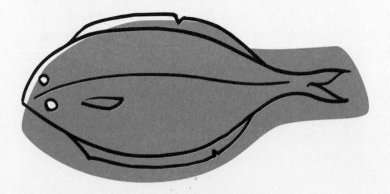

Seared Salmon Scallops with Warm Potato and Snap Pea Salad

12 very small new potatoes, scrubbed

3 cups Sugar Snap peas, stemmed and strung

4 pieces salmon fillet, 4 ounces each

Kosher salt and freshly ground pepper to taste

3 teaspoons olive oil

1 tablespoon fresh lemon juice

2 tablespoons chopped fresh dill

1. Put the potatoes in a medium saucepan and cover with cold water. Cook over medium heat until tender, about 12 minutes. Drain and halve the potatoes. Set aside. Meanwhile, bring a medium saucepan of salted water to boil. Add the peas and blanch for 3 minutes. Drain and set aside.

2. Season the salmon with salt and pepper. Heat a large heavy-bottomed non-stick skillet over medium heat until hot. Add 1 teaspoon of the olive oil. Add the salmon and sauté until just cooked through, about 2½ minutes per side. Place 1 piece of salmon in the center of each of 4 warm plates.

3. Transfer the potatoes and peas to the skillet and toss until warmed through. Remove from the heat and toss with the remaining 2 teaspoons of olive oil, the lemon juice, and salt and pepper to taste. Arrange around the salmon, sprinkle with dill, and serve immediately.

Serves 4 as a main course

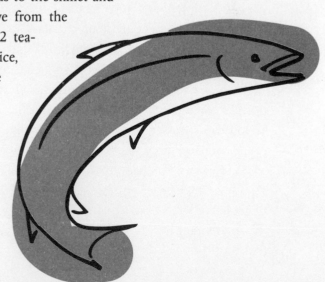

Sesame-Crusted Tofu with Carrots and Spinach

Five-spice powder is an aromatic combination of star anise, cassia bark, Sichuan peppercorns, fennel seed, and clove.

½ cup all-purpose flour
½ teaspoon five-spice powder
2 large egg whites
½ cup water or light vegetable broth
5 tablespoons teriyaki sauce
½ cup sesame seeds
1 pound fresh tofu, cut into 8½ × 3 × 2-inch pieces
1 cup thinly sliced carrots
2 teaspoons minced fresh ginger
1 teaspoon dark sesame oil
¾ pound spinach, cleaned and stemmed
⅛ teaspoon crushed red pepper
Vegetable oil spray

1. Combine the flour and five-spice powder on a plate. Combine the egg whites, 2 tablespoons water, and 2 tablespoons teriyaki sauce in a shallow bowl. Spread out the sesame seeds on a plate. Dip 1 side of each piece of tofu into the flour mixture, then into the egg white mixture, and then gently press into the sesame seeds. Place, seed side up, on a plate and set aside.

2. Combine the carrots, ginger, sesame oil, remaining water, and remaining teriyaki sauce in a medium saucepan. Cook, covered, over medium heat until the carrots are crisp-tender, about 4 to 5 minutes. Add the spinach and red pepper, cover, and cook until tender. Keep warm.

3. Heat a large heavy-bottomed nonstick skillet over medium heat until hot. Lightly coat with the vegetable oil spray. Add the tofu, seed side down, and sauté until golden brown, about 3 to 4 minutes. Turn and cook on the other side until brown.

4. Divide the carrot mixture with its liquid among 4 plates. Top each with 2 pieces of tofu and serve immediately.

Serves 4 as a main course

Pepper and Onion–Topped Chicken Paillards

SALAD

> 1 *each* red, green, and yellow bell peppers, seeded and sliced into thin strips
>
> 1 red onion, very thinly sliced
>
> 2 oranges, skin and pith peeled and cut between membranes into sections
>
> Kosher salt and freshly ground pepper to taste

CHICKEN

> ½ cup cornmeal
>
> ¼ cup all-purpose flour
>
> ¼ teaspoon cayenne
>
> ¼ teaspoon ground fennel seed
>
> 4 boneless and skinless chicken breast halves, flattened to $3/16$ inch
>
> 1 teaspoon olive oil

1. Toss the peppers, onion, oranges, and salt and pepper together in a glass or ceramic bowl and set aside. Combine the cornmeal, flour, cayenne, and fennel on a plate. Coat each piece of chicken in the mixture.

2. Heat a large heavy-bottomed nonstick skillet over medium-high heat until very hot. Add the oil. Place the chicken in the skillet and sauté until golden brown and cooked through, about 2 minutes per side. Place 1 piece of chicken on each of 4 plates, top with the salad, and serve immediately.

Serves 4 as a main course

Artichoke-Mint Salad over Lamb Chops

SALAD

    2 cups very thinly sliced defrosted frozen artichoke hearts
    2 tablespoons fresh lemon juice
    3 tablespoons minced fresh mint
    3 tablespoons minced Italian parsley
    ½ teaspoon kosher salt, plus more to taste
    Freshly ground pepper to taste

LAMB

    4 loin lamb chops, about ¾ inch thick
    Salt and freshly ground pepper to taste

1. Toss the artichoke hearts, lemon juice, mint, parsley, salt, and pepper together and set aside.

2. Heat a large heavy-bottomed nonstick skillet over medium-high heat until very hot. Place lamb chops in the pan and sauté until medium-rare, about 3 minutes per side. Sprinkle with salt and pepper. Place 1 lamb chop on each of 4 plates. Top with the salad and serve.

Serves 4 as a main course

Peppered Beef with Watercress and Cucumber

SALAD

   2 cups watercress leaves

   2 cucumbers, peeled, halved, seeded, and julienned

   4 teaspoons fresh lemon juice

   8 teaspoons olive oil

   ¼ teaspoon kosher salt

   Freshly ground black pepper to taste

BEEF

   1 pound beef tenderloin, cut into 4 equal pieces and flattened to almost ¼ inch

   2 tablespoons cracked black peppercorns

1. Toss the watercress and cucumbers together in a glass or ceramic bowl. Add the lemon juice, olive oil, salt, and pepper and toss to coat. Set aside.

2. Heat a large heavy-bottomed nonstick skillet over medium-high heat until very hot.

3. Meanwhile, coat each piece of beef on both sides with the peppercorns. Place in the pan and sauté until medium-rare, about 30 seconds per side. Place a piece of beef on each of 4 plates, top with the salad, and serve immediately.

Serves 4 as a main course

DRUIDS WITH 360-DEGREE VISION

Morels, the wrinkled, honeycombed, druid cap–shaped mushrooms that push through barely thawed earth in Italy, France, Switzerland, and northerly parts of the American Midwest, pay a certain homage to winter yet they are harbingers of gentler days. They look like mushrooms à la Disney. But since they are hollow little huts of cartilage, they deliver only a hint of the woodsy flavor of the late autumn cousins; their taste variously hints of hazelnuts or nutmeg, and even more vaguely of smoke. In general, they bring no-longer-winter, not-quite-spring nuance to a dish.

Unlike any other mushroom, a morel's charm lies more in its snap than its substance. In fact it is a phantom mushroom, bringing more air and suggestion than earthiness to the table. If a taster is blindfolded, it takes a significantly well honed palate to detect the presence of a morel. On sighting, however, a morel could be nothing else. A relative of the truffle, the morel is an ascomyceter; rather than having the gills and pores that give a fall mushroom girth, it has wrinkles and pocks in its spore-bearing cap. The mushrooms of late fall and early winter surge to beat the snow. Morels push against it, especially in Minnesota and Michigan, a valiant declaration of spring rising from the sandy soil with underlying chalk that lines the edges of woods, banks, or pastures. Like so many phoenixes, morels also push up from burned woodlands from late March to early May.

That morels must be cooked—raw they can be indigestible to some—makes the mushroom part of winter's last stand. That their hollow bodies and deep pores can harbor insects may be nature's reminder of summer things to come. Morels are on the fence. A little bit of winter, a little bit of summer: by deduction, then, completely spring. That they are cute and endearing, seeming as they do capable of being trees for Hobbits or other mystical beings, has probably increased the morel's charm.

At festivals such as the Harridan Mushroom Festival in Harridan, Michigan, and the aforementioned National Mushroom Hunting Championship in Boyne

City, Michigan, foragers are well aware of the distinction between edible morels and their poisonous look-alike *"Gyromitra esculenta,"* or false morel, whose honeycombed hat is free-form, as opposed to the symmetrically lobed bonnet of the edible version. They also know the difference between the two most delicious species, *Morchella esculenta* and *Morchella elata,* the former having a spongier appearance with a flesh-colored cap and cream-colored stem, the latter being more crisp than spongy and having a pale brown cap and white stem.

Gatherers such as Billy Mavis, an aficionado who grew up in the Upper Peninsula of Michigan, know to use a sharp knife and to cut the fungi as closely to the cap as a couturier cuts a garment to the body, thus avoiding the sandy stem parts. He knows that crispness is paramount in morels and rinsing can be anathema. He knows that a druid cap pierced by tiny holes signals insect infestation and makes thorough rinsing necessary, though running cold water may compromise the ultimate crunchiness of the fungus. He knows that whether rinsed or *au naturel,* a morel should be patted gently dry before cooking; moisture first promotes the fungi and then becomes the enemy, causing it to deteriorate. He knows that like asparagus, fiddleheads, corn, and many fish, the mushroom should be cooked immediately, as its passage from delicacy to discardability is remarkably short. Gently pressed dry between paper towels, morels can successfully be stored for several days, but they are at their best cooked within hours of picking. If buying the mushrooms, keep in mind that the stems are tough and are the most likely lurking place for sand; choose ones with the shortest stems. Dry stems or caps are not a problem, damp ones could be. The best morels are almost odorless; at first sniff, they may smell slightly nutty.

Billy Mavis does not know, however, what the big price that morels command is all about. "They're there for the taking, so you take them. They come before the grass or the fiddleheads, so you celebrate them. Still, their flavor is so mild that you wonder about them," he said.

What cook doesn't?

The tawny morel lacks the audacity of greener spring things. Unlike other offerings, it requires a contemplative taster to discern its presence, to say nothing of its nuance. Unlike most spring ingredients, the morel imbues rather than bestows. Its flavor is so subtle it is elusive. Therefore, the mushroom requires speed and agility in the kitchen; only the sauté expert can capture it at its best. Nevertheless, the mushroom is precious. It suggests a subtle warming, a nearly imperceptible lengthening of the sun, signals that are, for now, as elusive as the flavor of a morel.

Morels are high maintenance. They require much from the forager, and even more from the diner who must contemplate their flavor in order to appreciate their emergence. The morel is a luxury mostly because it is a lesson. Sometimes, you have to try very hard to receive what a season begets.

Morel Gratin

1 tablespoon unsalted butter
3 tablespoons chopped shallots
½ pound fresh morels, rinsed if sandy and dried well
1 teaspoon kosher salt
¼ cup heavy cream
2 tablespoons cognac
2 tablespoons freshly grated Parmesan cheese

Preheat the broiler. Melt the butter in a medium cast-iron skillet over medium-low heat. Add the shallots and cook until soft, about 3 minutes. Add the morels and salt and cook, stirring occasionally, for 10 minutes. Stir in the cream and cognac and simmer for 5 minutes longer. Sprinkle with the Parmesan and place under the broiler until browned. Divide among 4 plates and serve immediately.

Serves 4 as a first course or side dish

Fettuccine with Fresh Morels

1 pound dried fettuccine
Morel Gratin (page 24)
3 tablespoons chopped Italian parsley
Kosher salt and freshly ground pepper to taste

Bring a large pot of salted water to a boil. Add the fettuccine and cook until al dente. Drain. Toss with the morel gratin and the parsley. Season with salt and pepper. Divide among 4 plates and serve immediately.

Serves 4 as a main course

Potato, Leek, and Morel Salad with Truffle Oil Vinaigrette

SALAD

- 1 pound small new potatoes, scrubbed and halved
- 8 small leeks, trimmed and cleaned
- 2 teaspoons olive oil
- 3 tablespoons thinly sliced scallions
- ¾ pound fresh morels, rinsed if sandy and dried well, halved or quartered if large
- ½ teaspoon kosher salt

VINAIGRETTE

- ½ teaspoon Dijon mustard
- 2 tablespoons sherry vinegar
- ½ teaspoon kosher salt
- Freshly ground pepper to taste
- 2 teaspoons truffle oil

1. Place the potatoes in a large saucepan and cover with cold water. Simmer, covered, over medium heat until tender, about 15 minutes. Drain and set aside. Bring a medium pot of lightly salted water to a boil, add the leeks, and poach until tender, about 10 minutes. Drain and set aside.

2. Heat the olive oil in a large nonstick skillet over medium heat. Add the scallions and cook until soft, about 3 minutes. Add the morels and cook, stirring occasionally, for 10 minutes. Toss in the potatoes and season with salt.

3. Whisk together the mustard, vinegar, salt, and pepper in a small bowl. Whisk in the truffle oil. Add the vinaigrette to the morel mixture and toss. Cut the leeks in half lengthwise. Mound the salad in the center of 4 plates and lean the leek halves around the salad. Serve immediately.

Serves 4 as a first course

THE ASPARAGUS ALSO RISES

In western Massachusetts, there is a certain field where, after a deep freeze and slow thaw, after a warmish rain and a gentle sun, wild asparagus rise like a gangly army every year. It takes an acutely focused eye to discern the spears. Even if their tips have a lavender blush, wild asparagus are nearly indistinguishable from the grass and stems of purple, blue, and yellow wild flowers that precede them in the field. This is fitting for the asparagus which, like other members of the lily family, is a relative of the grasses. Hence, in the wild form at least, asparagus have a flavor that wine writers call "grassy" or "herbaceous" when found in a fresh white wine.

Pencil-thin wild asparagus also have a greater peel-to-inner-flesh ratio than their fatter, cultivated cousins, hence wild grass offers a taut, snappy, more fibrous, less mushy chew. The cultivated varieties tend also to have a milder taste; Chilean and other winter supermarket asparagus can even have a sugary flavor. But the passion for wild asparagus is more than simply a flavor and texture preference.

I shared the wild asparagus patch in western Massachusetts with a man who, every year, would station himself flat on his stomach over a likely protrusion on the floor of the field and remain there quietly for up to two hours, watching as an asparagus tip pushed through the damp earth. Like a sports fan cheering the lengthening and rising of a basketball player toward the hoop, or some other form of male prowess, he would mutter impassionedly: "Yes! Yes! Yes!"

An Elizabethan writer observed that the shape of the spear "manifestly provoketh Venus." The race of the human heart at asparagus rising, then, may have less to do with flavor than with structural fact. Like any natural spring drama, that of sprouting asparagus is progenerative. There is something brave and willful about the wispy, pale spears pushing through the soil. So much earth, so few spears.

Unlike the soft spring grass or delicate wild flowers, asparagus are impervious to gentle breezes; they rarely bend with rain. The spears remain resolutely straight and tall, reaching toward the sun. It is the sun that darkens their color, eventually toughening their stems and causing their budding tips to open and flower, which is good news for the asparagus population and bad news for sensitive palates. A vegetable peeler can make short work of thick skin, but once opened, nothing can restore an asparagus's clenched bud.

The asparagus plant generally produces male flowers on some plants and female flowers on others, relying on birds as matchmakers. But, particularly in the wild, the plant sprouts hermaphroditic blossoms in which both pistils and stamens are functional. Wild asparagus, in other words, is self-sufficient and complicated by nature; its flavor falters if further complicated by a cook.

Like most valiant lives, asparagus seems to prefer a quick and certain end. The Roman Emperor Augustus knew that asparagus should be quickly steamed or blanched. He is credited with having invented the Roman equivalent of our "faster than Jack Robinson": *Velocius quam asparagi coquantur,* faster than you can cook asparagus. When steaming, use a tall pot and stand the stalks on the thick end so that these soften at the same rate as the slimmer portions. Afterwards, a squeeze of lemon and/or a drizzle of butter or olive oil, along with salt, pepper, or nutmeg, flatter the flavor of asparagus best. The French are fond of coddling asparagus in cream, which to my taste yields a better-tasting cream than stalk. In some parts of Italy, asparagus are lightly breaded and deep-fried—which, when done well, is tastier than it sounds.

Used in tandem with other ingredients, blanched and piled on a paillard of chicken or veal, for instance, asparagus permeate any dish with a hint of renewal, the stamp of spring. The vegetable's ability to maintain its own distinct character and lend it to everything it touches may have prompted Jonathan Swift to write: "Oh, 'tis pretty picking/With a tender chicken!"

Then again, the poet may have had other things on his mind.

Steamed Asparagus

½ cup fresh lemon juice

½ cup olive oil

¼ cup water

1 pound asparagus, ends snapped off, stalks peeled

Combine the lemon juice, olive oil, and water in the bottom of a large pot and bring to a simmer. Place the asparagus in a steamer basket and place over the liquid. Cover and simmer until asparagus is crisp-tender, about 4 minutes. Divide among 4 plates and serve immediately.

Serves 4 as a first course

Asparagus and Farfalle with Lemon and Pepper

½ pound farfalle (also called bowtie pasta)

1 tablespoon olive oil

2 pounds asparagus, ends snapped off, stalks peeled and cut into 1½-inch
    lengths

1 cup cooked green peas

2 teaspoons grated lemon zest

1 teaspoon kosher salt, plus more to taste

⅛ teaspoon freshly ground black pepper

1 tablespoon grated Parmesan cheese

1. Bring a large pot of salted water to a boil. Add the pasta and cook until al dente. Meanwhile, heat 1 teaspoon of the olive oil in a large nonstick skillet over medium heat. Add the asparagus and sauté until tender, about 4 minutes. Toss in the peas.

2. Drain the pasta and put in a large bowl. Toss with the remaining olive oil, the asparagus mixture, lemon zest, salt, and pepper. Divide among 4 pasta bowls. Sprinkle with Parmesan and serve immediately.

Serves 4 as a main course

Asparagus and Mint Flan with Poached Scallops and Shrimp

FLAN

8 asparagus spears, ends snapped off, stalks cut into 1-inch pieces and tips halved lengthwise and reserved

⅓ cup heavy cream

¼ cup yogurt cheese (see Note)

2 teaspoons minced fresh mint

2 large eggs, lightly beaten

1 teaspoon kosher salt

Freshly ground pepper to taste

Vegetable oil spray

SAUCE AND SHELLFISH

½ teaspoon olive oil

½ pound medium shrimp, in the shell

½ pound bay scallops

2 tablespoons white wine

1 tomato, cored and chopped

½ cup water

2 teaspoons heavy cream

Kosher salt and freshly ground pepper to taste

GARNISH

1 teaspoon olive oil

Reserved asparagus tips

1 cup fresh shiitake mushrooms, stemmed and sliced

1. Preheat the oven to 325° F.

2. Steam the asparagus stalks until tender, 5 to 6 minutes. Put in a food processor and add the cream. Process until smooth. Add the yogurt cheese. Process until smooth, stopping once to scrape the sides of the bowl. Scrape the

mixture into a bowl and stir in the mint. Whisk in the eggs, salt, and pepper. Spray four 6-ounce ramekins with vegetable oil. Divide the mixture among the ramekins. Place in a roasting pan and pour in enough boiling water to reach halfway up the sides of the ramekins. Cover with aluminum foil. Bake until flans are set, about 30 minutes. Remove the ramekins from the pan and let cool slightly.

3. Meanwhile, heat the ½ teaspoon olive oil in a medium-size saucepan over medium heat. Add the shrimp and cook for 1 minute. Add the scallops and cook until opaque, about 1 minute longer. With a slotted spoon, remove the shrimp and scallops from the pan. Set aside.

4. Peel the shrimp, reserving the shells. Add the wine to the pan and cook, stirring with a wooden spoon, to deglaze the pan. Add tomato, water, and reserved shrimp shells. Simmer for 15 minutes. Pass sauce through a fine-mesh sieve into a clean pan. Add the cream, bring to a boil, and cook until sauce thickens, about 1 minute. Set aside.

5. Heat the 1 teaspoon olive oil in a nonstick skillet over medium heat. Add the asparagus tips and mushrooms and sauté until tender, about 5 minutes.

6. Run a knife inside the rim of each ramekin to loosen. Invert 1 flan onto each of 4 plates. Warm the sauce over low heat, add the shrimp and scallops and turn to coat. Divide among the plates, placing the mixture beside the flans. Place the asparagus tips and mushrooms over and around each flan. Serve immediately.

Serves 4 as a main course

To make yogurt cheese, place ½ cup plain lowfat yogurt in sieve lined with paper towels and place over a bowl. Set aside in refrigerator until yogurt is thick and liquid has drained out, several hours or overnight. Discard the liquid.

AS LIFE UNFURLS

Fiddlehead ferns epitomize vernal ephemera. Coiled as they are like tiny watch springs, edible when tight and young, they become when fully unfurled unfit for human consumption. In this way, the loosening of the frond is tantamount to the tick of a clock, a grunt and heave that defies winter, beckons summer, insists on spring. Fiddleheads are a sign. One that passes in a blink.

The forager, with sights set on eating and thus incorporating this herald of a gentler yet relentlessly determined life, races against the fiddleheads' own obscure and unpredictable biological clock. Ferns thrive in the shrouded remoteness of marshy woodlands. They are private, quiet, and delicate plants, which may explain much of their allure, particularly because their flavor is far from that of a shrinking violet. The tight fiddlehead combines grassy and herbaceous tones with the raw, searing effect of a barely cooked artichoke in the mouth and the meaty reassurance of a hardy green bean. Although shy when uncovered, they are surprisingly stout.

Fiddleheads are a growth stage, not a species. Many types of fiddleheads have been gathered from Virginia to New Brunswick since colonial times, but as Elizabeth Schneider writes in *Uncommon Fruits and Vegetables*, "there is considerable evidence that some . . . may be extremely carcinogenic." The bracken fern (*Pteridium aquilinum*) can lead to an uncomfortable evening, take it from one who has tried it. The Ostrich fern, however, the variety most commonly marketed, carries no death threat, only a surfeit of vitamins A and C, and obviously, lots of fiber, and of course, the taste of spring, duplicitous as it is.

When plucked and eaten in a hurry, the fiddlehead is supple and elastic, of contradictory flavor but nevertheless a yielding thing. When given time to consider its fate, as little as two days in a refrigerator, the spirals, while showing no sign of spoilage, get tough and fibrous and unsuitable as anything other than a garnish.

For those who want to preserve the memory of spring, a fiddlehead can be blanched, dipped in ice water, patted dry, and frozen to be used as a garnish in the future, a souvenir of spring in the seasons to come. For those whose desire is more primitive, who desire not so much to dance around the maypole as to become the maypole, eating a mess of fiddleheads is the logical prescription.

Delicate and changeable as they are, fiddleheads should not be misconstrued as low-maintenance. Their fibrous stems need to be snipped and the tight fronds must then be soaked and soaked again to wash away the tawny parchment shreds that protect each strand from the cold. The tight coils then need to be cooked, most gently.

I discovered fiddleheads when living in New England and thus can no more separate them from that area than Eve could an apple from Eden. The Japanese serve them blanched with soy and sesame seeds. The French bake them in cream, under a crust of mildly seasoned buttered bread crumbs. I favor the simple method of blanching the ferns and dousing them with melted butter, salt, pepper, and a touch of nutmeg. It is equally impossible to deny the attrac-tion of fiddleheads blanched and tossed when still warm with a soft lemon vinaigrette; blanched and then sautéed with pancetta or bacon; or blanched and tossed with a resolute and hence firmly herbaceous olive oil. In other words, treat a fiddlehead as you would an asparagus or green bean and settle into delicious conjugations of spring.

Chris Holmes of the New Penny Farm in Presque Isle, Maine, who gathers and ships fid-dleheads, says that the end result—whether blanched and tossed, marinated, or sautéed—is ancil-lary to the hunt. Squishing through the soft belly of the deep woods in spring yields intermittent glimpses of a firm and determined life. Fiddleheads are rare and fleeting, thus precious. Mostly because they are, from wood's floor to table, contentious little beings who had better things to do.

Fiddleheads Steamed in Lemon Oil

1 cup water
2 tablespoons Lemon and Parsley Oil (page 130)
3 cups fiddleheads, trimmed and cleaned as described on page 33
¾ teaspoon kosher salt, plus more to taste
Freshly ground pepper to taste

Combine the water and the oil in a pot with a steamer insert. Bring to a boil. Reduce to a simmer. Place the fiddleheads in the steamer basket, cover, and steam until tender, about 6 minutes. Remove from heat and season with salt and pepper. Divide among 4 plates and serve immediately.

Serves 4 as a first course or side dish

Sautéed Fiddleheads with Pancetta

4 cups fiddleheads, trimmed and cleaned as described on page 33
½ pound pancetta, cut into ¼-inch dice
Kosher salt and freshly ground pepper to taste

Bring a pot of lightly salted water to a boil. Add the fiddleheads and blanch for 5 minutes. Drain. Place the pancetta in a large skillet over medium heat and fry until browned. Add the fiddleheads and sauté for 2 minutes. Season with salt and pepper. Divide among 4 plates and serve immediately.

Serves 4 as a first course

Veal with Fiddlehead and Shiitake Sauce

¼ pound pancetta, cut into ¼-inch dice

4 veal cutlets, about 2 ounces each

Kosher salt and freshly ground pepper to taste

2 tablespoons all-purpose flour

1 teaspoon unsalted butter

2 cloves garlic, minced

½ cup sherry

8 fresh shiitake mushrooms, stemmed and cut into ¼-inch slices

½ cup fiddleheads, trimmed and cleaned as described on page 33

1. Place the pancetta in a large skillet over medium heat. Fry until pancetta turns light brown and fat is rendered. Remove pancetta from the skillet with a slotted spoon and set aside.

2. Season the veal cutlets with salt and pepper and dust with the flour. Add them to the skillet and sauté until just cooked through, about 3 minutes per side. Remove veal from pan and keep warm.

3. Melt the butter in the skillet. Add the garlic and cook for 1 minute. Add the sherry and deglaze the pan. Add the shiitakes, fiddleheads, and reserved pancetta and cook for 5 minutes. Divide the veal among 4 plates. Spoon the sauce over and serve immediately.

Serves 4 as a main course

THE YOUNG AND TENDER

Foragers stalk the woods, fields, and riverbanks in search of the first signs of spring, but gardeners and farmers use a different barometer. After the first turn of earth, even before the threat of frost has lifted, when, nevertheless, the rains yield to a few sunny days, peas begin to sprout.

Until recently in the United States, the small pale pea greens were simply a promise of things to come: a darkening expanse of leaves, a wild gander up the garden row, and an eventual sweet pea or snow pea for the taking. But the expanding global table has further spurred the understandable impatience of spring. Recently American growers have begun to harvest the pea sprouts and greens.

In Asia, the sprouting leaves have long been a delicacy, one that must be handled carefully and cooked quickly to preserve their tender nature. But here, the focus of the vernal equinox has been trained more on the wild than the cultivated, so that pea greens (and any number of lettuces) were spared an early harvest and left to grow—sometimes to a tough and bitter old age. Morse Pitts, who owns Windfall Farms in Montgomery, New York, only began to harvest the pea sprouts when the market demanded it last year. An increasing clamor for variety in the flavor of greens, he said, spurred him on.

The greens can be harvested in April and May, and again in the fall months in a temperate climate; they can be cultivated twelve months a year in a greenhouse. "I can find you pea greens any time of year," scoffed one epicure when I suggested we hunt them down in Chinatown as a rite of spring. "Name the month," he said. Even robbed of the romantic imperative, I continue to view the bundled greens as one of spring's early stirrings.

To me, pea greens seem like the ground-dwelling equivalent of morning glories, sprouting overnight, rambling here and there, turning the grower into a shepherd, at least for the duration. In New York's Chinatown, the plucked greens are sometimes poetically called "spiderwebs"; their spindly stems are fragile, and their leaves collapse at the merest hint of heat. But the greens are nonetheless a robust source of beta-carotene and other healthful vitamins, and like other feisty young greens of the season, add pepper and pizzazz to the spring kitchen.

Eaten raw in a salad mix, pea greens are tender, like young spinach. Like any living thing snatched up before its time, raw pea greens are sassy and hot. It's almost enough to make you think twice. When cooked, however, the greens wilt like ballerinas after a good show, lending their spice to the ingredients around them, a final adieu, a bittersweet memory, before collapsing limply and almost sweetly upon themselves.

The greens, which are sold through specialty grocers and in green markets, are sometimes called "pea sprouts." In cooking, they behave like something between a mung bean sprout and young spinach or watercress, either of which can be used as a substitute; if cooked quickly, their stems remain crisp and slightly bitter while their leaves turn buttery, soft, and herbaceously sweet. Pea greens are a tailor-made foil for tender things like crabmeat and shrimp and lobster; they can also hold their own with pork, veal, or chicken.

By co-opting the Cantonese technique of barely warming the greens, the cook can fashion a wilted salad with sesame dressing that makes a fine first course or an excellent accompaniment to steamed or sautéed chicken, veal, or pork. Pea greens can collaborate with early mint to enliven crabmeat or can be used with shrimp or squid along with garlic and ginger to make a sprightly sauce for pasta. Foolproof as an addition to any stir-fry, pea greens are also a sort of exotic watercress and can be substituted for it in French-inspired soups or even added to small pancakes, topped with lobster meat.

Whether handled in an Eastern or Western manner, the greens remain impetuous. Even if wrapped in damp towels, they can grow stubbornly woody and spitefully bitter in three days. Rather than suffer these recriminations, the cook should move quickly. Treated well, pea greens offer a chance to capture the moment between youthful audaciousness and the inevitable sighs of accommodation to come.

Wilted Pea Green Salad with Sesame Dressing

2 tablespoons fresh lemon juice
2 teaspoons canola oil
¾ teaspoon toasted sesame oil
¼ teaspoon kosher salt
8 cups pea greens, rinsed but not dried
2 teaspoons sesame seeds, lightly toasted

Whisk together the lemon juice, canola oil, sesame oil, and salt in a medium bowl. Heat a medium saucepan over medium heat until hot. Add the pea greens and cook, stirring, just until wilted. Place the pea greens in the bowl with the dressing and toss to coat. Divide among 4 plates and sprinkle with the sesame seeds. Serve immediately.

Serves 4 as a first course

Pea Green and Snow Pea Soup

5 cups chicken broth, homemade, or low-sodium canned broth
2 pieces fresh lemon grass, 5 inches each, finely chopped
2 teaspoons chopped fresh ginger
1 tablespoon Sichuan peppercorns, crushed
1 cup snow peas, strung
2 cups pea greens, rinsed and coarsely chopped
2 scallions, green parts only, thinly sliced
½ teaspoon kosher salt

Combine chicken broth, lemon grass, ginger, and peppercorns in a large saucepan over medium heat. Simmer for 40 minutes. Strain the broth and return it to the pan. Place over medium heat and bring to a simmer. Add the snow peas and cook for about 1 minute. Add the pea greens and scallions and cook for about 30 seconds. Remove from the heat and season with salt. Ladle into bowls and serve immediately.

Serves 6 as a first course or 4 as a main course

Linguine with Pea Greens and Shrimp

1 pound dried linguine
3 teaspoons canola oil
4 teaspoons ground coriander
2 cloves garlic, minced
3 teaspoons grated fresh ginger
1½ pounds large shrimp, peeled and deveined
4 cups pea greens, rinsed
1½ teaspoons kosher salt, plus more to taste
Freshly ground pepper to taste

1. Bring a large pot of salted water to a boil. Add the linguine and cook until al dente. Meanwhile, heat the oil in a large nonstick skillet over low heat. Stir in the coriander, garlic, and ginger and cook, stirring, for 30 seconds. Increase the heat to medium. Add the shrimp and sauté until just cooked through, about 5 minutes. Add the pea greens and sauté, stirring constantly, until the leaves turn bright green and begin to wilt. Season with salt and pepper.

2. Drain the linguine and place it in a large bowl. Toss in the shrimp and pea green mixture. Divide among 4 plates and serve immediately.

Serves 4 as a main course

A FAVORITE THING

While pea greens are still relatively rare and effete things, in most fields across the country, clumps of spinach are the greening that signals spring. Unlike the crinkly, deep-ribbed spinach of winter, which is usually sold as picked leaves in sealed plastic bags, spring's field spinach is tender: Its leaves are small and smooth and it tends to be sold by the bunch, rather than the bag. It is exquisite stuff.

The coarse spinach of winter makes fine soups and sauces and is perfectly passable when boiled, creamed, and pureed or baked *au gratin*. But young spring spinach has a delicate, mildly herbaceous flavor and a butter-tender leaf that requires only a whisper of heat. It can add a delicate touch of resistance to sautéed dishes, become a medium for assertive seasoning in side dishes, make an enviable salad.

Popeye boasted of being strong to the finish 'cause he ate all his spinach, implying a strong, tough green. But long before, a French gastronome described spinach as gentler stuff. The young leaf is so impressionable as to be "the virgin wax of the kitchen," he wrote. Spinach, in other words, absorbs flavor and bears the stamp of the tastes that surround it, rather than lending flavor.

Many are unmoved by the mild manner of spinach. To me, that is its charm and allure. It is happy to quietly absorb, leaving it to other ingredients to broadcast their flavors and needs.

The green's malleable nature may be why it was the first food I loved. Family lore has it that, as a toddler, coming to the last bite of creamed spinach from a baby food jar was one of the few things that could provoke me to a tantrum. I didn't know then, of course, that the puree was filled with butter and cream; it was spinach I wanted, spinach I sought, spinach I continue to dote on. I am a rare member of my generation in that I never understood the caption Carl Rose gave the cartoon that pictured a recalcitrant child diner: "I say it's spinach and I say to hell with it." The joke, I thought, was that this was a weird kid. But of course, the joke was on me. My brothers all hated spinach; every other child in the neighborhood hated spinach; the school didn't even try to serve spinach in the cafeteria.

My affection progressed from pureed baby food to steamed spinach and then to chopped spinach baked in cream under bread crumbs and Parmesan cheese. Then there was wilted spinach, made limp by hot bacon grease and vinegar, served with sliced mushrooms and hard-boiled egg. This was so disgusting to my brothers that they would leave the dinner table rather than watch me eat it. Soon after, I developed a mania for all things *à la florentine*, a tribute, it is thought, to Catherine de Médicis, the Tuscan princess said to have introduced, if not spinach, a certain passion for it to the fifteenth-century French court.

When I began cooking in restaurant kitchens, spinach soups—in cooler weather pureed with potatoes, chicken broth, and cream or with braised fennel, at warmer times of the year with yogurt, scallions, and garlic—were inescapable on my menus. Though not partial to baked oysters, I was passionate about oysters Rockefeller. I responded to requests for deviled eggs with eggs stuffed with a puree of yolk, mustard, mayonnaise, and, of course, spinach. This all occurred during the years of the quiche. I considered my mustard and spinach pies and my Greek-inspired feta and spinach pies to be masterpieces, though not all diners agreed. The pies were followed by French-style spinach *mousselines*, served alone as a first course timbale garnished with lobster or shrimp or used as a stuffing for flounder.

My abiding affection for spinach reflected my evolution as a cook. Gradually, I understood that spinach is more a vehicle than a destination. In Cantonese steamed or stir-fry dishes, spinach is a sponge for the flavors of garlic and soy, ginger and pepper. In Southeast Asian dishes, spinach absorbs perfume from lemon grass, chilies, and mint. In Indian dishes, pureed spinach carries the flavors of cardamom and curry when baked around fresh cheese, so that each bite is redolent.

These days, I'm less interested in creamed and pureed spinach, more interested in what the individual leaves can do when minced and tossed fresh into a warm, clear soup or over pasta, stirred into rice, or added at the last minute to give snap and a hint of the outdoors to a spring stew or sautéed dish. In fuller bodied soups, such as a chickpea and sweet pepper porridge, a chiffonnade of fresh chopped spinach lightens. In a lighter crab chowder, it enlivens. I remain convinced there is nothing spinach cannot do.

I champion the chameleon of greens, though it is probably best when young and malleable. The tough, old, crinkled spinach of winter seems innocuous, obsequious, and generally bland. A similar taste in the smooth, tender leaves of spring, on the other hand, seems merely understated and full of promise, possibility, and hope.

Spinach with Garlic and Lemon

3 teaspoons olive oil
4 cloves garlic, minced
3 pounds spinach, stemmed, washed, and torn
4 teaspoons fresh lemon juice
1 teaspoon kosher salt
Freshly ground pepper to taste

Heat 1 teaspoon of the oil in a large skillet. Add the garlic and cook, stirring constantly, for 20 seconds. Add the spinach by handfuls, tossing it in the skillet, until you can fit it all in. Cook, stirring, for about 2 minutes. Remove from heat, add the remaining olive oil, the lemon juice, salt, and pepper, and toss. Divide among 4 plates and serve.

Serves 4 as a side dish

Spinach Salad with Bacon and Oven-Dried Mushrooms

2 large portobello mushrooms, stemmed and cut into ⅛-inch slices
1 teaspoon rosemary oil or olive oil
½ teaspoon kosher salt, plus more to taste
Freshly ground pepper to taste
4 slices bacon, diced
4 teaspoons Dijon mustard
4 teaspoons apple cider vinegar
1 pound spinach, stemmed, washed, and torn

1. Preheat the oven to 200° F.

2. Brush the mushroom slices with the oil and spread them out on a baking sheet in a single layer. Sprinkle with ¼ teaspoon salt and pepper. Bake until dried, about 1 hour. Set aside.

3. Fry the bacon in a skillet over medium heat until brown and crisp, about 6 minutes. Remove the bacon with a slotted spoon and drain on a paper towel. Measure out 2 tablespoons plus 2 teaspoons of the bacon fat and place in a small bowl. Whisk in the mustard and then the vinegar. Add ¼ teaspoon salt and pepper.

4. Put the spinach leaves in a large bowl. Add the dressing and toss to coat. Season with additional salt and pepper if needed. Divide the salad among 4 plates. Top with the dried mushrooms and bacon and serve immediately.

Serves 4 as a first course

Spinach and Chickpea Pie

CRUST

2 cups chickpea flour (see Note)

¾ cup all-purpose flour, plus additional for rolling

1 tablespoon baking powder

1¼ teaspoons kosher salt

3 tablespoons cold unsalted butter, cut into small pieces

2 tablespoons plain lowfat yogurt

¾ cup lowfat milk

FILLING

2 teaspoons olive oil

2 medium onions, halved and thinly sliced

2 cans (15 ounces each) chickpeas, drained and rinsed

4 tablespoons balsamic vinegar

2 teaspoons kosher salt

Freshly ground pepper to taste

3 cloves garlic, minced

6 pounds spinach, washed and stemmed

½ cup crumbled feta cheese

Olive oil spray

1 egg, lightly beaten

1. Combine the chickpea flour, all-purpose flour, baking powder, and salt in a large bowl. Rub in the butter and yogurt until well combined. Add the milk and stir just until combined. Flour your hands and gather the dough into a ball. Wrap in plastic and refrigerate.

2. Heat 1 teaspoon of the olive oil in a large nonstick skillet over medium heat. Add the onions and cook until soft and golden, about 10 minutes. Add the chickpeas and the vinegar, turn the heat to low, and cook for 15 minutes. Stir in 1½ teaspoons salt and pepper. Set aside.

3. Heat the remaining teaspoon of oil in a large pot over medium heat. Add the garlic and cook, stirring constantly, for 30 seconds. Add the spinach, stir, cover

the pot, and steam for 5 minutes. Drain the spinach in a sieve, pressing out all the water. Coarsely chop the spinach, put in a bowl, and season with ½ teaspoon salt and pepper. Add the feta and toss. Set aside.

4. Preheat oven to 350° F. Lightly coat a 9-inch pie plate with olive oil spray.

5. Press a third of the dough over the bottom and up the sides of the pie plate. Spread half the spinach mixture over the crust. Top with half the chickpea mixture. Repeat.

6. On a lightly floured surface, roll out the remaining dough into a circle that will just fit the top of the pie. Place the dough over the top and pinch the bottom and top crusts together to seal. Brush the top of the pie with a little of the beaten egg. Make small steam vents with the tip of a sharp knife. Bake until the crust is browned, about 30 minutes. Cut into wedges and serve.

Serves 6 as a main course

Note: Chickpea flour is available by mail from Balducci's. Call (800) BALDUCCI.

THE HOURS BETWIXT INCARNATIONS

Spring taunts the watermen of the upper Chesapeake Bay. At one moment, March will flash a blue sky over Crisfield, Maryland. The next, a nasty little breeze snatches away the blue, quick and cold as a change of heart. By April, the sun lingers long enough to pop dogwood blossoms and coaxes the hopeful aroma of brine and bait and new eelgrass into the air. But the sun doesn't stick around long enough to rouse the blue crabs from their winter burrow in the crab grounds that run north from Tangier Island in Virginia to the Eastern Shore of Maryland. "Like as never ta git here," is how the local watermen discuss the arrival of the warm season and the molting crabs it brings.

James Michener called soft-shell crabs "the tastiest morsel in the bay." As perishable as the Chesapeake spring is impetuous, soft-shell crabs remained a regional delicacy until the railroad carried them up to Philadelphia and New York in the early nineteenth century, eventually turning a sideline business into a full-scale industry.

As the nation developed a taste for soft-shell crabs, fishermen began to catch them as far south as the Gulf of Mexico and as early as March. But these early risers have yet to ruffle the calendars of soft-shell crab connoisseurs. Spring means Maryland soft-shell crabs, or "soft crabs," as they are called there. It's a rite.

To the local watermen, the preseason interlopers are a symbol of a world that's racing against a faster and faster clock, a world whose finer aspects are often blurred. The late-rising Maryland crabs remain the sweetest. Pragmatists say Maryland's cool waters explain its superior crabs. Those of a more poetic nature credit the preponderance of marshlands around Crisfield and Smith Island, the spongy shallow flats thick with the slender, floating, grasslike stems of eelgrass where crabs shed one shell and wait for the new one to toughen. No one doubts that generations of following the water have given Maryland watermen a sixth sense about the private lives of crabs.

The watermen have an uncanny instinct about where to lower their pots, and can spot a crab that is ready to moult—a "peeler," or "paler," as it is pronounced locally—at a glance. After they are trapped, peelers are placed in holding tanks called floats, which are the size of small wading pools and hold up to two hundred crabs. The peelers soon get about the sometimes painful business of slowly backing out of their old shells. Their new shell hardens within hours, so watermen pace the piers and check their floats at least four times a day. When a shed crab is spotted, the watermen use a long-handled net to swoosh the water like Venetian gondoliers. When they come up with one, they look triumphant as a child who has netted a butterfly.

True connoisseurs (and every self-respecting waterman) want soft-shell crabs that are removed from the water within ten minutes of shedding. The new shell should look wrinkled and feel like wet parchment. Within twelve hours, it will be leathery; within a day it will be as hard as armor.

No group has had more experience handling soft-shell crabs than the watermen around Crisfield. Their touch is, perhaps, another reason why their crabs reach the market sweeter, more tender, and less bruised than others. From May to October, watermen around Crisfield catch up to 30 bushels of peelers a day. Every year, at least 3.6 million crabs are inspected by Federal inspectors, cleaned, packed in eelgrass in flat cardboard boxes, and sent out from the John T. Handy Company, the largest in the world.

"It's gold-rush time," says Johnny Brittingham, a thirty-one-year-old Crisfield waterman. Brittingham's "blood runs a little faster," and he gets "nervous-like, excited," when the spring sun first begins to bleach the piers that fence the tip of Crisfield like a protective picket. By late March, Brittingham fidgets with his 600 crab pots, watching the sky for signs of a mild and early spring. Restraints like water temperature and the law keep Brittingham—like most local watermen—patient. (Virginia law prohibits Maryland watermen from chugging south to Virginia's warmer waters, where the crabs can get lively by late March.)

"We're willin' to wait fer the best, that we are," he says. But soon the wait is "aggravatin." He worries about the peelers and the season. "Changes every year. Like watermen, if you ask me—no two are the same," he says.

Though in one way every waterman is the same; none can resist the vernal tides. Year after year they fall for the tides' encouragements; year after year they rail against their caprice. By mid-April, most dawns find them chasing spring across the bay.

It is 5 A.M. on Easter Monday, and Brittingham is steering his 33-foot boat, the *Star-Gazer*, from Crisfield out into a gray-gauze dawn. The water slaps the stern, and Brittingham squints for signs of the red-tipped buoys that mark his pots. He slams down his morning Pepsi and reaches for the microphone of his citizens' band radio.

"Boiling today, isn't she?" he says. The cackle of the radio joins the caw of the gulls, the diesel chug, the slap of the tide as Brittingham waits for a response.

"Nasty," comes the reply.

"Hard job ta git a purdy day," comes another.

These are the words of spring, as reliable, says Brittingham, as the slight reddening of the female crab's claws that appears when the water warms and the crabs begin to rustle around below.

For three hours, Brittingham heaves his pots. The pots' split-level cubes, made of chicken wire, look like giant dice coming over the side of the boat. One carries three hard crabs, another has more than a dozen. Not one crab shows signs of being "rank," or ready to peel. Brittingham hauls and empties the traps, separating the male and female hard crabs into different bushel baskets, rebaiting, and resinking the pot.

Hard male crabs bring $40 a bushel; females, with their smaller yield of flesh, bring $20. Soft-shell crabs will be worth triple that. "The first, you know, are the tiniest and sweetest," he says. "Prices are sky high." Like a gambler at the table, he keeps a running tab.

Years ago, I watched the soft-shell minuet, and it went like this: On shore, the Handy Company set out floats and opened its processing plant. About 250 seasonal workers had been promised jobs, and they wandered by, gauging starting day by the progress of the sun. Five miles away, on tiny Smith Island, a haven for peelers, octogenarian Frances Kitching, who ran a boardinghouse and served family-style meals in her Smith Island home for thirty years, oiled her cast-iron skillet.

Around the Chesapeake, she was a legendary cook, but she saw herself as only a supporting character. "The best thing you can do to a crab is let it be," she said. "Clean it, fry it, and watch that it doesn't pop in the skillet and burn your arm."

Like most who have a touch for frying crabs, she frowned on breading and deep-frying and preferred to dust the crabs with a light filigree of flour and sauté them quickly. Later in the summer, when Smith Island palates have been jaded by several months of crabs, she tossed them on the grill, for variety. It's easy to overwhelm a soft-shell crab; it's hard to insult one, for its sweet flavor is endlessly adaptable.

Even the best crab needs a good cleaning, she said. The gills, external aprons, and eyes must be removed. If you are squeamish, have the fish store do the honors, and then, right before cooking, simply dust the crabs with a little flour, put a little butter or oil in a pan, and get it just hot enough so it makes the flour sizzle. Up the shore in Baltimore, crabs are slipped into a milk bath before the flour dusting, making an even crisper crust.

In either case, the sound of the first crabs sizzling in a pan is like the sound of the fans cheering the Orioles up the bay in Baltimore. It means spring.

Just before noon on Easter Monday that year, spring settled into the sound between Crisfield and Smith Island. The sun sent the mercury up the thermometer. It was well over 70 degrees when the *Donna Carol*, a 33-foot crab boat, nuzzled the bow of Brittingham's *Star-Gazer*. No words were exchanged, but a single crab was tossed to Brittingham. He caught it, studied it, and smiled like a kid with seats behind home plate on opening day.

"We got us a peeler," he said.

Soft-shell Crabs Sautéed in Brown Butter

2 cups lowfat milk

2 teaspoons Tabasco

1 teaspoon mustard powder

1 teaspoon cayenne

1 teaspoon freshly ground white pepper

½ teaspoon kosher salt, plus more to taste

2 teaspoons sugar

2 cups all-purpose flour

8 soft-shell crabs, cleaned

8 tablespoons unsalted butter

1 cup fresh lemon juice

½ cup Italian parsley, minced

1 teaspoon freshly ground pepper, plus more to taste

1. Combine the milk and Tabasco in a bowl. Mix the mustard powder, cayenne, white pepper, salt, sugar, and flour in a shallow dish. Dip the crabs in the milk and dredge in the flour mixture. Heat 2 tablespoons butter in a large sauté pan over medium-high heat until bubbling. Working in batches, place the crabs in the pan and sauté for 3 minutes. Turn and sauté until tender, about 2 more minutes. Drain on paper towels.

2. Add ½ cup lemon juice to the pan and boil over high heat until it glazes the pan. Stir in the remaining butter and cook over medium heat until brown, about 5 minutes. Skim off any foam that rises to the surface. Take the pan off the heat. Whisk in the remaining ½ cup lemon juice and parsley and season with salt and pepper. Place 2 crabs on each of 4 plates. Pour sauce over the crabs and serve.

Serves 4 as a main course

Soft-shell Crabs with Black Bean Sauce

2 cups lowfat milk
2 teaspoons Tabasco
2 cups all-purpose flour
½ teaspoon kosher salt
1 teaspoon freshly ground pepper
8 soft-shell crabs, cleaned
1 tablespoon sesame oil
½ cup white wine
1 cup Chinese black bean sauce
1 tablespoon hoisin sauce
2 teaspoons chili paste (see Note)
2 tablespoons grated fresh ginger
4 scallions, minced

1. Combine the milk and Tabasco in a bowl. Mix the flour, salt, and pepper in a shallow dish. Dip the crabs in the milk and dredge in the flour mixture. Heat the oil in a heavy-bottomed skillet over medium-high heat. Working in batches, place the crabs in the pan and sauté for 3 minutes. Turn and sauté until tender, about 2 more minutes. Drain on paper towels.

2. Wipe the pan clean. Return the skillet to the heat. Pour in the white wine, black bean sauce, hoisin sauce, chili paste, and ginger. Turn the heat to medium-high and simmer until the sauce thickens, about 3 to 5 minutes. Place 2 crabs on each of 4 plates. Pour sauce over crabs. Sprinkle scallions on top and serve immediately.

Serves 4 as a main course

> Note: Chili paste (sometimes seen as chili paste with garlic) is found in supermarkets along with black bean sauce and hoisin.

Thai Soft-shell Crabs

2 cups lowfat milk

2 teaspoons Tabasco

2 cups all-purpose flour

½ teaspoon kosher salt

1 teaspoon freshly ground pepper

8 soft-shell crabs, cleaned

1 tablespoon sesame oil

½ cup white wine

½ cup orange juice

2 limes, juiced

2 Thai chilies, seeded and minced

4 scallions, minced

¼ cup mint leaves, minced

¼ cup basil leaves, minced

½ cup coriander leaves, minced

1. Combine the milk and Tabasco in a bowl. Mix the flour, salt, and pepper in a shallow dish. Dip the crabs in the milk and dredge in the flour mixture. Heat the oil in a heavy-bottomed skillet over medium-high heat. Working in batches, place the crabs in the pan and sauté for 3 minutes. Turn and sauté until tender, about 2 more minutes. Drain on paper towels.

2. Drain the fat from the pan. Return the skillet to the stove. Add the wine, orange juice, lime juice, chilies, and scallions. Turn the heat up to medium-high and simmer until sauce reduces to ⅓ cup, about 3 to 5 minutes. Place 2 crabs on each of 4 plates. Drizzle with the sauce and garnish with minced mint, basil, and coriander leaves and serve.

Serves 4 as a main course

A LOOSE NET AND A VERY SHARP KNIFE

For as long as the history of fields and streams has been recorded, Hudson River shad have been an icon of a world warming and stirring. Bucking the spring runoff from the Adirondacks the fish are propelled, writes Robert H. Boyle in his natural history *The Hudson River*, by "ancestral fury."

On the banks of the river their predators, the fishermen, seem caught in an equally instinctive dance as they mend their gill nets and sharpen their knives. The river men study the banks for the yellow forsythia and white-budded shadbush that blossom when the water temperature rises a few degrees above 50, luring shad from the Atlantic in search of a flat, shallow spawning ground. The rivermen also study the surface of the water for the swarms of shadfly and brown caddis fly that a warm sun brings, sand the pine planks for smoking the fish, scrub the flat tin drums that the roe is fried on.

In the mutable world following a thaw, life is possible; the female shad, bloated in the literal sense with her twin sacks of caviar, is also pregnant with the possibilities of beginning again.

Among river men, the metaphor seems as powerful as an actual taste for the delicate fish and its rich, pungent roe. "I love the drift as much as the fish," said Tom Turck, whose family has fished for shad and sturgeon for five generations in Kingston, New York. At night, from late March until mid-May, Turck and his brothers "drift" the gill nets from their boats to capture the migrating fish. While awaiting their prey, the brothers Turck drift as well, close enough to witness a nibble in the tug and bob of the white Clorox bottle buoys they use to mark their trap. "By that time, you done everything a river man can do and you wait, knowing that something good's going to happen, just not knowing when or how much," he said.

Generally, by late April and early May, the shad run is steady enough to incite shad fries along the mid-Hudson. In the style of a church supper, fishermen and their wives fire up coals under halved oil drums in parking lots or flat grassy spots near the river. They fry slabs of bacon and then, after dusting the shad roe in flour, fry it in the grease. In some Hudson River towns, shad fillets are fried, too, but more often the fillets are tacked to a pine plank upwind from a hardwood fire. A planked shad looks like crucifixion. River men tend to eschew whatever shamanistic properties the nailed, splayed, and smoked fillet might have, preferring to eat fried roe on sandwich buns topped with bacon. Everyone else lines up for plates heaped high with planked shad, fried roe, bacon, baked potatoes, and coleslaw. It is the Thanksgiving meal of spring along the Hudson.

Sunday is the favored day for such fetes, perhaps because the state law to protect shad stock decrees that nets can't be drifted and set from dusk on Friday until dusk on Sunday, perhaps because Sunday lends itself to being fortified by a totem of fertility. Shad itself, which was so plentiful in colonial times that the fish was considered "common" and wasn't eaten in polite circles, is a member of the herring family; *sapidissima*, the Latin species name of American shad, means "most delicious." The female shad fillets are fat, easy to fry, and have a delicate flavor and fine flake. The male shad fillets are smaller, though tasty. The roe is easiest to handle if left to rest in iced water for fifteen minutes, then quickly (and carefully) blanched. Lightly dusted with seasoned flour and fried, it is as pungent as other forms of caviar, though gamier and smaller grained.

Shad has its ways of avenging itself. In addition to a ribbed skeleton that extends from the backbone, the fish has two rows of intramuscular floating ribs on each fillet. These can defy the sharpest knife and tend to surface, like hidden porcupine quills, after cooking.

But don't let that inhibit you. In *Foods of the Hudson*, Peter G. Rose bemoans the fact that boning shad takes a surgeon's precision and points to the long cooking or pickling methods that can soften the bones and make them edible.

However, it *is* possible to excise the floating bones, first by running a finger along the flesh side of the fillet to locate them, then following with a sharp blade along both sides of the ribs. Lift the end nearest the head and tug gently toward the tail. If the entire section does not lift out intact, tweezers may be in order.

Short of that, you can do what the Hudson river men do to avoid a thorny encounter. They recommend stuffing a shad with a vegetable mixture and vinegar or baking the fillets under a vinegary topping to soften or dissolve that second set of ribs. With nothing sharp to distract them, the river men get to enjoy completely a meal meant to signal a new beginning.

Shad Fillets Braised with Wild Mushrooms and Tomatoes

FISH

    2 shad fillets, about 2 pounds each

    1 cup white wine

    1 cup fresh lemon juice

    1 clove garlic, minced

    1 small onion, minced

    1 bay leaf

    3 black peppercorns, cracked

    ¼ pound fresh porcini mushrooms, stems trimmed, caps and stems cut into
        ½-inch slices

    ¼ pound fresh shiitake mushrooms, stemmed and cut into ½-inch slices

    ½ pound fresh morels, rinsed if sandy, and dried well

    4 plum tomatoes, peeled, cored, seeded, and quartered

SAUCE

    2 ounces dried porcini

    5 cups water

    1 teaspoon kosher salt

    Pinch sugar

    1 tablespoon soy sauce

    1 scallion, thinly sliced

1. Place the fish, skin side down, in a glass or ceramic baking dish. Cover with the wine, lemon juice, garlic, onion, bay leaf, and peppercorns. Marinate for 1 hour.

2. Preheat the oven to 300° F.

3. Transfer the fish to a clean baking dish. Sprinkle 2 tablespoons of the marinade over the fish. Arrange the porcini, shiitake, and morel mushrooms over the top. Add the tomatoes. Cover tightly with foil and bake until the small bones dissolve, about 3 to 4 hours.

4. Meanwhile, combine the dried mushrooms and water in a saucepan and bring to a boil. Reduce the heat and simmer for 30 minutes. Stir in the salt, sugar,

and soy sauce. Add the scallion and simmer until reduced to 1 cup, about 25 minutes. Strain. Set aside.

5. Remove the fish from the oven. Cut the fillets in half and divide among 4 plates, with the mushrooms over the fish. Spoon the sauce over the shad and serve immediately.

Serves 4 as a main course

Potted Ginger Shad

1 tablespoon kosher salt

1 tablespoon freshly ground pepper

1 teaspoon ground allspice

½ teaspoon ground clove

2 shad fillets, 2 pounds each, skinned and cut in half crosswise

1 cup grated fresh ginger

2 cups apple cider vinegar

2 cups water

1. Preheat the oven to 200° F.

2. Combine the salt, pepper, allspice, and clove. Sprinkle a small amount of the spice mixture into a small ovenproof crock that you can pack the fish into tightly. Top with a layer of shad, cover with a thin layer of ginger, and sprinkle with spice mixture. Continue layering the fish, ginger, and seasonings until you have used all the fish. Pour in the vinegar and water. Cover with foil and top with pie weights. Bake for 6 hours. Cool. Remove shad from vinegar and serve or wrap in plastic. Keeps in the refrigerator for 3 days.

Serves 4 as a main course

A WILL AND A DESTINY

Shortly after the Chesapeake Bay warms and blue crabs start shedding their shells, some Pacific salmon get restless in their ocean feeding grounds, turn tail, and surge en masse—first against the tides and then against the currents—up different rivers of the Pacific Northwest. The salmon's is a lethal instinct, as well as the ultimate love story: They will spawn, then they will die. Or they will be caught in the midst of the effort.

It is not clear whether wild salmon, as opposed to farmed salmon, have an option for a different sort of life; most marine biologists believe the fish is incapable of refusing the call of its nature. Nevertheless, the salmon's unflinching focus on returning home inspires awe among observers on the banks of the rivers. Passionate, single-minded determination is an admirable thing. Especially to beings overwhelmed by choice.

Indigenous Americans in the Pacific Northwest tried to soften the edges of the salmon's fate. Some believed that the fish was the incarnation of a benevolent god who took piscine form in order to feed his people and that this spirit rose with the smoke from the cooking fire to observe their thankfulness. In the *The Great American Seafood Cookbook*, Susan Herrmann Loomis, who spent many years in the Northwest, writes that after the ceremonial cooking of the first of the season's salmon, the bones were carefully laid on the river bank, pointing upstream to insure a continued run and the return of the salmon the following spring.

Farm-raised salmon, which is available year round, has dimmed that anticipation. Still, watching salmon run in Washington, Canada, Alaska, and Ireland, I felt a certain rush of the heart. It's impossible not to cheer the surging fish. Even when planning dinner. Such is the predators' dilemma.

I also got spoiled. Once one has cooked and eaten chinook salmon, which runs up the Columbia River between Oregon and Washington, or wild Atlantic salmon, which plies the rushing creeks of the Connemara region of Ireland, it is difficult to sing the praises of what is available all year.

Common salmon nomenclature doesn't help those seeking the fattest and fittest and freshest salmon. Despite appellations such as "Irish," Scottish," or "Norwegian," there are two basic types of salmon: Atlantic and Pacific.

Atlantic salmon (*Salmo salar*) once clogged rivers up and down America's eastern seaport until pollution caused them to vanish. Waverley Root quotes Jonathan Norton Leonard as saying "any salmon trying to navigate the lower Connecticut River, which drains the sewage of city after city, would have to make the trip in a space suit." True Atlantic salmon, which is fatty, pale pink, and has a large, fine flake, can still be caught in Canada and throughout northern Europe, but because it is legally an endangered species, wild Atlantic salmon cannot be sold. Most farmed salmon is the Atlantic variety.

Native Americans claimed there were five tribes of salmon, and there are indeed five varieties of Pacific salmon in American waters; a sixth plies those of Japan. In general, the more rapid a salmon's home river is, the richer its flesh will be. The longer a salmon spends feeding in the ocean prior to heading up the river home, the finer, fatter, and tastier it is. Of the four most toothsome varieties the deep pink king or chinook salmon, which spends a leisurely four to five years at sea, is, to my taste, unrivaled. Sockeye, though, which spends three to four years feeding, is a very fine fish as well. It has a dark orange-pink color and is almost as fatty as the king. The pink salmon is the smallest and quickest to mature; it has a pale pink color and an indistinct flavor. Like the yellow-fleshed chum salmon, it is best suited for canning or for using in fish cakes or croquettes.

Equally significant is when the fish is caught. The best fish are homeward bound. Like body builders preparing for the competition of a lifetime, they have spent years feeding their muscle; they are pumped up, powerful, and ready for the journey. After spawning, the fish are spent, and the flesh is spongy and tasteless; captured too far ahead of time, the meat can be flabby. In other words, to indulge in the finest salmon is to devour future generations.

Until very recently, this fact caused little crisis of conscience. Salmon was so plentiful that, during the American colonial era, contracts for indentured servants stipulated that they could not be fed the fish more than once a week, or lobster either for that matter. Today, their employers would be hard pressed to afford both marine delicacies in a week. Scarcity, it seems, not quality, confers preciousness; as wild salmon stocks have been drastically depleted, farmed salmon has eroded the image of the fish.

Nevertheless, being in the right place at the right time is, in the case of salmon, as with many other things in life, the most precious commodity of all. A fact that hasn't changed since Longfellow described a Boston Brahmin as "a solid man of Boston / A comfortable man, with dividends, / And the first salmon, and the first green peas."

Salmon with Sugar Snaps and Potatoes in Shrimp Broth

2 cups water
1 teaspoon kosher salt
2 tablespoons fresh lemon juice
16 large shrimp
1 cup chardonnay wine
8 small red potatoes, scrubbed and quartered
1 cup frozen pearl onions, defrosted
4 salmon fillets, 5 ounces each
Freshly ground pepper to taste
2 cups Sugar Snap peas, stemmed and strung
2 teaspoons chopped Italian parsley

1. Combine the water, ½ teaspoon salt, and lemon juice in a medium saucepan and bring to a boil. Add the shrimp and simmer for 5 minutes. Drain, reserving the liquid. When cool enough to handle, peel the shrimp, reserving the shells.

2. Put the shrimp shells and the cooking liquid back in the saucepan and bring to a boil. Reduce heat and simmer, covered, for 15 minutes. Strain into a large saucepan, add the wine, and bring to a boil.

3. Add the potatoes, reduce the heat, and simmer for 10 minutes. Add the onions, cover, and simmer for 5 minutes.

4. Season the salmon with ½ teaspoon salt and pepper. Place over the potatoes, cover the pan, and poach for 3 minutes. Add the peas and the shrimp, return to a simmer, cover, and cook for 5 minutes. Divide the salmon, shrimp, and vegetables among 4 shallow soup bowls and ladle some of the broth over the mixture. Sprinkle with parsley and serve immediately.

Serves 4 as a main course

Teriyaki Salmon Steaks

4 salmon steaks, 8 ounces each
¼ cup teriyaki sauce
2 scallions, thinly sliced

Preheat the grill or broiler. Place the salmon steaks in a shallow dish and cover with 3 tablespoons of teriyaki sauce. Let stand for 10 minutes. Grill or broil the salmon until almost cooked through, about 4½ minutes per side. Divide among 4 plates and sprinkle with the remaining teriyaki sauce and the scallions. Serve immediately.

Serves 4 as a main course

Stuffed and Roasted Whole Salmon

1½ cups kosher salt
1 salmon, 7 pounds, head and tail on
Spiced Corn and Rice Stuffing or Roasted Potato-Onion Stuffing (recipes follow)

1. Preheat the oven to 425° F.
2. In a large roasting pan, make a bed of salt that runs the length and width of the salmon. Place the salmon on top of the salt. If the salmon tail hangs out of the pan, wrap it in aluminum foil. Fill the inside of the salmon with one of the stuffings. Place any stuffing that doesn't fit in the salmon in a covered baking dish. Tie the salmon with string in 3 places to hold in the stuffing.
3. Roast the salmon until just cooked through, about 45 minutes. Start baking the additional stuffing after about 25 minutes. Carefully transfer the salmon to a platter and remove the string. Gently pull the skin off the top of the salmon. To serve, lift pieces of salmon off the bone.

Serves 8 to 10 as a main course

Spiced Corn and Rice Stuffing

2 packages frozen corn, defrosted (10 ounces each)
½ cup lowfat milk
4 cups cooked white rice
2 teaspoons kosher salt
Freshly ground pepper to taste
1 teaspoon ground cumin
2 tablespoons minced cilantro

Place half the corn in a food processor with the milk and process until smooth. Place the rice in a bowl and stir in the corn puree. Stir in the remaining corn, salt, pepper, cumin, and cilantro.

Serves 8 to 10 as a side dish

Roasted Potato-Onion Stuffing

8 small onions, halved and thinly sliced

24 small red potatoes, scrubbed and thinly sliced

4 teaspoons olive oil

3 teaspoons kosher salt

Freshly ground pepper to taste

2 tablespoons minced Italian parsley

2 cloves garlic, minced

½ teaspoon grated lemon zest

Preheat the oven to 375° F. Toss the onions and potatoes with the olive oil and divide between 2 baking sheets. Sprinkle with salt and pepper. Roast until brown and tender, turning once, about 25 minutes. Place in a bowl and toss with the parsley, garlic, and lemon zest.

Serves 8 to 10 as a side dish

FLOUNDERING AROUND

Like most Americans raised landlocked during the 1950s, I was deeply suspicious and a little afraid of any fish that was not square, breaded, and deep-fried until I moved to Provincetown, Massachusetts, in the mid-1970s. The town's ambient aroma of fish and brine seemed romantic, if a little scary. I tried to act unfazed when boats from the fishing fleet docked and wooden boxes of glassy-eyed fish were heaved onto the town pier, but I was as unsettled by the fishermen's vernacular as I was by the fishes' stare.

Words like "dabbin'," as in "Hey bub, you been doin' some dabbin'," or "flukin'," or "backin'" reminded me that, at least that first spring, I was The Other, an outsider. I had no idea what they meant.

My cluelessness followed me to work where I was a young cook. When the chef first ordered me to "grab ya a fill-it, darlin'," I searched frantically for containers to fill. Only the process of elimination taught me that, in Provincetown, a fill-it is actually a fish fillet, pronounced to distinguish it from a filet of beef.

A town so intimate with the ocean has volumes of fish phraseology. It was years before I was fluent in the precise language that denoted particular species, their size, quality, and rarity or commonness at any given time of the year. That first summer I learned about backs and dabs, yellowtail and flukes. In other words, like most people I found the four major varieties of flounder that populate the waters off Cape Cod ("flounda" in local parlance) the least threatening of fish.

This was partly because of the sweet and subtle flavor of the fish. It also was because, despite the alacrity required to cook the more delicate fillets, the flounder is a simple fish to fry. As well as to bake or to broil, to sauté or to poach.

Yellowtail flounder (not to be confused with the tuna of the same name) were typically small fillets, pearly and nearly translucent near the tail, otherwise snow white, fine flaked, and excessively lean. Their flavor was so sweetly of the sea that they needed nothing more than a quick sauté, a judicious seasoning, a squeeze of lemon, and a sprinkling of parsley.

A Portuguese fisherman taught me to soak the fillets in milk and dust them in lightly seasoned flour to seal in the moisture, protect the fish from the sizzle of butter, and give them a delicate crust. It was a lesson I used on mild fillets of fluke, a flounder that also abounds in New England's summer waters. With its coarser flake, it needed a foil like scallions, mushrooms, or a handful of fresh chopped herbs to distract from its lack of finesse.

Gray sole (also called witch flounder) is stockier and hence has thicker and narrower fillets than most flounders. Large flaked, white with an occasional tinge of pink, gray sole is the meatiest of all flounder and was best steamed or baked. It rolled well and could be stuffed with mussels, oysters, or crab. It could even stand up to a rich flavor like one of the traditional mustard sauces, or to the flavors of onions, garlic, or wild greens.

Blackbacks—or winter flounder—and dabs, which are also called American plaice, are also generally large and sturdy fish. Like all flounder, they are white and lean, although these have a larger flake than most members of the flounder family. They arrived as the weather cooled and were delicious poached in tomato sauce or baked or steamed with full-flavored vegetables. By that time, I considered myself a flatfish connoisseur. Many consider flatfish synonymous with sole. Technically, in United States waters, the family includes flounder, fluke, plaice, dab, and halibut.

Knowing the family readied me for mackerel and tinkers and whitebait, left me unfazed by eel or even by a whole tuna so large it required a crew of three to clean it. I didn't realize then, however, that it wasn't simply the pure simple flavor of the flounder, nor its ease of preparation, that had emboldened me and opened the door to other fish. The blessing of flounder was its lack of skin and bone.

When cut along the dorsal fin, the fillet lifts easily from either side of an intact skeleton, leaves it forever and without any shards. When the fillet is placed skin side down and a sharp knife is passed between the skin and the flesh, the fillet rolls easily away from the skin, no tearing, no remnants, no mess. The landlocked American wants no reminder of the past, no souvenir, no second thoughts about her fish. Like many, I got comfortable with fish by getting to know flounder. Its fillets are a pristine white canvas, fishy enough to hint of the sea, simple enough to make it seem safe.

A Fisherman's Perfect Sole Meunière

½ cup lowfat milk

1 teaspoon Tabasco

1 cup all-purpose flour

2 teaspoons kosher salt, plus more to taste

Freshly ground pepper to taste

1½ teaspoons unsalted butter

4 white flatfish fillets, such as sole or flounder, about 5 ounces each

½ cup fresh lemon juice

4 teaspoons chopped Italian parsley

1. Stir together the milk and Tabasco in a shallow bowl. Place the flour in a shallow dish and season with salt and pepper. Melt the butter in a large nonstick skillet over medium heat. Dip the fish in the milk and then coat with flour on both sides.

2. Sauté the fish until just cooked through, about 2 minutes per side. Carefully remove from the skillet with a spatula and place 1 fillet on each of 4 plates. Lower the heat, add the lemon juice to the skillet, and stir just to scrape up any browned bits in the skillet. Spoon over the fish, season with salt and pepper, and sprinkle with parsley. Serve immediately.

Serves 4 as a main course

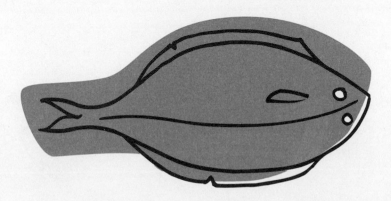

Sole with Mushrooms, Scallions, and Parsley

2 teaspoons unsalted butter

2 cloves garlic, minced

1 pound mushrooms, thinly sliced

4 white flatfish fillets, such as sole or flounder, about 5 ounces each

2 teaspoons kosher salt

3 tablespoons fresh lemon juice

3 tablespoons chopped Italian parsley

2 tablespoons thinly sliced scallions

½ cup white wine

Freshly ground pepper to taste

1. Melt the butter in a large nonstick skillet over medium heat. Add the garlic and cook, stirring, for 30 seconds. Add the mushrooms and sauté for 5 minutes. Place the fish in the skillet, rounded side down, and sauté for 5 minutes. Sprinkle with 1 teaspoon salt. Turn the fillets over and sprinkle with the remaining salt.

2. Add the lemon juice, parsley, scallions, and wine and simmer for 5 minutes longer. Season with pepper. Divide among 4 plates and serve immediately.

Serves 4 as a main course

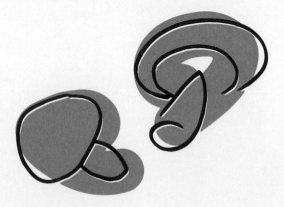

Sole with Ramps, Asparagus, and Roasted Potatoes

12 small red potatoes, scrubbed and halved

2 teaspoons unsalted butter

5 teaspoons olive oil

32 ramps or small scallions, trimmed

½ cup white wine

½ cup water

3½ teaspoons kosher salt

Freshly ground pepper to taste

16 asparagus spears, tough ends snapped off

½ cup all-purpose flour

½ cup cornmeal

4 white flatfish fillets, such as sole or flounder, about 6 ounces each

2 cloves garlic, minced

2 heads escarole, trimmed and cut across into ¼-inch strips

2 tablespoons chopped Italian parsley

1. Preheat the oven to 450° F.

2. Put the potatoes in a large saucepan, cover with water, and bring to a boil. Reduce the heat and simmer, covered, until almost tender, about 15 minutes. Drain, place in a baking dish, and toss with 1 teaspoon butter. Roast until browned and crisp, about 30 minutes.

3. Meanwhile, heat 2 teaspoons of the oil in a large wide pot over medium heat. Add the ramps and cook until just wilted, about 4 minutes. Add the wine and water, cover with a sheet of parchment paper, reduce the heat and braise until tender, about 25 minutes. Season with ½ teaspoon salt and pepper. Set aside, keeping warm. Blanch the asparagus in boiling salted water for 5 minutes. Drain and set aside.

4. Combine the flour, cornmeal, 2 teaspoons salt, and pepper in a shallow dish. Coat the fish in the mixture on both sides. Heat 2 teaspoons of the oil in a

large nonstick skillet over medium heat. Add the fish and cook until golden brown, about 3 minutes per side. Remove from the pan and keep warm.

5. Wipe out the pan and add the remaining 1 teaspoon of oil. When hot, add the garlic and cook, stirring, for 30 seconds. Add the escarole and stir-fry until wilted, about 3 minutes. Remove from the pan and keep warm. Wipe out the pan again and add 1 teaspoon butter. Add the asparagus and cook for 3 minutes. Toss the potatoes with 1 teaspoon salt, pepper, and parsley. Place 1 sole fillet in the center of each of 4 plates. Mound the ramps, potatoes, and escarole around the fish and cross the asparagus over it. Serve immediately.

Serves 4 as a main course

SPRING CHICKEN

That the term "spring chicken" has become quaint is a woeful sign of the times. The fluffy chick that pecks and feeds indiscriminately has its charms. In epicurean terms, the charms of very young poultry include an embarrassing tenderness and a mild, amiable flavor that happily absorbs any aromatics with which it comes in contact. In human terms, the seductive power of innocence, connoting as it does a lack of judgment and a bald acceptance of the world-as-it-is-found, can never be underestimated.

After all, "chicks" came to mean girls, in rock-and-roll vernacular, specifically the kind who hung around backstage. Likewise, "chicken" came to mean the young and easily exploited in gay circles. Both are nervous-making concepts, as undignified as chicks dyed pink, blue, or green in an Easter basket, and, while society was busy cleaning up the image of backyard chicks, amiable chicken, and dip-dyed Easter basket accoutrement, for all the right reasons, agribusiness was just as busy, extincting the notion of spring chicken. Perhaps the poultry industry harbored less altruistic reasons. They wanted to create a year-round commodity. Under heating lamps that simulated the seasons, hens could hatch eggs as easily in November as in April.

A chicken in every pot became a reality. Poultry growers developed an inexhaustible supply of chicken with the supple, nondescript nature once celebrated as spring chicken. But with no gamey summer chicken, no stringy fall chicken, no preserved winter chicken as contrast, the eternal spring chicken seemed bland. As unbelievable as the women who, through various cosmetic procedures, strive to remain spring chickens.

Every meaning of spring chicken became a joke. But only because the little bird was plucked, as if of so many feathers, of its primordial integrity. Rather than being a salutation to the young and feisty urges of spring, chicken became a pose.

This is not an intractable situation. Growers who raise free-range or organic birds can supply the tender chicken of spring. When accompanied by other spring ingredients, even a small commercially bred bird can summon the gods of hope, resilience, and tender, impressionable youth to a table. Like baby lamb, baby arti-chokes, or blindly flailing soft-shell crabs, baby chicken has an inherent magic: You eat it, and you become young, living a life without boundary or prohibition, at least for a moment.

As the original proponent of a chicken in every pot, King Henri IV of France wasn't just promising dinner. He was suggesting good fortune and the possibility of eternal youth. Properly roasted, a young chicken's skin becomes crisp as gold leaf; its flavor is forever-young. Who wouldn't vote "yes" on proposition chicken? The rationalists, that's who.

Good fortune, as well as a horror of indiscriminate gains, has plagued chicken through the ages. According to Margaret Visser in her *Much Depends on Dinner,* some African tribes eschew eating chicken. The bird is seen as a sacred messenger. The attitude is mirrored in Southeast Asia and Iran where the hen, in particular, is considered promiscuous and careless of both family structure and dietary discrim-ination. The fact that a chicken will wantonly peck a worm nauseates Buddhists, makes the bird anathema to high-caste Indian Hindus, and distinguishes both groups from Muslims, who love chicken.

In 817, the Council of Aachen ruled chicken too sumptuous for fast days and relegated its consumption to the feast days preceding Easter and Christmas. A rul-ing that must have brought a smirk from the Jews, who have long included chicken in both Passover and Rosh Hashanah celebrations.

Even today, a freshly killed chicken is, among some major league baseball players of Caribbean extraction, a good-luck totem in the locker room on opening day. The superstition that pays homage both to innate expertise and those lucky enough not to imagine another, more jaded world. And yes, I'd like to live there, even if only for dinner.

The fleeting nature of spring chickens is the essential charm. The totem-power of a young chicken, on the other hand, is unleashed by the first blast of heat, whether from the oven or grill, the frying pan or fricassee pot, and abides both for the duration of dinner and the hours before sleep. Chicken, even stripped of its folkloric draping, is light and lending. It makes a hopeful meal.

Chicken with Morels, Fava Beans, and Spring Potatoes

(Adapted from Le Cirque, Manhattan)

1 teaspoon kosher salt
1 pound fresh fava beans, shelled
2 tablespoons vegetable oil
1 chicken, about 3½ pounds, cut into 8 pieces
½ pound small new potatoes, scrubbed and halved
16 cloves garlic, unpeeled
8 small shallots, peeled
1 tablespoon fresh thyme leaves
2 bay leaves
1 teaspoon freshly ground pepper
4 cups fresh morels, stems removed, rinsed if sandy and
    dried well, cut into ½-inch slices
1½ cups chicken broth, homemade, or low-sodium canned broth
3 tablespoons minced fresh chives

1. Add ½ teaspoon salt to a large pot of boiling water and cook the fava beans for 1 minute. Drain, submerge them in ice water, drain again, and peel off the skins. Set aside.

2. Preheat the oven to 425° F.

3. Heat 1 tablespoon oil in a large cast-iron skillet over medium-high heat. When hot, add the chicken, skin side down, and cook until golden brown, about 3 minutes. Remove from the heat, turn the chicken, and add the potatoes, garlic, shallots, thyme, and bay leaves. Add the remaining salt and the pepper and put the skillet in the oven.

4. Meanwhile, heat the remaining oil in a large sauté pan over high heat. When hot, add the morels in 1 layer, in batches if necessary, and sauté until golden brown. Add the chicken broth, bring to a boil, and remove from heat.

5. When the chicken has roasted for 10 minutes, pour the morels over the chicken. Stir until the vegetables are coated with broth. Continue to bake the chicken, basting with the pan juices, until tender, about 20 to 25 minutes longer.

6. Add the fava beans and chives to the chicken. Stir until the beans are coated with the pan juices and bake for 2 to 3 minutes more. Remove the bay leaves. Arrange the pieces of chicken in the center of a warm platter, pour the vegetables and pan juices over the meat, and serve.

Serves 4 as a main course

Herb-Crumbed Roasted Chicken with Watercress

2 cups buttermilk

2 chicken breasts, split in half, and 2 chicken legs, separated at the joint, skinned

2 cups bread crumbs

1½ tablespoons chopped fresh rosemary

2 tablespoons chopped fresh thyme

¼ cup chopped Italian parsley

2½ teaspoons kosher salt

Freshly ground pepper to taste

1 cup all-purpose flour

Olive oil spray

6 bunches watercress, about 6 ounces each, thick stems removed, leaves washed
    but not dried

1 teaspoon fresh lemon juice

1 teaspoon olive oil

1. Pour the buttermilk into a large, shallow dish. Add the chicken pieces and turn to coat. Cover and let stand for 1 hour. Combine the bread crumbs, rosemary, thyme, parsley, 1½ teaspoons salt, and pepper in a shallow dish. Spread the flour in another shallow dish.

2. Preheat the oven to 400° F. Lightly coat 2 baking sheets with the olive oil spray.

3. Remove the chicken from the buttermilk and coat each piece with flour. Dip each piece back into the buttermilk and then coat with the bread crumb mixture. Place the chicken on the baking sheets, spacing pieces as far apart as possible. Bake until the chicken is cooked through and the crust is crisp, about 45 minutes.

4. Heat a large saucepan over medium heat. Add the watercress and toss until just wilted. Add the lemon juice, olive oil, the remaining salt, and pepper. Divide the chicken and the watercress among 4 plates and serve immediately.

Serves 4 as a main course

Roast Chicken with Bread Salad

(Adapted from Zuni Cafe, San Francisco)

CHICKEN

    1 chicken, about 2½ pounds
    1½ teaspoons kosher salt
    Freshly ground pepper to taste
    4 sprigs fresh thyme
    4 cloves garlic, lightly crushed

SALAD

    1 teaspoon red wine vinegar
    1 tablespoon warm water
    1 tablespoon dried currants
    6 cups stale country-style bread, most crust removed and cut into 1-inch cubes
    4½ teaspoons olive oil
    2 teaspoons Dijon mustard
    4 tablespoons champagne vinegar
    ½ teaspoon kosher salt
    Freshly ground pepper to taste
    3 cloves garlic, slivered
    4 scallions, thinly sliced
    3 cups mixed young bitter greens, such as arugula, chicory, or frisée

1. The day before serving, sprinkle the chicken with salt and pepper. Run your fingers between the skin and flesh of the breasts and thighs to make 4 small pock-

ets. Stick a sprig of thyme and a garlic clove in each pocket. Wrap the chicken in plastic and refrigerate overnight.

2. About 2 hours before serving, combine the red wine vinegar and water in a small bowl, add the currants, and let stand for 1 hour. Put the bread in a large bowl and toss with 2 teaspoons of the olive oil. Toast the bread under the broiler for about 2 minutes. Set aside.

3. Preheat the oven to 425° F.

4. Place the chicken, breast side up, in a shallow roasting pan. Roast for 30 minutes. Turn the chicken over and roast until the juices run clear when pricked in the thickest part of the thigh, about 15 to 20 minutes longer. Let stand for 10 minutes.

5. Whisk together the mustard, champagne vinegar, ½ teaspoon salt, and pepper in a large bowl. Slowly whisk in 2 teaspoons of the olive oil. Add the bread and toss to coat. Set aside. Heat the remaining ½ teaspoon of olive oil in a small nonstick saucepan over medium heat. Add the garlic and scallions and cook for 2 minutes. Add the garlic and scallions to the bread mixture. Drain the currants, add them, and toss the salad. Place in a baking dish.

6. When the chicken is done, place the salad in the oven and bake for 5 minutes. Turn off the oven and leave the salad in for 10 minutes. Carve the chicken into 8 pieces, reserving the pan juices. Toss the salad with 2 tablespoons of the pan juices and the greens. Divide the salad among 4 plates, top each with 2 pieces of chicken, and serve.

Serves 4 as a main course

INNOCENCE AND DINNER

Wherever there have been grassy knolls and people, there has been lamb. The animal and the people who tend it have symbolized the gentle, pastoral spirit of a culture. Like Mary and her little lamb, the animal and its shepherd wander freely, intimately though not restrictively connected, from one grassy patch to the next, without destination or deadline. Theirs is an innocent freedom. It makes sense that lamb has long symbolized the season of renewal.

Monotheists like the Jews, and later the Christians and Muslims, presumably borrowed the symbol from the pagan cultures that preceded them. As early as 600 B.C. in China, the *Book of Songs* gave a description of the propitiatory spring sacrifice of lamb. To sacrifice an innocent is to acknowledge a basic human dilemma. We take life in order to live. At the same time, the ritual incarnates hope. After the initial wince, those who baste young lamb on a spit at a Greek Easter, Sephardic Passover, or during the final days of the Muslim Ramadan celebration feel chastened and protective. Reminded of their dark side, they look toward the light. It is spring. From Jakarta to Sonoma County, lamb is in the air.

Even removed from the messy sacrifice, modern mortals commune with the season whenever they tuck into a meal of spring lamb. Born in February or March, the lamb has generally grazed solely on young grass or, in the case of the French *pré-salé* lamb or the succulent young lamb of the Connemara region of Ireland, on salty marsh grass and herbs by the time it reaches the market in late April. The delicate herbaceousness of lamb meat is like an edible postcard from the animal's hometown. Spring lamb from Provence has a savor of rosemary, wild fennel, and thyme; from Colorado, the meat tastes like clover and has a faint suggestion of balsam. A spring lamb from Sonoma County can have a subtle hint of wild garlic.

Some cooks, like Madeleine Kamman, describe these flavors as "built-in seasoning" and consider them sufficient. Others take a cue from the residual flavors in spring lamb and use similar herbs to bolster its flavor. Yet to preserve the inherent nuance of spring lamb takes an ineffably delicate hand in the kitchen.

Spring lamb's lean, finely grained, light pink meat requires less cooking time and gentler cooking techniques than older lamb. The meat is more impressionable than older lamb or mutton, both of whose flavors will dominate any dish. Young lamb, on the other hand, like spring chicken, impressionably absorbs the character of any ingredient with which it is cooked; unlike spring chicken, though, it gives, in turn, its own perfume. The cool weather of early spring gives the season's lamb a fine, creamy layer of white fat. Which is a good thing. Without this natural basting material, the lean spring meat would be dry.

New Zealand and Australia have led the way in delivering young lamb nearly twelve months a year. This particular spring lamb is frozen and, therefore, slightly tougher than fresh lamb. It also lacks the idiosyncratic taste of its origin that makes young lamb compelling. So I prefer to play roulette at the butcher, accepting his word about the provenance of the lamb and using common sense to judge whether a leg of lamb is truly "spring," or merely all-season. The more a leg of lamb weighs, the older it is. A leg of spring lamb weighs five to seven pounds. Large enough to make a company meal, it is still small enough to engender a protective, coddling spirit in the cook.

Rack of Lamb with Feta-Garlic Crust

1 rack of lamb, at room temperature
2 teaspoons Dijon mustard
½ cup bread crumbs
2 large cloves garlic, minced
2 tablespoons crumbled feta cheese
2 tablespoons chopped Italian parsley
½ teaspoon kosher salt
Freshly ground pepper to taste

1. Preheat the oven to 400° F.

2. Rub the fat-covered side of the lamb with the mustard. Put the bread crumbs, garlic, feta, and parsley in a mixing bowl and rub the mixture between your fingers until the cheese is mixed into the bread crumbs. Season with salt and pepper.

3. Pat the crumb mixture over the mustard and over the sides of the lamb. Place on a baking sheet and roast until medium rare, about 30 minutes. Let stand for 10 minutes before carving.

Serves 4 as a main course

Greek Lamb and Artichoke Stew

2 teaspoons olive oil

1½ pounds lamb shoulder, trimmed and cut into 1½-inch cubes

1 large onion, coarsely chopped

3 medium carrots, cut into 1-inch pieces

8 fresh artichoke hearts, quartered

8 scallions, chopped

½ cup plus 2 teaspoons chopped Italian parsley

1 cup water

1 cup white wine

4 tablespoons fresh lemon juice

1 tablespoon cornstarch

2 teaspoons kosher salt

Freshly ground pepper to taste

1. Heat the olive oil over medium-high heat in a medium-size pot. Add the lamb and brown on all sides, about 7 minutes. Lower the heat to medium, add the onion and carrots, and cook, stirring occasionally, for 5 minutes. Add the artichoke hearts, scallions, ¼ cup parsley, ½ cup water, the wine, and 3 tablespoons lemon juice. Simmer, uncovered, until the lamb is tender, about 45 minutes to 1 hour.

2. Gradually stir the remaining water into the cornstarch and stir the mixture into the stew. Cook for 1 minute longer. Stir in the salt, pepper, ¼ cup parsley, and the remaining lemon juice. Divide among 4 bowls and garnish with the remaining parsley. Serve immediately.

Serves 4 as a main course

Middle Eastern Tomato, Split Pea, and Lamb Stew over Rice

2 teaspoons olive oil
1 pound lamb shoulder, trimmed and cut into 1-inch cubes
1 medium onion, chopped
¼ teaspoon turmeric
¼ teaspoon ground cinnamon
Pinch ground ginger
Pinch ground clove
Pinch ground cardamom
1 teaspoon kosher salt, plus more to taste
¼ teaspoon freshly ground pepper
2 cups water
1 cup yellow split peas, rinsed and picked over
2 cups canned crushed tomatoes
3 cups cooked white rice
2 teaspoons chopped cilantro

1. Heat the olive oil in a deep large skillet over medium-high heat. Add the lamb and brown on all sides, about 5 minutes. Remove the lamb from the skillet and set aside. Add the onion and cook until soft, about 5 minutes. Stir in the lamb, spices, salt, and pepper and cook for 1 minute. Add the water and bring to a boil. Reduce heat, and simmer, uncovered, for 30 minutes.

2. Stir in the split peas, cover the skillet, and cook until the peas are soft but still retain their shape, about 20 minutes. Stir in the tomatoes. Simmer, uncovered, until the mixture is thick, about 15 minutes longer. Taste and add more salt if needed. Divide the rice among 4 plates and spoon the stew over it. Garnish with cilantro and serve immediately.

Serves 4 as a main course

FOREVER FRESH

Lemons, like most edible parts of modern life, are no longer bound by seasonal constraints. The most acidic of all citrus fruits, lemons are arguably at their best from December to March, but a squeeze of lemon merely freshens winter's typically rich dishes and is less apparent for what it is than for what it does. It is in the spring, when ingredients and cooking techniques are delicate, that the force and personality of lemons are most apparent, most insistently young, most indisputably alive.

There is something eternal about the freshness a lemon imparts, though Her Royal Yellow Bitterness is actually a fairly modern fruit. Botanists are divided as to whether the fruit was initially cultivated in Malaysia, China, or the Indus valley, but they agree that lemons haven't been grown for much more than two thousand years. The lemon is riddled with contradictions. The lemon tree, after all, is a subtropical evergreen with tender lush leaves ("very pretty," as the song goes) and an intoxicatingly fragrant flower ("and the lemon flower is sweet"). But the fruit of most lemon trees "is impossible to eat."

Its acidity is intractable. The lemon possesses so few carbohydrates that it must ripen on the tree; once picked, it will, unlike most tree fruits, not sweeten at all. And yet the fruit itself is such a cheerful-looking, self-contained little universe that generation after generation of curious eaters fall for its charm. How they pucker and gnash their teeth, how they heap reprisals on the false-faced fruit whose seed-bearing sections bitterly punish any intruder. And yet it is difficult to sustain fury at anything as purely itself as the lemon is. Unable to relish the whole, the cook endeavors to use its parts.

In India—and, after colonial reign there, in England—lemons are soaked in mustard oil and fierce spices; their acidity thereby matched or subdued, preserved or pickled lemons become an interesting condiment. In Morocco, salt is used to mitigate a lemon's sourness with a more subtle result. Part of the lemon's contradictory nature is that its juice can actually sear or partially cook meat or fish when used as a marinade. Lemon juice is an oxymoron: liquid fire. Used sparingly, the juice brightens savory dishes or, if sweetened with sugar, gives a fresh edge to desserts.

A lemon's very acidity is blithe, and, however chastening, it is a flavor that people seem seldom to tire of. Fresh lemon juice is better than that prepared ahead of time, as the juice tends to separate and even become acrid in the air. Likewise, lemon zest should contain only the yellow part of the skin, as the white spongy pith tends toward the acrid as well. Otherwise, besides using lemons judiciously and to taste, there are few caveats a cook need observe. Between lemons and humans nothing is irreversible. There is always sugar.

And for many, like the poet Pablo Neruda, there is even a sort of awe surrounding the fruit.

"Delicate merchandise!" he wrote in his poem "A Lemon." "The harbors are big with it / —bazaars / for the light and the / barbarous gold. / We open / the halves / of a miracle, / and a clotting of acids / brims / into the starry / divisions: / creation's / original juices, / irreducible, changeless, / alive: / so the freshness lives on / in a lemon, / in the sweet-smelling house of the rind, / the proportions, arcane and acerb."

Preserved Lemons with Cardamom and Black Pepper

This condiment can give a fresh flavor to chicken or veal stews, couscous dishes, tomato or other vegetable salads, and any lamb dish. Use it sparingly to taste.

7 lemons
½ cup kosher salt
1 tablespoon cardamom pods
2 teaspoons black peppercorns
¼ cup fresh lemon juice, plus more if needed

1. Cut the lemons in quarters lengthwise, leaving them attached at 1 end. Rub the cut surfaces of the lemons with a little of the salt. Place 1 tablespoon of the salt in the bottom of a 1-quart glass jar. Layer the lemons in the jar alternately with the remaining salt, cardamom pods, and peppercorns, pressing them with a wooden spoon as you put them in. Pour in enough lemon juice to barely cover the lemons.

2. Cover the jar and refrigerate, shaking the jar daily, for 2 to 3 weeks before using. To use, rinse the salt off the lemons, scrape out the pulp, and cut into pieces. Preserved lemons will keep for several months in the refrigerator.

Makes 7 preserved lemons

Lemon Roasted Chicken

4 large lemons
1 chicken, 4 to 5 pounds
1 teaspoon kosher salt
Freshly ground pepper to taste
2 small onions, quartered

1. Preheat the oven to 425° F.

2. Using a vegetable peeler, remove the zest from one of the lemons in long thin strips. Loosen the skin over the chicken breasts and insert the zest between the skin and the meat. Cut the lemons in half lengthwise and then across into ¾-inch slices. Squeeze the juice from one of the slices over the skin of the chicken.

3. Season with salt and pepper. Stuff half the lemon slices and half the onions into the cavity of the chicken. Put the rest in the center of a roasting pan and place the chicken on top of them. Roast for 15 minutes. Turn the oven down to 375° F. Continue roasting until the juices run clear when pricked with a fork in the thickest part of the thigh, about 1 hour and 15 minutes longer. Let stand for 10 minutes. Carve, divide among 4 plates, and serve.

Serves 4 as a main course

Lemon Curd Tart with Candied Almond Topping

CURD

    6 eggs

    1½ cups sugar

    1 tablespoon grated lemon zest

    1 cup fresh lemon juice

    4 tablespoons (½ stick) unsalted butter, cut into small pieces

CRUST

    ⅓ cup slivered almonds

    2½ tablespoons sugar

    1 tablespoon grated lemon zest

    ¾ cup all-purpose flour, plus additional for rolling

    ½ teaspoon kosher salt

    6 tablespoons (¾ stick) cold unsalted butter, cut into small pieces

    1 large egg yolk

    1 tablespoon water

    ¼ teaspoon almond extract

TOPPING

    ¾ cup sugar

    1 tablespoon grated lemon zest

    1 cup sliced almonds

    2 large egg whites, whisked until foamy

1. To make the curd, combine the eggs and sugar in a medium nonreactive saucepan and whisk until thickened and light in color. Whisk in the lemon zest and juice. Place over low heat and cook, whisking constantly, until thick, about 10 minutes. Do not boil. Remove from the heat and whisk in the butter. Let cool. Refrigerate until cold.

2. Meanwhile, make the crust: Combine the almonds, sugar, and zest in a food processor and process until ground. Add the flour and salt and pulse just to com-

bine. Add the butter and pulse until the mixture resembles coarse meal. Whisk together the egg yolk, water, and almond extract. Add to the flour mixture and process just until the mixture starts to come together. Press into a ball, flatten into a disk, wrap in plastic, and refrigerate for 30 minutes.

3. Preheat the oven to 350° F.

4. Roll out the dough and fit it into a 10-inch quiche dish. Line with foil and fill with pie weights or dried beans. Bake for 20 minutes. Remove the foil and weights and bake until the crust is lightly browned, about 5 minutes longer. Let cool.

5. To make the topping, turn the oven down to 300° F. Lightly butter a baking sheet. Combine the sugar and zest in a bowl and set aside. Whisk the egg whites until foamy, add the almonds and stir to coat. Drain the almonds and toss with sugar. Spread out on the baking sheet and bake, until the almonds are dried, about 30 minutes. Let cool.

6. Spoon the lemon curd into the pastry shell and top with the sugared almonds. Keep refrigerated until ready to serve. Just before serving, sift a little confectioners' sugar over the top and cut into wedges.

Serves 8

A WORLD OF ONE'S OWN

There is the cherry and of course there are the pits. Perhaps I was lucky to learn this lesson between the ages of five and eight, when my best friend and next-door neighbor, Anne Stutz, and I, along with our imaginary friends, Karen and Leslie, respectively, raided the tree in her backyard for three seasons running, an activity that yielded swift and certain punishment, which left us, nevertheless, undeterred. We weren't bad. We were, however, seemingly incapable of resisting the siren call of that gnarled and ancient tree in the suburban backyard.

We were Famous Naturalists, coolly appraising the bud and white clustered bloom of the tree, with occasional stints as Tourists ("Today it is cherry blossom time in Washington, D.C."). When the hard green berries appeared, we were Famous Farmers, appraising the crop. No matter how much we tried to avoid it we inevitably became Hansel and Gretel, surviving on wild berries in the forest. Then what choice did we have but to become Young George Washington, telling the painful and hideous truth. We never attempted to chop down the tree, but we never ceased picking its fruit.

Due either to the impatience of youth or the boredom of July days in the backyard, we picked them at first blush and they were truly horrible, yellow and scarlet, bitter and hard. But we ate them voraciously, even sucking the stems. Then we spent a long time trying to figure out how to get rid of the stain on our hands and to blame the birds for the balding.

Our early harvest seemed to bother Mrs. Stutz the most: "They are not even ready; they are not even for eating. These cherries are for pies." My mother had a passing concern for stomachs and an enduring concern for the understated wrath of Mrs. Stutz. "Why?" she would rail. "Tell me why. Didn't you have enough to eat for lunch?"

But lunch and the culinary destiny of the cherries had nothing to do with the two real and two imaginary girls who climbed and pillaged the tree. A cherry is impossible to resist, even in full knowledge of the pits. A cherry is a world of one's own, to regard and to relish, something one is never expected to share. The American poet Lucien Stryk understood this when he wrote:

> *Because I sit eating cherries*
> *which I did not pick*
> *a girl goes bad under*
>
> *the elevator tracks, will*
> *never be whole again.*
> *Because I want the full bag.*

At least I picked my own. Still, the selfish ethos of any cherry echoes part of the summer appetite.

There are over a hundred natural species of cherries, most being found in Asia from whence they came, though Italy can be credited with initiating the cultivation of the trees. In Europe and the United Sates, about a dozen different varieties are cultivated and, for the sake of simplicity, can be placed in three categories. Black cherries, such as the Bing and Schmidt varieties, are actually deep red or purple and may be sweet or sour. White cherries, such as the Royal Anne cherry, are often yellow with a pale red tinge, white only by comparison to the black variety; they are usually sweet. Sour cherries, which are also called pie cherries or tart cherries, comprise the bulk of the world's, and one hundred percent of Mrs. Stutz's harvest, are most often red as in the case of the European Morello or yellow in the case of the Amarello and the famed French Montmorency. Sour cherries are the premier cooking cherry. Sweet cherries bleed depressingly. Any variety should be firm, shiny, and dry when purchased and should be rinsed well before using.

Many people relish sour cherry compotes, chutneys, and salsas or pickled cherries with grilled meat. I am not one of them. In Traverse City, Michigan, which along with Door County in the same state and sandy lake regions in the Pacific Northwest is the cherry basket of the nation, the annual crop has been honored since 1924 in a celebration called "The Blessing of the Cherries." There, over the years, I have tasted cherry turkey stuffing, cherry chicken on linguine, pork and cherry empanadas and cherry pizza, all of which were surprisingly good, though apparently not good enough to change my personal predilection.

I love macerating sweet cherries in kirsch or even, if they are right at the edge, macerating them in sugar, lemon juice, and balsamic vinegar. I like cherries cooked in pies, simmered down into jellies, wrapped in turnovers, drowned in Manhattan cocktails, garnishing fresh cheese, or dried and baked in cakes, muffins, or scones. But I still prefer to eat my cherries fresh.

To hold a cherry by the stem and nibble it, as most people would a peach, in small bites, each one reminded by the pit of the pit, each one risking lip and hand stain, each one delivering a sweet or sour, a musky or fresh flavor, is, to me, a singularly selfish satisfaction.

Sour Cherry Crumble

4 cups pitted sour cherries
4 tablespoons sugar
½ cup all-purpose flour
¼ cup whole wheat flour
⅓ cup (packed) light brown sugar
½ teaspoon kosher salt
½ teaspoon ground cinnamon
6 tablespoons (¾ stick) cold unsalted butter, cut into pieces
¼ cup chopped walnuts
¼ cup rolled oats

1. Preheat the oven to 375° F.

2. Combine the cherries and the sugar and let stand for 10 minutes. Pour into a sieve and let drain very well. Place in a 9-inch pie plate and set aside.

2. Combine the all-purpose and whole wheat flours, brown sugar, salt, and cinnamon in a medium bowl. Rub in the butter until the mixture resembles coarse meal. Add the walnuts and oats and toss lightly to combine. Cover the cherries with the topping and bake until the topping is crisp and the juices are bubbling, about 40 minutes. Place on a rack to cool slightly before serving.

Serves 4

Mostly Cherry Fruit Soup with Shortbread Croutons

SOUP

    1 large peach

    2 cups sweet white dessert wine, such as a late harvest Riesling

    2 cups water

    ½ cup sugar

    1 tablespoon fresh lemon juice

    1 strip of lemon zest, 3 × ½ inch

    1 bay leaf

    4 sprigs fresh thyme

    1 cinnamon stick

    2 medium plums, halved, pitted, and cut into ½-inch pieces

    2 cups pitted sour cherries, with their juice

CROUTONS

    1 cup all-purpose flour

    ¼ cup sugar

    3 tablespoons cornstarch

    ½ teaspoon kosher salt

    ¼ pound (1 stick) unsalted butter, cut into small pieces

    ½ teaspoon almond extract

1. To make the soup, bring a small pot of water to a boil. Add the peach and boil for 1 minute. Place immediately in a bowl of cold water and slip off the skin. Halve and pit the peach and cut it into ½-inch pieces. Set aside.

2. Place the wine, water, sugar, and lemon juice in a large saucepan over medium heat. Tie the lemon zest, bay leaf, thyme, and cinnamon stick together with a string and add to the pan. Bring the mixture to a boil. Reduce heat to a simmer and add the peach, plums and cherries. Simmer until the fruit is tender, about 5 to 10 minutes. Remove the spices.

3. Transfer 1 cup of the soup to a food processor or blender and process until smooth. Stir the mixture back into the soup. Refrigerate until cold.

4. Preheat the oven to 350° F. Butter an 8-inch baking pan.

5. To make the croutons, sift the flour, sugar, cornstarch, and salt together into a medium bowl. Rub in the butter. Add the almond extract and use your hands to gently work the mixture until it comes together to form a dough. Lightly flour your fingertips and press the dough into the pan in an even layer. Bake until the dough is very lightly browned, about 15 to 20 minutes. While the shortbread is still warm, cut into 1-inch squares. Let cool.

6. To serve, ladle the soup among 4 bowls. Just before serving, garnish each bowl with some shortbread croutons.

Serves 4

Cream Cheese–Cherry Pound Cake with Sour Cherry Sauce

TOPPING

4 tablespoons (½ stick) cold unsalted butter, cut into small pieces

½ cup plus 2 tablespoons sugar

½ cup all-purpose flour

Pinch kosher salt

⅛ teaspoon grated nutmeg

CAKE

1 cup dried sour cherries

¼ pound (1 stick) unsalted butter, at room temperature

8 ounces cream cheese, at room temperature

1¼ cups sugar

3 large eggs, at room temperature

2 teaspoons vanilla extract

2 cups all-purpose flour

1½ teaspoons baking powder

½ teaspoon kosher salt

2 tablespoons milk

SAUCE

    3 cups pitted sour cherries

    ¾ cup sugar

    ¼ teaspoon ground cinnamon

    1½ teaspoons balsamic vinegar

    ¾ teaspoon cornstarch dissolved in 1 teaspoon water

1. To make the topping, place butter, sugar, flour, salt, and nutmeg in a bowl and rub between your fingers until mixture resembles coarse meal. Set aside.

2. To make the cake, preheat the oven to 350° F. Butter and flour a 9-inch tube pan.

3. Put the dried cherries in a bowl and pour boiling water over them. Let stand for 5 minutes. Drain.

4. Using an electric mixer, cream the butter, cream cheese, and sugar until light and fluffy, stopping to scrape the bowl from time to time. Add the eggs, one at a time, beating well after each addition. Mix in the vanilla.

5. Sift together the flour, baking powder, and salt. Add to the butter mixture in thirds. Gently stir in the milk and the cherries. Scrape the batter into the pan and top with the crumb mixture. Bake until a skewer inserted into the center of the cake comes out clean, about 1 hour. Place on a rack to cool for about 15 minutes. Turn the cake out of the pan, invert, and let cool completely.

6. To make the sauce, combine the cherries, sugar, and cinnamon in a medium saucepan over medium heat. Simmer, stirring occasionally, for 10 minutes. Stir in the vinegar. Stir in the cornstarch mixture and cook until the sauce begins to thicken, about 2 minutes longer. Strain. To serve, cut the cake into slices, place on plates, and spoon a little of the sauce around each slice.

Serves about 10

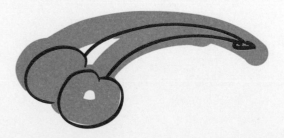

THE BITTER AND THE SWEET

Most spring ingredients symbolize regeneration and renewal, but raspberries are different. Both the ramble of wild raspberry bushes that hem either woods or pastures and the low cultivated clusters that line gardens or fields are perennial plants, but their drama is not simply one of reemergence. Rather, ripening like a hard-won sweetness from a prickly tangle of stems and leaves, the raspberries signal the triumph of tenderness amidst adversity.

Theirs is no jammy, cloying sweetness but one veiled by bitter notes and enhanced by an exotically spicy perfume. The sweetness of the raspberry is neither uncomplicated nor undefended. The "rasp" in raspberries may not be coincidental.

Anyone who has ever picked the berries knows that the harvest is similar to cutting wild roses: Hands, legs, and arms bear scratches that last longer than the flavor of the fruit or the scent of the rose. And yet while the bushes scrape and scar, the berry itself adamantly demands a soft, gentle hand. Heedless picking brings nothing but sauce. Careless tossing into a pail yields jam.

Anyone who has tucked into a bowl of raspberries and cream knows how easy it is to be seduced by the berry's soft giving body and velvety jacket, but the tough little seeds hiding in a raspberry's drupelets can be a rude wake-up call. There is the additional betrayal of the occasional bitter berry, plucked from the same bough as half a dozen that are bursting with sweet perfume. Even cultivated raspberries are not far removed from the wild varieties. In their own small, seemingly soft way, raspberries are a savage fruit.

A native of eastern Asia (where there are more than two hundred known species), the raspberry can be used to give an exotic sweet-and-sour tone to lamb or duck, the necessary astringency to a marinade, or a flowery note to vinegar for salads. A dash of raspberry vinegar in water over ice can be an oasis on a humid afternoon; a splash of French raspberry liqueur (Chambord), raspberry brandy (framboise), or homemade raspberry cordial or "wine" in champagne does much the same trick.

Having grown up on homemade raspberry jam, I find it difficult to imagine mornings without it. It is equally difficult to *plan* to cook the berries. Only after I've eaten my fill of them fresh, only when the fragile tempestuous little things threaten to rot, do I think of heating and sweetening them. Which, of course, happens on a fairly regular basis from late April to early June.

The sight of half-pint cardboard cartons filled with raspberries makes me greedy, mostly for their flavor, which can be relied on to be unreliable. Thus the raspberry's parable. It is a difficult, fragile, and complicated fruit. That it is these things and still sweet is compelling, inspiring, irresistible.

Raspberries have summoned such response for as long as there has been spring. "Raspberries grow by the way, / With pleasure you may assay," said an unnamed poet from the Crusades.

Raspberry-Tarragon Vinegar

1 bottle (17 ounces) good quality white wine vinegar
1 pint fresh raspberries
¼ cup fresh tarragon leaves and stems, bruised slightly
1 tablespoon honey

1. Pour the vinegar into a nonreactive saucepan over low heat and heat until warm. Place the raspberries and tarragon in a sterilized wide-mouth jar. Pour in the warm vinegar. Seal tight. Let stand in a warm place for 2 weeks.

2. Strain the vinegar, pressing the raspberries firmly into a nonreactive saucepan. Add the honey and bring to a boil. Reduce the heat and simmer, uncovered, for 10 minutes. Pour into a sterilized bottle and seal with a new cork. Keep refrigerated.

Makes 2 cups

Raspberry Sorbet

2 cups sugar
1 cup water
3 pints fresh raspberries
4 tablespoons fresh lemon juice

1. Combine the sugar and water in a small saucepan over medium heat. Simmer for 5 minutes and set aside to cool.

2. Place the raspberries, sugar syrup, and lemon juice in a blender and puree until smooth. Strain through a fine-mesh sieve. Refrigerate until cold. Freeze in an ice cream machine according to the manufacturer's directions.

Serves 6

Raspberry-Champagne Soup with
Rosemary-Raspberry Sorbet

SORBET

    1 cup sugar

    ½ cup water

    1½ pints fresh raspberries

    2 tablespoons balsamic vinegar

    2½ tablespoons chopped fresh rosemary

SOUP

    ½ cup sugar

    ½ cup water

    1½ pints fresh raspberries

    2 cups good quality champagne or other sparkling wine, chilled

1. To make the sorbet, combine the sugar and water in a small saucepan over medium heat. Simmer for 5 minutes and set aside to cool. Place the raspberries, sugar syrup, vinegar, and rosemary in a blender and puree until smooth. Let stand for 1 hour. Strain through a fine-mesh sieve. Refrigerate until cold. Freeze in an ice cream machine according to the manufacturer's directions.

2. To make the soup, combine the sugar and water in a small saucepan over medium heat. Simmer just until the sugar dissolves. Let cool. Set aside ½ cup of raspberries. Place the rest in a blender. Add the sugar syrup and puree until smooth. Strain through a fine-mesh sieve and refrigerate until cold.

3. Just before serving, divide the soup mixture among 4 bowls and add ½ cup of champagne to each. Place a scoop of the sorbet in the soup and garnish with the reserved raspberries.

Serves 4

ALMOST
SUMMER

ACT NOW, EAT LATER

*T*hough Memorial Day weekend signals a new season in entertaining and warm-weather cooking, this may have less to do with what's on the shelves than what's on our minds. The fixings for simple summer dishes—home-grown tomatoes, eggplants and zucchini, a panoply of lettuces, shell beans and herbs—are mere sprouts in most of the country. Yet the appetite for them is inflamed by the first suggestion of a long weekend in May.

Ready or not, here come the cooks of summer.

In addition to this hankering for sun-baked flavor, there is the annual urge to cook ahead of time, to prepare large quantities of food that can be used to make a cold dinner buffet, a lunch, or a late-afternoon nibble. It takes a clever cook to do this when the best the market has to offer is the remnants of the spring larder—asparagus and rhubarb, the first tiny potatoes and spinach—foods that are usually too delicate for the full-bodied marinades and robust cooking techniques of summer.

So, like a consummate politician, the cook must appear to coddle the summer appetite while dealing with the reality of fresh, chilly mornings and cool sundowns.

In addition to awakening a deceptive appetite, the early weeks of summer refuel childhood dreams. Softball sluggers oil their gloves, swimmers practice flip-turns, rollerbladers skate fierce figure eights—and hosts begin to flex their conviviality muscles when days get longer and the air turns warm and sweet. Summer entertaining is the ultimate playhouse fantasy. One part technique, 99 parts strategy.

Planning dishes for a summer weekend is not dissimilar from planning a wardrobe. The idea is to create a collection that can be mixed-and-matched, that can appear in different incarnations at different meals. If the cook prepares large quantities of each recipe, there will be leftovers, all fair game for imaginative recycling over a weekend's entertaining. A host expecting guests should shop ahead and, well before guests arrive, prepare the recipes that will keep, saving the most perishable for the last minute.

On Friday, large grain or bean salads can be made, meat or fish can be marinated for later barbecues, and other food that needs to be cooked and chilled can be prepared. Only lighter salads require last-minute attention. Knowing that the pasta served Friday night can become a salad for Saturday lunch, or that cold grilled vegetables can find their way into sandwiches or salads or become garnishes for grilled meat, gives a cook a Zen-like calm.

Cooks with a larder and a plan are imperturbable people, even if temperatures suddenly shoot up and five unexpected guests arrive for dinner. Summer grants the leisure for such cooking. The season also issues a challenge of balancing kitchen work with the charms of an endless afternoon. Summer weekends are a rare opportunity to have it all, if, at the outset, there is a plan.

Used in almost any combination, doubled or tripled as the crowd calls for, the following recipes can be a backbone of summer weekend meals.

RECIPES TO MAKE ONE DAY AHEAD

Parsley Pickled Mushrooms

Use these mushrooms as part of a dinner buffet and combine leftovers with beef tenderloin on French bread sandwiches.

1 teaspoon kosher salt
¼ cup fresh lemon juice
½ teaspoon freshly ground pepper
¾ cup olive oil
1 cup Italian parsley, stemmed and minced
2 pounds white mushrooms, stemmed and quartered
1 pound shiitake mushrooms, stemmed and quartered

1. Half fill a large pot with water and bring to a boil.

2. Dissolve the salt in the lemon juice in a large bowl. Add the black pepper. Slowly drizzle the olive oil into the lemon juice, whisking constantly. When all the oil has been added, stir in the parsley and refrigerate.

3. When the water is boiling, add the white and shiitake mushrooms and blanch for 1 minute. Immediately drain the mushrooms and pat them dry with paper towels. Stir the mushrooms into the lemon-parsley vinaigrette and chill for at least 1 hour before serving.

Serves 8 as a side dish

Grilled and Chilled Japanese Eggplant

16 small Japanese eggplants, no longer than 5 inches
1 cup chicken broth, homemade, or low-sodium canned broth
2 tablespoons dried bonito flakes (see Note)
2 teaspoons soy sauce
1 teaspoon sweet rice wine (Mirin) (see Note)
4 tablespoons grated fresh ginger

1. Prepare a charcoal fire. Grill the eggplants over hot coals, turning frequently, until soft, about 10 to 15 minutes. Remove and set aside until cool enough to handle.

2. Combine the chicken broth, bonito flakes, soy sauce, and rice wine in a saucepan. Simmer for 5 minutes. Add the ginger and remove from the heat. Slice the eggplants lengthwise into 4 slices, without cutting through the stem end. Fan each eggplant out on a platter and drizzle with the sauce. Refrigerate until completely cool or up to 24 hours before serving.

Serves 8 as a side dish

Note: Dried bonito flakes and sweet rice wine are available in Asian markets and by mail order from Katagiri, 224 East 59th Street, New York, New York 10022; (212) 755-3566.

Provençale Chickpea Salad

Marinated chickpeas make a vibrant one-dish lunch when tossed with spiral or bowtie pasta.

3 cups dried chickpeas, soaked in water overnight and drained
4 fresh rosemary branches
¼ cup red wine vinegar
1 medium head garlic, roasted and peeled (page 175)
2 tablespoons plus 2 teaspoons olive oil
4 teaspoons chopped fresh rosemary leaves
¾ cup chopped Italian parsley
¼ cup chopped pitted green olives
¼ cup chopped pitted imported black olives
3 teaspoons kosher salt, plus more to taste
Freshly ground pepper to taste

1. Put the chickpeas in a large pot and cover with cold water. Add the rosemary branches and bring to a boil over high heat. Reduce heat and simmer until the chickpeas are tender, about 2 hours, adding more water if necessary to keep them covered. Drain the chickpeas, place in a large bowl, and discard the rosemary.

2. Whisk together the vinegar and roasted garlic. Whisk in the olive oil. Stir in the chopped rosemary, parsley, and green and black olives. Toss the olive mixture with the chickpeas. Stir in the salt and pepper. Serve at room temperature.

Serves 8 as a side dish

RECIPES TO MAKE A FEW HOURS AHEAD

Farfalle, Arugula, and Tomato Salad

½ pound farfalle (also called bowtie pasta), cooked, drained, and rinsed

3 cups stemmed and torn arugula

½ cup chopped fresh basil

2 large tomatoes, cut into ½-inch dice

1 teaspoon grated lemon zest

3 tablespoons olive oil

1 tablespoon fresh lemon juice

2 teaspoons kosher salt

Freshly ground pepper to taste

Place the farfalle in a large bowl. Add the remaining ingredients and toss until well combined. Serve at room temperature.

Serves 8 as a side dish

Fresh Lima Bean and Romaine Lettuce Slaw with Orechiette

2 large ripe tomatoes, cut into small dice

½ cup minced fresh chives

¼ cup minced pitted green olives

2 tablespoons olive oil

2 cups fresh or frozen lima beans

½ pound orechiette

2 teaspoons kosher salt, plus more to taste

Freshly ground pepper to taste

1 small head romaine lettuce, cut across into thin strips

1. Toss together the tomatoes, chives, olives, and olive oil in a large bowl. Set aside. Cook the lima beans in simmering water until tender. Drain and add to the tomato mixture.

2. Bring a large pot of lightly salted water to a boil. Add the orechiette and cook until al dente. Drain. Add the warm pasta to the salad and toss. Add the salt and pepper. Toss in the lettuce just before serving.

Serves 6 as a main course or 12 as a side dish

Tomato Bread Salad

5 large ripe tomatoes, cut into small dice

1 red onion, cut into small dice

3 cloves garlic, minced

½ cup chopped Italian parsley

1 tablespoon chopped fresh rosemary

1 tablespoon olive oil

1 tablespoon red wine vinegar

1 tablespoon grated orange zest

1 tablespoon kosher salt, plus more to taste

Freshly ground pepper to taste

1 loaf stale crusty French or Italian bread

1. Combine the tomatoes, onion, garlic, parsley, and rosemary in a large bowl. Add the olive oil, vinegar, zest, salt, and pepper and mix well.

2. Slice the bread in half lengthwise. Pour on enough water to completely moisten the bread. Let stand for 10 minutes. Squeeze out excess water. Finely chop the bread, add it to the salad and toss. Season with salt and pepper and serve.

Serves 6 as a main course or 12 as a side dish

Smoked Fish Brandade

1 pound boiling potatoes, peeled
8 cloves garlic, peeled
½ cup heavy cream
2 pounds smoked whitefish, skinned, boned, and cut into 1-inch chunks
¼ cup olive oil
Dash Tabasco
2 teaspoons kosher salt, or to taste
2 cups oil-cured black olives
Toast points or crackers

1. Put the potatoes in a pot of cold water, and boil over high heat until tender, about 15 minutes. Drain the potatoes and refrigerate until cool.

2. Put the garlic and the heavy cream in a small saucepan and simmer over medium heat until the garlic is tender, 8 to 10 minutes. Refrigerate the cream and garlic mixture.

3. When the potatoes and garlic are cool, put two of the garlic cloves and 1 tablespoon of the heavy cream in a food processor. Add a quarter of the fish and an eighth of the potatoes and pulse to combine. Do not overprocess. Remove the first batch to a serving bowl and repeat the procedure until all the garlic, fish, and potatoes are used.

4. Using a rubber spatula, stir half the olive oil and a dash of Tabasco into the fish mixture and season with salt. Smooth the top of the brandade and drizzle the remaining olive oil over it. Decorate with black olives and serve with toast points or crackers.

Serves 8 as a first course

Thai Beef Salad

1 cup fresh lime juice
½ cup Thai fish sauce (see Note)
1 tablespoon sugar
2 teaspoons minced Thai chili or jalapeño pepper
2 small tomatoes, peeled, cored, seeded, and diced
2 small cucumbers, peeled, seeded, and diced
2 pieces flank steak, 12 ounces each
1 cup fresh mint leaves

1. Prepare a charcoal fire. Combine the lime juice, fish sauce, sugar, and chili in a large glass or ceramic bowl. Add the tomatoes and cucumbers and toss. Refrigerate.

2. Grill the steaks over hot coals until medium rare, about 3 to 5 minutes per side. Let stand for 5 minutes. Slice the meat across the grain into thin slices. Add to the salad. Add mint leaves and toss well. Serve at room temperature.

Serves 8 as a first course

Note: Thai fish sauce, or *nam pla*, is available in Asian markets and by mail order from Kam Man, 200 Canal Street, New York, New York 10002; (212) 571-0330.

SUMMER

THE SEASON OF BRASHNESS
AND LANGUOR

Compared to the fair maiden of spring, the summer appetite is like an indecisive lover. Subdued, or perhaps subordinated, by heat and the mixed blessing of long, slow days, warm-weather hunger is laconic and lackadaisical. It is loath to commit to a full meal, looking to be convinced.

The season obliges with overabundance, bigger flavors, and the magnet of fresh air. In a macho capitulation to summer's lush charms, you rush to the grill and the barbecue. In calmer, quieter moments, you reinvent the salad and contemplate ways of preparing food ahead without suspending every edible particle in oil. You face the season's plenty, mounds of zucchini, corn, eggplant, and tomatoes, all dancing the tenuous line between the ripe and the rotten, and hope that imagination prevails over panic.

Heat breeds hyperbole in ingredients. But it begs the cook for finesse. Dog-day hunger is a complicated thing. It can be sated by a brash barbecue and left still wanting something gentler and cooler. It is no coincidence that the season's tender berries become icy sorbet, a shale of violent glassy crystals. The summer appetite summons extremes.

A SLOW BURN

Grilling and barbecuing are the hallmark of summer, and each is a male thing. Oh, women can appreciate a properly charred brisket or rib. I've sat swatting mosquitoes with other women, allowing the aroma from a charcoal grill to carry us back to the days of Coppertone tans and AM radio.

Still, we remain spectators. Many women do take pride in their prowess at the grill. But we don't share that primal pull to an open flame any more than we share whatever it is that can make a man's eyes grow misty at the sight of a Little League park.

Just as men have analyzed every thunk and slide of the summer game, many tend to be quite exacting about barbecue. American or National League fans are no more loyal or impassioned than fans of grilling (quick cooking over intense heat) as opposed to those who favor the long, slow fire of a traditional barbecue. The sauce and fuel debates can continue to heat up long after the coals have crumbled and cooled.

With all due respect, both barbecue and grilling come down to two things: food and fuel.

On the second point, the most lucid analyst I know is Don Hysko, co-owner of Nature's Own, a company that sells chunked charwood in Attleboro, Massachusetts. The mere mention of a word like "briquette" makes him cringe. Even the various hardwood "charcoals" that are proliferating as grilling becomes a year-round sport make him uneasy.

"What kind of wood do they use?" Hysko asks. "Maybe scrap lumber! Even wood pallets! The only way to have mellow, sweet, consistent flavor and a wood that burns hot is to use *virgin* wood." His company cuts such wood in Rimouski, Quebec, dries it for up to a year, and chars it for seven days in a two-story kiln.

Charred virgin wood is to grilling what real grass is to an infield. Adding soaked herb branches or vine cuttings to the grill can enhance the woodsy flavor.

And then there is the food. Chris Schlesinger, co-owner of the East Coast Grill in Cambridge, Massachusetts, and author, with John Willoughby, of *The*

Thrill of the Grill, is a regular Red Barber when it comes to the play of ingredients on the grill. Fish, vegetables, steaks, and chops stand up well to grilling, but, Schlesinger advises, "be careful not to cremate them." Heavier cuts of meat can take a slow, smoky fire. Make sure that all food is brought to room temperature before grilling.

As if debating a pitching strategy, Schlesinger considers the marinade question. "Now, I might occasionally use a marinade to impart flavor, but only when using cuts with a very large surface area, such as a flank steak," he writes. "This is because in a 24-hour marinating period, the actual penetration of the marinade into the food is minimal, so you really gain nothing but surface flavor. In general, I prefer a dry rub, which not only imparts surface flavor more efficiently, but also aids in the formation of a flavorful crust or feel. Of course a rub is not practical for all situations. . . ."

In those occasional non-rub situations, when you want to grill fish fillets, for instance, or vegetables, or lighter cuts of meat, exotic marinades make up in flavor what they may lack in the crust-making department. And with countless grilling scenarios to play out this season, you need a range of marinating strategies as well as a repertory of well-spiced rubs.

MAIL ORDER SOURCES FOR HARDWOODS
AND HARDWOOD CHARCOALS

Humphrey Charcoal Corporation, P. O. Box 440,
Brookville, PA 15825
(814) 849-2302
Nature's Own, 453 S. Main St.,
Attleboro, MA 02703
(800) 289-2427
People's Woods, 75 Mill Street,
Cumberland, RI 02864
(401) 725-2700

Tuscan Marinade

This marinade is particularly good with vegetables, as in the following recipe, or with chicken paillards or flank steak. Always bring food to room temperature before grilling. For chicken, pound chicken breasts a quarter inch thick. Marinate in the refrigerator for four hours. Grill over hot coals until tender, about two to three minutes per side. For flank steak, marinate in the refrigerator for eight hours. Grill over hot coals until medium rare, three to four minutes per side.

2 cups red wine
⅔ cup olive oil
4 cloves garlic, minced
2 tablespoons grated orange zest
2 tablespoons minced sage leaves
4 teaspoons minced rosemary leaves
4 teaspoons black peppercorns, crushed
2 teaspoons kosher salt

Combine all ingredients in a glass or ceramic bowl.
Refrigerate in an airtight container for up to 3 days.
Makes about 2 cups

Tuscan Grilled Summer Vegetables

1 purple eggplant, about 1 pound, cut across into 2-inch slices

1 white eggplant, about ½ pound, cut into 2-inch slices

2 zucchini, cut in half lengthwise

2 yellow squash, cut into 2-inch slices

1 tablespoon kosher salt

3 large ripe tomatoes, cut into 2-inch slices

1 yellow bell pepper, seeded and cut lengthwise into 2-inch slices

1 red bell pepper, seeded and cut lengthwise into 2-inch slices

1 medium red onion, cut across into ½-inch slices

1 cup coarsely chopped fresh basil

2 cups Tuscan Marinade (page 114)

Put the eggplants, zucchini, and yellow squash in a colander. Toss with the salt and let drain for 30 minutes. Rinse, pat dry, and place in a large shallow glass or ceramic dish. Add the tomatoes, yellow and red peppers, onion, and basil. Cover with the marinade. Refrigerate for 8 hours, turning the vegetables once. Bring to room temperature and grill over hot coals until tender, about 5 to 10 minutes per side. Serve hot or at room temperature.

Serves 4 to 6 as a side dish

Korean Barbecue

A wonderful marinade with pork chops, flank steak, or chicken wings. Bring food to room temperature before grilling. Marinate pork chops in the refrigerator overnight. Grill over hot coals until medium-rare, about five minutes per side. For flank steak, marinate in the refrigerator for at least eight hours. Grill over hot coals until rare, about three to four minutes per side.

1 tablespoon grated fresh ginger
1 medium-size ripe papaya, peeled and coarsely chopped
1 small pear, chopped
1 small onion, chopped
1 small clove garlic, minced
1 tablespoon honey
¼ cup soy sauce
⅓ cup pineapple juice
1 tablespoon sake or dry white wine
½ teaspoon freshly ground pepper
½ teaspoon sugar
2 tablespoons sesame oil
½ teaspoon sesame seeds
¼ cup minced scallions

Put the ginger, papaya, pear, onion, garlic, honey, soy sauce, pineapple juice, sake, pepper, sugar, and sesame oil in a blender. Puree until smooth. Pour the marinade into a glass or ceramic bowl. Add the sesame seeds and scallions. Refrigerate in an airtight container for up to 3 days.

Makes 2 cups

Spice Island Marinade

Use this marinade to lend a pungent Indian flavor to chicken, beef, or ribs. It works particularly well with tuna steaks or fish fillets. Marinate the steaks in the refrigerator for four hours. Bring to room temperature before grilling. Grill over hot coals until rare, about three minutes per side.

1 medium-size ripe papaya, peeled and diced
½ pound ripe apricots, pitted and finely chopped
¼ cup fresh lime juice
2 cloves garlic, minced
2 small Thai chilies or jalapeño peppers, seeded, deveined, and minced
1 tablespoon grated fresh ginger
1 tablespoon cardamom pods, crushed
2 tablespoons coriander seeds, crushed

Combine all of the ingredients in a large glass or ceramic bowl. Refrigerate in an airtight container for up to 2 days.

Makes 2 cups

RUBBING THE BELLY OF THE BEAST

Grilled food is the bass note of summer dining. The smoky flavor and crusty texture of grilled meat, chicken, or fish can be counted on to recur at regular hot-weather intervals. Side dishes provide contrast, nothing more, nothing less. But it takes the serendipitous jolt of the condiments in a savory rub to give grilled food the surprising pow that wakes up summer eating.

Rather than add a superficial shellac, herb mashes and seasoned salts permeate food deeply, creating contrasting layers of flavor. But these condiments are sneaky. They leave no mark while managing to alter everything. Once applied, they insinuate themselves, changing not only the flavor of chicken or fish but their own taste as well.

Rubbed into chicken, for instance, an Afghan blend of black peppercorns, cumin seeds, turmeric, cardamom, and coriander adds a subtle but pungent heat to the bird. In the process, the blend itself becomes sweeter, lending the crust the faint flavor of cinnamon toast. Rubbed into fish, however, the same peppery blend sweetens the taste of the host while taking on a fiery flavor of its own.

Condiments are like that—they're chameleons. That's part of their charm.

At Vong, the Thai-French restaurant in Manhattan, chef Jean-Georges Vongerichten uses star anise, cinnamon, Sichuan peppercorns, cloves, cumin, and celery seed to season kosher salt. This Thai-inspired confection is then used in place of table salt, adding an exotic note to flat bread or plain steamed rice. When rubbed into chicken, it imparts a rich, husky flavor. On fish, it works to sharpen and freshen an already briny taste.

Seasoned salts and herb pastes also deliver a subtle sense of place. A paste of cilantro, garlic, chili peppers, and soy sauce, for instance, points chicken, fish, lobster, or shrimp in an unmistakably Asian direction, evoking hot, thick days and the flavors that serve as an antidote.

It would be wrong to underestimate how many flavor combinations condiments can incite: A pantryful equals an unlimited culinary repertoire. Besides, their mere presence enables the cook to be spontaneous and creative; most rubs and pastes are simple to make and keep nearly indefinitely. They can be used to perk up sandwiches or salads, leftover pasta or rice, as well as to transform meat, chicken, and seafood with hardly any fuss or bother.

Just as they change the character of food and their own nature, seasoned salts, spice blends, and herb mashes change the character of the summer cook. Armed with secret seasonings, the cook becomes a sorcerer, a potential maestro, not just another lackey minding the grill.

Zvia's Hawayej

Rub this spice blend devised by Zvia, an Afghan street vendor in New York City, all over beef, pork, or chicken two hours prior to grilling. It also adds a pungent note to tuna, swordfish, bluefish, and bass; rub it on both sides of the steaks or fillets about an hour before grilling. In either case, the rub can be left on the meat or fish while grilling to make a blackened seasoned crust. Used as a spice, hawayej, pronounced HA-wayj, can be stirred into boiled rice or summer soups to taste.

3 tablespoons black peppercorns
3 tablespoons cumin seed
2 tablespoons turmeric
1 tablespoon ground cardamom
1 tablespoon ground coriander

Grind all the ingredients together with a mortar and pestle or in a spice grinder. Store in an airtight container.

Makes about ⅓ cup

Spiced Salt (Adapted from Vong, Manhattan)

This Thai-spiced salt is used in place of table salt at Vong Restaurant. It is particularly good with chicken or any fish steak or fillet; rub it in about an hour before grilling. The salt can be left on during the grilling to create a mildly spiced crust. It also adds zing to cold rice, pasta salads, or even grilled vegetables when used in place of table salt and pepper. For more intense flavor, cumin and celery seed can be added.

2 heaping tablespoons star anise
2 cinnamon sticks, broken into pieces
3 tablespoons Sichuan peppercorns
2 tablespoons cloves
2 teaspoons cumin seed (optional)
1 teaspoon celery seed (optional)
½ cup kosher salt

Grind the star anise, cinnamon sticks, peppercorns, cloves, and cumin seed, if using, separately in a spice grinder. If using celery seed, leave whole. Combine the spices and salt in a bowl and mix thoroughly. Store in an airtight container.

Makes 1 cup

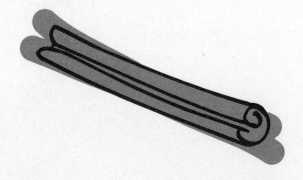

Cilantro-Soy Paste

A potent Asian mixture that makes a good marinade for chicken, shrimp, or fish like bluefish. Cover with the paste for three hours before grilling; turn in the marinade frequently. Wipe off excess marinade before grilling.

⅔ cup fresh cilantro leaves
4 cloves garlic, chopped
2 jalapeño peppers, stemmed and seeded
6 tablespoons soy sauce

Combine all ingredients in a blender. Process until smooth, stopping as needed to scrape down the sides of the jar. Refrigerate in an airtight container for up to 2 days.

Makes ½ cup

A Spice Paste for the Thrill of the Grill

Adapted from a recipe of Chris Schlesinger's, this paste is wonderful with steaks, chicken, or veal chops. Rub the chops with the spice paste and refrigerate for four to six hours before grilling. Bring to room temperature and grill over hot coals until medium rare, about four minutes per side.

2 tablespoons cumin powder
2 tablespoons curry powder
2 tablespoons sweet paprika
2 tablespoons coriander seed, cracked
2 tablespoons black peppercorns, cracked
1 tablespoon ground cinnamon
1 teaspoon kosher salt
¼ cup olive oil
2 cloves garlic, minced
2 tablespoons minced fresh oregano
¼ cup minced fresh cilantro

Combine the cumin, curry powder, paprika, coriander seed, peppercorns, cinnamon, and salt in a small cast-iron skillet. Dry roast over medium-low heat until spices begin to smoke but not burn, about 3 to 5 minutes. Transfer the roasted spices to a large bowl. Add the olive oil, garlic, oregano, and cilantro and mix well. Refrigerate in an airtight container for up to 3 days.

Makes ¾ cup

THE QUICK FIX: SALSA FOR GRILLED FOOD

Salsa has entered its salad days. Salsa has long been a Mexican staple, a pounded or pureed substance made of peppers or tomatoes or both, something between a sauce and a condiment that was used either way. But now it has expanded into a wide variety of ethnic permutations. Unlike a marinade, spice paste, or herbal rub, salsa can be added to food after it is grilled to give a layer of youthful freshness, some whimsy, and some verve.

The change in salsa came slowly. After generations of obscurity on grocery shelves north of the border, last year salsa outsold ketchup in the United States. Even as it became the king of American condiments, salsa was undergoing a transformation. It was taking in seasonings from India, Asia, and the Mediterranean. It was opening up to cucumbers, onions, mangos, and sweet corn. Nearly *everything* seemed to have salsa potential. And the stuff kept getting chunkier.

Salsa was now making appearances on grilled meat and fish and as a dressing for pasta and grains. On toast points or cucumber rounds, salsa became an hors d'oeuvre. Spooned on a heap of greens, salsa could even be a first course or an intermezzo. In California recently, I had a green mango salsa sorbet served with a sizzling main course. It had potential.

Salsa, in other words, has become a concept.

Now, this is good news for the health-conscious who are still searching for the meaning of life after *beurre blanc.* Salsa is, by nature, high fiber and low fat, and salsa variations are limited only by the whim of any given cook. To culinary purists, on the other hand, expansion on the salsa front is a travesty. Calling minced mango a salsa, one preservationist told me, is like calling grape juice a Bordeaux. I share an abiding affection for the primal salsa, but I'm just as uncomfortable with the assumption that any change in salsa is automatically a change for the worse. Besides, I've tasted some marvelous variations.

I do sympathize with etymologists, to whom the expansion of the salsa definition is nervous-making. Salsa can mean something soupy and chip friendly, or something chutneylike. More and more, salsa can mean a feisty and piquant salad that takes the place of a sauce.

This can be viewed as shocking behavior for a salsa. Or it can be seen as a sweet and gradual evolution whereby an exotic substance is transmogrified in order to assume a position on a traditional dinner plate. Didn't your mother pile the iceberg lettuce on the same plate with the roast beef and mashed potatoes?

Thai Cucumber and Mint Salsa

A wonderful salsa to serve with grilled fillet of sea bass or red snapper.

3 medium cucumbers, peeled, seeded, and cut into ¼-inch dice
2 cloves garlic, minced
1 small Thai chili, seeded, deveined, and minced
¼ cup fresh lime juice
1 tablespoon vegetable oil
¼ cup chopped fresh cilantro
¼ cup chopped fresh mint
¼ cup chopped fresh basil
2 scallions, minced
1½ teaspoons kosher salt, plus more to taste
½ teaspoon freshly ground pepper, plus more
   to taste

Combine all the ingredients in a large glass or ceramic bowl, cover, and refrigerate for at least 2 hours before serving. Season with more salt and pepper, if needed. Store, refrigerated, in an airtight container for up to 2 days.

Makes 3 cups

Fiery Melon and Peanut Salsa

This salsa has a sweet and spicy taste that complements grilled shrimp or full-bodied fish like tuna. It also makes an unusual salad when garnished with chilled strips of grilled pork or chicken.

¼ cup unsalted dry-roasted peanuts, coarsely chopped
3 cloves garlic, minced
1 tablespoon brown sugar
¼ cup Thai fish sauce (see Note)
2½ teaspoons grated lime zest
¼ cup fresh lime juice
1 medium jalapeño pepper, seeded, deveined, and minced
½ cup minced fresh cilantro
1½ cups honeydew melon, peeled, seeded, and cut into ¼-inch dice
1½ cups cantaloupe, peeled, seeded, and cut into ¼-inch dice
½ cup coarsely chopped Italian parsley

1. Preheat the oven to 350° F.
2. Place the peanuts on a baking sheet and toast in the oven until golden brown, about 10 minutes. Set aside to cool.
3. Combine the garlic, brown sugar, fish sauce, lime zest, lime juice, jalapeño, and cilantro in a large glass or ceramic bowl. Add the peanuts, melon, cantaloupe, and parsley. Toss well. Cover and refrigerate for at least 1 hour before serving. Store, refrigerated, in an airtight container for up to 3 days.

Makes 3 cups

Note: Thai fish sauce, or *nam pla*, is available in Asian markets and by mail order from Kam Man, 200 Canal Street, New York, New York 10002; (212) 571-0330.

Roasted Corn Salsa

Adapted from Red Sage in Washington, this salsa can be used as a dip for chips or on grilled fish, pork, chicken, or beef. Tossed with arugula, it makes a lovely salad.

5 ears fresh corn
1 tablespoon olive oil
1 cup fresh shiitake or other wild mushrooms, cleaned and diced
2 large poblano chilies, roasted, peeled, seeded, and diced
1 teaspoon minced fresh marjoram
1 clove roasted garlic, peeled (page 175)
½ teaspoon sherry vinegar
1 tablespoon fresh lime juice
1 teaspoon kosher salt, plus more to taste

1. Cut the corn kernels from the cobs. Heat a cast-iron skillet over high heat until almost smoking. Add 1 layer of kernels and dry roast, tossing constantly, until the corn is smoky and dark, about 5 minutes. Place in a large bowl and repeat until all the corn is cooked.

2. Heat the olive oil in a sauté pan over medium-high heat. Add the mushrooms and sauté until tender, about 5 to 10 minutes. Add to the corn. Add the remaining ingredients and mix well. Season with additional salt, if needed. Serve at room temperature. Store, refrigerated, in an airtight container for up to 2 days.

Makes 3 cups

Moroccan Orange, Red Onion, and Black Olive Salsa

A great accompaniment to cold grilled veal chops, roast tenderloin of pork, or whole poached salmon.

4 navel oranges, peeled, sectioned, and each section cut across into 3 pieces
1 medium red onion, coarsely chopped
2 cloves garlic, minced
1½ teaspoons kosher salt, plus more to taste
1 teaspoon sweet paprika
1 cup coarsely chopped Italian parsley
½ teaspoon ground cumin
¼ teaspoon cayenne
2 tablespoons olive oil
¾ cup oil-cured black olives, pitted and coarsely chopped

Combine the oranges, onion, garlic, salt, paprika, ¼ cup parsley, cumin, cayenne, and olive oil in a glass or ceramic bowl. Taste and season with additional salt, if needed. Store, refrigerated, in an airtight container for up to 2 days. Add the olives and remaining parsley just before serving.

Makes 4 cups

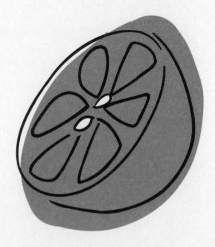

TO FLAVOR A FINE OIL

For me, summer mornings have always been the time when I was best able to understand the nuances of the day, the direction of its wind, the thickness of its air, and its consequent mood come dinner. In the hours between sunrise and noon, it is still possible to see past the insistent demands of sun-baked desire. It is possible to cook with a cool and even hand.

Working in a resort in Provincetown, Massachusetts, we knew in the morning, for instance, that evening would welcome a light though warm summer vegetable soup; that a hearty fish stew, though anathema at noon, would be soothing after sunset; that vegetables would actually be more satisfying when gently cooked and allowed to nap in marinade.

The best of summer cooking is like that—an act now, eat later sort of thing. By minding this fact, the cook remains sensitive to the season. Young vegetables, impressionable greens, new corn, and soft berries all require the kind of finesse that gets lost in the heat of the day.

In her classic book *Summer Cooking,* Elizabeth David writes that the aim of her recipes is to present fresh food with a "new outlook." To do so requires not only thought but also the kind of gentle medium that will prolong and enhance the flavor of summer edibles.

Food that is completely cooked is a done deal. Food gently handled and embossed with something like a flavored oil is food in suspended animation; ripening is slowed but not completely quelled. More important, food that has been treated with infused oil takes on new life when it is heated, or brought to room temperature, or just put into a warm mouth.

To me, simply made oils, like basil oil and its lemon-and-parsley variation, encompass the lustiness of the season while encouraging in the cook the sort of restraint that brings a slower and more sustained satisfaction.

These infused oils literally taste of the season. But because they are a part of a meal, rather than the whole, their flavors do not overwhelm. Use a flavored oil like the perfume that it is, not like the fatty lubricant it seems to be. This is summer.

Such oils can be used to dress pasta, rice, or potato salads; chicken, lobster, or fish. They can be used as the basis of a vinaigrette for young greens or slaw, for ripe tomatoes, or for mélanges of young vegetables that have been briefly blanched. I've used these (and other oils) to make cold soups or to garnish warm soups that were made in the morning and heated for dinner. I've also brushed infused oils on grilled food. Their flavors linger as freshness is sacrificed to the char. In whatever manner they are employed, these oils will coat other ingredients like a summer morning, when everything seems young and anything seems possible.

THE OILS

Basil Oil

2 bunches (¾ pound) fresh basil, stems on, washed
2 cups plus 7 tablespoons extra-virgin olive oil

1. Bring a large pot of water to a boil. Add the basil and blanch for 30 seconds. Drain and rinse under cold running water until cool. Drain and dry well. Place in a food processor with 5 tablespoons of the olive oil. Process until a thick puree forms, stopping several times to scrape down the sides of the bowl. Transfer to a clean glass jar and pour in 2 cups of the oil. Shake well and refrigerate for 1 or 2 days.

2. Strain the oil through a fine-mesh sieve. Pour the remaining 2 tablespoons oil through a coffee filter to dampen the filter. Fit the filter inside the rim of a clean glass jar. Pour some of the oil into the filter and let it drip into the jar. Continue pouring and letting the oil drip until all has passed through the filter; this will take several hours. Store in the refrigerator for up to 2 weeks.

Makes about 1½ cups

Lemon and Parsley Oil

2 bunches (½ pound) Italian parsley, stems on, washed
2 cups plus 7 tablespoons extra-virgin olive oil
2 teaspoons chopped lemon zest

1. Bring a large pot of water to a boil. Add the parsley and blanch for 30 seconds. Drain and rinse under cold running water until cool. Drain and dry well. Place in a food processor with 5 tablespoons of the olive oil. Process until a thick

puree forms, stopping several times to scrape down the sides of the bowl. Transfer to a clean glass jar and pour in 2 cups of the oil. Add the lemon zest, shake well, and refrigerate for 1 to 2 days.

2. Strain the oil through a fine-mesh sieve. Pour the remaining 2 tablespoons oil through a coffee filter to dampen the filter. Fit the filter inside the rim of a clean glass jar. Pour some of the oil into the filter and let it drip into the jar. Continue pouring and letting the oil drip until all has passed through the filter; this will take several hours. Store in the refrigerator for up to 2 weeks.

Makes about 1½ cups

APPLYING THE OILS

Zucchini with Basil Oil and Mint

4 small zucchini, cut across into ¼-inch slices
2 teaspoons Basil Oil (page 130)
1 teaspoon fresh lime juice
1 tablespoon minced fresh mint leaves
1 teaspoon kosher salt, plus more to taste
Freshly ground black pepper to taste

Bring a medium pot of lightly salted water to a boil. Add the zucchini and blanch for 45 seconds. Drain and immediately place under cold running water until cool. Drain again and pat dry. Place zucchini in a bowl and toss with the oil, lime juice, mint, salt, and pepper. Taste and adjust seasoning if desired. Serve cold or at room temperature.

Serves 4 as a side dish

Potato and Shrimp Salad with Peas and Basil Oil

8 small red potatoes, steamed until tender and quartered
1 pound cooked and peeled shrimp
1 cup shelled fresh green peas, cooked until tender
1 jalapeño pepper, stemmed, seeded, and minced
4 teaspoons Basil Oil (page 130)
1 teaspoon kosher salt, plus more to taste
Freshly ground pepper to taste

Combine the potatoes, shrimp, peas, and jalapeño in a bowl. Add the oil, salt, and pepper and toss. Taste and adjust seasoning if desired. Serve cold or at room temperature.

Serves 4 as a main course

Poached Leeks with Lemon and Parsley Oil

8 medium leeks, white and light green parts only, washed well
2 teaspoons fresh lemon juice
2 teaspoons Lemon and Parsley Oil (page 130)
½ teaspoon kosher salt, plus more to taste
Freshly ground pepper to taste

Bring a large pot of lightly salted water to a boil. Reduce to a simmer. Add the leeks and cook until tender, about 25 minutes. Drain well and set aside to cool. Place leeks on a plate and drizzle with the lemon juice and oil. Sprinkle with salt and pepper. Serve cold or at room temperature.

Serves 4 as a first course

Squid Salad with Lemon and Parsley Oil

1½ pounds cleaned squid, tentacles separated, bodies cut across into ⅛-inch
   rings
6 scallions, thinly sliced
4 stalks celery, thinly sliced
2 teaspoons Lemon and Parsley Oil (page 130)
1 teaspoon kosher salt, plus more to taste
⅛ teaspoon cayenne
Freshly ground black pepper to taste

Bring a medium pot of water to a boil. Add the squid and blanch for 1 minute. Drain and set aside to cool. Place the squid in a bowl, add the scallions, celery, oil, salt, cayenne, and pepper, and toss. Taste and adjust seasoning if desired. Serve cold or at room temperature.

Serves 4 as a first course

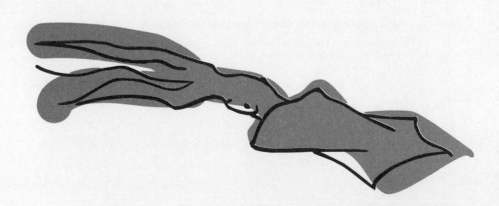

DISTILLING THE SEASON:
A User's Guide to Deploying Vegetable Juices

*I*n summer, the urge to eat lightly, however powerful, is easily sabotaged. A pristine tumble of greens, for instance, becomes a rich meal when tossed with a vinaigrette and topped with oil-baked croutons, cold meat, or cheese. A light summer soup turns hefty with a dollop of cream. And the addition of a butter or olive oil sauce can transform the leanest poached fish into a dietary hazard—leaving the diner feeling as logy as a hot, humid night.

To eat lightly while still savoring the vivid flavors of summer is a challenge. Grilling, sans sauce, and salad, hold-the-dressing, is dining interruptus. Cooking with infused vinegars and oils is one solution to the season's predicament. Using vegetable juice is another. The technique entails less potential to damage the beach physique and more potential to appease the quieter side of summer hungers.

When passed through a commercial juicer (Champion is a popular model), vegetables yield an intensely flavored essence, unmitigated by the crunch of pulp and flesh. The juices are in fact such a strong distillation that the cook should beware: Vegetables with bitter undertones, like eggplant or onion, will yield a juice that packs quite a sting.

But ripe vegetables like sweet red peppers and tomatoes yield an especially sunny perfume. Because they contain a balance of sweet, herbaceous, and sour tones, their essences make alluring cold soups, dressings, and sauces and can be used as poaching liquids. These juices can also be used to make vinaigrettes. More will be said about their use on salads later on. For now, suffice it to say that vegetable vinaigrettes can give pizzazz to a panoply of first and main course dishes, served warm or cold. The juices, in other words, are as versatile as the vegetables they come from.

After juicing the vegetables, the liquid should be allowed to drip through a fine-mesh sieve. Most can be strained quickly, but the tomato is as slow as a dog-day afternoon. In any case, the result is a tart and faintly sweet liquor. Lacking a commercial juicer, these essences can be made by pureeing the vegetable in a food processor to a fine pulp, pushing it through a fine-mesh strainer, and then re-straining the resulting liquor. More work. Less money.

Strained tomato juice is an excellent poaching medium for scallops as well as sea bass. Chilled and garnished with minced scallions, tomatoes, and cucumbers, it becomes an elegant gazpacho; frozen in an ice-cream maker, tomato essence can be turned into a granita that's superb when served with a splash of tequila or vodka.

Like tomatoes, sweet red peppers can be juiced and strained to make a vinaigrette that becomes the basis of an alluring corn chowder or provides a delicious medium for poaching salmon and dressing Sugar Snap peas. Like its tomato cousin, pepper juice can be frozen to make granita; and it also makes an interesting base for a Bloody Mary.

Tomato and sweet red pepper juice are like liquid summer. The juice from vegetables like cucumbers and celery, on the other hand, tastes cooler, like a garden distilled.

Being better known for its crunch than its flavor, the cucumber seems an unlikely candidate for juice. But after the pulp and skin have been removed by the juicer, cucumber juice has a full, though delicate, flavor. Like other vegetable juices, that of a cucumber can be used in place of most of the olive oil in a traditional vinaigrette. When perked up with lime or lemon juice and garnished with additional minced cucumber, scallions, basil, chili pepper, and mint, the juice makes a startling cold soup.

Since vegetable juices quickly lose their pizzazz in the refrigerator, they are best used immediately or frozen in small containers for future use. Nature has conveniently color-coded these essences. Red is for warm sunny dishes. Pale green is for creating moments in the shade.

THE JUICES

Sweet Red Pepper Juice

16 medium red bell peppers, stemmed and seeded

Pass the peppers through a juice extractor. Strain through a fine-mesh sieve. Skim off the foam.

Makes 6 cups

Tomato Juice

8 large tomatoes

Pass the tomatoes through a juice extractor. If using to make a vinaigrette, do not strain. Otherwise, let stand overnight. Place a fine-mesh sieve over a large bowl and let the juice drip through the sieve. Stir from time to time but do not push the pulp through the sieve. This will take about 1 hour.

Makes 4 cups

Cucumber Juice

4 large cucumbers, peeled

Pass the cucumbers through a juice extractor. If using in a vinaigrette, do not strain. Otherwise, skim off the foam. Strain through a fine-mesh sieve.

Makes 4 cups

USING THE JUICES

Cold Red Pepper and Corn Chowder

4 medium ears fresh corn
1 pound medium shrimp, peeled and deveined
½ teaspoon olive oil
4 cups cold Sweet Red Pepper Juice (page 136)
1 small red onion, finely chopped
1 jalapeño pepper, stemmed, seeded, and minced
2 teaspoons white wine vinegar
2 teaspoons kosher salt
Freshly ground pepper to taste
2 tablespoons minced fresh cilantro

1. Heat a grill until very hot. Pull the husks back from the corn and remove the silks. Rewrap the corn in the husks. Soak in water for 15 minutes. Grill the corn, turning frequently, until tender, about 20 minutes. Set aside to cool.

2. Thread the shrimp on metal skewers and brush with the olive oil. Grill just until cooked through, 2 to 3 minutes per side. Take the shrimp off the skewers. Remove the husks from the corn and cut the kernels off the cob. Place the pepper juice in a large bowl. Stir in the corn, onion, jalapeño, vinegar, salt, and pepper. Ladle the soup into 4 bowls. Garnish with the shrimp and sprinkle with cilantro.

Serves 4 as a main course

Scallops Poached in Tomato Juice with Orzo Salad

1 cup Tomato Juice (page 136)
1 tablespoon chopped fresh basil
1 tablespoon chopped Italian parsley
¼ teaspoon kosher salt, plus more to taste
Freshly ground pepper to taste
24 sea scallops, cleaned
1½ cups cooked orzo
1½ teaspoons grated lemon zest
1 tablespoon chopped fresh thyme
1 teaspoon olive oil
2 teaspoons fresh lemon juice
½ cup diced tomato
12 basil leaves, cut across into thin strips

1. Pour the tomato juice into a small saucepan. Stir in the chopped basil, parsley, salt, and pepper. Bring to a simmer over medium heat. Adjust heat so that liquid barely simmers. Add the scallops and poach until just cooked through, about 2 minutes.

2. Place the orzo in a bowl, add the lemon zest, thyme, olive oil, and lemon juice, and toss. Season with salt and pepper.

3. Remove the scallops from the poaching liquid with a slotted spoon and divide among 4 plates. Strain the liquid and spoon some over the scallops. Garnish the scallops with the diced tomato and basil strips. Spoon the orzo salad beside the scallops and serve immediately.

Serves 4 as a main course

DRESSING LIGHTLY

When the air grows heavy and the human spirit wilts, a salad is the best revenge. A seemingly innocent tangle of greens is neither gentle nor mild. It is alive. Fierce both in its inherent crispness and in the varying pepper of individual varieties, it appeals to the brutal side of the summer appetite. Eating a salad is like cracking a whip against languor and ennui. Salad emboldens. It is raw, not cooked. Eating a salad is not about satiating physical hunger but about satisfying a psychological urge.

Making a green salad, on the other hand, is an intellectual endeavor. One must know the character and potential of each individual green.

One must know, for instance, that head lettuces are the crispest and usually the mildest flavored choices and are therefore good candidates for becoming the canvas upon which an interesting salad is created.

The pale-leafed and much maligned iceberg lettuce, when sliced in thin ribbons, gives a satisfying, long-lasting crunch and a quick rush of juice and then disappears, leaving almost no flavor to remember it by. Buttercrunch lettuce, on the other hand, while remarkably crisp and sturdy, has a leaner leaf, is best torn by hand and lends a delicious, fresh flavor to a salad. Boston lettuce is softer than most head lettuces, and its tender leaves and faint taste of the garden will not happily suffer large quantities of full-flavored greens, herbs, or dressing. Bibb or lime-stone lettuce, a loosely folded head with leaves as tender though more substantial than Boston's, lends a sweet taste to a salad bowl. The same can be said for red or green leaf lettuce.

In general, as the color of lettuce deepens, the flavor tends to sharpen and the crunch of the leaves becomes more brittle, at times even tough. The great exception, of course, is romaine lettuce, whose body is nearly as stout as iceberg's and whose flavor is only mildly sharp. This lettuce can stand being cut with a knife and is not easily bruised. Only when the green outer leaves and the paler (and more sharply flavored) inner leaves are combined, does romaine, in and of itself, form a remarkable salad.

But unlike head lettuce like romaine, most leaf lettuces and greens are bold and full of flavor. Watercress and arugula, young dandelion and nasturtium greens are fierce and peppery. They are somewhat tougher to the tooth, but their spicy flavor can punctuate the crisp, tender, mild mannered head lettuces. Appraise the color, taste, and texture of each green and combine them thoughtfully, keeping in mind that finding the perfect balance of crispness and spice offers an innate pleasure.

Members of the cabbage family like endive, radicchio, and chicory, or frisée, as it's come to be called from the French, can add a subtle and alluring bitterness to the spice and herb flavors of summer's more traditional greens. For all their crunch, these greens suggest a hint of cooler weather as well, compromising, at least a little, the freshness of a summer salad. Nevertheless, variety and the unexpected are as welcome in the salad bowl as they are in most other parts of life.

A mélange of torn fresh herbs, shaved cucumber, minced red onion or pepper, and tomatoes, of course, can add another dimension to a summer salad. And then there is the dressing.

For a thoughtfully constructed green salad, there is probably nothing as perfect as a traditional vinaigrette: one part vinegar, three (or four) parts oil. There are also few substances as dietarily deceptive. Several tablespoons can turn a light dish into a total daily allowance for fat. Commercial food manufacturers have spent billions trying to develop full-bodied dressings that use little oil. The slippery substances manufacturers have created are a palliative to the natural urge for a dose of oil with one's cellulose. An unusual flavor, on the other hand, can divert the fat tooth while dressing the salad. Enter, once again, fresh vegetable juices.

The juice of tomatoes or red peppers, cucumber or celery, can replace half the oil used in a traditional vinaigrette and make a satisfying foil for the simplest salad. The juice of fresh corn lends a creamy, nutty satisfaction to salads as well. For the more ambitious, these juices can also be used to create more complex dressings. The juices can be combined with unusual vinegars and oils or enriched with pureed roasted vegetables, nonfat yogurt, or even a touch of fresh ricotta or cottage cheese.

The more complicated dressings, of course, seem to beg more complicated salads. Simple greens are where it all begins, but the urge to create salads in summer is a progressive sort of addiction. It may come down to the fact that while physiological hunger is abated by sating a psychological urge, it doesn't completely disappear. Something more substantial is required.

Whether it's cold pasta, potatoes, roasted vegetables, shellfish, meat, beans, or grains that's being used, contrasting flavors and textures remain as paramount to a substantial salad as they are to a simple one. One cannot underestimate the power of crunch, the shock of cold, the pleasure of a rush of moisture in the languid season.

Cucumber Dill Vinaigrette

Drizzle this dressing over steamed fish or toss with a salad of rice and crisp cucumber.

1 cup Cucumber Juice (page 136)
6 tablespoons buttermilk
2 tablespoons chopped fresh dill
½ teaspoon kosher salt, plus more to taste
Freshly ground pepper to taste

Whisk the juice and buttermilk together in a medium bowl. Whisk in the dill, salt, and pepper. Taste and correct seasoning if needed.

Makes 1½ cups

Cucumber Vinaigrette with Basil and Garlic

This is delicious with tiny steamed potatoes or as a dressing for a bulgur and feta salad stuffed into pita pockets.

1 cup Cucumber Juice (page 136)
2 tablespoons plain lowfat yogurt
4 teaspoons finely chopped scallions
2 teaspoons finely chopped fresh basil
1 medium clove garlic, minced
½ teaspoon kosher salt
Freshly ground pepper to taste

Whisk the cucumber juice and yogurt together in a medium bowl. Whisk in the scallions, basil, garlic, salt, and pepper. Taste and correct seasoning if needed.
Makes 1 cup

Tomato, Basil, and Mint Vinaigrette

Dress an orzo salad with this or drizzle it over warm goat cheese toasts.

1 cup Tomato Juice (page 136)
4 teaspoons chopped fresh basil
4 teaspoons chopped fresh mint
2 teaspoons chopped scallions
½ teaspoon olive oil
½ teaspoon kosher salt
Freshly ground pepper to taste

Combine the juice, basil, mint, and scallions in a medium bowl. Whisk in the olive oil, salt, and pepper. Taste and correct seasoning if needed.
Makes 1 cup

Tomato Tarragon Vinaigrette

Serve as a dip for steamed mussels or spoon over poached chicken.

1 cup Tomato Juice (page 136)
2 teaspoons chopped fresh tarragon
2 teaspoons finely chopped shallots
½ teaspoon olive oil
½ teaspoon kosher salt
Freshly ground pepper to taste

Combine the juice, tarragon, and shallots in a medium bowl. Whisk in the olive oil, salt, and pepper. Taste and correct seasoning if needed.

Makes 1 cup

Red Pepper Balsamic Vinaigrette

Drizzle this slightly sweet dressing over lobster or roasted vegetables.

1 cup Sweet Red Pepper Juice (page 136)
1 teaspoon balsamic vinegar
½ teaspoon fresh lemon juice
2 teaspoons olive oil
½ teaspoon kosher salt
Freshly ground pepper to taste

Combine the pepper juice, vinegar, lemon juice, olive oil, salt, and pepper in a food processor and process for 30 seconds. Taste and correct seasoning if needed.

Makes 1 cup

Red Pepper and Cumin Vinaigrette

This is delicious teamed with a warm wild mushroom salad or tossed with quinoa, zucchini, and yellow squash.

1 cup Sweet Red Pepper Juice (page 136)
1 teaspoon sherry vinegar
1 teaspoon almond oil
⅛ teaspoon ground cumin
½ teaspoon kosher salt
Freshly ground pepper to taste.

Combine the pepper juice, vinegar, oil, cumin, salt, and pepper in a food processor and process for 30 seconds. Taste and correct seasoning if needed.
Makes 1 cup

Couscous and Crab Salad with Cucumber Juice and Mint

1 cup Cucumber Juice (page 136)
½ cup uncooked instant couscous
2 cups lump crabmeat, picked over for cartilage and shells
15 small cherry tomatoes, quartered
1 small red onion, halved and thinly sliced
1 tablespoon chopped fresh mint leaves
½ teaspoon grated lemon zest
½ teaspoon grated lime zest
1 teaspoon kosher salt
Freshly ground pepper to taste

1. Place ¾ cup cucumber juice in a saucepan and bring to a boil. Add the couscous, cover, and remove from heat. Let stand for 5 minutes. Uncover and stir with a fork. Place in a bowl and set aside to cool.

2. Add the crabmeat, cherry tomatoes, onion, mint, and lemon and lime zest and toss to coat. Add in the remaining cucumber juice and toss. Season with salt and pepper. Divide among 4 plates and serve immediately.

Serves 4 as a first course

Chicken Salad with Red Pepper Vinaigrette and Wilted Spinach

2 boneless and skinless chicken breasts, split

¾ teaspoon kosher salt

Freshly ground pepper to taste

2½ pounds spinach leaves, stemmed and washed but not dried

4 tablespoons chopped fresh basil

2 tablespoons chopped fresh mint

½ cup red pepper vinaigrette (pages 143–44)

4 tablespoons finely diced red bell pepper

1. Preheat a grill or broiler until hot. Grill or broil the chicken breasts until cooked through, about 5 minutes per side. Cut on the diagonal into ¼-inch strips. Season with ¼ teaspoon salt and ground pepper.

2. Put the spinach in a large saucepan over medium heat. Cook, stirring, until spinach is barely wilted. Place in a bowl and toss in the basil, mint, remaining ½ teaspoon salt, and pepper. Mound the spinach mixture on each of 4 plates. Fan the chicken strips to the side of the spinach. Spoon the vinaigrette over the chicken, sprinkle with diced pepper, and serve.

Serves 4 as a main course

COLD SNAP

The appetite of summer doth protest too much.

"Just something light," goes the refrain from May to September, "something easy, something refreshing, something cool." So unvaried and unceasing are these demands that the cook begins to suspect they're a cover-up for more complicated yearnings. And, of course, they are.

Beneath the plea for cooling food, one suspects, is the desire to be jolted by a cold shock. Truly soothing food, with its velvety texture and mild seasoning, usually leaves those who have requested it hankering for something more.

Cold soups epitomize the double-edged yearnings of summer. They appear to be a bowlful of everything the season demands. They can be made ahead and are therefore "easy." In fact, for most, the flavor actually improves with time. But without a hidden punch, a cold soup can leave you sullenly tapping your spoon to the tempo of "Is that all there is?"

A lettuce and buttermilk soup, for instance, is smooth and soothing but uneventful until one enriches the texture with French bread and enlivens the flavor with garlic and lemon juice. You can also deepen the intrigue with scallions and a variety of fresh herbs, which stipple the smooth puree as well as boost the taste.

Flavors and textures are not the only way to punch up a cold soup. The sheer girth of a walnut and watercress pesto, for example, plays against the smooth, silky texture of a potato soup while underscoring the peppery bite of the green. In a vibrant tomato soup, balls of cumin and cucumber–scented ice deliver a giant wallop of contrast, especially when floating next to chunks of sweet poached lobster meat.

Because this particular restorative should take your breath away, it must be served icy cold. (Some cooks rest the serving bowls on dishes of shaved ice; others simply cool the soup plates in the freezer for several hours before serving.) The arctic temperature, which is the charm of a cold soup, requires that all seasoning be intensified, as the cold tends to mute it. So always taste before serving and adjust with more salt, pepper, vinegar, lemon, or herbs.

Finally, summer isn't kind to the congenitally wimpy. No matter what people say they want for dinner, they also need (unconsciously, perhaps) something bold, something cold, something *shocking!* to wake up an ornery appetite.

Lettuce and Herb Soup

1 cup white wine
1 cup water
4 small heads Boston lettuce, cored
2 cups cubed stale French bread
2 cups buttermilk
4 cloves garlic, chopped
4 teaspoons minced scallions
4 tablespoons chopped fresh oregano
4 teaspoons chopped fresh rosemary
4 teaspoons chopped fresh thyme
½ cup chopped fresh basil
4 teaspoons fresh lemon juice
1 teaspoon kosher salt, plus more to taste
Freshly ground pepper to taste

Bring the wine and water to a simmer in a large pot. Place the lettuce in a steamer over the wine mixture, cover, and steam until wilted, about 3 minutes. Transfer the lettuce to a blender and add the bread, buttermilk, and garlic. Blend until smooth. Stir in the scallions, oregano, rosemary, thyme, basil, lemon juice, salt, and pepper. Refrigerate until chilled. Taste and adjust seasoning. Divide among 4 bowls and serve immediately.

Serves 4 as a main course

Potato Watercress Soup with Watercress-Walnut Pesto

SOUP

4 medium red potatoes, scrubbed

2½ pounds watercress, stemmed

1½ cups plain lowfat yogurt

1½ cups 1% milk

2 teaspoons Dijon mustard

2 teaspoons kosher salt, plus more to taste

Freshly ground pepper to taste

PESTO

2 cups stemmed watercress

¾ cup walnuts, toasted and chopped

1 large clove garlic, chopped

3 tablespoons olive oil

¼ teaspoon kosher salt

1 teaspoon black mustard seeds

1. Cook the potatoes in boiling water until tender, about 30 minutes. When cool enough to handle, slip off the skins and pass through a ricer. Set aside.

2. Bring a large pot of water to a boil. Add all but 2 cups of the 2½ pounds of watercress and blanch for 5 seconds. Immediately drain and refresh under cold running water. Drain and squeeze out excess water.

3. Transfer to a blender, add the yogurt, and blend until smooth. Scrape into a bowl and whisk in the potatoes, milk, mustard, salt, and pepper. Coarsely chop the remaining 2 cups watercress and stir into the soup. Refrigerate until chilled.

4. Meanwhile, make the pesto. Blanch the watercress as in step 2. Drain, squeeze out excess water, and coarsely chop with a knife. Transfer to a blender, add the walnuts, garlic, olive oil, and salt and blend until smooth, stopping as necessary to scrape down the sides of the jar.

5. Taste the soup and adjust seasoning. Ladle the soup among 4 bowls. Place 2 teaspoons of the pesto in the center of each bowl and sprinkle the mustard seeds around it. Serve immediately.

Serves 4 as a main course

Tomato, Lobster, and Pepper Soup with Tomato-Cumin and Cucumber-Coriander Ices

TOMATO ESSENCE

8 large, ripe tomatoes, cored and quartered

TOMATO ICE

1 cup tomato essence (Step 1)
½ teaspoon ground cumin
½ teaspoon kosher salt
Freshly ground pepper to taste

CUCUMBER ICE

2 medium cucumbers, peeled and coarsely chopped
1 teaspoon kosher salt
½ teaspoon ground coriander
1 teaspoon fresh lemon juice
Freshly ground pepper to taste

SOUP

3 cups tomato essence (Step 1)
2 red bell peppers, stemmed, seeded, and cut into small dice
2 yellow bell peppers, stemmed, seeded, and cut into small dice
1 teaspoon kosher salt, plus more to taste
1 tablespoon fresh lime juice
⅛ teaspoon cayenne
2 lobsters, steamed, meat removed and cut into ½-inch pieces
2 teaspoons chopped fresh chives

1. To make the tomato essence, place half the tomatoes in a food processor and process until finely chopped. Press through a medium-fine sieve. Discard the pulp. Repeat with the remaining tomatoes. You should have about 4 cups of tomato essence.

2. To make the tomato ice, combine 1 cup of the tomato essence with the cumin, salt, and pepper. Pour into a 9-inch pie plate and freeze, stirring every 30 minutes, until firm but not frozen solid, about 2 hours.

3. To make the cucumber ice, liquefy the cucumbers in a food processor. Sprinkle with ½ teaspoon salt and let stand for 20 minutes. Strain through a medium-fine sieve. Stir in the remaining salt, coriander, lemon juice, and pepper. Pour into a 9-inch pie plate and freeze, stirring every 30 minutes, until firm but not frozen solid, about 2 hours.

4. To finish the soup, place the remaining tomato essence in a large bowl and stir in the red and yellow peppers, salt, lime juice, cayenne, and lobster meat. Refrigerate until chilled. Taste and add more salt if needed. Divide the soup among 4 shallow soup bowls. Scoop the ices into balls with a spoon and place 1 ball of each one in the center of each bowl. Sprinkle with chives and serve immediately.

Serves 4 as a main course

TO MAKE A COOL AND SUPPLE GRAIN

G rains are stalwart little soldiers. Whether milled for bread or cooked as nibs sufficient unto themselves, they can be counted on to add heft and forbearance to a meal. But there is also an inherent nuttiness to a grain, a teasing flavor that counters its stodgy and reliable qualities. Likewise the bean, which, whether dried or fresh, would be a humdrum denizen of the kitchen if not for its buttery nuance, the snap of its outer membrane, the satiny mush of its interior, its unending willingness to become either the soul of a meal or its complement and soul mate.

Together or combined with shellfish, herbs, or a soupçon of meat, grains and beans can be fashioned into sturdy, do-ahead meals, becoming a particular staff of life in summer. When handled with care and panache, the sturdy staples step out, becoming more of themselves and therefore more alluring. Isn't that always the way.

History and current events collide in any bean or grain. The Romans called bulgur, a wheat berry derivative, *cerealis*, for Ceres, goddess of agriculture. Bulgur is still held holy by Arabic people, who believe that it was a giant wheat plant and its wheat berry, not an apple, that seduced Eve. The ancient Israelites were more practical, calling this form of wheat *dagan*, or bursting kernel of grain.

This particular moniker reflects the process of preparation rather than the poetic possibility of bulgur, which is wheat that has been steamed, dried, and milled into various grinds. Because it has been precooked, bulgur requires only a short soaking or brief cooking to swell and soften. Coarse grind bulgur has a self-explanatory texture and is best used for pilafs or stuffings; a medium or all-purpose grind is best for salads; the fine grind is delicate enough for breads and desserts.

The grind gradations for cracked wheat are similar to those of bulgur, but the cereal is uncooked wheat that has been dried and milled. Cracked wheat, therefore, requires longer soaking or simmering to become palatable.

Whether by dint of a resurgent primitivism, popular health conceits, or both, wheat nibs began moving slowly from the health food fringes into the mainstream over the past decade. It began with tabbouleh, and now the cereals are used in place of potatoes, rice, or pasta in artful cuisine as well as styled into the sorts of salads that are the one-pot dishes of summer.

Parsley and Bulgar Salad

1 cup medium-grind bulgur
3 cups boiling water
¾ cup chopped Italian parsley
2 tablespoons plus 2 teaspoons fresh lemon juice
1 teaspoon olive oil
1 teaspoon kosher salt, plus more to taste
Freshly ground pepper to taste

Pour the boiling water over the bulgur and soak until tender but firm, about 10 to 12 minutes. Drain well, transfer to a medium bowl and let cool. Add the parsley, lemon juice, olive oil, salt, and pepper and toss. Divide among 4 plates and serve.

Serves 4 as a first course

Barley, Corn, and Lobster Salad

2 lobsters, 1½ pounds each
2 cups cooked barley, cooled
2 ears corn, cooked and kernels cut from cob
1 tablespoon fresh lemon juice
2 teaspoons olive oil
3 tablespoons chopped fresh basil
1 teaspoon kosher salt, plus more to taste
Freshly ground pepper to taste

Steam the lobsters for 10 minutes. Set aside until cool enough to handle. Remove the meat and cut into large chunks. Toss the lobster, barley, and corn together. Add the lemon juice, olive oil, basil, salt, and pepper and toss until well combined. Divide among 4 plates and serve.

Serves 4 as a main course

Mediterranean Lentil Salad with Lemon-Thyme Vinaigrette

SALAD

    1 cup lentils

    5 cups water

    1 tomato, cored and chopped

    ½ cup oil-cured black olives, pitted and coarsely chopped

    ½ cup crumbled feta cheese

    2 stalks celery, trimmed, peeled, and thinly sliced

    Salt and freshly ground pepper to taste

VINAIGRETTE

    ¼ cup fresh lemon juice

    2 large cloves garlic, minced

    2 teaspoons minced fresh thyme leaves

    2 tablespoons plus 2 teaspoons olive oil

    ½ teaspoon kosher salt

    Freshly ground pepper to taste

    1 tablespoon chopped Italian parsley

1. Combine the lentils and water in a large saucepan and bring to a boil. Reduce the heat and simmer until tender but not mushy, about 20 minutes. Drain, transfer to a large bowl, and let cool. Add the tomato, olives, feta, and celery and toss.

2. Whisk together the lemon juice, garlic, and thyme in a medium bowl. Slowly whisk in the olive oil. Whisk in the salt and pepper. Pour the vinaigrette over the salad, toss, and season to taste. Divide among 4 plates, garnish with chopped parsley, and serve.

Serves 4 as a first course

White Bean and Shrimp Salad with Tarragon Vinaigrette

SALAD

    1 cup dried navy beans, soaked in water overnight and drained

    4 cups water

    2 sprigs fresh thyme

    1 bay leaf

    1 clove garlic, crushed

    1 pound large shrimp, cooked and peeled

    1 cup slivered fennel

    1 teaspoon kosher salt

    Freshly ground pepper to taste

VINAIGRETTE

    4 teaspoons sherry vinegar

    4 teaspoons olive oil

    2 tablespoons chopped fresh tarragon

    ¼ teaspoon kosher salt

    Freshly ground pepper to taste

    2 tablespoons chopped fresh chives

1. Combine the beans, water, thyme, bay leaf, and garlic in a medium saucepan and bring to a boil. Reduce the heat to a simmer, cover, and cook until the beans are tender but not mushy, about 1 hour. Drain and remove and discard thyme, bay leaf, and garlic. Transfer beans to a large bowl and set aside until cool. Add the shrimp, fennel, salt, and pepper and toss.

2. Whisk together the vinegar, olive oil, tarragon, salt, and pepper. Pour over the salad and toss. Divide among 4 plates, garnish with the chives, and serve.

Serves 4 as a main course

CONSIDERING TOMATOES

Since the sixteenth century, when the Spanish brought tomatoes back to Europe from the Andes, tomatoes have been a palimpsest upon which societies scribbled their fears and fetishes. First considered poisonous, then aphrodisiac, tomatoes were finally viewed as rather pitiful, a position from which, even today, only the rare sun-ripened tomato escapes.

A full two centuries after Italy was wallowing joyfully in tomatoes, England and the United States viewed the fruit with the disapprobation generally reserved for the common. As late as 1860, *Godey's Lady's Book* admonished proper American housewives that tomatoes should "always be cooked for three hours." Through diligent effort even the tomato could be redeemed, presumably hygienically and perhaps gastronomically.

A taste for cooked tomatoes may have spawned the tomato canning industry in the mid-nineteenth century; without a doubt, this industry gave rise to the demand for meaty, thick-walled, and easily transportable tomatoes. And these tough customers, in turn, gave the current generation plenty to screech and write about.

By now, the words "cottony" and "cardboard" have a symbiotic relationship with the word tomato. The symbiosis is social. When one disdains a tomato as cottony or finds in the fruit qualities reminiscent of cardboard, one is really saying that he or she is above the banal, too special to accept the mass-produced. One is also announcing the ability to discriminate and implying that he or she has access, whether now or in some idealized past, to a world in which life is simple, food is fresher, and tomatoes ripen on the vine.

Still, I find it difficult to imagine anything better than a fat tomato straining at its skin, straddling the fence between the ripe and the rotten. Call me a prisoner of context.

Much has been written about the joy of snatching a tomato still warm from the vine and biting into it, sloppy juices be damned. I won't bore you. I prefer tomatoes at cellar temperature, barely cooled, like an elegant red wine. Besides, my idealized tomato is the Ohio beefsteak that my mother liked to slice and layer with shaved purple onion, salt, and pepper for dinner on August nights. Everyone has her private pastoral; mine happens to be slightly suburban. Nevertheless, my mythical tomato and its personal context remain as tyrannical as that of those who conjure visions of fields and vines.

I'd been cooking for over a decade before I considered tomatoes as anything other than a talisman of summer, a memory of Mom, the red underneath purple onions. Gradually, I came to discern the infinitely varied flavor of tomatoes, the unpredictable balance between their essential acidity and their sweetness, the miracle of such a powerful, juicy universe being contained in such fragile, tentative housing. Of course, it took me a long time to appreciate my mother, too.

The worst thing about commercial tomatoes (which, I am embarrassed to say, means cotton or cardboard) is that they are not time bombs. There is no sense of urgency about them, no chance that one will miss one's chance, no opportunity to deliver them from certain explosion and sorry, weeping rot. I've kept them for months in a refrigerator; they rot not. Commercial tomatoes are constant. The only thing constant about a garden tomato is change, and change is a challenge. Commercial tomatoes don't need people. Garden tomatoes do, desperately. Isn't it gratifying?

Modern life offers so few chances to be a hero. Tomatoes beg for heroes, at least in the kitchen. And to be a hero one needs only to sense the moment just before the tomato will surrender its self-contained world, burst its skin, and seep outward. At that moment, the tomato is the most itself that it will ever be.

By nature, a tomato is bound to assimilate. Fleshier plums and globes glory and mellow when cooked. Juicy globes offer the best of themselves raw. Tomatoes at their best lend rather than absorb. They require a cook to appreciate context, both of origin and of possibility.

It is probably no coincidence that tomatoes occur naturally in summer. It is probably wise to appreciate them as punctuation marks. At their best, tomatoes deliver a jolt, the end of a phrase, the question of what is to be, which inevitably curves back to the question of what was.

My Mother's Tomato and Red Onion Salad

4 large ripe tomatoes, cut into ¼-inch slices
1 small red onion, thinly sliced
2 teaspoons red wine vinegar
4 teaspoons extra-virgin olive oil
Kosher salt and freshly ground pepper to taste
15 fresh basil leaves, cut across into thin strips

Arrange the tomato and onion slices on 4 salad plates in slightly overlapping layers. Sprinkle with vinegar and drizzle with the olive oil. Season with salt and pepper. Sprinkle basil strips over the top of each salad and serve immediately.

Serves 4 as a first course

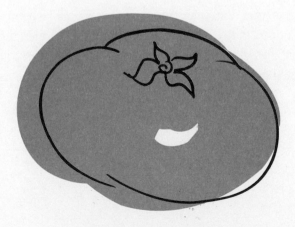

Tomato-Lemon Chutney

1½ teaspoons kosher salt
2 tablespoons plus 2 teaspoons sugar
½ cup water
1 lemon, quartered and sliced ⅛ inch thick
3 medium-size ripe tomatoes
1 teaspoon olive oil
3 large shallots, thinly sliced
1 teaspoon balsamic vinegar
Freshly ground pepper to taste

1. Combine 1 teaspoon salt, 2 tablespoons sugar, the water, and lemon pieces in a small saucepan and bring to a boil over medium heat. Reduce the heat and simmer for 15 minutes. Drain, reserving the liquid, and set aside.

2. Bring a medium saucepan of water to a boil. Add the tomatoes and blanch for 10 seconds. Peel the tomatoes and cut them into large dice. Heat the olive oil in a medium saucepan. Add the shallots and cook until soft but not brown, about 3 minutes.

3. Add the tomatoes, the remaining sugar, and 1 tablespoon of the reserved lemon liquid. Bring to a boil over medium-high heat. Reduce the heat and simmer, stirring often, until the mixture is thick, about 35 minutes. Stir in the lemons, the vinegar, the remaining salt, and pepper. Let cool and store in the refrigerator.

Makes 1 cup

Fresh Tomato Sauce with Olives and Basil

This salsa can be tossed with pasta or rice, used to top pizza, or used as a sauce for chicken or seafood.

2 teaspoons extra-virgin olive oil
3 cloves garlic, minced
1 medium onion, finely chopped
4 medium-size ripe tomatoes, diced
1 cup fresh basil leaves, coarsely chopped
3 tablespoons chopped pitted green olives
3 tablespoons chopped pitted imported black olives
½ teaspoon kosher salt, plus more to taste
Freshly ground pepper to taste

1. Heat 1 teaspoon of the olive oil in a medium nonstick skillet over medium heat. Add the garlic and onion and cook, stirring often, for 5 minutes. Stir in the tomatoes and cook for 5 minutes.

2. Meanwhile, combine the basil and olives in a mixing bowl. Stir in the tomato mixture and let cool to room temperature. Stir in the remaining olive oil and season with salt and pepper. Serve within a few hours.

Makes 3 cups

Tomato Bisque

3 teaspoons extra-virgin olive oil

4 cloves garlic, minced

2 small onions, diced

2 teaspoons ground cumin

1 teaspoon ground coriander

2 cups chicken broth, homemade or low-sodium canned broth

8 medium tomatoes, seeded and diced

4 slices stale crusty bread, 1 inch thick, torn into pieces

1 teaspoon grated orange zest

1 teaspoon kosher salt, plus more to taste

Freshly ground pepper to taste

1. Heat 1 teaspoon of the olive oil in a large saucepan. Add the garlic and onions and cook for 2 minutes. Stir in the cumin and coriander and 1 tablespoon of the broth. Cook until the onions are very soft, about 5 minutes longer. Add the tomatoes and the remaining broth and bring to a boil. Reduce the heat and simmer for 30 minutes.

2. Stir in the bread pieces and the orange zest and cook for 5 minutes longer. Transfer half the soup to a food processor and process until smooth. Place in a clean saucepan. Repeat with remaining soup. Stir in the salt and pepper. Heat over low heat until hot. Ladle the soup into 4 bowls and swirl ½ teaspoon of the remaining olive oil into each one. Serve immediately.

Serves 4 as a first course

Windfall Pie

1 tablespoon olive oil

1 large egg yolk

2 large egg whites

2 cups fine dried bread crumbs, freshly made

2 teaspoons chopped fresh oregano

½ teaspoon kosher salt

1 teaspoon freshly ground pepper

3 pounds green tomatoes, cut into ¼-inch slices

2 pounds ripe tomatoes, peeled, cored, seeded, and diced

1 teaspoon grated orange zest

1 small clove garlic, minced

1 bay leaf

½ cup crumbled feta cheese

1. Preheat the oven to 350° F. Brush the inside of a 9-inch fluted tart pan with the olive oil.

2. Lightly beat the egg yolk and whites together. Set aside. Combine the bread crumbs, oregano, salt, and pepper. Set aside. Dip the green tomato slices in the egg mixture. Dredge in the bread crumb mixture. Lay the slices on a baking sheet. Bake until the bread crumbs are golden, about 15 minutes per side. Set aside.

3. Combine the red tomatoes, orange zest, garlic, and bay leaf in a nonstick skillet. Cook over medium-low heat until the sauce thickens, about 30 minutes. Remove and discard the bay leaf. Set aside.

4. Spread a thin layer of tomato sauce on the bottom of the tart pan. Cover with a layer of green tomato slices and another thin layer of sauce. Sprinkle with a small amount of feta cheese. Repeat until all the ingredients are used up, ending with a generous layer of feta. Cover with foil and bake for 2 hours. Let cool slightly, divide among 6 plates, and serve.

Serves 6 as a main course

ESSENTIAL EGGPLANT

*I*saw my first eggplants in 1974 in Fuller's Market in Granville, Ohio. The shiny purple orbs were piled next to the beefsteak tomatoes and sweet corn that Paul Bennett, a local gardener and poet, had grown. With their curling stems and thick ruffled leaves, they looked like the work of a fantasist, like something out of "Jack and the Beanstalk." And they must have scared everybody as much as they did me, because that purple pyramid remained intact while the tomatoes disappeared and the corn dwindled to pale, orphaned husks and strands of forsaken silk.

Ohioans have definite ideas about summer dinner. And that summer we were more definite than usual. Watergate was everywhere. WCOL played Don McLean singing "American Pie" so often that even the rednecks were starting to believe it and the rest of us were finding out that being right doesn't necessarily feel right. Everyone cleaved to the familiar, which didn't include eggplant. The only reason I bought one was that Paul Bennett seemed so sad looking at his undiminished supply.

Bye Bye Miss American Pie. Hello Eggplant Parmesan. I made the dish as often as WCOL played the song. It was a long time before I appreciated eggplant as anything other than a breadable, fryable, bakeable medium.

Like most Americans, Paul Bennett grew Black Beauties, which look like giant, deep-purple goose eggs and are about as absorbent as a household sponge, and only slightly more nutritious. Nearly every eggplant will immediately soak up oil, sauce, or any liquid that it is cooked in, up to four times its own weight. And then, in some moment of catharsis known only to eggplants, one drop of oil becomes too much and the eggplant begins evicting all it had so graciously taken in. The patient cook is rewarded with a silky texture and incomparably rich, nutty flavor. So what if they are 92 percent water.

Within weeks of my first purchase, I'd figured out that small eggplants are usually more bitter than larger and more mature ones. There was only one type to contend with, Black Beauties. Though today there are other varieties—Oriental

Purple, the long, sweet-tasting fruit with thin, light violet skin; Albino, which generally comes from Holland and has the most silken texture, and tiny virginettes—Black Beauty remains king, of the home garden, of the commercial grower, and of almost any recipe.

I've used Black Beauties in Greek moussaka, baba ganoush, ratatouille, caponata, and Provençale eggplant caviar. I've roasted them in the Serbian manner, with green pepper and garlic puree, served them with Georgian walnut sauce, stuffed them in both the Turkish and Creole style, and fashioned them into a Persian kookoo, an eggplant soufflé with soy sauce and walnuts. Eggplant is so adaptable that it is easy to miss its singular shocking quality. When most itself, the fruit that clings to an umbilical vine close to the earth tastes not at all of the earth, but of the sea.

Paul Bennett tried to explain this in a poem. "The embodiment of sun, seed, this vegetable is what it wants to be," he wrote in "Jottings of an Ohio Gardener." "Enterprising egg, royal black wholeness, known when tongue buds taste the open seas far inland, a faint oyster breeze."

I've rarely tasted the eggplant being its surprising self. The most recent time was a simple Japanese preparation at Rissa, a restaurant in St. Helena, California. The first time was the night that Richard M. Nixon resigned. A bunch of us were grilling steaks over a hardwood fire in the backyard when WCOL interrupted its programming with the news bulletin. We tried to cheer, but our mouths were full so instead we chewed while the crickets screamed and WCOL played.

"Oh my God the eggplant," said Juan Carlos Durante.

"The eggplant," said Jude Ogsburg.

"The eggplant," said Alice Merrill.

I'd dropped it on the grill and forgotten it, leaving it to blister and get soft and sweet as butter over the dying coals. When we finally ate it, each spoonful hinted of a world beyond the obvious, something underneath the surface, under water, beyond our shores.

The cookbook author Paula Wolfert swears it was the fuel. Recently she gave me a recipe for whole grilled eggplant whose extraordinary flavor, she insists, is a result of using fresh, local eggplant and cooking only over virgin hardwood charcoal. I keep wishing there were more to it than that. But her eggplant tastes much better than the one I cremated so many years ago by mistake, just as shocking, even more itself.

Rissa's Eggplant

1 cup miso paste (see Note)
1 cup soba sauce (see Note)
1 cup (packed) brown sugar
1½ teaspoons crushed red pepper
2 medium eggplants, trimmed and cut lengthwise into ⅓-inch slices, each slice
    scored diagonally
1 tablespoon canola oil

1. Combine the miso paste, soba sauce, brown sugar, and red pepper in a large bowl. Place the eggplant slices in a shallow dish and pour the marinade over them. Let stand at room temperature for at least 30 minutes.

2. Preheat the oven to 350° F. Use 1½ teaspoons oil to grease a jelly-roll pan.

3. Drain the eggplant and place on the pan. Bake in lower third of oven for 30 minutes. Remove from the oven.

4. Preheat the broiler. Lightly brush the remaining oil over the eggplant. Broil for 2 minutes. Turn slices over and broil for 1 minute more. Divide among 4 plates and serve.

Serves 4 as a first course or side dish

> Note: Miso paste and soba sauce are available in
> Asian markets and by mail order from Katagiri,
> 224 East 59th Street, New York, New York
> 10022; (212) 755-3566.

Arabic Eggplant

2 pounds eggplant, cut across into ½-inch slices
1 tablespoon kosher salt
2 ripe tomatoes, peeled
¼ cup olive oil
2 cloves garlic, roasted and peeled (page 175)
½ teaspoon ground cumin
1 teaspoon sweet paprika
½ cup lemon juice
½ cup fresh coriander leaves

1. Place the eggplant in a colander and toss with the salt. Let drain for 30 minutes.

2. Core, seed, and dice the tomatoes over a bowl to collect the juice. Set the juice and tomatoes aside. Rinse the eggplant under cold water and pat dry. Brush both sides of the eggplant with the olive oil and grill over hot coals until golden brown. Set aside to cool.

3. Combine the tomatoes and juice, garlic, cumin, paprika, and lemon juice in a large salad bowl. Add the eggplant and toss. Season to taste with salt and pepper. Divide among 4 plates and serve.

Serves 4 as a first course

Roasted White Eggplant Soup

1 cup plain lowfat yogurt

1 large red bell pepper, roasted, seeded, and peeled

4 pounds white eggplant

1 teaspoon olive oil

1 onion, coarsely chopped

2 cloves garlic, chopped

4 cups chicken broth, homemade, or low-sodium canned broth

½ teaspoon kosher salt

1 teaspoon freshly ground pepper

1. Scrape the yogurt into a sieve lined with paper towels, set over a bowl, and let drain in the refrigerator for 3 hours.

2. Put the roasted pepper in a food processor or blender and puree until smooth. Set aside.

3. Preheat the oven to 425° F.

4. Place the eggplants on a baking sheet. Roast until soft, about 35 minutes. Set aside to cool. Peel the eggplant, cut in half lengthwise, lift out the small seed sacs, and discard. Chop the remaining pulp.

5. Combine the olive oil, onion, garlic, and eggplant in a large pot. Cook over low heat until the onions are soft, about 10 minutes. Add the broth and simmer for 10 minutes. Season with salt and pepper.

6. Ladle the soup into 4 bowls, garnish each with a dollop of thickened yogurt and a swirl of red pepper puree, and serve.

Serves 4 as a main course

AN EMBARRASSMENT OF RICHES

Zucchini are the embarrassment of August, so many, so big, and often so bland. The first crop of the green squash inspires, like most first encounters, a flush of excitement. They are small and firm, with a delicate, willing, and herbaceous taste. But as the summer squash itself and its numbers grow, appreciation diminishes. The larger the zucchini, the more water and the less flavor it has; the more zucchini there is, the less precious and inspiring it seems.

By the last Saturday in August, when the International Zucchini Festival is held in Harrisville, New Hampshire, freak zucchini—specimens the size of dolphins, Siamese zucchini, and ones that grew curled like giant bagels—grab attention. Normal zucchini, those six to eight inches long and one to two inches thick, are nearly invisible in the glut. Only an eye trained to nuance can appreciate the charm of their individual shape and crook, their various striations, their sheen.

Perhaps the glut also numbs us to the zucchini's subtle charms. Reams of recipes have been written in an effort to save zucchini from itself. Even the *Dictionnaire de l'Académie des Gastronomes* insists that zucchini "call for help from without to augment their flavor."

Au contraire according to the French gastronomic writer James de Coquet, who wrote that the zucchini position of the *Dictionnaire* constituted "a slanderous charge" as well as a sorry statement of the times.

"We must be living in an epoch in which discretion does not pay, since it is reproached for the subtlety of its taste." "To pretend . . . that foods are to be valued in proportion to the intensity of their flavor is to arrive at the conclusion that the finest of all dishes is pickled herring."

Only connoisseurs, claimed M. de Coquet, can appreciate zucchini. He was, of course, referring to tiny squash unembellished: disks of zucchini sautéed in butter or olive oil, baked whole, or minced or grated raw into a salad. The tiniest zucchini, in fact, require little help from without.

Small, young zucchini can be shredded and tossed with olive oil and lemon juice to make a sprightly slaw, or they can be cut into small dice and used like cucumber to give salad a surprise. But the larger zucchini (I'm sorry, M. de Coquet), need help. Their essence is diluted, and it must be bolstered to taste of much of anything at all. A small zucchini is an entity; a larger one is a vehicle.

A large zucchini can be shredded like a small one, but it needs torn herbs and perhaps even slivered red peppers to become a comely slaw. A touch of garlic or onion can, in fact, overwhelm a small zucchini. A big zucchini appreciates the thought.

In fact, the big guys of the bumper crops are wonderful when chopped and sautéed with garlic, onion, and tomatoes to make a ratatouille, baked as a gratin, turned into a savory bisque, or stuffed with chopped vegetables or meat. Pungent seasonings like curry or chili peppers don't overpower large zucchini. Instead, their bold flavors render the summer vegetable a mild background and redeem a squash left too long on the vine.

Zucchini Gratin with Parsley and Thyme

    3 medium zucchini, cut into ¼-inch rounds
    2¼ teaspoons kosher salt
    1 tablespoon white wine
    1 teaspoon olive oil
    1 teaspoon chopped Italian parsley
    ¼ teaspoon chopped fresh thyme
    Freshly ground pepper to taste

1. Sprinkle the zucchini rounds with 2 teaspoons salt, place in a sieve, and let drain for 1 hour. Pat dry.

2. Preheat the oven to 350° F.

3. Arrange the zucchini in concentric circles in a 10-inch quiche dish, overlapping the pieces slightly. Whisk together the wine, oil, parsley, thyme, remaining salt, and pepper and spoon the mixture over the zucchini. Bake until zucchini is tender but not too soft, about 25 minutes. Divide among 4 plates and serve immediately.

Serves 4 as a side dish

Zucchini Pasta with Fresh Tomato Sauce

½ teaspoon olive oil

1 medium zucchini, diced small

3 cloves garlic, minced

2 medium tomatoes, seeded and diced small

2 tablespoons chopped Italian parsley

3 tablespoons thinly sliced basil leaves

1 teaspoon kosher salt, plus more to taste

Freshly ground pepper to taste

4 medium zucchini, halved lengthwise

1. Heat the olive oil in a medium nonstick skillet over medium heat. Add the diced zucchini and cook until browned, about 4 minutes. Stir in the garlic and cook for 1 minute. Add the tomatoes, parsley, basil, ¾ teaspoon salt, and pepper and cook until heated through, about 1 minute longer.

2. Bring a large pot of lightly salted water to a boil. Place the zucchini on a work surface, cut side down, and cut lengthwise into thin strips. Place in the pot and cook for 3 minutes. Drain well. Place in a large bowl, sprinkle with the remaining salt, and toss with the tomato sauce. Taste and adjust seasoning if needed. Divide among 4 plates and serve immediately.

Serves 4 as a main course

Indian-Spiced Zucchini-Coconut Soup

1 teaspoon olive oil

1 medium onion, chopped

2 cloves garlic, chopped

4 medium zucchini, cut into ½-inch dice

1 teaspoon ground cumin

½ teaspoon turmeric

Pinch cayenne

1½ teaspoons kosher salt

Freshly ground pepper to taste

1½ cups chicken broth, homemade, or low-sodium canned broth

½ cup unsweetened coconut milk

2 teaspoons chopped fresh cilantro

2 teaspoons chopped fresh mint

½ teaspoon grated orange zest

1 teaspoon grated unsweetened coconut

1. Heat the oil in a large pot over medium heat. Add the onion and garlic and cook for 5 minutes. Add the zucchini and cook for 5 minutes more. Stir in the cumin, turmeric, cayenne, salt, and pepper. Stir in the broth and coconut milk. Bring to a boil. Reduce the heat and simmer until the zucchini is soft, about 25 minutes.

2. Scrape the soup into a blender and process until smooth. Pour into a saucepan and heat over low heat just until hot. Combine the cilantro, mint, and orange zest in a small bowl. Divide the soup among 4 soup bowls. Sprinkle with the grated coconut and then the herb mixture. Serve immediately.

Serves 4 as a main course

GARLIC YOUNG AND OLD

Garlic looks deceptively innocent. From a distance, a bulb appears to be a pudgy, amiable jobber, rustic and reminiscent of hardscrabble lives. Like ears of corn or branches of chili peppers hung up to dry, a braid of garlic promises to deliver a note of summer to a bleak winter's night dinner. Perhaps because its flavor is so fiercely sunny, garlic has been relied on too, folklorically, as a purifier, an antiseptic, an antibiotic, a deterrent to vampires.

A friend of mine was forced to wear a garlic necklace to school when she was young. She was a healthy girl, but this could have had as much to do with the fact that other children gave her a wide berth as with the preventative powers of garlic. Even so, I make a tea of chicken soup, chili peppers, and twenty cloves of garlic at the first pang of a cold. Vulnerability has a way of sending moderns scurrying back in time. And garlic, it seems, has always had a way of being there. Recipes for the venerable Greek skordalia, the Roman aglio e olia, the Spanish sopa de ajo and the French aïoli can be read as prescriptions as easily as they can be consulted as blueprints for dinner.

But the utility and versatility of garlic veils something essential about this member of the allium family, whose cousins include chives and onions, shallots and leeks. On closer inspection, a head of garlic has the elegance of an egg, a self-contained universe revealing little of itself, waiting.

Unlike an egg, however, a bulb of garlic is not a single life, but a community. The cloves strain against their parchment cloak, as if they cannot wait to be free of each other, but they are joined at the root. Individual cloves swell away from the bulb but inevitably each curves back toward the whole. Garlic is determinedly social, which may explain the marriage of garlic and Italy in the American mind. Anyone who has strolled an Italian piazza at dusk is aware of the national tendency to know oneself in relationship to others.

Likewise garlic is best known by what it does. Unpeeled, so that no juices escape, garlic gives a mildly sunny perfume when warmed in oil for pasta, buried in lamb or stuffed in chicken; when peeled, the effect of the whole clove will be warmer, insistently a summer day. Sliced or minced, raw or cooked garlic becomes more pronounced, almost spiteful. Mashed, garlic is overbearingly itself; no other ingredient can get a taste in edgewise.

Garlic can be subtle and sweet, or it can be a big bully with acrid underpinnings. It all depends on how and with what garlic is used, as well as on how long garlic is cooked. The cook chooses. Garlic obliges. Then garlic changes everything. Garlic just wants to have fun.

Americans have long feared garlic, not so much for what it is, but for what it does. Anyone who knows garlic recognizes this fear as personal misgiving tinged with a terror of the unquantifiable and the unknown. You can choose fresh garlic and employ it either judiciously or with abandon. But you cannot really predict the effect of garlic, you can only smell and taste and judge garlic as you go along.

Those who do not know garlic are content to parrot the common garlic slur. They call garlic anti-social. Will Rogers described Gilroy, California, a town on the Monterey peninsula that claims to be the garlic capital of the world, as "the only town in America where you can marinate a steak by hanging it on the clothesline." The aspersion has not deterred Gilroy: every July the town sponsors a garlic festival that features garlic scampi, garlic tamales, garlic fried ravioli, escargot kebabs in garlic butter, pickled garlic, garlic jelly, and garlic ice cream. The festival also offers garlic and rose perfume which promises "He may forget your name, but he'll know you've been there."

Where you've been individually or, in the case of America, culturally, is reflected in your relationship to garlic. The potent and unpredictable bulb has been around at least as long as the bible, and whether you cook with it, cure with it, or wear it as perfume, you place yourself on a continuum. It takes a certain confidence to boldly embrace something that appears lowly, as well as a certain wit to contend with the elegance and uncharted possibility beneath the veneer.

America is currently in love with garlic. The nervous nature of the infatuation, however, can be witnessed in the way that whole bulbs of garlic are now roasted and served, rather than butter, with bread in restaurants from Gilroy to Columbus, Ohio. Roasting intensifies the sweetness of garlic, reduces the cloves to a caramelized bass note and effectively limits the tunes—acerbic, petulant, insistent, and intense as they might be—that garlic can play. Roasted garlic is not a bad beginning, but it shouldn't be the end.

Sometimes I roast garlic. I like the soft, unctuous way roasted cloves squirt from their fragile apartments to sweeten bread or pizza, bean or grain salads, or to serve as a complement to grilled meat or fish. But in the summer, when garlic is firm and insistent, I like it better raw or cooked barely golden, still insouciant, a worker of magic, not magic itself.

My preference for roasted garlic is more personal than it is about garlic. When I was learning to cook in restaurants, I was regularly assigned the task of peeling five gallons worth of garlic cloves. Garlic became, therefore, precious to me. To witness trays of bulbs being roasted, or cups of cloves smashed with basil to make pesto still makes me wince. To me, each clove of garlic is an inscrutable friend. The only way I can know its distinct disposition is to witness its effect on others. Garlic rarely acts alone.

Roast Garlic

Garlic can be roasted ahead of time and stored, well covered, in the refrigerator for up to a week. It can be used in a wide variety of recipes, and can also be mashed with warm olive oil and served on bread, or tossed with pasta or rice.

4 medium heads garlic
2 teaspoons olive oil
½ teaspoon kosher salt
Freshly ground pepper to taste.

1. Preheat the oven to 350° F.
2. Smash the heads of garlic lightly to loosen but not completely separate the cloves. Place on a large sheet of aluminum foil or in a small casserole with a lid. Drizzle with the olive oil and season with salt and pepper. Wrap the foil into a tight package or cover the dish. Roast until the garlic is soft, about 1 hour. When cool enough to handle, peel the garlic by squeezing each clove at 1 end so that it pops out of the skin.

About ⅔ cup mashed garlic

Linguine with Garlic and Lemon

1 pound dried linguine
2 teaspoons olive oil
12 large cloves garlic, minced
2 teaspoons grated lemon zest
4 teaspoons fresh lemon juice
2 teaspoons kosher salt
Freshly ground pepper to taste
½ cup chopped Italian parsley

Bring a large pot of salted water to a boil. Add the linguine and cook until al dente. Meanwhile, heat the olive oil in a small nonstick skillet over medium-low heat. Add the garlic and cook, stirring constantly, for 45 seconds. Do not let the garlic brown. Drain the pasta and transfer it to a large bowl. Add the garlic and oil. Add the lemon zest, lemon juice, salt, pepper, and parsley and toss to coat well. Divide among 4 plates and serve immediately.

Serves 4 as a main course

Garlic Broth with Lobster or Chicken

2 quarts water
1 head garlic, cloves smashed well
3 cups country-style bread, cut into 1-inch cubes
2 teaspoons olive oil
4 small lobsters, steamed, or 1 chicken, roasted
1½ teaspoons kosher salt
2 teaspoons fresh lemon juice
2 tablespoons coarsely chopped Italian parsley
¾ cup seeded and diced tomato

1. Combine the water and garlic in a large saucepan and bring to a boil over medium-high heat. Reduce the heat and simmer until reduced to 1 quart, about 2 hours. Strain, reserving the broth. Discard the garlic.

2. Preheat the oven to 350° F.

3. Toss the bread cubes with the olive oil and bake until crisp, about 12 minutes.

4. Remove the tail and claw meat from the lobsters or carve the chicken, separating the legs at the joint and quartering the breast.

5. Stir the salt, lemon juice, and parsley into the broth. Reheat if necessary. Divide the lobster meat or chicken among 4 large shallow soup bowls. Ladle the broth over them and sprinkle with the diced tomato. Top with croutons and serve immediately.

Serves 4 as a main course

Garlic Custard with Shrimp and Tomato Broth

3 cups canned tomato juice

1 cup milk

6 large cloves garlic, chopped

1 pound shrimp, peeled and deveined

½ teaspoon kosher salt, plus more to taste

Freshly ground pepper to taste

Olive oil spray

2 large eggs

½ teaspoon olive oil

1 red bell pepper, seeded and diced

1 yellow bell pepper, seeded and diced

4 teaspoons chopped chives

1. Strain the tomato juice through a sieve lined with a paper towel, stirring occasionally. This will take about 1½ hours.

2. Place the milk and garlic in a medium saucepan over medium heat. Bring just to the simmering point and remove from heat. Let stand until cool.

3. Place the tomato juice in a nonreactive saucepan and bring to a simmer. Reduce the heat, add the shrimp, and cook until done, about 1 minute. Season with salt and pepper to taste.

4. Lightly coat four ½-cup ramekins with the olive oil spray. Whisk the eggs in a large bowl. Whisk in the cooled milk and ½ teaspoon salt. Strain through a fine sieve and divide among the ramekins. Bring water in a steamer to a boil and adjust to a low simmer. Place the ramekins in the steamer, cover, and steam until set, about 20 minutes.

5. Meanwhile, heat the olive oil in a medium nonstick skillet over medium heat. Add the peppers and cook until crisp-tender, about 3 minutes. Rewarm the tomato broth.

6. Unmold the custards into the center of 4 shallow soup bowls. Ladle some of the tomato broth around each custard, dividing the shrimp evenly among the bowls. Place the peppers around the custards and sprinkle the top with chives. Serve immediately.

Serves 4 as a main course

FRESH SHELL BEANS

There is something Gone With the Wind about shelling beans. The activity seems made for rocking chairs on a shaded verandah and is best done in a group and accompanied by gossip. Shelling beans is also a little like birthin' babies. Splitting a lima, fava, or cranberry bean pod reveals a row of perfectly formed, incipient lives. The cook is overwhelmed by the responsibility, and then by the possibilities.

In the sixth century B.C., the Greek philosopher Pythagoras forbade his followers to eat fava beans, the most common shell bean of antiquity. He claimed the pods held the souls of the dead. Others believed the stalks were the passage to the underworld. Even a humdrum bean isn't as easy as it seems.

In America, the small baby lima bean and its larger cousin, the Fordhook, have inured the public to the shell bean's inherent mystery and charm. About 60 million pounds of the beans are stripped, partially cooked, packaged and frozen each year; lima beans are the tenth most popular frozen vegetable in the country. The beans freeze very well but tend not to have the tender, sweet butteriness of the freshly shelled.

But to get that sweetness, the cook must battle the indolence of summer with its slowed sense of time. Like corn and fresh peas, shell beans begin converting their own natural sugars to starch the moment they're picked. The cook who dawdles will get not a toothsome bean but one that is mealy and blasé. The nature of the bean is to challenge the cook and the nature of the season.

For one used to the Stepford Wives quality of frozen lima beans, fresh ones re-align reality. Ranging from creamy white to pale spring green, the beans are sweet, mildly herbaceous, and, though delicate, unexpectedly sassy. Once shelled, fresh limas should be dumped into boiling water and simmered until tender, which takes five to fifteen minutes depending on their size. Then they should be drained and cooled quickly under cold water. Their skins are tender enough to provide a subtle contrast to the almost buttery density within.

Lima beans with fresh corn, à la the Algonquin musicickquatash or succotash, is a difficult combination to improve upon. Lobster or shrimp can add a briny, sweet counterpoint; exotic mushrooms like shiitake can give a woodsy hint to the bean. Fresh succotash and aromatic rice could redefine Louis Armstrong's signature "red beans and ricely yours." But then again, succotash and ricely yours lacks a certain ring. I've yet to find an herb that flatters lima beans as well as salt and pepper.

Fava beans, on the other hand, those thick, bright green pods with pale green beans often called broad beans, have a more robust flavor, are less buttery than they are earthy, and, as the Italian, Greek, and other Mediterranean cuisines know, can stand up to peppery olive oil, intense herbs, and full-flavored cheese.

It is difficult to do better by a fava than to shell it, boil it, chill it, remove its leathery skin, and toss it in olive oil and lemon juice to serve under wafers of pecorino cheese. The same salad can be used to top pasta or can be stirred into risotto in the final moments of cooking. The bean makes a fine counterpoint to shaved prosciutto and holds its own with minced onion. Moreover, if the fava beans are young, the shells are tender enough to be minced and used as a garnish. Cook fava beans from one to ten minutes, depending on their age and whether they need some bite for a salad or more softness for a puree.

Cranberry beans, mottled pink inside their rust and cream colored striped shell, are called "shellouts" in the American South. Falling somewhere between lima and fava beans in taste and texture, they can be shelled and simmered until soft, about thirty minutes. While fresh cranberry beans are more delicate than dried ones, both can be used the same ways, as long as one adjusts the cooking time and tempers the seasoning.

Cranberry Beans with Garlic and Rosemary

3 cups cooked cranberry beans
1 tablespoon fresh lemon juice
1 tablespoon extra-virgin olive oil
2 small cloves garlic, minced
1 tablespoon minced fresh rosemary
¾ teaspoon kosher salt
Freshly ground pepper to taste

Place the cranberry beans in a bowl, add the remaining ingredients, and toss.
Serve as a salad, an accompaniment for grilled meats, or toss with cooked pasta.
Serves 4 as a side dish

Fava Bean Pudding with Shiitakes, Bacon, and Wilted Arugula

PUDDING

    5 pounds fresh fava beans, shelled

    2 large eggs

    ¼ cup yogurt cheese (page 31)

    2 scallions, green parts only, minced

    1 teaspoon kosher salt

    Freshly ground pepper to taste

    Olive oil spray

GARNISH

    3 slices bacon, diced

    3 cups stemmed and sliced shiitake mushrooms

    2 cups arugula leaves

    ½ teaspoon kosher salt

    Freshly ground pepper to taste

1. Bring a large pot of water to a boil. Add the fava beans and blanch until soft, about 10 minutes. Drain and rinse under cold running water. Slip the skin off each bean. Set aside ½ cup of beans and place the rest in a blender. Add the eggs, yogurt cheese, scallions, salt, and pepper and blend until smooth.

2. Lightly coat four 6-ounce ramekins with the olive oil spray and divide the bean mixture among them. Place the ramekins in a steamer basket over barely simmering water. Cover and steam until the puddings are set, about 25 minutes.

3. Meanwhile, cook the bacon in a medium nonstick skillet until browned. Remove the bacon with a slotted spoon and set aside. Pour off the fat. Add the shiitakes to the skillet and cook over medium heat until softened, about 5 minutes. Add the arugula and cook until almost wilted. Remove from the heat and stir in the bacon, salt, and pepper.

4. To serve, run the tip of a small knife around the inside edge of each ramekin to loosen the pudding. Invert onto the center of each of 4 plates and surround with the shiitake mixture. Sprinkle with the reserved fava beans and serve immediately.

Serves 4 as a main course

Lima Bean Ragout with Grilled Shrimp

SHRIMP

> 6 large cloves garlic, minced
>
> 2 jalapeño peppers, seeded and minced
>
> Juice of 2 lemons
>
> 1 tablespoon olive oil
>
> ½ teaspoon kosher salt
>
> ½ teaspoon freshly ground pepper
>
> 1½ pounds large shrimp, unpeeled

RAGOUT

> 1 teaspoon olive oil
>
> 1 medium onion, diced
>
> 1 medium red bell pepper, seeded and diced
>
> 1 cup corn kernels
>
> 2 cups cooked lima beans
>
> 1 medium tomato, diced
>
> 1 jalapeño pepper, seeded and minced
>
> 2 teaspoons fresh lime juice
>
> 2 tablespoons coarsely chopped fresh cilantro
>
> 1½ teaspoons kosher salt
>
> Freshly ground pepper to taste

1. Combine the garlic, jalapeños, lemon juice, 1 tablespoon olive oil, salt, and pepper in a shallow dish. Add the shrimp and toss to coat. Refrigerate for 1 hour. Meanwhile, light the grill.

2. Heat 1 teaspoon of the oil in a large nonstick skillet over medium heat. Add the onion and sauté until soft, about 5 minutes. Add the red pepper and corn and cook for 2 minutes. Add the lima beans, tomato, and jalapeño, reduce the heat, and cook for 8 minutes. Remove from the heat and stir in the lime juice, cilantro, salt, and pepper. Keep warm.

3. Grill the shrimp until cooked through, about 2 minutes per side. Mound the ragout onto the center of 4 plates and surround with the shrimp. Serve immediately.

Serves 4 as a main course

WHY CORN WON'T GO AWAY

One who grows up with corn is forever affected by corn, unspeakably moved by acres of the plants in their straight, leafy green rows, reassured of a certain order and predictable cycle to life. Such people know the difference between good corn and bad corn early in life and have the confidence that comes from being able to discriminate between the two. Most people like this are Midwesterners, like me, and hence are by nature down-to-earth. But our rootedness is laced with a capacity for wonder. Sitting in cornfields late at night, we've heard corn grow. The rustling sound is easily explained: as it grows, the cornstalk expands like a telescope, its internode sliding out from a leaf sheath. But to a child hiding in a cornfield, the sound is tantamount to seeing a flying saucer. You feel selected to share a secret of life and spend years wondering exactly what the secret is.

The imponderable makes you part of a chain that stretches unbroken for nearly six thousand years. Indigenous to America, corn is the New World's most important agricultural contribution to the Old World and was cultivated as early as 3500 B.C. in Central America. Its planting and harvest gave order to life, and it was the root of the Mayan language, rituals, and calendar.

Corn was so important, so sacred, to the Maya that they fertilized its seeds with the blood of their enemies as well as that sacrificed by their own kings. "For the Maya a single kernel of corn is symbolic of what Christians symbolize by the holy cross—the tragic and monstrous truth that the seed of life is death," writes Betty Fussell in *The Story of Corn*, a superb compendium of the myths, history, culture and agriculture of the crop. Other peoples worshipped the grain as "tears from the sun" or as a gift of gold from the gods. There were, therefore, millennia of corn rituals and devotion before 1862, when Henry Thoreau wrote in "Walking," "I believe in the forest, and in the meadow and in the night in which the corn grows."

But a sturdy practicality is wrapped as tightly as green leaves around the myth of corn. In her book, Fussell quotes a passage from "A Childhood" by Harry

Crews: "So much of farming was beyond a man's control, but at least he could have whatever nature allowed to grow laid off in straight rows. And the feeling was that a man who didn't care enough to keep his rows from being crooked couldn't be much of a man." A grain second only to wheat in acres planted and sustenance given worldwide is worth marshaling.

Of the five basic types of corn—pop and flint corn, dent corn (primarily animal fodder), flour corn, whose name connotes its use, and sweet corn—only the last offers instant gratification. Picked young in life, usually during July and August when its nibs are still firm and milky, ears of sweet corn are trophies. To select the best corn, make sure its silky tassel is neither brittle nor rotting, look for a moist stem and kernels that are plump and tight on the cob and bleed a milky juice when pricked. Like all corn, sweet corn is a curious grain: Rather than converting starch to sugar as it ripens, it converts sugar to starch.

I am pretty sure that my mother put a huge pot of water on to boil before rushing to Warner's Corn Stand in Columbus, picking several dozen ears and rushing home where we all husked them in a frenzy and plunked them into the pot. If she didn't, she meant to. Sweetness is what makes corn precious and to conserve it, human effort must move faster than vegetable biology.

We were of the Mark Twain school of sweet corn. "There ain't nothing in the world so good when it's cooked right," said Huckleberry Finn. Cooking right, for us, was boiling it, buttering it, salting and peppering it, that was all. It is not possible to describe the pleasure of gnawing corn nibs from a cob. Most people who grew up with corn, I've noticed, tend to deforest the ears in the same manner in which the plants are set, in long, straight rows. When we were young, my brothers and I were mesmerized and a little repulsed by the one of us who ate corn in random patches from the cob. The rituals of corn run deep, though they are not always significant: The haphazard corn eater turned out just fine and still eats corn the same way.

I, on the other hand, learned, via clambakes on Cape Cod, the pleasure of corn roasted over coals on the beach, corn that in fact steamed in its own husks. I developed a taste for grilled corn, both charcoal grilled and grilled in a pan on the stove. My brothers find these variations disgusting and claim that my deviance is a result of living so far from Ohio corn. They are of a similar opinion when I use corn as an ingredient, rather than serving it unadorned. They may be right.

Still, I prefer to believe that roasting and steaming bring out the smoky element of corn. The individual nibs that were, for the Maya, a cosmic globe condensing all of human history into a single germ of life contain, when roasted or steamed, the flavors of a full life cycle: the milk of spring, snap of summer, and tough smokiness of fall.

Basic Corn on the Cob

4 ears corn
4 teaspoons softened plain or flavored butter (optional), recipes follow
Kosher salt and freshly ground pepper to taste

1. Pull back the corn husks without detaching them from the cobs. Pull out all of the silk. Spread the corn with butter, if desired. Pull the husks back over the corn.

2. To steam the corn, bring a large pot of water to a boil. Reduce the heat to a simmer and place the corn in a steamer over the water. Cover and steam until the corn is tender, about 12 minutes.

3. To roast the corn, preheat the oven to 375° F. Roast the corn until tender, turning it twice, about 35 minutes.

4. Pull the husks off the corn and season with salt and pepper. Serve immediately.

Serves 4 as a side dish

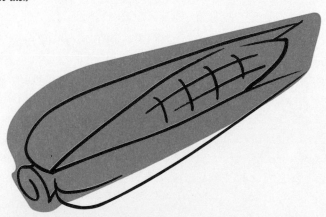

Lime Butter

4 tablespoons (½ stick) unsalted butter, softened
2 teaspoons grated lime zest
½ teaspoon kosher salt
2 teaspoons finely chopped fresh mint (optional)
1 tablespoon fresh lime juice

Cream the butter with the lime zest, salt, and mint, if using, in a small bowl. Gradually stir in the lime juice. Use immediately or store in the refrigerator.

Makes ¼ cup

Ancho Chili–Garlic Butter

1 small ancho chili
4 tablespoons (½ stick) unsalted butter, softened
1 small clove garlic, minced
¼ teaspoon kosher salt, plus more to taste

1. Stem the chili, break it open, and shake out all the seeds. Bring a small saucepan of water to a boil. Reduce the heat, add the chili, and simmer until softened, about 5 minutes. Drain and let cool. Use a small knife to scrape the flesh of the chili from the skin. Chop the flesh until it forms a paste. You should have about 1½ teaspoons.

2. Cream the butter with the chili in a small bowl. Stir in the garlic and salt. Use immediately or store in the refrigerator.

Makes ¼ cup

Lime-Marinated Chicken over Creamed Corn

5 tablespoons fresh lime juice
1 pound boneless and skinless chicken breasts
Kernels from 6 large ears corn
½ cup 1% milk
1¼ teaspoons kosher salt
Freshly ground pepper to taste
4 teaspoons chopped fresh cilantro
1 teaspoon minced jalapeño pepper
½ teaspoon grated lime zest
1 teaspoon olive oil

1. Place 4 tablespoons of the lime juice in a small shallow dish. Add the chicken and turn to coat on both sides. Marinate for 1 hour.

2. Meanwhile, put half the corn in a food processor and pulse just enough to coarsely chop. Scrape into a medium saucepan. Put the remaining corn in the food processor with the milk. Process until pureed. Scrape into the saucepan. Place the pan over medium heat and simmer, stirring often, until the mixture is thick, about 10 minutes. Season with 1 teaspoon salt and pepper. Keep warm.

3. Preheat a grill or broiler. Remove the chicken from the lime juice and grill or broil until just cooked through, about 4 minutes per side. While the chicken is cooking, stir together the remaining lime juice and salt, the cilantro, jalapeño, lime zest, and olive oil.

4. Divide the corn mixture among 4 plates, placing it in the center. Lay a piece of chicken over the corn and spoon the cilantro mixture on top. Serve immediately.

Serves 4 as a main course

Corn and Lobster Pie in a Chili-Polenta Crust

POLENTA

    2⅔ cups water

    ⅔ cup yellow cornmeal

    1 teaspoon chili powder

    ¾ teaspoon kosher salt

    Freshly ground pepper to taste

    Olive oil spray

CUSTARD

    3 cloves roasted garlic, peeled (page 175)

    2 large eggs

    1 cup milk

    1 teaspoon kosher salt

    Freshly ground pepper to taste

    Kernels from 2 large ears corn

LOBSTER MIX

    Kernels from 1 large ear corn

    2 lobsters, steamed, meat removed and cut into ½-inch dice

    1 yellow bell pepper, stemmed and cut into ¼-inch dice

    1 red bell pepper, stemmed and cut into ¼-inch dice

    1 jalapeño pepper, seeded and minced

    1 tablespoon chopped fresh cilantro

    2 scallions, chopped

    1 tablespoon fresh lime juice

    ½ teaspoon kosher salt, plus more to taste

    Freshly ground pepper to taste

1. To make the polenta, bring the water to a boil in a medium saucepan. Stir together the cornmeal, chili powder, salt, and pepper. Whisking constantly, add the cornmeal to the water in a slow, steady stream. Switch to a wooden spoon, reduce the heat slightly, and cook, stirring constantly, until the mixture is very thick,

about 25 minutes. Lightly coat a 9-inch pie plate with the olive oil spray and spoon the polenta into it. Place a large sheet of plastic wrap over the polenta and press the polenta out evenly to cover the bottom and sides of the pie plate. Remove the plastic and set aside.

2. Preheat the oven to 325° F.

3. To make the custard, place the roasted garlic in a mixing bowl and whisk to puree it. Add the eggs and whisk lightly. Add the milk, salt, and pepper and whisk just until well combined. Stir in the corn. Pour the mixture into the polenta shell. Place the pie plate in a large roasting pan and fill the pan with enough hot water to come halfway up the sides of the pie plate. Bake until the custard is set, about 1 hour.

4. To make the lobster mix, toss together the corn, lobster, yellow and red peppers, jalapeño, cilantro, and scallions. Add the lime juice, salt, and pepper. Taste and adjust seasoning if needed. Spoon the mixture evenly over the custard. Cut the pie into wedges and serve immediately.

Serves 6 as a main course

LAST CALL FOR THE LEAN AND THE SWEET

Let us now praise sweet peppers.

Vivid mounds of red, yellow, green, and orange peppers, bell shaped and banana shaped, are a blast of color, the climax of summer, in farmers' markets. At the same time, sweet peppers are a reminder of a vivid season and its passing. Raw, they have a sweet, sometimes herbaceous, always sunny crunch; when cooked, sweet peppers become toothsome and sweetly intense, while carrying a smoky aftertaste that hints of things to come. Who among us doesn't experience a moment of awe when catching a glimpse of the rococo barrage of summer's last bounty?

Of course, the sweet pepper is no longer a denizen only of August and early September. California grows colorful peppers from late winter to mid-summer; Holland supplies brash red and neon yellow peppers from fall to early spring; Florida weighs in with a crop of sweet peppers early in the spring. Other than price, there is nothing objectionable about off-season peppers. They can be roasted, grilled, fried, or sautéed; pickled, marinated, turned into a chutney, a sauce, or a puree. Off-season peppers, like most high-strung hybrids, tend to be thicker in flesh and hence not as yielding as their thin-bodied summer cousins, but only one hungry for raw peppers could take offense.

Nevertheless, the intensity, sheer volume, and unpredictable character of field-grown peppers brings, after awe, an urge to create. Inspiration is unbridled in times of bounty or scarcity. Lacking either, the cook tends toward the predictable.

The peck of peppers Peter Piper picked would be, by the Italians, fried in fruity olive oil, perhaps scented with garlic and certainly seasoned with salt and pepper and eaten *au naturel*. In the south of France, the same harvest might be roasted, peeled, layered with olive oil and capers, and served, for weeks afterwards, as an adjunct to first or main courses. In the southern Mediterranean, a plethora of peppers might be turned into a spiced paste; in the eastern Mediterranean, the same peppers would be diced and pickled. Historically, New Englanders picked up on the pickle, making preserves, a memento of peppers for the months to come.

California can probably be credited with turning to the grill in times of pepper plenty. This technique exaggerates the smoky potential that lies deep within any sweet pepper, placing it squarely between summer and fall.

The terms sweet pepper and bell pepper are used interchangeably when referring to a mild pepper (as opposed to a chili pepper) of a puffed and proud shape. Sweet also denotes the elongated yellow, red, orange, and green peppers that Italians dote on, particularly when fried. Sweet peppers are the mildest members of the otherwise fiery *Capsicum* family, and like most mild-mannered family members are accommodating in the kitchen.

All begin life green, gaining color as they ripen. Peppers will progress from the mildly herbaceous green pepper to the slightly sweeter yellow pepper, and for the varieties whose colors change, continue on to orange, red, purple, and chocolate brown, gradually acquiring more sweetness in their travels along the spectrum. Green peppers are picked earlier and keep longer, in inverse proportion to the other hues of the pepper mosaic. Aside from the color they offer in the end, they all cook the same. The delicate require less heat than the sturdy. That's life.

In *Home Cooking*, the late Laurie Colwin wrote that, as far as peppers are concerned, for her, "redder is better." We shopped for peppers together once and both instinctively reached for the same: red, orange, and yellow ones; delicate, long, and skinny; everything, in other words, that we were not. Sweetness and the atavistic desire to capture the sun guides most pepper-buying hands. If tempered with a soupçon of common sense, the hand instinctively gravitates toward the brightest, firmest peppers, seeks the svelte contours that offer an alluring skin-to-flesh ratio, avoids the wrinkled or the bruised. After all, these are the final days of a season that allows such a choice.

For imperfect humans, there is a secret relief in the encroaching season of covered flesh. The pleasure of a pepper, on the other hand, is its naked perfection, its eagerness to please, its guileless charm. Get it while you can.

Roasted Peppers

Roasted peppers have the best flavor when charred on a charcoal grill, but a gas burner is a close second. While broiling pepper won't give them a smoky flavor, it is the most efficient method for cooking peppers in large quantities. Use roasted peppers as an appetizer with fresh mozzarella and prosciutto; marinate them in balsamic vinegar, olive oil, and garlic and layer them on smoked turkey sandwiches; or puree them to sauce pasta, grilled fish, and meats.

4 bell peppers, any color

1. To grill peppers, start a charcoal fire. Grill the peppers until well charred on all sides, about 12 to 15 minutes. On a gas range, cook peppers over a medium flame until well charred on all sides, turning them with tongs, about 7 to 10 minutes. To broil peppers, preheat broiler. Cut the peppers in half and place, cut side down, on a baking sheet. Broil until well charred, about 12 minutes.

2. Place the peppers in a brown paper bag, seal the top, and set aside for 10 minutes. Rub the skin off the pepper with a paper towel or scrape it off with a paring knife. Cut off the top, remove the core and cut the pepper in half. Scrape out the seeds and ribs. Store in the refrigerator, wrapped in plastic for up to 3 days or covered with olive oil for up to 1 week.

Serves 4 as a side dish

Sweet Pepper Tapenade

  2 red bell peppers, roasted and seeded (page 193)
  1 red bell pepper, seeded
  3 cloves garlic, chopped
  2 teaspoons ground almonds
  ½ teaspoon olive oil
  2 teaspoons fresh lemon juice
  1 teaspoon kosher salt
  Freshly ground pepper to taste
  2 teaspoons chopped Italian parsley

Coarsely chop the peppers and combine with the garlic and almonds in a food processor. Process until smooth. Add the olive oil, lemon juice, salt, and pepper and process until combined. Scrape into a fine-mesh sieve and drain well. Stir in the parsley. Store refrigerated in an airtight container up to 2 days.

Makes about ⅔ cup

Roasted Pepper Bisque with Zucchini-Shrimp Salsa

BISQUE
  ½ teaspoon olive oil
  6 yellow bell peppers, roasted and cut into large pieces (page 193)
  2 red bell peppers, roasted and cut into large pieces (page 193)
  4 medium onions, chopped
  2 cups chicken broth, homemade or low-sodium canned broth
  2 cloves garlic, minced
  6 tablespoons plain nonfat yogurt
  2 tablespoons fresh lemon juice
  1 teaspoon kosher salt
  Freshly ground pepper to taste

SALSA

1 small zucchini, trimmed and cut into ⅛-inch dice

12 large shrimp, cooked, peeled, and finely diced

2 tablespoons minced scallion

¼ cup chopped fresh basil

2 tablespoons fresh lemon juice

1 teaspoon kosher salt

Freshly ground pepper to taste

1. Heat the olive oil in a large pot over medium-low heat. Add the peppers, onions, and ½ cup broth. Simmer, stirring occasionally, for 20 minutes. Stir in the garlic and cook for 5 minutes. Cover and cook for 20 minutes longer. Scrape the mixture into a food processor and process until smooth. Add the remaining broth, yogurt, lemon juice, salt, and pepper and process until combined. Transfer to a saucepan.

2. Preheat the oven to 375° F.

3. Place the zucchini on a baking sheet and roast until tender, about 20 minutes. Transfer to a bowl and let cool. Add the remaining salsa ingredients and toss to combine. Heat the soup over low heat just until hot. Ladle the soup among 4 bowls. Top with a mound of salsa and serve immediately.

Serves 4 as a first course

Sweet Peppers Stuffed with Chilies and Corn

½ teaspoon olive oil
2 cloves garlic, minced
1 small onion, finely chopped
2 large ears corn, kernels cut from the cob
1 can (1 pound) hominy, drained and rinsed
2 large eggs
2 small hot chilies, seeded and minced
1½ teaspoons kosher salt
Freshly ground pepper to taste
4 red, green, or yellow bell peppers, or a combination
4 teaspoons grated monterey jack cheese
1 scallion, chopped

1. Preheat the oven to 375° F.

2. Heat the oil in a medium nonstick skillet over medium heat. Add the garlic and cook, stirring, for 20 seconds. Add the onion and cook until soft, about 5 minutes. Let cool. Combine half the corn and half the hominy in a food processor. Add the eggs and process until smooth. Scrape into a bowl and stir in the onion mixture, the remaining corn and hominy, the chilies, salt, and pepper.

3. Slice the tops off the peppers. Remove the cores and scrape out the seeds and ribs. Trim the bottoms so the peppers will stand straight, being careful not to cut all the way through. Fill the peppers with the corn mixture. Place in a shallow baking dish large enough to hold them without crowding and pour in 1 cup of water. Cover with aluminum foil and bake for 30 minutes. Uncover and continue baking until peppers are tender when pierced with a small knife, about 30 minutes longer. Sprinkle the tops with the cheese and bake just until melted. Divide the peppers among 4 plates, sprinkle with the scallion, and serve.

Serves 4 as a main course or side dish

A FULL MOON IN JUNE

The silver-blue flash of the season's first striped bass strikes the backwaters of Provincetown at the first full moon every June, but every year their appearance comes as a shock. Sport fishermen get crazy hunting eels for bait; commercial fishermen get crazy casting lines; and everyone gets worked up about the best way to cook a striper.

All of this, of course, is a way of avoiding the real anxiety: Once the striped bass have arrived, summer is no longer anticipated, summer *is*. Human longings cannot focus any more on the future of blue skies and endless days. And that reservoir of excuses, the one everyone draws on from year to year, suddenly goes dry.

Summer is the way people mark time. More than any other season, it promises to stay forever and then, abruptly, departs. And striped bass, more than any other fish, is a witness to that.

Take a 45-pound striped bass who's spent the last decade or so swimming up and down the Atlantic coast between winter dips in Florida and summers in Maine. In those ten years, a child has grown up, and maybe a marriage has ended. On some level, to reel in a bass is to take stock of one's life.

Land dwellers tend to mark time by appraising what they have accomplished against natural odds. Bass, on the other hand, carry with them every nuance of the waters they ply. In the South, where they feed on crustaceans, they become sweet; in the North, where they chase herring and menhaden, they acquire a gamier flavor. And while they may taste like diesel fuel when taken from heavily trafficked waters, striped bass generally survive quite nicely in polluted areas, their glistening silver-and-indigo skin giving no hint of the compromised flavor of the flesh beneath it.

To the experienced eater, the first bass of summer are an epicurean barometer, revealing not only the age and travels of a fish but the current state of the waters. Striped bass have the allure of the unknown, the intrigue of a message in a bottle.

A younger fish, weighing between six and eight pounds, has a firm yet delicate flake and is sweet enough to be panfried, eaten as sushi, or filleted and broiled. An older, larger fish tends to become coarse and is best cut into thick steaks and marinated before being broiled, grilled, or stewed.

For reasons more atavistic than gustatory, it is the large striper that makes an angler's heart race. The big ones, who instinctively followed feed and warming tides, somehow got lucky. And perhaps it's this defiance that the angler finds appealing: a large bass so close to the shore, all blind strength, beauty, and instinct.

In his book *Outdoors*, Nelson Bryant describes striped bass "running straight into the moon's path over the tumult of smaller waves beyond the unrolling white scrolls of surf."

For those who court the season's first stripers, there is a drama in the battle between fish and line. For a few moonlit moments, time stops, as a being that bears the stamp of its past communes with one trying to outrun its future.

Bass Broiled with Mustard Mayonnaise

¼ cup mayonnaise
1 tablespoon Dijon mustard
Pinch cayenne
¼ teaspoon kosher salt
4 bass fillets, about 4 ounces each, all bones removed
1 lemon, cut into wedges

Preheat the broiler. Stir the mayonnaise and mustard together until well combined. Season with the cayenne and salt. Coat the flesh side of the bass fillets with the mayonnaise and place on a baking sheet, skin side down. Broil until the fish is just cooked through and the top browns, about 5 minutes. Place 1 fillet on each of 4 plates and serve immediately with lemon wedges.

Serves 4 as a main course

Bass Steaks with Tomato and Black Olives

1 large ripe tomato, cored and quartered

½ cup white wine

1 teaspoon grated lemon zest

½ teaspoon kosher salt, plus more to taste

8 bass steaks, 1 inch thick, about 2 ounces each

¼ cup chopped tomatoes

1 tablespoon chopped pitted imported black olives

1 teaspoon chopped fresh rosemary

Freshly ground pepper to taste

1 teaspoon chopped fresh chives

1. Place the tomato in a food processor and process until finely chopped. Press the mixture through a fine sieve. Discard the pulp. You should have about ½ cup tomato liquid. Combine the tomato liquid, wine, lemon zest, and ½ teaspoon salt in a medium nonreactive saucepan and bring to a boil over medium heat. Reduce the heat so the liquid simmers. Add the bass, cover and poach until just cooked through, about 7 minutes.

2. Remove from the heat and carefully mix in the chopped tomatoes, olives, and rosemary. Place 2 bass steaks in each of 4 shallow bowls and spoon some of the sauce over them. Season with salt and pepper, sprinkle with chives, and serve immediately.

Serves 4 as a main course

Seared Bass with Roasted Shallot and Garlic Puree and Caramelized Leeks   (Adapted from Elka, San Francisco)

FISH

    1 teaspoon coarsely ground black pepper

    1 teaspoon coarsely ground white pepper

    1 teaspoon sugar

    1 teaspoon finely chopped fresh rosemary

    6 bass fillets, about 6 ounces each

PUREE

    3 cloves garlic, unpeeled

    12 whole shallots, unpeeled

    2 teaspoons kosher salt

    1 teaspoon freshly ground black pepper

    2 tablespoons olive oil

    ¼ cup heavy cream

LEEKS

    1 cup water

    ½ cup sugar

    2 teaspoons grated lemon zest

    1 cup thinly sliced leeks, white part only

VINAIGRETTE

    1 cup extra-virgin olive oil

    ½ cup lemon vinegar or white wine vinegar

    4 shallots, finely chopped

    1 teaspoon sugar

    Kosher salt and freshly ground black pepper to taste

    1 tablespoon finely chopped fresh chives

    1 teaspoon unsalted butter

    2 teaspoons olive oil

1. To prepare the fish, combine the black and white peppers, sugar, and rosemary. Use a sharp knife to make crosshatch marks on the skin of each fish fillet. Rub the spice mixture into the skin and marinate for 1 hour.

2. Meanwhile, preheat the oven to 375° F.

3. Place the garlic and shallots in a small baking dish. Sprinkle with salt, pepper, and 2 tablespoons of the olive oil. Cover with aluminum foil and bake until soft, about 30 minutes. Let cool to room temperature. Peel the garlic and shallots and puree in a food processor with the heavy cream. Set aside.

4. While the garlic mixture roasts, prepare the leeks. Combine the water, sugar, and lemon zest in a medium saucepan. Simmer over medium heat until the mixture turns a golden color. Oil a baking sheet. Stir the leeks into the caramel and immediately scrape onto the baking sheet. Cool. Separate the leeks and set aside.

5. To make the vinaigrette, put 1 cup of the olive oil, vinegar, shallots, sugar, salt, and pepper in a blender and blend until well combined. Stir in the chives and set aside.

6. Melt the butter in a large nonstick skillet over medium heat. Add 2 teaspoons of the olive oil. When the pan is hot, add the fish, skin side down, and sauté until browned, about 2 to 3 minutes. Turn the fish and cook until it is firm to the touch, about 1 to 2 minutes.

7. Spoon even portions of the shallot and garlic puree in the center of 6 plates. Place the fish over the puree, sprinkle with the caramelized leeks, and pour some of the vinaigrette in a circle around the fish. Serve immediately.

Serves 6 as a main course

THOSE WHO FOLLOW

Bass glide like bolts from Thor, their power and elegance a lesson in reason and restraint. A school of bluefish, on the other hand, is a blur of senseless aggression. To see a school of blues feeding is to see a blind frenzy of unfettered rapacity.

The appetite of summer is very Jekyll and Hyde. One is aware of craving the delicate, the refined, and the cool, and yet just beneath the surface lurk the season's predatory cravings. Striped bass and bluefish, the two marine species that herald warm weather in the northern Atlantic, mirror the conflicting sides of human nature as well as the discordant desires of summer.

In *The Encyclopedia of Fish Cookery*, A. J. McClane quotes a nineteenth-century report to the United States Fish Commission that likens bluefish to "an animated chopping-machine" whose "trail is marked by fragments of fish and by the stain of blood in the sea."

The primary business of the chopping machine, the report says, "is to cut to pieces and otherwise destroy as many fish as possible in a given space of time."

Due to the constant, castanetlike clacking of their razor-sharp teeth, baby bluefish (weighing under a pound) are called "snappers," while more mature bluefish (anywhere up to 30 pounds) are called "choppers." Like striped bass, they migrate from north to south in the fall; from south to north in the spring. Unlike bass, they spawn in northern salt water, limiting the sweet-tasting snappers to the region between the Chesapeake Bay and New England.

Every summer, there are stories about choppers wreaking revenge on the forearms, fingers, and thighs of their captors. Some of the tales recall the final scene of *Carrie*, but rather than a hand from the grave, it is an apparently subdued blue that arches up from a bucket for one last gnash. Aggressiveness is, therefore, all the more merited in the fisherman, as well as the cook.

Nelson Bryant recounts an evening on Martha's Vineyard, fishing with his brother for striped bass. "I wish I could banish them from the ocean!" his brother complained after disengaging his tenth bluefish from the line. "They ruin your plugs, they fray your leader, they cut your line, they keep good fish away and they taste like manure."

In fact, only bluefish that are cleaned and cooked immediately defy such aspersion. Like mackerel, salmon, bonito, albacore, and other oily fish, a bluefish deteriorates quickly, its potentially sweet, milky flesh acquiring the flavor of rancid cod liver oil. And because of its oily nature, bluefish is a prime candidate for broiling, grilling, baking, or smoking.

The last is easily accomplished on a covered grill over very low coals. The result, when served on toasted bread with minced Bermuda onion, makes a tasty appetizer. Smoked bluefish can also be coated with an orange and black olive salsa to make a sandwich or tossed with onions, chopped vegetables, and mayonnaise to make a satisfying salad.

There is a certain poetic justice in the fact that a bluefish requires aggressively spiced and acidic sauces and marinades. Such a foil packs a mean, long-lasting punch that can stand up to its stout, fatty flesh. Without really knowing or understanding why, one feels calmed by such bold, inflammatory flavors. For the dark side of the summer appetite, there is nothing like fire and spice.

Soy, Ginger, and Mustard–Coated Bluefish with Grilled Scallions

1 bluefish fillet, about 1½ pounds
1 teaspoon Dijon mustard
2 teaspoons soy sauce
2 teaspoons minced fresh ginger
12 scallions, trimmed

1. Start a charcoal grill. Cut diagonal slashes in the skin of the bluefish. Combine the mustard, soy sauce, and ginger, and rub the mixture over the flesh side of the bluefish. Let stand for 10 minutes. Place the fish on the grill, flesh side down. Grill for 7 minutes. Carefully turn the fish over and grill until just cooked through, about 5 minutes more.

2. Meanwhile, place the scallions on the grill and grill, turning once, until ten-

der, about 10 minutes. Cut the fish in half lengthwise, then cut again crosswise, making roughly equal pieces. Place 1 piece of fish and 3 scallions on each of 4 plates and serve immediately.

Serves 4 as a main course

Chili-Lime Bluefish Grilled with Red Peppers and Corn

6 tablespoons fresh lime juice
2 jalapeño peppers, seeded and minced
1 teaspoon olive oil
½ teaspoon kosher salt, plus more to taste
Freshly ground pepper to taste
1 bluefish fillet, about 1½ pounds
4 ears corn
2 red bell peppers, seeded and quartered

1. Combine the lime juice, jalapeños, olive oil, salt, and pepper in a large shallow glass or ceramic dish. Cut diagonal slashes in the skin of the bluefish and place, skin side up, in the marinade. Spoon some of the marinade over the skin. Cover and refrigerate for 2 hours.

2. Start a charcoal grill. Pull back the husk of the corn, remove the silk, and cover the corn with the husks again. Soak in water for 10 minutes. Place the corn on the grill for 10 minutes, turning the ears one quarter turn after 5 minutes.

3. Place the fish, skin side up, on the grill with the corn. Place the peppers on the grill. Grill the fish for 7 minutes. Turn it over carefully and grill until just cooked through, about 5 minutes more. Grill the peppers until charred, about 5 minutes per side. Grill the corn until tender, about 10 minutes longer, turning twice.

4. Cut the fish in half lengthwise, then cut again crosswise, making roughly equal pieces. Season with salt. Place 1 piece of fish, 1 ear of corn, and 2 pieces of red pepper on each of 4 plates and serve immediately.

Serves 4 as a main course

Coconut and Curry–Marinated Bluefish with Lima Bean Dal

1½ teaspoons coriander seed
1 teaspoon cumin seed
1½ cups unsweetened coconut milk
1 teaspoon curry powder
2 teaspoons seeded and minced hot chilies
½ teaspoon dry mustard
1½ teaspoons kosher salt, plus more to taste
1 bluefish fillet, about 1½ pounds
1 package (10 ounces) frozen lima beans
2 cups water

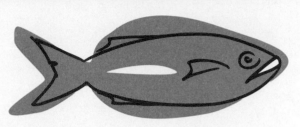

1. Heat a small skillet over medium heat until hot. Add the coriander and cumin seeds and shake the pan until the seeds are toasted, about 30 seconds. Crush the seeds, place in a bowl, and stir in the coconut milk, curry powder, chilies, dry mustard, and 1 teaspoon of salt. Reserve 1 cup of the mixture. Pour the remaining liquid into a large shallow glass or ceramic dish.

2. Cut diagonal slashes in the skin of the bluefish and place, skin side up, in the marinade. Spoon some of the marinade over the skin. Cover and refrigerate for 2 hours.

3. Combine the lima beans and water in a medium saucepan and bring to a boil. Reduce the heat, cover and simmer until the beans are very soft, about 20 minutes. Drain. Place about a quarter of the beans in a blender with ½ cup of the reserved coconut mixture and puree. Scrape the mixture into a saucepan and stir in the remaining reserved coconut mixture, lima beans, and ½ teaspoon salt. Place over low heat, cover, and simmer for 10 minutes, stirring occasionally.

4. Start a charcoal grill. When the coals are red hot, remove the fish from the marinade and wipe dry. Place the fish on the grill, flesh side down. Grill for 7 minutes. Turn the fish over carefully and grill until just cooked through, about 5 minutes more. Cut the fish in half lengthwise, then cut again crosswise, making roughly equal pieces. Season with salt. Warm the beans. Place 1 piece of fish on each of 4 plates and divide the dal among them. Serve immediately.

Serves 4 as a main course

TO CAPTURE AND COOK A DINOSAUR

Before I consumed lobster, which was before the decade that I lived and cooked on Cape Cod, I was wary of it. Like most Midwesterners I believed the creatures of the deep-blue, especially those of a dinosaurean incarnation, merited a wide berth. Modern life is such that by contending with the primordial, one earns a certain status. But it was years before I got past the fits and spasms of a cooking lobster and the ensuing alarm inherent in its red cooked shell to indulge a sense of entitlement in the sweetness of its meat.

In addition to the crustacean's penchant for vacuuming up everything in its path on the ocean floor, its slow, laborious growth, its warrior-like disposition replete with cannibalism, and the confusing tender moments of its romantic life force one to confront a number of dichotomies.

Most who can afford to order lobster in a restaurant, for instance, can ill afford the embarrassment of being befuddled by a lobster's armor. Since I got to know lobster as an ingredient, rather than as dinner with drawn butter and a lemon crown, I bypassed this stage. But one of my brothers came from Ohio to visit me once, and I served him steamed lobster to celebrate his arrival. He is a big, strapping, blustery fellow who is afraid of little and befuddled by less, but the lobster stopped him. "What the heck am I supposed to do with this guy?" he asked. He looked sort of pitiful with a bib around his neck and a useless utensil in either hand. I took the plate back to the kitchen and served the lobster again, out of its shell.

For those who lack a sister in the kitchen, the key is this: Bend the tail back from the head and release it. Do not worry about the possible spatter of juice. Use the small fork provided to gently tug the meat from the tail. Then use a standard table knife to cut the tail meat into bite-size medallions, which should be drenched in warm butter, sprinkled with lemon, seasoned with salt and pepper, and devoured.

The claws are more challenging. Seek to use brute strength or a nutcracker to break them at their vulnerable points. One is found where the claw joins the crusher or ripper, the second in the joint of the claw. Once again, employ the small fork. Tug. Pull. Pray. If you are ambitious, driven by the possibility of pleasure, direct either fork or fingers to every crevice within the shell where sweet morsels might hide. You may even suck the legs. Only the shell and the small sacs found behind the eyes and the feather gills at the base of the legs are inedible; if a lobster is taken from clean, unpolluted waters, even the tomalley and roe are edible, though these delicacies are best avoided if the geographic origin of the lobster is unknown.

The lobster itself is familiar with the backward squirm it takes to break free of an old shell. Every year male lobsters molt by wriggling free of their constricting armor and patiently waiting for the new shell to form; for a female, the process occurs every other year. It takes a lobster five years to weigh a pound, up to twenty years to reach four pounds and become a suitable dinner for three.

For the female, molting is freighted. Only after shedding her shell and standing soft and defenseless on the ocean floor is she open to male and procreative charms. He mounts with unspeakable tenderness and afterward remains, scavenging around near the crevice or cave to which the female has retreated, for the six to eight weeks it takes for her shell to harden. Then she, he, and their possible zoeae, are on their own. Maybe lobsters are more modern than they appear. Lobster mating is the single gentle punctuation in a brutal life. It is important for the fainthearted cook to note that a lobster is more brutal than anything it encounters on the ocean floor.

It is, perhaps, the inherent brutality of a lobster, any lobster, that makes it possible for the cook to cast it in boiling water, or (as I prefer) steaming water, wine, and aromatics. Oh, it thrashes. It protests. It flips pan lids aside. A lobster goes not willingly to its destiny, if its destiny happens to be the table. I used to be rattled by this, later I was inured. Still later, I came to appreciate the sweet remnants of a lobster's ferocious life.

For years, I couldn't understand the big fuss and big price attached to lobsters. They're fine and sweet, and, in the months when they are not molting and weak of shell, they are meaty enough to seem to merit the effort they entail. But I'd cooked them for years before I ate one that made me understand their incalculable thrill. Mine was in black bean sauce at a Chinatown restaurant; yours might be simply steamed, or sautéed with a savory sauce, or tossed with potatoes, pasta, or gnocchi to make a salad.

In any case, the moment one appreciates lobster is the moment one understands that the sweet is not without a particular history, ferocity, or will. The life of a lobster, the trapping of a lobster, the cooking of a lobster, the eating of a lobster are all about making sense of the fact that the bitter can be very, very sweet.

Basic Steamed Lobsters

2 cups white wine
1 cup water
2 cloves garlic, minced
3 tablespoons fresh lemon juice
2 tablespoons sherry
1 teaspoon kosher salt
4 lobsters, each 1½ pounds

1. Combine the wine, water, garlic, lemon juice, sherry, and salt in a pot large enough to hold the lobsters. Bring to a rolling boil over medium-high heat. Quickly place the lobsters in the pot and cover with a lid. Cook until the lobsters turn bright red, about 12 minutes.

2. Remove the lobsters from the pot and set aside until cool enough to handle. To remove the meat, twist off the claws. Crack them with a hammer or nutcracker, break them open, and pull out the claw meat. Gently pull the tail from the body. Turn the tail so that the hard shell side is down and use a knife or scissors to cut through the tail. Pull the shells apart and take out the meat.

Serves 4 as a main course

Lobster and Wild Mushroom Salad

¼ cup plus 2 teaspoons olive oil

1½ teaspoons grated lemon zest

4 cups stemmed shiitake mushrooms, halved or quartered if large

¼ teaspoon kosher salt, plus more to taste

Freshly ground pepper to taste

2 lobsters, 1½ pounds each, steamed, meat removed and cut into ½-inch pieces
    (page 208)

2 tablespoons chopped scallions

2 tablespoons chopped Italian parsley

2 tablespoons fresh lemon juice

1. Heat ¼ cup of the olive oil in a small saucepan. Place in a small glass jar and add the lemon zest. Let stand for 1 to 2 hours. Strain and set aside.

2. Heat 2 teaspoons of the olive oil in a medium nonstick skillet over medium heat. Add the mushrooms and sauté until tender, about 8 minutes. Season with ¼ teaspoon salt and pepper. Toss the mushrooms with the lobster meat, scallions, parsley, and lemon juice in a medium bowl. Add in 1 tablespoon of the lemon oil (reserve the rest for another use) and toss again. Season with salt and serve.

Serves 2 as a main course or 4 as a first course

Lobster Chowder

2 lobsters, 1½ pounds each, steamed (page 208)

8 cups water

1 cup white wine

2 teaspoons olive oil

2 shallots, minced

8 small red potatoes, each cut into 8 wedges

2 cups fresh corn kernels

6 saffron threads

Freshly ground pepper to taste

4 teaspoons chopped Italian parsley

1. Remove the lobster meat from the tails and claws and cut into ½-inch pieces. Cover and refrigerate. Place the lobster shells in a large pot. Add the water and the wine and place over medium heat. Simmer for 1 hour and strain. Set aside.

2. Heat the oil over medium heat in a large saucepan. Add the shallots and cook until soft, about 3 minutes. Pour in the lobster broth and bring to a simmer. Add the potatoes and cook until almost tender, about 10 minutes. Add the corn and the saffron and cook for 5 minutes. Stir in the pepper and the reserved lobster. Divide among 4 soup bowls, sprinkle with parsley, and serve immediately.

Serves 4 as a main course

Lobster with Tomatoes, Basil, and Gnocchi

2 cups white wine
1 cup water
¼ cup sherry
1½ tablespoons fresh lemon juice
1 teaspoon kosher salt, plus more to taste
2 lobsters, 1½ pounds each
1 pound gnocchi (see Note)
2 medium tomatoes, cored and chopped
½ cup fresh basil leaves, torn
Freshly ground pepper to taste

1. Combine the white wine, water, sherry, lemon juice, and salt in a large pot over medium-high heat and bring to a boil. Add the lobsters, cover, and steam for 10 to 12 minutes, until lobsters are bright red. Remove the lobsters from the pot and set aside to cool. Strain and reserve the liquid.

2. Remove the lobster meat from the tails and claws and cut into ½-inch pieces. Set aside. Place the cooking liquid in a large skillet over medium-high heat and bring to a boil. Cook until reduced by half.

3. Meanwhile, bring a large pot of water to a boil, add the gnocchi, and cook for about 4 minutes. Drain. Stir the tomatoes and basil into the sauce and cook until sauce thickens. Stir in the gnocchi and lobster meat and cook for 2 minutes. Season with salt and pepper. Divide among 4 plates and serve immediately.

Serves 4 as a main course

Note: Gnocchi is available at specialty food stores and in the frozen food department at some supermarkets.

TENDER MONSTERS

I was able to resist squid longer than most people of pretentious palate. Many budding connoisseurs hone their taste for the cephalopod on French *calmar*, stuffed delicately with minced crayfish and crab or simmered gently in bouillabaisse. Or they warm to the idea of squid through sampling the Italian *calamari*, pickled with lemon and garlic, or cut into rings and deep-fried, or tossed with tomatoes and pasta. Some get used to the dense white flesh in the Chinese salt-baked or stir-fried squid or Thailand's *yum pla meuk,* flash-fried squid with chilies, basil, mint, and lime. All of these preparations taste predominantly of the culture, secondarily of squid. Therefore, one passes across the threshold of revulsion as easily as if it were a border between a ho-hum place and the promised land.

I had no such golden parachute. I awoke to the possibility of taste in Provincetown, at a time when squid was still thrown back in the drink, kept as bait or, when the catch was really pitiful, taken home for dinner. It was also stewed at Cookie's Tap, a Portuguese saloon in the west end of town, in a manner that required any taste-abiding epicure to wrinkle his nose in contempt: in ketchup. Ketchup! The first time I sat at Cookie's Tap with someone who ordered squid stew I averted my eyes.

"Don't be such a little priss," my companion, Howard Mitcham, scrawled on a paper napkin. I raised my eyebrows in the time-honored manner of status-one-upmanship.

"Taste isn't all pretty pictures in *Gourmet* magazine," he scribbled. I sighed, patiently.

"True delight is the fine line between a dream and a nightmare," he wrote, and then he made horselike guffawing noises and slurped his squid stew.

My relationship with the author of the *Provincetown Seafood Cookbook, Creole Gumbo and All that Jazz,* and *Clams, Mussels, Oysters, Scallops & Snails* continued like this for years. In the summers, I'd find him creeping along the west-end break-water looking for mussels and periwinkles or getting drunk at the Focsle, waiting for a fisherman to bring him a pail of slimy squid, whitebait, or tinkers. Anything that produced a gag-response in polite society prompted Howard Mitcham to roar and wheeze with delight, and he'd grab a knife, throw on an apron, and start cooking.

In the winters, I'd find him stumbling through the French Quarter in New Orleans, making gasping sounds that he imagined mimicked a saxophone or slurping oysters at Acme. He lost his hearing when he was a toddler. I probably should have perceived sooner that the loss of one sense had inflamed several others, including his sense of taste and his sense of observation. But I was too busy establishing myself as morally superior to ketchup. It was years before I understood that, at least in terms of squid, ketchup was a red herring.

Squid, like a lot of things that society disdains, is primordial, a free-floating monster, voracious predator and skillful pretender that sidles right beneath the surface of the sea, the stuff of nightmares. Even Howard Mitcham called it an "octopus-faced monstrosity." And it lurks in every ocean except the Black Sea, in numerous species and dozens of families.

The Pacific flying squid, which belongs to the *Ommastrephidae* family, constitutes about 75 percent of the world catch and dominates Asian kitchens. The *Loligo pealei*, or long-finned squid, also known as bone and winter squid, is the most common Atlantic variety and is cousin to the *Todarodes sagittatus*, the French *calmar*. The *Illex illecebrosus*, or short-finned squid, is also caught in the Atlantic, primarily during the summer months when warm water brings it closer to the shore.

Like cuttlefish and octopus, squid is a highly developed mollusk. It grows between eight and eleven inches, and the cellophane-like quill that runs through its mantle is, in fact, a vestigial shell. Nature doesn't make tough squid—they are fragile animals that rarely live longer than two years—sloppy cooks make tough squid.

The first time I saw a school of squid pulsing beneath the surface of the Cape Cod Bay, I was transfixed. They move by hydraulic propulsion, in a fierce, tidelike rhythm, as free, uncontrollable, and inevitable as a monster in a dream. When frightened, they expel an ink that creates a cloud of phantom squid, foiling pursuers and allowing the real squid to jet into hiding—"like many men I know," writes A. J. McClane in *The Encyclopedia of Fish Cookery*. But even the phantoms are netted and hauled overboard.

The Japanese still catch three quarters of the world's squid, but recently, squid has come into vogue in the United States. Nearly twelve million tons of squid were landed here in 1990 according to the Northeast Fisheries Center in Woods Hole, Massachusetts, an increase of 75 percent over the average catch in the century before.

Health concerns—squid is very lean and contains a high amount of protein—and the influence of Italian and Asian cooks on the mainstream have probably accounted for the sudden popularity of squid, said Denis F. Durante of B-G Lobster and Shrimp Corporation in North Bergen, New Jersey. His company now distributes Grippa Brand squid rings and squid steaks to restaurants and groceries across the country.

But fifteen years ago, squid was still suspect. The first time I ate it was one June in Provincetown, when a boat captain hauled in a passel of thumb-size squid and fried them on his boat's exhaust pipe. I was in the company of fishermen. There was no escape. And I was surprised at the sweet tenderness of the squid, surprised at the elation that comes from nibbling away at some little fear, surprised at the transcendence.

I became messianic about squid. I baked it, stuffed it, turned it into paillards, tossed it with pasta. Flash cooked or simmered forever, squid is toothsome. There is only that troublesome time in between when it is tough. I even worked on a gastronomically correct variation of Cookie's ketchup routine, roasting tomatoes and poblanos to make a squid stew.

"Don't turn into some little Yuppie snot," scrawled Howard Mitcham, when I proudly dished out this invention.

"Don't get all puffed up reinventing the wheel," he wrote. He had to write these things. Because he was slurping and smacking his lips and howling like a saxophone, making a sound that definitely resembled "Hooray," and wildly signaling thumbs up with every spoonful.

Marinated Squid

6 stalks fresh lemon grass, minced, or ½ cup dried lemon grass
1 tablespoon crushed red pepper
½ cup fresh lemon juice
¼ cup fresh lime juice
1 teaspoon grated fresh ginger
1 tablespoon olive oil
1 pound small squid, cleaned and cut into ¼-inch circles, tentacles reserved
½ teaspoon kosher salt
1 teaspoon freshly ground pepper
1 red bell pepper, seeded and cut into thin slivers
1 green bell pepper, seeded and cut into thin slivers
1 cup shredded scallions
1 cup fresh cilantro leaves
1 head iceberg lettuce, shredded

1. Combine the lemon grass, red pepper, lemon juice, lime juice, ginger, and 1 teaspoon of the olive oil in a large bowl. Pour half into a small bowl. Refrigerate. Blanch the squid bodies and tentacles in boiling salt water for 1 minute. Drain. Rinse under cold running water until chilled. Add to the remaining vinaigrette. Cover and refrigerate overnight.

2. Drain the squid. Set aside. Strain the reserved vinaigrette through a fine mesh strainer and then pour into a large glass or ceramic bowl. Whisk in the remaining olive oil. Season with the salt and pepper. Add the squid, peppers, scallions, and cilantro. Toss to combine. Divide the lettuce among 4 plates. Top with the salad and serve immediately.

Serves 4 as a first course

Squid, Tomato, and Roasted Poblano Stew

1 teaspoon vegetable oil

2 cloves garlic, peeled and minced

1 onion, peeled and minced

3 poblano chilies, roasted, peeled, and seeded

2 serrano chilies, roasted, peeled, and seeded

2 pounds ripe tomatoes, cored and quartered

½ cup red wine

1 teaspoon minced fresh marjoram leaves

4 cups cold water

½ teaspoon kosher salt

1 teaspoon freshly ground black pepper

½ teaspoon Tabasco

2 medium baking potatoes, peeled and cut into 1-inch cubes

1½ pounds squid, cleaned and cut into ¼-inch rings, tentacles reserved

2 tablespoons minced Italian parsley

1 tablespoon minced fresh cilantro

1. Combine the oil, garlic, and onions in a large saucepan. Cover and cook over low heat until the onion softens, about 15 minutes, stirring often. Add the peppers, tomatoes, wine, and marjoram. Add the water and bring to a boil. Reduce the heat and simmer for 40 minutes.

2. Pass the sauce through a food mill. Add salt, pepper, and Tabasco. The sauce can be made ahead of time and kept for up to 4 days in the refrigerator.

3. One hour before serving, warm the sauce in a large saucepan. Add the potatoes and the squid and simmer until tender, about 40 minutes. Serve in warm bowls garnished with parsley and cilantro.

Serves 4 as a main course

Paillard of Squid

SQUID

    16 small squid, cleaned
    ½ cup fresh orange juice
    ½ cup fresh lemon juice
    ½ cup fresh lime juice
    1 small red onion, minced
    3 cloves garlic, minced
    1 small Thai chili or jalapeño pepper, seeded and minced
    2 tablespoons grated fresh ginger

SALAD

    2 teaspoons sherry vinegar
    1 tablespoon grated orange zest
    1 tablespoon olive oil
    3 poblano peppers, roasted, peeled, seeded, and diced
    1 red bell pepper, seeded and cut into fine julienne
    1 large yellow bell pepper, seeded and cut into fine julienne
    3 carrots, grated
    1 cup pomegranate seeds
    6 scallions, minced
    1 cup Italian parsley leaves
    ½ cup minced fresh mint leaves
    ½ teaspoon kosher salt, plus more to taste
    1 teaspoon fresh ground pepper, plus more to taste

1. Cut each squid sac open and lay it flat. Score it by cutting deep slices across the meat in 1 direction, but do not cut through the flesh. Peel off the skin. Repeat in the opposite direction to create perfect squares. Set aside. Combine the orange, lemon, and lime juices, onion, garlic, chili, and ginger in a large glass or ceramic bowl. Add the squid and toss to coat well. Cover and marinate in the refrigerator for 4 hours.

2. Combine the vinegar and orange zest in a large glass or ceramic bowl.

Whisk in the olive oil. Add all the peppers, the carrots, pomegranate seeds, scallions, parsley, and mint. Season with salt and pepper.

3. Grill the squid over hot coals until cooked through, about 3 minutes. Add to the salad and toss. Serve immediately.

Serves 4 as a main course

BLUE SKIES AND BERRIES

The blueberries I first knew were indistinguishable from their constant companion, sugar. Blueberries were sugared and baked to a bubbling syrup under lattice-work crust, sugared and sprinkled on pancakes, sugared and folded into muffins, sugared and served with cream when I was growing up. Blueberries and sugar made a nice couple, but like many nice couples, each tempered something essential about the other. Each accommodated something in the other's nature, masked it, and made it more palatable, if not for the world, at least for the marriage. Sugar mediated the spiciness of blueberries, and the berries gave sugar a hint of pepper, the suggestion that sugar's one-note sweetness was more complex than perhaps it was.

Meeting blueberries without sugar was like meeting Laurel without Hardy or Ozzie without Harriet along a hiking trail, which was where I was at the time, on a mountain in Maine. The local radio station had played Simon and Garfunkel as we drove through a heavy mist to the trailhead that morning, and the idea of Simon without Garfunkel was as unthinkable as an African drum solo in the middle of "The Sound of Silence." Things change.

My companion and I were too young to understand the extent to which disrupted assumptions force one to reconsider oneself. Everyone on Mount Desert Island had warned us that there was a mad bull moose on the mountain, a seven-hundred-pound adolescent who'd been causing all sorts of trouble and had evaded every effort to capture him. They told us to sing and make noise as we hiked. We made impromptu arrangements of Girl Scout songs and Simon and Garfunkel as we climbed through evergreens and scrub.

Clomp, clomp. "I love to go a'wandering along the mountain track." Pant, pant. "Hello darkness, my old friend, I've come to talk to you again." Even an insane moose wouldn't bother charging two twenty-year-old girls so bent on stitching together their innate wholesomeness and the deep and meaningful and ever so solitary poetic poses they strove to assume. The moose had enough trouble. And we had the usual vexations: scratches from briars, nascent blisters, the disappointment of switchbacks that seemed to promise the mountain top and then dipped deep into rocky shade for miles.

It was a mean Maine day. The northeast was withholding its wind, and the sun was white. On the occasional crest, the Atlantic stretched like a hard, uncut agate below the mountain; the sky was a gentle blue that kept evading us. The blueberries were tiny, nearly black beads veiled with a white dust. Clustered on gnarled scrub along the trail, they looked like sapphires that needed a good polish. They did not look like lunch.

We'd outwalked the hope one feels at the foot of a mountain and were still miles from the exhilarating gratefulness one feels at the top. We were mad at what the mountain demanded, and so we took every blueberry we could. The blueberries, and possibly the mountain, however, got the last laugh.

If you've climbed hard and sung relentlessly, you get a feeling of entitlement and sovereignty on the top of a mountain. For an instant, you are mistress of all you survey. From the mountain top, you see the folds of geologic order, carpets of deciduous and coniferous trees and, in Maine at least, how the ocean marshals the land and the land marshals the ocean. There is a deep contentment of knowing your place.

For me, that glorious mountaintop moment was shattered by a handful of blueberries. They were spiteful and peppery and tart. They bore no relationship to the blueberries I'd known. They were blueberries alone and for a second they made me question everything, especially because I liked them. I liked how strong they were, how herbaceous and spicy they tasted. They were like soft black peppercorns with an aftertaste of fruit—that bold. Rather than being seduced by a veneer of sweetness, you had to chew deep to find it. Ultimately, this wouldn't change my taste for a good blueberry pie, it would simply make me appreciate blueberries more.

We sat too long, getting to know the blueberries and ourselves. By the time we got off the mountain, dusk and fog shrouded the narrow, familiar road as we drove home. It was surreal. We were contemplative. We didn't see the dinosaurlike apparition that blocked the road until we were less than ten feet away from it. It was the moose. He was bigger than our Saab 96. He charged it twice, denting the hood and one of the doors and nearly rolling the car over before we had the sense to stop screaming and turn off the lights.

Singing was out of the question. All we could do was wait. The moose circled the car for nearly two hours. After a while, we ate the rest of the blueberries. By then, and ever since, I've never missed sugar at all.

Blueberry-Ginger Sorbet

1 cup plus 2 tablespoons sugar
1 cup plus 2 tablespoons water
3 tablespoons grated fresh ginger
3 pints fresh blueberries, cleaned
¼ cup fresh lemon juice

Combine the sugar, water, and ginger in a medium saucepan and bring to a boil. Reduce the heat and simmer for 5 minutes. Let stand until cool. Pour the ginger syrup into a blender. Add the blueberries and lemon juice and blend

until smooth. Strain through a fine-mesh sieve. Refrigerate until cold. Freeze in an ice cream machine according to the manufacturer's directions.

Serves 4

Blueberry Muffins

6 ounces (1½ sticks) unsalted butter, at room temperature
1 tablespoon grated lemon zest
1½ cups plus 1 tablespoon sugar
2 large eggs, at room temperature
1½ teaspoons vanilla extract
3 cups cake flour
1 tablespoon baking powder
2 teaspoons kosher salt
2 cups fresh blueberries, cleaned
¾ cup milk

1. Preheat the oven to 375° F. Line a muffin pan with 4-ounce paper muffin cup liners.

2. Using an electric mixer, combine the butter and lemon zest. Add 1½ cups of the sugar and beat until light. Mix in the egg and then the vanilla.

3. Sift together the flour, baking powder, and salt. Place the blueberries in a bowl and toss with ¼ cup of the flour mixture. Add the remaining flour mixture to the butter mixture alternately with the milk, mixing just to combine. Gently fold in the blueberries.

4. Spoon the batter into the cups, filling them about three quarters full. Sprinkle the tops with the remaining sugar. Bake until muffins are lightly browned and spring back when touched in the center, about 30 minutes. Let cool slightly before serving.

Makes 12 muffins

Cold Blueberry Soup with Orange-Herb Sorbet

SORBET

3½ cups fresh orange juice

2 tablespoons honey

5 tablespoons fresh lemon juice

1½ tablespoons grated orange zest

2 teaspoons grated lemon zest

¼ cup finely chopped fresh basil

¼ cup finely chopped fresh mint

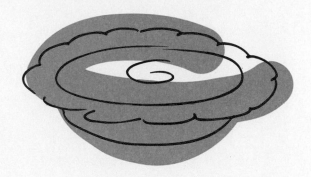

SOUP

¼ cup sugar

¼ cup water

6 cups fresh blueberries, cleaned

3 tablespoons fresh lemon juice

2 cups cold seltzer

2 oranges, peeled and sections cut from membranes

4 mint sprigs

1. To make the sorbet, combine ½ cup of the orange juice and the honey in a small saucepan and heat just to dissolve the honey. Stir into the remaining orange juice. Stir in the remaining sorbet ingredients. Refrigerate until cold. Freeze in an ice cream machine according to the manufacturer's directions.

2. Meanwhile, make the soup. Combine the sugar and water in a small saucepan and bring to a boil. Simmer for 2 minutes and let cool. Set aside 1½ cups of the blueberries. Put the remaining blueberries in a blender and puree until smooth. Strain through a fine-mesh sieve. Stir in the sugar syrup and the lemon juice. Refrigerate until cold.

3. Just before serving, combine the blueberry puree and the seltzer and divide among 4 bowls. Place a scoop of the sorbet in the center of each bowl and surround with the orange sections and reserved blueberries. Garnish with mint and serve immediately.

Serves 4

Blueberry Lattice Pie

CRUST

    2½ cups all-purpose flour

    2 teaspoons sugar

    2 teaspoons kosher salt

    ¼ pound (1 stick) cold unsalted butter, cut into small pieces

    6 tablespoons cold vegetable shortening

    6 to 8 tablespoons ice water

FILLING

    ½ cup plus 2 tablespoons sugar

    ½ teaspoon ground cinnamon

    ¼ cup all-purpose flour

    1 teaspoon grated orange zest

    6 cups fresh blueberries, cleaned

    1 egg beaten with 1 teaspoon water

1. To make the crust, combine the flour, sugar, and salt in a large bowl. Use your fingers to rub in the butter and shortening until the mixture resembles coarse meal. Gradually and lightly mix in just enough ice water for the dough to be gently pressed into a ball. Flatten into a disk, wrap in plastic, and refrigerate for 1 hour.

2. Preheat the oven to 400° F.

3. To make the filling, combine ½ cup of sugar, cinnamon, flour, and orange zest. Add the blueberries and toss to coat. Divide the dough in half and roll out 1 piece on a lightly floured surface and fit into a 9-inch pie plate. Place the filling in the dish. Roll out the remaining dough, cut into ½-inch-wide strips, and weave into a lattice top. Seal, trim, and crimp the edges. Brush the top pastry with the egg wash and sprinkle with the remaining sugar.

4. Bake for 30 minutes. Reduce the temperature to 325° F. and bake until the crust is browned and the filling is set, about 20 minutes longer. Place on a rack to cool. Cut into wedges and serve.

Serves 8

A GEORGIA PEACH

With the exception of the tomato, no fruit has been denatured like the peach. Drafted for long-distance shipping, it's often plucked before its time and sentenced to hard labor, like being processed and canned. Of all the fruit grown in America, only apples are harvested in larger numbers. This results in the need for a certain consistency. Peach growers are forever seeking perfect symmetry, with a predictable crease and a cosmetically correct blush. But consistency, as we know, is the enemy of character. This is true for peaches as well as people.

I have always felt self-righteous about hating a peach. Having encountered my first one from a can (those half-moons that look like giant egg yolks and are often stuffed with cottage cheese), I felt entitled to a degree of antipathy, even if the occasional peach cobbler or fragrant pie tugged against the bias. Granted, some canned peaches can be put to exceptional use, but that's an altogether different thing from an exceptional peach, one that begs to be intimately fondled.

Like anyone with a prejudice, I needed to be taught. I needed to learn how the peach has suffered at the hands of man.

"Tender them," an old-time grower at a farmers' market in North Carolina admonished me several summers ago. I was prodding and squeezing his crop, oblivious to its nuance, not really thinking about how hard it is to be a ripening peach in this vacu-sealed world.

"Sniff, don't pinch," he said. "The blush don't matter," he said. "The rosiness, that's just Maybelline." He sounded like a father offering marriage advice to his son.

"The shape don't count, it's just a feeling you get when you look and take a whiff of the perfume, and make your mind up to take a chance."

He jolted me from canned life to real life, and I've yet to regret the shift. Having now experienced the perfect peach and its honey-like nectar, I understand all too well the need for compensation. For peaches plucked before their time and destined to become ice cream, pies, and cobblers, one should administer a compassionate dose of honey, brown sugar, or bourbon. For delicacies like the puree of peaches that forms the basis of Italy's champagne cocktail, the Bellini, a dash of sugar is in order.

I also came to understand that the sweetness of a peach is a balancing act between bitterness and nectar, between the tickling fuzz, the delicacy of the skin, the lushness of the pulp, and the danger of the pit.

Though the peach was thought for centuries to have originated in Persia, hence its botanical name, *Prunus persica*, botanists are now certain that as early as the fifth century B.C. the peach was cultivated in China, where it is called *tao*, and is a symbol of immortality.

Beneath the sweet, giving flesh, there is, inevitably, the pit, which contains a cyanide compound that gives the peach its almond undertone, and makes for it a bittersweet conundrum.

In the case of clingstone peaches, the pit clutches the fruit in a most unliberated fashion, and it is therefore better suited for industrial canning than home cooking. Freestone peaches, on the other hand, fall gratefully from their stones. If purchased from a farm stand or specialty producer and allowed to ripen at room temperature, they are sublime eaten plain, served with prosciutto, or steeped in vinegar as an accompaniment for rich meats.

Sight and smell are the most infallible guides to buying peaches. In other words, don't buy a hard, unyielding peach that looks green beneath its bionic blush and don't buy a peach that doesn't smell like a peach.

Once you have picked well, you are ready for one of life's peak experiences, according to Brillat-Savarin in *The Physiology of Taste*. The initial bite, he wrote, induces the eater to continue, to chew his juicy mouthful. But the peach does not truly reveal its perfume until fully swallowed. Only then, writes the philosopher, will the taster stop and say to himself, "How delicious."

Peach Butter

9 large ripe peaches, peeled, pitted, and cut into large chunks
½ cup plus 1 tablespoon water
¾ cup (packed) light brown sugar
6 strips orange zest, 2 × ¼ inches each
2 tablespoons fresh orange juice
5 tablespoons fresh lemon juice
¾ teaspoon ground cinnamon
⅜ teaspoon ground nutmeg
¼ teaspoon ground clove

1. Combine the peaches and the water in a large saucepan over low heat. Cook, stirring and mashing the peaches, until soft, about 12 minutes. Remove from the heat and pass through a food mill.

2. Transfer the pureed peaches to a clean pan and place over medium heat. Stir in the brown sugar, orange zest, orange juice, 3 tablespoons of the lemon juice, the cinnamon, nutmeg, and clove. Cook, stirring frequently, until mixture is very thick, about 8 minutes. Remove and discard the orange strips and stir in the remaining lemon juice. Pour into hot sterilized jars and seal or let cool, place in a covered container, and refrigerate for up to 1 week.

Makes 2 cups

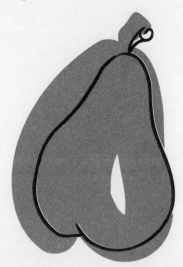

Honey Peach Ice Cream

5 large ripe peaches, peeled, pitted,
    and coarsely chopped
⅓ cup sugar
1 cup milk
1 cup heavy cream
⅓ cup honey

Put the peaches and 2 tablespoons of the sugar in a food processor. Process until smooth. Whisk together the milk, cream, remaining sugar, and honey in a large bowl. Whisk in the peach puree. Refrigerate until cold. Freeze in an ice cream machine according to the manufacturer's directions.

Makes about 4 cups

Peach-Almond Turnovers

4 ripe peaches, peeled, pitted, and cut into ½-inch chunks
2 tablespoons peach liqueur
1 tablespoon fresh lemon juice
¼ teaspoon ground nutmeg
½ cup plus 3 tablespoons sugar
3 tablespoons all-purpose flour
½ cup sliced almonds
2 sheets frozen puff pastry, defrosted
1 egg beaten with 1 teaspoon water

1. Place the peaches in a bowl and toss with the peach liqueur, lemon juice, nutmeg, and ½ cup sugar. Let stand for 10 minutes. Add the flour and the almonds and toss to coat well.

2. Preheat the oven to 350° F. Line a large baking sheet with parchment paper.

3. On a lightly floured surface, roll 1 sheet of the pastry out into a square

slightly larger than 10 × 10 inches. Trim to form a 10-inch square with very straight sides. Cut into four 5-inch squares. Brush the egg mixture lightly around the edges of each piece.

4. Place about ⅓ cup of the filling slightly off center on each square. Fold over the pastry to form a triangle and pinch the edges together to seal securely. Place the turnovers on the baking sheet. Repeat with remaining sheet of pastry and filling. Brush the tops with a little of the egg mixture and sprinkle with the remaining sugar. Bake until golden brown, about 25 minutes. Serve warm.

Makes 8 turnovers

A JOLT OF COOL

Like the bell of an ice-cream truck cutting through the still air of a summer afternoon, sorbet or granita can give you a start, the temperature, simultaneously lip-numbing and a relief to the soul, evoking the double-edged thrill of a childhood Popsicle. And then the freeze fades to flavor, with another jolt. Made well, fruit ices are hyperbole, more intensely fruit than the fruit they're wrought from. They take your breath away.

Considering the shocking nature of the confection, Harold McGee, author of *The Curious Cook*, suggests that sorbet and granita "blend the unadorned flavor of intense life with a startling, lifeless cold." "The combination refreshes," he says. "It brings us back to first things, back to earth." Life at its ripest, death at its coldest, can do that to a person. At the very least, it's enough to rouse you from the hammock of your own inertia.

Many a Little League coach has altered the course of a sandlot game by offering Popsicles all around. Is it possible to calculate the number of life paths changed by detours to the slushy stand? And these iced fruits are the pale, commercial cousins of the original, alchemic confection: ripe fruit pureed with sugared water, then frozen.

So potent and precious is the substance that the Roman Emperor Nero is said to have executed any general who, dispatched to get ice from the Alps for granita, let it melt. The only thing worse than melted ice is ice that won't yield: Anyone who has made granita that has, after a few hours in the freezer, became granite, or sorbet that has turned into a glazed brick overnight, can understand the Emperor's impulse. Commercial producers possess the golden fleece: gums and artificial stabilizers. Home *gelatieres* rely on sugar.

Basically, the higher the sugar content, the finer and more snowlike the frozen confection. Italian granita is probably the oldest rendition. Low in sugar, the fruit (or espresso, or perfumed water mixture) was traditionally frozen on flat trays and stirred occasionally so that it formed glassy crystals and clumps. Granita spoons easier than it scoops. In the bowl, it forms determinedly jagged and random peaks; it is best eaten soon after it is frozen. Later it becomes glacial.

Sorbet generally has more sugar, which makes it denser. It is mixed constantly as it freezes, which creates infinitesimal crystals and a fine, almost smooth texture. Sorbet can be scooped, and will form soft little hills on a cone or in a cup. When the sugar content is very high, it will remain snowlike for days in the freezer.

In his search for a "comprehensive theory of ices," McGee found that "ice-making is one of the very few culinary operations that comes down to arithmetic." Using a computer program, he determined the sugar content of dozens of fruits and created charts showing the percentage of sugar, by weight, needed to render everything from a granita to a moderately sweet and grainy sorbet to a sweet and fine sorbet.

Personally, I can't stomach weight charts of any sort during swimming season. So I putter along with the fruit, the water, the sugar, the lemon, and the advice of friends. Eventually I come up with recipes that are like edible perfume, the sort of dish that life seems to serve up just when you settle into stasis. Often with a cookie on the side.

Grapefruit Sorbet

1½ cups water
¾ cup sugar
1½ cups freshly squeezed pink grapefruit juice, strained
    and chilled
1 tablespoon vermouth

1. Pour the water in a saucepan. Add the sugar and bring to a boil. Reduce the heat and simmer for 5 minutes, stirring until all the sugar has dissolved. Refrigerate until chilled.

2. Combine the sugar mixture, grapefruit juice, and vermouth in a bowl. Freeze in an ice cream machine according to the manufacturer's directions.

Serves 4 to 6

Watermelon Granita   (Adapted from Remi, Manhattan)

3 cups watermelon puree
⅓ cup superfine sugar
¼ cup fresh lemon juice
4 sprigs fresh mint

Combine the watermelon puree, sugar, and lemon juice in a large shallow pan. Put it in the freezer and stir every 20 minutes until no liquid remains, about 1½ to 2 hours. Serve with sprigs of mint.

Serves 4 to 6

Bittersweet Chocolate Sorbet

4 ounces bittersweet chocolate, finely chopped
¼ cup cocoa powder
2 cups water
½ cup sugar

1. Combine all the ingredients in a small saucepan. Bring to a boil. Reduce the heat and barely simmer for 5 minutes, stirring constantly. Strain through a sieve lined with cheesecloth. Refrigerate until chilled.

2. Stir the mixture until smooth. Freeze in an ice cream machine according to the manufacturer's directions.

Serves 4 to 6

Espresso Granita

2 cups espresso
2 tablespoons sugar
1 tablespoon Sambuca or anisette
1 cup heavy cream, whipped

Combine the espresso, sugar, and Sambuca. Refrigerate until cold. Pour the mixture into a large shallow pan and put it in the freezer. Stir the mixture every 20 minutes until there is no liquid in the bottom of the pan, about 1 hour. Spoon the granita into 4 chilled dessert glasses. Top with a dollop of whipped cream and serve.

Serves 4 to 6

ALMOST AUTUMN

SUMMER'S LAST STAND

Like many last stands, summer's is a rococo barrage, a smug and swollen plethora with no apparent end. Farmstands sag under the weight of summer's green beans, lima beans, corn and tomatoes, zucchini and eggplant, as well as mounds of the early autumn cauliflower and squash. The diversity is at first exhilarating and then a little embarrassing. These are the vulgar days of plenty: plenty of food, plenty of heat and, as summer's lethargic sunsets continue to creep into evening, still plenty of time.

Traditionally, the late summer harvest signaled a race against ripeness. It was a time to pickle and sun-dry, to smoke, freeze, and can: acts of thrift in a time of riches. Late summer is like an overfed creature, lolling and lazy, just begging to be pricked by lack; the urge to put food by is not dissimilar from the urge to quilt. The activities are equally archaic, but the impulse to insulate against cooler winds remains.

The glib salads and quick meals of early summer begin to seem silly and insubstantial. The ingredients they are crafted from is not the problem. It is the body, complexity, and weight of those dishes that become unsatisfying. Summer's end seems to ask for deeper, huskier flavors, the kinds born of roasting, toasting, slow simmering, and baking. Romancing summer and reveling in the new gives way to a relationship. It's time to tend.

Tiny new potatoes, thumb-size zucchinis and slender beans needed nothing but to be their youthful selves in June and July. By September, the mature vegetables are harder to contend with. Ultimately, they offer more in terms of flavor and substance. Like life, hopefully. At the same time, like any living creatures, mature produce carries more baggage.

Eggplant grows bitter and needs either to be seeded or sliced in half lengthwise and salted for an hour and then rinsed and dried before cooking. Rather than being chopped for salads or halved and tossed on a grill, late summer's bat-size zucchini need to be sliced and cooked more slowly to balance their nascent bitterness and complement the spiciness they have acquired through the long, hot months. Likewise, the season's heftier green beans lend themselves to slower cooking. These are the days of Southern-style green beans simmered with fatback, soft boiled beans, or beans in a vinaigrette that partially pickles them, permeating their woodier facade, softening their edges.

Late summer tomatoes are bloated. They no longer ask to bask on the windowsill but instead demand immediate attention. Oven-drying is one quick way of preserving them, while allowing their sugar to caramelize into the sort of husky, pungent flavor that late summer requires. The tomatoes can be covered with oil and stored in the refrigerator in a glass container for up to two weeks. They can be used on pasta or pizza, baked with chicken, fish, or pork, or turned into a soup with a touch of curry to accentuate their roasted flavor.

The season's elephantine peppers become sweeter and more intense when roasted or grilled. Once peeled, peppers can be layered with oil and stored for up to a week in the refrigerator. They can be served as an appetizer with cheese, used to garnish grilled food or to give color and a smoky sweetness to a late summer vegetable pie.

Like tomatoes and peppers, September's corn is swollen. Its kernels grow milkier as they stretch against their jackets and their flavor becomes less concentrated. Grilling the ears gives the kernels a pleasantly smoky nuance when sautéed with chicken, mushrooms, and chilies. Grilled corn gives variety to succotash and, when combined with minced cilantro, makes an alluring chutney or salsa to garnish grilled fish or pork.

Grilling and oven-drying are segues to autumn, techniques for coping with the bounty of late summer while lending the flavor and chewier textures that are harbingers of the season to come. When sunflowers turn from gaudy Van Gogh to dry seed in the field, the only hope is renewal, and its necessary long, slow sowing begins to inform the appetite. After a summer's hiatus, the oven beckons and heavy pots on the stove say "slow simmer." Both techniques soften the thick skins of late-harvested vegetables and turn the almost bitter to butter.

It is probably no coincidence that one lowers cooking temperatures and begins to reach for dried grains and beans during summer's last stand. The dried and the fresh reflect the fettered and the free. They form a meal that mirrors the uneasy cusp between summer and fall.

A SUPPLE MATURITY: OVEN-DRYING

As the slant of the sun becomes more oblique, the urge to capture its flavor by using its heat is a primordial one. Indigenous people have long placed sliced vegetables and fruits on drying trays, hung meat and fish on lines to dry, and hoped for the warm breeze and low humidity it takes to coax the moisture out of food and preserve it for the months to come. Before refrigeration, meat and fish were heavily salted to insure that the enzymes which support bacteria would be neutralized; sweet peppers, squash, corn, and fruit were often blanched briefly to soften them for the sun's rays.

Refrigeration and the global pantry have eliminated the need to put food by. Yet the taste for a memory of summer abides. The ubiquity of commercial sun-dried tomatoes is a sign of the universality of an appetite for summer. So is the proliferation of dried vegetable chips, fruits, and the fruit leathers, which are made by pureeing overripe fruit and putting thin layers of the puree out to dry. The soft, chewy texture and sweet, lightly baked flavor of dried vegetables and fruit is satisfying and reassuring, particularly as friendly breezes turn to nasty little gusts.

As drying food was converted from a necessity to a luxury, stove-tops, home ovens, and even electric food dryers were drafted to create new flavors and techniques. When a tomato is being dried in order to be put by for the duration, 98 percent of its inherent moisture must be sacrificed in order to extinguish the possibility of decay. When, on the other hand, a tomato can be refrigerated and is being dried purely for its flavor, little more than 50 percent of its water content needs to be removed, leaving a succulent, still pliable ingredient of complicated flavor—chewy but still soft and giving at its heart.

Drying a summer crop to feed a family for the winter, we can assume, was not an activity that lent itself to creating delicacy and subtlety in the food. The challenge was to beat the rains and preserve as much food as possible. The challenge of drying food for flavor, on the other hand, is not to the elements but to the imagination. Judiciously seasoning tomatoes, for instance, with basil, thyme, or a mixture of rosemary and orange builds another layer of flavor and increases the inventive possibilities of dishes to come.

Seasoned, oven-dried tomatoes can become a sauce or a pesto to use on pasta, meat, or fish dishes. They can be layered on grilled bread with cheese, grilled vegetables, or meat to make a fine sandwich. Their soft bodies can be further plumped up by heat and used to top sautéed chicken or fish, lending a mellow acidity that is an ode to summer, a hint of fall. They make the foundation for a delicious smoky bisque as well.

Tomatoes, of course, aren't the only things that can profit from a partial drying. Green and yellow beans, sliced beets, celery, cauliflower, corn, onions, leeks, eggplant, zucchini, and mushrooms can be dried, as can sweet peppers and potatoes. Any vegetable but lettuce, in fact, can be transformed with a low slow heat. Generally, four pounds of produce will dry to a pound.

If one lives in a warm, arid climate, candidates for drying can be laid flat on screens in the sun and checked periodically. Depending on the heat of the days, vegetables can take as little as three hours or as long as three days to dry to the cook's taste.

In an electric dryer (the best are available through cookware and outdoor supply stores) the same results can be had in an hour, and the cook doesn't have to worry about rain or bugs. In a home oven at a very low heat, most ingredients will become dense and slightly dry while still remaining faintly juicy in a few hours. It is impossible to write a precise formula for drying any ingredient, as ovens vary almost as widely as the sun and individual taste. The cook must simply mind the first few batches and remove them from the heat when satisfied. Drying summer squash, mushrooms, onions, or potatoes for chips clearly takes more time than drying slices of sweet pepper, nibs of corn, or halved tomatoes. In the first case, the object is to parch brittle, in the second, merely to condense.

In general, vegetables and fruit should be sliced thin and placed on screens or directly on the oven rack to dry. In the case of tomatoes, use the plum variety, slice them in half lengthwise, and place them, skin side down, on a standard baking tray for the most succulent result. Do not overcrowd the tray or the oven.

If only life were as kind to its youth as a slow oven can be to summer produce. Gently dried and thoughtfully seasoned, the brash vegetables and fruits of summer can be tempered without withering and can become more complicated and interesting without becoming bitter.

Apples, pears, apricots, peaches, berries, cherries, and even citrus peel (cut clean of the bitter white pith) can all be dried on racks in a slow oven. Hard fruit like apples or pears should be sliced a quarter to a half inch thick; stone fruit need only be pitted and cut in half. Small berries can be left whole; cherries should be pitted and sliced.

Nothing surpasses the seedless grape for accord with the winy air of autumn. Used with seasoned oven-dried tomatoes, in particular, the grapes, which are dried less than raisins so that they retain some liquid, can make a lasagna, a sauce, or a salad that screams "harvest"—in other words, a satisfyingly sweet and mildly sour meal.

Whether sundrying on mesh trays, using an electric dryer, or a home oven, the only real judge of dryness is the cook. One of the better handbooks for home-preserving is *Stocking Up*, a preserving guide by Carol Hupping and the staff of the Rodale Food Center. The following recipes dry produce only partially, leaving it juicier, more fragile, and of a less indefinite life-span than the book suggests, therefore obviating the need for a preliminary blanching. In general, common sense, some basic parameters and a cook's own keen eye and nose insure produce that is dried but still succulent.

As with much of life, the more perfect the vegetable or fruit specimen is to begin with, the better it will meet the challenges of drying and heat. The exception to this rule is fruit used to make fruit leathers: Overripe peaches, apricots, apples, or berries can be pureed and spread in a thin layer on a nonstick tray and dried. All other drying candidates should be unbruised, unblemished, and ripe, but not overly so.

Therefore, selecting ingredients to dry is not unlike selecting ingredients suitable for dinner. One strokes, sniffs, fondles, and appraises each candidate for what it is, knowing that this is the single best indicator for what it will become. What a convenient excuse for dawdling at the market in the days when sweet peppers start to crowd out tomatoes and winter squash and onions edge onto the shelves. It seems fitting that, as the world's shadows lengthen, cooks become preoccupied with selecting the best of the passing season to distill and condense and preserve as a Baedeker for the next.

Basic Oven-Dried Tomatoes

28 medium plum tomatoes, core end cut off and halved lengthwise
2½ teaspoons extra-virgin olive oil
1 teaspoon kosher salt
Freshly ground pepper to taste

Preheat the oven to 200° F. Using a pastry brush, coat the skin side of each tomato half lightly with olive oil. Place, skin side down, on a large baking sheet. Sprinkle with salt and pepper. Bake the tomatoes until they shrink to about a quarter of their original size but are still soft and juicy, 4 to 6 hours. Let the tomatoes cool on the baking sheet. Place in a container and store in the refrigerator.

Makes 2 cups

Rosemary-Orange Oven-Dried Tomatoes

For basil oven-dried tomatoes, substitute 1 tablespoon Basil Oil (page 130) for the rosemary and orange oils.

1 tablespoon rosemary oil (see Note)
½ teaspoon orange oil (see Note)
28 medium plum tomatoes, core end cut
    off and halved lengthwise
1 teaspoon kosher salt
Freshly ground pepper to taste

Note: Rosemary oil and orange oil are available in some specialty food stores and by mail order from Williams Sonoma; (800) 541-2233.

Preheat the oven to 200° F. Combine the rosemary and orange oils in a small bowl. Using a pastry brush, coat both sides of the tomato halves lightly with the oil mixture. Place, skin side down, on a large baking sheet. Sprinkle with salt and pepper. Bake the tomatoes until they shrink to about a quarter of their original size but are still soft and juicy, 4 to 6 hours. Let the tomatoes cool on the baking sheet. Place in a container and store in the refrigerator.

Makes 2 cups

Oven-Dried Mushrooms

   6 cups sliced (about ¼ inch) white mushrooms
   1 tablespoon porcini oil (see Note) or olive oil
   1½ teaspoons kosher salt
   Freshly ground pepper to taste

Preheat the oven to 200° F. Using a pastry brush, lightly coat the mushroom slices with the oil. Place on baking sheets in a single layer. Sprinkle with salt and pepper. Bake until the mushrooms shrink to about half their original size, about 1 hour and 20 minutes. Let cool. Place in a container and store in the refrigerator.

Makes 2 cups

Note: Porcini oil is available in some specialty food stores and by mail order from Williams Sonoma; (800) 541-2233.

Oven-Dried Summer Squash

   2 medium zucchini, cut across into ¼-inch slices
   2 medium yellow summer squash, cut on the diagonal into ¼-inch slices
   2 teaspoons olive oil
   1 teaspoon kosher salt
   Freshly ground pepper to taste

Preheat the oven to 200° F. Using a pastry brush, lightly coat the squash with the olive oil. Place on baking sheets in a single layer. Sprinkle with salt and pepper. Bake, turning once, until the squash slices shrink to about half their original size, about 2 hours 20 minutes. Let cool. Place in a container and store in the refrigerator.

Makes 3 cups

Oven-Dried Grapes

4 cups seedless white or red grapes (or a combination), cut in half
¾ teaspoon kosher salt
Freshly ground pepper to taste

Preheat the oven to 200° F. Spread the grapes out in a single layer on 2 baking sheets. Bake for 1½ hours. Remove from the oven and season with salt and pepper. Return to the oven and bake until the grapes shrink to about a quarter of their original size but remain plump and juicy, about 1 hour longer. Let the grapes cool on the baking sheets. Place in a container and store in the refrigerator.

Makes 1 cup

Oven-Dried Tomato Pesto

This pesto is excellent on pasta, veal, or chicken.

1 cup Basic Oven-Dried Tomatoes (page 242)
4 tablespoons slivered blanched almonds, toasted
2 tablespoons bread crumbs
4 medium cloves garlic, coarsely chopped
½ teaspoon grated lemon zest
2 teaspoons olive oil
½ cup plus 2 tablespoons Strained Tomato Juice (recipe follows)
½ teaspoon kosher salt, plus more to taste
Freshly ground pepper to taste

Combine the tomatoes, almonds, bread crumbs, garlic, lemon zest, olive oil, and tomato juice in a food processor and process until smooth, stopping several times to scrape down the sides of the bowl. Add ½ teaspoon salt and pepper. Process to blend. Taste and add more salt, if needed. Scrape into a jar and store in the refrigerator.

Makes about 1½ cups

Strained Tomato Juice

3 cups canned tomato juice

Strain the tomato juice through a sieve lined with a paper towel, stirring occasionally. This will take about 1½ hours.

Makes about 1½ cups

Fall Vegetable Salad with Oven-Dried Tomatoes, Squash, Mushrooms, and Grapes

VINAIGRETTE

¼ cup Basil Oven-Dried Tomatoes (page 242)
¾ cup Strained Tomato Juice (see above) or water
1 tablespoon balsamic vinegar
1 teaspoon kosher salt
Freshly ground pepper to taste

SALAD

1 teaspoon olive oil
4 cups torn radicchio
4 cups torn chicory
1 cup Basil Oven-Dried Tomatoes (page 242), halved
2 cups Oven-Dried Mushrooms (page 243)
2 cups Oven-Dried Summer Squash (page 243)
1 cup Oven-Dried Grapes (page 244)
Kosher salt and freshly ground pepper to taste

1. To make the vinaigrette, combine the tomatoes, tomato juice, vinegar, salt, and pepper in a blender and blend until smooth, stopping to scrape down the sides of the jar as necessary. Scrape into a small saucepan and set aside.

2. To make the salad, heat the olive oil in a large nonstick skillet over medium heat. Add the radicchio and chicory and toss until wilted slightly, about 2 minutes. Place in a large bowl. Add the dried tomatoes, mushrooms, squash, and grapes and toss to combine.

3. Warm the vinaigrette over low heat. Pour the vinaigrette over the salad and toss to coat. Season with salt and pepper. Divide among plates and serve immediately.

Serves 4 as a first course or 2 as a main course

Penne with Oven-Dried Tomatoes and Basil

    1 pound penne
    2 cups Basic Oven-Dried Tomatoes (page 242), cut lengthwise into thin strips
    2 tablespoons chopped pitted imported black olives
    2 medium cloves garlic, minced
    1 small jalapeño pepper, seeded and minced
    ½ cup fresh basil leaves, cut across into thin strips
    2 teaspoons extra-virgin olive oil
    2 teaspoons kosher salt
    Freshly ground pepper to taste

Bring a large pot of lightly salted water to a boil. Add the penne and cook until al dente. Drain and transfer to a large bowl. Add the tomatoes, olives, garlic, jalapeño, and basil and toss to combine. Add the olive oil, salt, and pepper and mix well. Divide among 4 plates and serve immediately.

Serves 4 as a main course

Linguine with Oven-Dried Tomatoes, Mushrooms, Grapes, and Anchovies

1 pound dried linguine

4 medium cloves garlic, minced

6 anchovy fillets, cut across into thin slices

2 cups Rosemary-Orange Oven-Dried Tomatoes (page 242), quartered

1 cup Oven-Dried Mushrooms (page 243)

¾ cup Oven-Dried Grapes (page 244)

½ teaspoon crushed red pepper

1 tablespoon extra-virgin olive oil

Kosher salt and freshly ground pepper to taste

Bring a large pot of lightly salted water to a boil. Add the linguine and cook until al dente. Drain and transfer to a large bowl. Add the garlic, anchovies, dried tomatoes, mushrooms, and grapes and the red pepper and toss well. Add the olive oil and salt and pepper and toss to combine. Divide among 4 plates and serve immediately.

Serves 4 as a main course

Halibut Topped with Oven-Dried Tomatoes, Shiitakes, and Broccoli Rabe

1 pound broccoli rabe, trimmed and cut into 2-inch pieces

1 teaspoon olive oil

2 cloves garlic, minced

3 cups stemmed and sliced shiitake mushrooms

1 cup Basic Oven-Dried Tomatoes (page 242), thinly sliced

3 teaspoons kosher salt

Freshly ground pepper to taste

3 tablespoons fresh lemon juice

4 halibut steaks, 6 ounces each

1. Bring a large pot of water to a boil. Add the broccoli rabe and blanch for 5 minutes. Drain, refresh under cold running water, and set aside.

2. Heat the olive oil in a large saucepan over medium heat. Add the garlic and cook, stirring constantly, for 30 seconds. Add the mushrooms and cook for 5 minutes. Add the broccoli rabe and cook for 3 minutes. Add the tomatoes and cook for 2 minutes. Stir in 2 teaspoons of the salt, pepper, and 4 teaspoons of the lemon juice. Remove from the heat and keep warm.

3. Preheat the oven to 400° F.

4. Place the halibut steaks on a baking sheet and sprinkle with the remaining salt, pepper, and lemon juice. Bake until the fish is cooked through, about 15 minutes. Place 1 halibut steak on each of 4 plates and spoon the vegetables over the top. Serve immediately.

Serves 4 as a main course

SMOKED FOODS

Smoke is a potent medium. It can be gentle; it can be fierce; it never goes unnoticed. Smoke, after all, is the ghost and indelible mark of fire, the ultimate transformer. A bonfire of brown and broken leaves is thrilling because it banishes the sad spectacle of death. Likewise, a hint of smoke in food says that time and decay have been thwarted, at least for the moment. Small wonder that autumn appetite waxes for smoky flavors.

On the surface, these flavors resonate with the smell of fall air. But the long tradition of preserving summer's bounty by smoking touches a deeper chord as well: To smoke food is to seize the present and change it subtly, thereby insuring its future.

Suspending food over hot smoke tempers its raw, youthful flavor; smoke enriches and mellows. Both the process and product of smoking give the archaic satisfaction of having battened down the hatches and hence a sense of well-being as nights begin to cool.

The interstice between the end of summer and the undeniable arrival of fall calls for the bold, quick hint of hot-smoked food, not the interminable dirge of a long, cool smoke.

Food that has been cured and set in a slow smoke—like commercially smoked trout, mussels and oysters, salmon, and ham hocks—is dried and preserved. It tastes more of smoke than it does of itself and can be used as an ingredient to lend an autumnal mood to the last of summer's shell beans, peppers, or corn.

But food that is uncured and flash smoked—placed over a hot, contained fire for a short period of time on a stove top or in an electric smoker—can be dinner. It is imbued with smoky flavor but is not completely preserved. Chicken or lobster or other shellfish is enriched, vegetables are deepened and mellowed, but all remain supple and juicy under the bold flavor of smoke. Summer survives, albeit as a fading bass note to the treble taste of autumnal smoke.

It is unclear whether the trace of carcinogenic chemicals in the smoke are offset by how little added fat smoked food requires to become an unctuous meal. So smoked food, from a health perspective, may be a mixed blessing. Both cool and hot smoking are chemical treatments. Unlike the water, broth, or wine used for braising or the simple heat used to cook food in an oven or on a stove, smoke has over two hundred chemical components including alcohols, acids and phenolic compounds that inhibit the growth of microbes and the oxidation of fatty acids.

The sweeter smelling the wood, the more alluring the traces the smoke leaves behind. Hickory, other nut or fruit woods, maple, oak, and alder chips, dried grapevine trimmings and herb branches give sweet smoke to foods placed above them in a closed container for less than an hour.

A stove-top smoker consists of a long deep pan, not unlike a cake pan, in which dry wood chips can be placed, a drip tray, and a rack for food that's to be smoked, as well as a lid. Once the smoker has been arranged, it is placed, uncovered, over medium heat until the wood chips begin to smolder. Then the lid is put on. Electric models work on the same premise.

Smoking, like aging or the season of autumn, occurs slowly and is probably best done unobserved. Despite the campfire aroma that drifts through the kitchen, smoked food itself is a surprise. Something has irreversibly altered, yet the food remains very much itself. Protected by the guardian angel of smoke, the character of food cast in the fumes of burning wood survives and abides and at least temporarily defies decay.

Smoked Autumn Vegetables

Toss these vegetables with pasta, stuff them into a chicken before roasting, or stir them into a creamy squash soup. The mushrooms also make a great pizza topping.

2 tablespoons wood chips
½ medium butternut squash, peeled, seeded, and
    cut lengthwise into ½-inch slices
2 medium sweet potatoes, peeled and cut into
    ½-inch-thick rounds
Kosher salt and freshly ground pepper to taste
6 shallots, peeled
2 portobello mushrooms, stemmed
4 cremini mushrooms, stemmed

1. Put half the wood chips in the bottom of a stove-top smoker and spread the squash and sweet potatoes on the rack over the chips. Season lightly with salt and pepper. Place over medium heat until the wood begins to smolder. Cover and cook until tender, about 30 minutes.

2. Remove the vegetables from the rack and keep warm. Add the remaining wood chips to the smoker. Spread the shallots and mushrooms on the rack, season, cover, and cook until tender, about 40 minutes. Thinly slice all of the vegetables and serve.

Serves 4 as a side dish

Smoked Vegetable Salad

3 tablespoons sherry vinegar
2 teaspoons Dijon mustard
1 tablespoon olive oil
½ teaspoon kosher salt
Freshly ground pepper to taste
½ teaspoon chopped fresh rosemary
6 cups arugula, stemmed
1 recipe Smoked Autumn Vegetables (page 251)

Whisk the vinegar and mustard together in a small bowl. Slowly whisk in the olive oil. Add the salt, pepper, and rosemary. Toss all but 1 tablespoon of the dressing with the arugula. Divide among plates. Arrange the smoked vegetables over the arugula and drizzle with the remaining dressing. Serve immediately.

Serves 2 as a main course or 4 as a first course

Smoked Chicken Breasts

Smoked chicken makes delicious salads, sandwiches, and fillings for burritos or enchiladas. It also makes an interesting garnish for corn chowder or nachos.

1 tablespoon wood chips
2 skinned chicken breasts, split

Put the wood chips in the bottom of a stove-top smoker and place the chicken on the rack over the chips. Set over medium heat until the wood begins to smolder. Cover and cook until the chicken is cooked through, about 45 minutes.

Serves 4 as a main course

Smoked Tomato and Chicken Pasta

2 skinned chicken breasts, split

1½ tablespoons wood chips

12 plum tomatoes, cored and halved lengthwise

1 teaspoon kosher salt, plus more to taste

Freshly ground pepper to taste

1 pound farfalle (also called bowtie pasta)

¼ cup basil leaves, cut across into thin strips

1. Smoke the chicken breasts as described on page 252, using 1½ tablespoons of wood chips. Sprinkle the tomatoes with ¼ teaspoon of the salt and pepper. Remove the chicken from the rack and add the tomatoes, cut side up. Cover and smoke until the tomatoes are soft, about 25 minutes.

2. Meanwhile, take the chicken off the bone and shred. Cut the tomato pieces in half crosswise.

3. Bring a large pot of salted water to a boil. Add the farfalle and cook until al dente. Drain the pasta and transfer to a large bowl. Add the chicken, tomatoes, remaining salt, pepper, and basil and toss. Divide among 4 plates and serve.

Serves 4 as a main course

Smoked Lobsters

Use to make rich brioche sandwiches; a hearty chowder of lobster, bacon, and potatoes; a pizza topping with sundried tomatoes, an elegant garnish for gazpacho, or in the recipe that follows.

4 lobsters, 1½ pounds each
1 tablespoon wood chips

Steam the lobsters for 10 minutes as described on page 208. When cool enough to handle, remove the tail and claw meat. Place the wood chips in the bottom of a stove-top smoker and place the lobster meat on the rack over the chips. Place over medium heat until the wood begins to smolder. Cover and smoke for 10 minutes.

Serves 4 as a main course

Smoked Lobster with Corn and Peppers over Soft Polenta

1 teaspoon olive oil
1 cup corn kernels
4 Smoked Lobsters, cut into large chunks (see above)
2¾ teaspoons kosher salt
Freshly ground pepper to taste
1 red bell pepper, seeded and cut into thin strips
1 yellow bell pepper, seeded and cut into thin strips
1 green bell pepper, seeded and cut into thin strips
4 cups water
1 cup yellow cornmeal
1 tablespoon chopped Italian parsley

1. Heat the olive oil in a large cast-iron skillet over medium heat. Add the corn and cook until browned, about 5 minutes. Transfer to a bowl, add the lobster,

¼ teaspoon of the salt, and pepper, and toss. Keep warm. Put the peppers in the skillet and sauté over medium heat until crisp-tender, about 3 minutes. Keep warm.

2. Bring the water to a boil in a medium saucepan. Whisking constantly, add the cornmeal in a slow, steady stream. Switch to a wooden spoon, reduce the heat, and stir until thick, about 10 minutes. Stir in the remaining salt.

3. Spoon the polenta onto the center of 4 plates. Surround the polenta with the peppers. Top with the lobster mixture and sprinkle with parsley. Serve immediately.

Serves 4 as a main course

Smoked Trout in Caramelized Apple and Onion Broth

2 teaspoons unsalted butter
2 large onions, peeled, halved lengthwise, and thinly sliced
4 Granny Smith apples, cored and thinly sliced
¼ cup dry sherry
6 cups water
½ cup finely diced stemmed shiitake mushrooms
½ cup finely diced peeled butternut squash
½ cup finely diced peeled carrot
½ cup finely diced celery
1 teaspoon kosher salt, plus more to taste
Freshly ground pepper to taste
1 smoked trout, skinned and filleted, each fillet halved lengthwise and crosswise
1½ teaspoons chopped fresh sage

1. Heat 1 teaspoon of the butter in a large heavy skillet over medium-high heat. Add the onions and sauté until caramelized, about 10 minutes. Transfer the onions to a large pot. Add the remaining butter and the apples to the skillet. Sauté until caramelized, about 10 minutes. Add the apples to the pot. Pour the sherry into the skillet and cook, scraping the pan with a wooden spoon, about 1 minute. Add this liquid and the water to the pot.

2. Bring to a boil, reduce the heat, and simmer for 1 hour and 15 minutes. Strain through a fine-mesh sieve. Place in a medium saucepan and add the mushrooms, squash, carrot, and celery. Simmer until tender, about 20 minutes. Season with salt and pepper. Ladle into 4 shallow bowls. Place 2 pieces of the trout in each bowl, overlapping them slightly at one end. Sprinkle with sage and serve.

Serves 4 as a first course

Pasta with Smoked Mussels and Tomatoes

1 pound dried linguine
¼ cup plus 2 teaspoons olive oil
3 cloves garlic, minced
8 plum tomatoes, cut into ½-inch dice
2 small cans smoked mussels, drained
5 tablespoons chopped Italian parsley
½ cup fresh basil leaves, cut across into thin strips
3 teaspoons kosher salt
Freshly ground pepper to taste

1. Bring a large pot of salted water to a boil. Add the linguine and cook until al dente.

2. Meanwhile, heat ¼ cup of the olive oil in a medium skillet over medium heat. Add the garlic and sauté for 1 minute. Do not brown. Add the tomatoes and cook just until heated through, about 4 minutes. Remove from the heat and stir in the mussels, parsley, basil, salt, and pepper.

3. Drain the linguine and transfer it to a large bowl. Add the mussel mixture and the remaining 2 teaspoons of olive oil and toss. Divide among 4 plates and serve immediately.

Serves 4 as a main course

Spaghetti Squash Topped with Smoked Oyster and Watercress Ragout

1 medium spaghetti squash, about 1½ pounds

2 medium carrots, julienned

1 small can smoked oysters, drained with 1 teaspoon of the oil reserved

2 teaspoons olive oil

2 cloves garlic, minced

2 shallots, minced

12 medium shiitake mushrooms, stemmed and thinly sliced

½ cup chicken broth, homemade or low-sodium canned broth

6 cups stemmed watercress

2 teaspoons kosher salt

Freshly ground pepper to taste

1. Preheat the oven to 400° F.

2. Cut the squash in half, scoop out the fibers and place, cut side down, on a baking sheet. Roast until tender, about 45 minutes.

3. Meanwhile, bring a saucepan of water to a boil. Blanch the carrots for 3 minutes, drain, and set aside.

4. When the squash is nearly done, heat the reserved oyster oil and the olive oil in a medium nonstick skillet over medium heat. Add the garlic and shallots and sauté until golden, about 2 minutes. Add the mushrooms and sauté until they begin to soften, about 3 minutes. Stir in the carrots and broth and cook for 2 minutes, scraping up the bottom of the pan with a wooden spoon. Add the oysters and the watercress and stir until just wilted, about 1 minute. Season with 1 teaspoon of the salt and pepper. Keep warm.

5. Use a fork to scrape out the squash flesh in spaghettilike strands. Place in a bowl and gently toss with the remaining salt and pepper. Divide the squash among 4 plates, mounding it in the center. Spoon the ragout over the squash and serve immediately.

Serves 4 as a main course

AUTUMN

A BITTERSWEET SEASON

Fall doesn't descend. It seeps slowly over the landscape and into the human spirit as thick summer air with its sweet perfume is swept away by cooler breezes tinged with the aroma of decay and smoke. Gradually you begin to bend inward, and one day you are surprised to find yourself immersed in yourself. Elizabeth Tudor wrote, "Old age came upon me suddenly, like a frost." But it is the realization of age, like the realization of fall, that is sudden. Each marches slowly but determinedly. It is easy to be unaware of the campaign until time at last comes to claim you. The finality is as sudden as the reality was slow to dawn.

Nevertheless, there you are, wanting a sweater.

The last gasp of summer, its peppers, tomatoes, and corn, contrasts sharply with the burgeoning bittersweetness of its evenings. Hunger becomes a hoot owl, more and more insistent, less easily understood. There is binary urge to be both diverted and comforted, a hankering for the familiar and, at the same time, as the fresh herbs of summer wither and dry, an increasing appetite for exotic spices.

Smoky flavors match the early fall mood. And as the season leans more toward winter and squash changes from summer's watery sponge to dense gourds, life slows down and so does cooking, gradually. First you think of chowders, then soups, then bisques. In the end, everything is stew.

The slow, contemplative pace of simmering on the stove or braising in the oven suits the autumnal mood and the ingredients of fall. Lacking the surging juices of summer's ingredients, fall produce generally benefits from slow, moist cooking. So does the human soul.

One has to think and imagine when layering ingredients and flavors to simmer in a pot. Likewise, as one dons more layers, one dives, however briefly, layer by layer, into the self. Fall is a season of second thoughts and subsequent shedding. Stew is a truth teller. Its ultimate character reflects a series of decisions made by the cook, as well as patience. It takes taste and creativity to plan a stew. It takes discipline to allow a stew to take its course.

Making a meat stock and reducing it to a glaze extends this paradigm to its ultimate extreme. The act of using water and heat to pull a second life from dead bones requires a certain faith as well as extreme restraint. In general, the rich, vibrant flavors that fall hankers for come, like the season itself, slowly. Likewise, it takes time to coax the natural sugars from fall fruit, time to wed spices with the season's produce, fish, and meat, time for all of these aromas to permeate the kitchen and seep into the soul.

Time is what there is most of in the fall. Like spring, autumn is a wrinkle, some days taut and other days loose, between summer and winter. It is a season of waiting and subtle foreboding, hence a season in slow motion rift with yearning. The cook becomes an alchemist. She turns the hard into the yielding, the dry into something unctuously moist, brings the dead back to life, finds the buried caramel or honey in the bitterness. All in her own sweet time.

SOOTHING AN AMBIVALENT APPETITE

Stew occupies a precarious place in the collective culinary unconscious. When the slow simmer of a potful of food yields a mellow whole far greater than its parts, the dish has triumphed over the mundane, becoming an edible synthesis of a culture, whether Hungarian goulash or Creole gumbo. When, on the other hand, a stew fails to reconcile its disparate ingredients, it can be a poignant reminder of the limits of human effort, sad to think about, horrible to taste.

Desire flirts with the possibility of disaster when you hanker for a stew. But few primitive appetites have ever been risk-free, so to stew is to hope, hope that the ingredients you choose will meld felicitously as they mellow together in a pot. Instinct is needed to season properly and to temper the developing stew with basic touches—more broth or water, a counterpoint of vinegar or lemon, a blast of fresh herbs.

Anyone who stews depends on the patience it takes to soften onions and carrots tenderly, so that the aromatics caramelize and lend a sweetness to the pot. Toasting spices and browning meat require a certain plodding vigilance as well.

In the end, the mandatory slow simmer is the most exhausting aspect of a stew. Yet the best thing a cook can offer is the extraordinary restraint it takes to let something become the best it can be, unhampered. The cook can stir and adjust seasoning but is basically little more than a witness to the adagio of a low flame warming the underside of a big pot, while it works a slow alchemy. Rushing ruins the whole thing. High heat, like bitter cold, tends to force food to stiffen rather than soften, making a polarized muddle rather than a nuanced mélange. Since rushing head down in the wind is a cold season's preferred state, there is something cosmically dissonant about rendering the slow surrender that is stew. But therein lies the lure of a one-pot dish on a cold night.

Old-fashioned Beef Stew

¼ cup all-purpose flour

¼ teaspoon freshly ground pepper, plus more to taste

1 pound beef stewing meat, trimmed and cut into 1-inch pieces

5 teaspoons vegetable oil

2 tablespoons red wine vinegar

1 cup red wine

3½ cups beef broth, homemade, or low-sodium canned broth

2 bay leaves

1 medium onion, peeled and chopped

5 medium carrots, peeled and cut into ¼-inch rounds

2 large baking potatoes, peeled and cut into ¾-inch cubes

2 teaspoons kosher salt

1. Combine the flour and pepper in a medium bowl, add the beef and toss to coat well. Heat 3 teaspoons of the oil in a large pot over medium-high heat. Working in batches, add the beef, a few pieces at a time, to the pot. Cook, turning the beef when browned on the bottom, until pieces are browned on all sides, about 5 minutes. Add more oil as needed between batches.

2. Remove the last batch of beef from the pot and add the vinegar and wine. Cook over medium-high heat, scraping the pan with a wooden spoon to loosen any browned bits. Put the beef back in the pot. Add the broth and bay leaves. Bring to a slow simmer.

3. Cover and cook, skimming the broth from time to time, until the beef is tender, about 1½ hours. Add the onion and carrots and simmer, covered, for 10 minutes. Add the potatoes and simmer until the vegetables are tender, about 30 minutes more. Season with the salt and pepper. Remove and discard the bay leaves. Ladle into 4 bowls and serve.

Serves 4 as a main course

Goulash

2 teaspoons unsalted butter

2 medium onions, thinly sliced

2 tablespoons sweet Hungarian paprika

1 teaspoon caraway seeds

1 pound beef stewing meat, trimmed and cut into 1-inch cubes

¼ cup all-purpose flour

2 cups beef broth, homemade, or low-sodium canned broth

1 tablespoon fresh lemon juice

2 teaspoons kosher salt, plus more to taste

¼ teaspoon freshly ground pepper

1. Melt the butter in a large pot over medium heat. Add the onions and cook, stirring frequently, until wilted, about 10 minutes. Stir in the paprika and caraway seeds and cook 1 minute more. Toss the beef with the flour to coat well. Add the beef to the onion mixture. Cook, stirring, for 2 minutes.

2. Add ½ cup of the broth, stirring and scraping the bottom of the pot. Gradually stir in the remaining broth. Bring to a slow simmer. Cover and cook, skimming the broth from time to time, until the beef is tender, about 1½ hours. Stir in the lemon juice, salt, and pepper and serve.

Serves 4 as a main course

Curried Root Vegetable Stew with Mace-Currant Dumplings

STEW

    1½ teaspoons unsalted butter

    1 small onion, peeled and chopped

    3 cloves garlic, peeled and minced

    1½ teaspoons curry powder

    4 cups Roasted Vegetable Broth (page 372) or chicken broth

    2 medium carrots, peeled, halved lengthwise, and cut across into ½-inch pieces

    2 large parsnips, peeled, thick end halved lengthwise, and cut across into ⅛-inch rounds

    1 small celery root, trimmed, peeled, and cut into ¼-inch dice

    1 medium sweet potato, peeled and cut into ½-inch dice

    3 tablespoons all-purpose flour

    2 teaspoons kosher salt

    Freshly ground pepper to taste

    1 tablespoon chopped Italian parsley

DUMPLINGS

    1 cup all-purpose flour

    1½ teaspoons baking powder

    ¾ teaspoon kosher salt

    ½ teaspoon ground mace

    2 tablespoons cold unsalted butter, cut into pieces

    ¼ cup currants

    6 tablespoons milk

1. Melt the butter in a large pot over medium heat. Add the onion and cook for 3 minutes. Stir in the garlic and curry powder and cook for 30 seconds. Stir in the broth, carrots, and parsnips and bring to a boil. Reduce to a simmer, cover and cook for 15 minutes. Stir in the celery root and sweet potato and cook for 10 minutes longer.

2. Meanwhile, combine the 1 cup of flour, baking powder, salt, and mace in a mixing bowl. Rub in the butter until the mixture resembles coarse meal. Mix in

the currants. Stir in the milk, just to combine. On a lightly floured surface, with floured hands, shape the dough into 1-inch balls.

3. Stir ¼ cup of the cooking liquid into the 3 tablespoons of flour to form a smooth paste. Stir the mixture into the stew and season with the salt and pepper. Bring the stew to a simmer if necessary. Place the dumplings on top of the stew, cover, and cook for 15 minutes. Divide the stew and dumplings among 4 bowls. Garnish with parsley and serve.

Serves 4 as a main course

COOKING DOWN TO THE BONES

Meat stock is the nexus of modern cooking. In the fourteenth century, when the French began shrugging off the medieval palette with its flavors of mustard, cinnamon, vinegar, and sugar in favor of sauces built from the rich essence of meat, Guillaume Tirel (aka Taillevent) began writing down the formula for broths as well as sauces that could moisten a variety of dishes. Carême and later Escoffier built on Taillevent's efforts to codify the saucier's repertoire—which, in fact, has changed very little in almost seven hundred years.

Some eras are partial to the rich, brown *sauce espagnole,* while others favor *velouté,* the white stock enriched with cream or butter. Whatever the reigning fashion, the foundation remains the same. Rich, clear, intensely flavored stock is the springboard for seemingly rich cooking.

Current taste aspires to the lean but is loath to abandon the rich. Stock is amenable to these opposing desires. Simmered and then reduced to syrupy glaze, beef stock can give a suppleness to vegetable, pasta, or tofu dishes that is tantamount to olive oil; it can lend a glossy beefiness to fish or shellfish and the illusion of heft to lean cuts of beef.

These modern-sounding applications are, in fact, simply history repeating itself. Taillevent's *Le Viandier,* finished around 1380, when meat was precious and reserved for the wealthy, mentions using beef glaze to enrich vegetables and seafood.

Likewise, the basic method for making a beef glaze remains unchanged. It requires patience and vigilance, a willingness to mind the pot as the flavors from the bones, meat particles, and vegetables are slowly drawn forth, like shy guests at a dinner party. Calibrated heat is to beef bones what charm is to bashfulness: Each is capable of bringing out an essential nature.

Making a glaze is more than work. It is a project. Which is why I make vats of it several times a year, storing the glaze in small, one-cup containers either in the refrigerator, where it keeps almost indefinitely, spawning a harmless fur easily removed with a sharp knife, or the freezer, where the glaze will keep for six months before losing its flavor.

There is a certain sympathy between autumn and stock-making. Perhaps it is the pervasive aroma that fogs the kitchen windows as the broth simmers and thickens, imbuing a home with a sense of well-being. Or it may simply be the act itself—transforming solid bones with their inaccessible flavor into an endlessly adaptable essence, giving hope to the season's brittle landscape.

In any case, the fundamentals are important. A heavy-gauge pot that can hold 20 to 40 quarts of liquid is worth the investment. So is a skimmer—a perforated disk with a long handle—for removing particles. Ask your butcher to crack the bones, fresh ones with lots of meat. If you do it yourself, crack them lengthwise with carefully executed karate chops.

To give the glaze a toasted, caramelized flavor, roast the bones and vegetables before simmering. After roasting, transfer the bones and vegetables to a large stockpot, add cold water, and place over low heat. Warmth causes the meat to release albumin, the soluble protein that, when forced from the meat too quickly, clouds the stock, creating a dull, greasy flavor.

The trick to making a clear, full-flavored glaze is slow simmering, which patiently pries the protein, gelatin, and fat from the bone, allowing large clumps to coagulate on the sides of the pot or rise to the surface in a gray scum. This can easily be lifted from the broth with a skimmer; the detritus that falls to the bottom or clings to the side will remain there as long as the cook resists the temptation to stir.

After the liquid has been reduced by about a third, run it through a fine-mesh strainer. Allow it to cool at room temperature for one hour. Refrigerate for twelve hours, lift the fat from the top and then simmer again to reduce the broth to a thick glaze.

In the late, great era of nouvelle cuisine, meat glazes were used to create soups and sauces that were intensely flavored but gluey and sticky. To avoid this, a beef glaze should be diluted with five parts water to one part glaze to create a soup broth. The glaze itself should be extended with other liquids—soy sauce, wine, the juice from tomatoes—for a balanced sauce.

A chicken glaze, on the other hand, requires slightly less time to make than a beef glaze, but it offers a similar challenge. The cook must remain vigilant and unobtrusive throughout the simmering, only to become resourceful and imaginative when using the resulting elixir.

Unlike a broth, a glaze has a suppleness that enables it to replace cream in some sauces and to moisten pasta, rice, or roasted winter vegetables without cooking oil. For all its body and rich caramel undertones, a beef glaze will always taste stridently and irrevocably meaty (which makes it the perfect dramatic counterpoint to seafood); a chicken glaze is more mutable, more influenced by the aromatic vegetables and herbs around it.

Traditional stock recipes call for veal knuckles to boost the gelatin content of the eventual glaze. I've found that turkey wings along with chicken wings and legs render just as stout a substance, without distracting from the poultry flavor. The ensuing nectar can accommodate and enrich almost any dish. It can lend a hearty, winter soul to pasta with chickpeas and spinach, to eggplant steaks or a mélange of steamed vegetables. It makes a tasty paprika sauce for chicken over noodles.

As with any stock, constructing the broth that will then be reduced to a syrupy glaze is a study in purity and order. Spread out fresh turkey wings and chicken parts in a roasting pan. Pan surfaces not covered by meat become hot spots during roasting, causing the fat to burn and develop an acrid taste that no amount of simmering can abate.

Theoretically, a dash of salt can marshal and mitigate the flavors. But salt becomes more, not less, pronounced as a stock reduces. And since it acts like an acerbic comment that cannot be undone, I prefer the safety of adding it to the finished dish. (Kosher chicken, with its residual salt, may well provide its own soupçon of salinity.)

In any case, the cook must roast the fowl until it is golden, turning the pieces several times to promote the even browning that will, in the end, provide a caramel flavor to the broth. When the fowl is golden, remove it, carefully drain off the fat, and deglaze the roasting pan with cold water. Then transfer the meat and the drippings from the pan to a large stockpot, add water, and settle in for the duration.

Coaxing the full flavor from the turkey and chicken parts takes about a third less time than it does from beef bones. But it is still a slow process that offers the cook only olfactory diversion.

As the broth simmers, a subtle meaty aroma slowly builds to a heady blast. The liquid sinks at a pace so gradual it requires time-lapse photography to show. But eventually, the meat relents and falls from the bones. There is a poignant pleasure in this languid alchemy, as the cook—stripped of any useful act, like stirring—is reduced, as the stock itself, to mere pot gazing.

Nothing more to do.

Rich Chicken Glaze

4 turkey wings, halved at the joint
5 pounds chicken wings and legs
3 yellow onions, unpeeled and quartered
2 carrots, peeled and coarsely chopped
2 stalks celery, coarsely chopped
1 teaspoon black peppercorns
1 small bay leaf
5 quarts plus 2 cups water

1. Preheat the oven to 450° F.

2. Place the turkey wings in a roasting pan and roast until well browned, stirring from time to time, about 40 minutes. Transfer the turkey wings to a large stockpot and add the chicken wings and legs, onions, carrots, celery, peppercorns, bay leaf, and 5 quarts of water.

3. Pour off the fat from the roasting pan. Place the pan over medium-high heat and add the remaining 2 cups of water. Cook, stirring and scraping the bottom of the pan with a wooden spoon, until all of the browned bits are loosened. Add the mixture to the stockpot and bring the stock to a boil over medium-high heat. Reduce the heat and simmer slowly, uncovered, for 3 to 4 hours, skimming as necessary.

4. Strain the stock through a fine-mesh sieve. Let cool at room temperature and then refrigerate for 12 hours. Lift the fat from the top and discard. Pass the liquid into a clean pot and simmer over medium heat until reduced to 5 cups. Store in the refrigerator or freezer.

Makes 5 cups

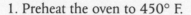

Beef Glaze

12 pounds meaty beef bones, cut into 2-inch pieces
2 large onions, unpeeled and coarsely chopped
3 carrots, peeled and cut into 1-inch pieces
2 stalks celery, cut into 1-inch pieces
2 leeks, cleaned and cut into 1-inch pieces
2 large tomatoes, quartered
8 quarts plus 2 cups water
10 sprigs fresh thyme
2 teaspoons black peppercorns

1. Preheat the oven to 450° F.

2. Place the bones in a very large roasting pan or 2 roasting pans and roast them for 25 minutes, turning twice. Add the onions, carrots, celery, leeks, and tomatoes. Roast until the bones are dark brown and the vegetables are caramelized, about 25 minutes longer.

3. Transfer the bones and vegetables to a large stockpot. Discard the fat from the roasting pan and place it over medium-high heat. Stir in 2 cups of water. Cook, scraping the bottom of the pan with a wooden spoon, until all of the bits stuck to the bottom of the pan are loosened. Add this mixture to the stockpot. Repeat if doing in batches.

4. Add the remaining water to the stockpot and bring to a simmer over medium-low heat. Reduce the heat and simmer slowly, uncovered, skimming as necessary, until the liquid has reduced by a third, 4 to 5 hours. Strain the stock through a fine-mesh sieve. Let cool at room temperature and then refrigerate for 12 hours. Lift the fat from the top and pour the liquid into a clean pot. Simmer over medium heat until reduced to about 2½ cups. Store in the refrigerator or freezer.

Makes 2½ cups

Vegetables Steamed in Chicken Glaze

1 cup Rich Chicken Glaze (page 271)
4 large boiling potatoes, peeled and cut into 8 chunks
4 medium carrots, peeled and cut on the diagonal into 1½-inch chunks
1 large fennel bulb, trimmed, cored, and cut into 8 wedges
8 medium leeks, white parts only, washed well
1 teaspoon kosher salt
Freshly ground pepper to taste

1. Put ¾ cup of the glaze in the bottom of a large wide pot over medium heat, add the potatoes, carrots, fennel, and leeks, and bring to a boil. Reduce the heat so that the liquid is at a slow simmer. Cover and cook until the vegetables are tender, about 25 minutes, adding water if necessary to keep liquid in the bottom of the pot at all times.

2. Preheat the broiler. Transfer the vegetables to a 9-inch pie plate. Spoon the remaining chicken glaze over the top and season with the salt and pepper. Place the dish under the broiler until the top is lightly browned. Divide among 4 plates and serve immediately.

Serves 4 as a side dish

Orecchiette with Chickpeas and Spinach

1 pound orecchiette pasta

1 teaspoon olive oil

2 large red bell peppers, seeded and diced

2½ pounds spinach, stemmed and coarsely chopped

1 teaspoon chopped fresh rosemary

½ cup Rich Chicken Glaze (page 271)

1 can (1 pound) chickpeas, drained and rinsed

1 teaspoon kosher salt, plus more to taste

Freshly ground pepper to taste

1. Bring a large pot of lightly salted water to a boil. Add the orecchiette and cook until al dente.

2. Meanwhile, heat the olive oil in a large nonstick skillet. Add the peppers and sauté until softened, about 5 minutes. Stir in the spinach and cook just until wilted. Stir in the rosemary, chicken glaze, and chickpeas. Cook for about 2 minutes. Stir in 1 teaspoon of the salt and pepper.

3. Drain the orecchiette and transfer to a large bowl. Add the spinach and chickpea mixture and toss to combine. Season to taste with additional salt and pepper. Divide among 4 pasta bowls and serve immediately.

Serves 4 as a main course

Egg Noodles with Paprikás Sauce

2 teaspoons olive oil

2 large onions, halved and thinly sliced

2 tablespoons sweet Hungarian paprika

1 cup Rich Chicken Glaze (page 271)

1 package (10 ounces) frozen baby peas

½ cup plain lowfat yogurt

1 tablespoon kosher salt

Freshly ground pepper to taste

1 pound wide egg noodles

1. Heat the olive oil in a large nonstick skillet over medium-low heat. Add the onions and cook until very soft, about 15 minutes. Sprinkle the paprika over the onions and continue cooking for 5 minutes. Stir in the chicken glaze and cook 5 minutes. Add the peas and cook until tender, about 2 minutes. Remove from the heat and whisk in the yogurt. Stir in the salt and pepper.

2. Bring a large pot of lightly salted water to a boil. Add the noodles and cook until tender. Drain the noodles and divide among 4 plates. Spoon the sauce over the noodles and serve immediately.

Serves 4 as a main course

Eggplant Steaks with Chinese Black Bean Sauce

2 large eggplants, unpeeled, cut across into ½-inch rounds
1 tablespoon kosher salt
1 teaspoon olive oil
1 cup Rich Chicken Glaze (page 271)
2 tablespoons minced fermented black beans (see Note)
1 tablespoon oyster sauce (see Note)
Freshly ground pepper to taste
⅓ cup thinly sliced scallions, green parts only

1. Place the eggplant rounds on a double thickness of paper towels and sprinkle with the salt. Let stand for 1 hour. Pat the eggplant dry. Heat the olive oil in a large skillet, preferably a cast-iron skillet. Add the eggplant in batches, cooking until blackened on both sides, about 3 to 4 minutes. Set aside.

2. Heat the chicken glaze in a medium saucepan over medium-high flame. Whisk in the black beans, oyster sauce, and pepper. Cook until reduced to ½ cup. Place the eggplant rounds on a broiler pan, brush the tops generously with the black bean sauce, and broil about 1 minute. Turn and brush the other side of each round with the sauce. Broil about 1 minute. Divide the eggplant among 4 plates and top with any remaining sauce. Sprinkle with scallions and serve immediately.

Serves 4 as a main course

> Note: Fermented black beans and oyster sauce are available in Asian markets and by mail order from Kam Man, 200 Canal Street, New York, New York 10002; (212) 571-0330.

Salmon Fillet with Ginger-Soy Beef Glaze

1 teaspoon olive oil
4 pieces salmon fillet, 4 ounces each
Kosher salt and freshly ground pepper to taste
1 tablespoon minced fresh ginger
⅓ cup warmed Beef Glaze (page 272)
2 teaspoons soy sauce

1. Heat the olive oil in a large nonstick skillet over medium heat. Season the salmon with salt and pepper and place in the pan. Sear until barely cooked through, about 1½ to 2 minutes per side. Remove from the pan, set aside, and keep warm.

2. Add the ginger to the skillet and cook for about 15 seconds. Stir in the glaze and the soy sauce. Cook until the sauce thickens slightly, about 1 minute. Season with salt and pepper. Place 1 piece of salmon on each of 4 plates and spoon the glaze over the top. Serve immediately.

Serves 4 as a main course

Roasted Vegetables with Spiced Beef Glaze and Couscous

1 medium butternut squash, peeled, seeded, and cut into ½-inch dice

2 sweet potatoes, peeled and cut into ½-inch dice

2 parsnips, peeled and cut into ½-inch rounds

2 carrots, peeled and cut into ½-inch rounds

1 medium onion, peeled and diced

2 teaspoons olive oil

1½ cups water

1½ teaspoons kosher salt, plus more to taste

½ teaspoon ground cumin

¼ teaspoon ground coriander

¼ teaspoon ground turmeric

1 cup uncooked instant couscous

½ cup Beef Glaze (page 272)

¼ teaspoon ground cinnamon

⅛ teaspoon ground clove

¼ teaspoon crushed red pepper

Freshly ground pepper to taste

2 tablespoons chopped pistachios

1. Preheat the oven to 400° F.

2. Place the squash, sweet potatoes, parsnips, carrots, and onion in a large roasting pan. Drizzle with the olive oil and toss to coat. Roast vegetables, stirring from time to time, until tender, about 25 minutes.

3. Pour the water into a small saucepan, add 1 teaspoon of the salt, the cumin, coriander, and turmeric, and bring to a boil. Stir in the couscous, cover, and set aside.

4. Spoon the glaze into a large nonstick skillet over medium heat. Stir in the cinnamon, clove, and red pepper. Cook for 1 minute. Add the vegetables and turn to coat them in the glaze. Cook until heated through, about 2 minutes. Season with the remaining salt and pepper. Adjust seasoning to taste.

5. Divide the couscous among 4 plates. Spoon the vegetables over the couscous, sprinkle with the pistachios, and serve.

Serves 4 as a main course

Scallops with Beef Glaze and Mushrooms

2 teaspoons olive oil

1 pound sea scallops

1 shallot, minced

4 cups stemmed and thinly sliced shiitake mushrooms

½ cup warmed Beef Glaze (page 272)

2 teaspoons kosher salt

Freshly ground pepper to taste

1 tablespoon chopped fresh thyme

1 large tomato, seeded and minced

1. Heat 1 teaspoon of the olive oil in a medium nonstick skillet over medium heat. Add the scallops and sauté until just cooked through, about 2 to 3 minutes. Remove the scallops from the pan and set aside.

2. Add the remaining teaspoon of the olive oil to the skillet. Add the shallot and cook until softened, about 30 seconds. Add the mushrooms and 2 tablespoons of the glaze and cook until tender, about 3 minutes. Stir in the remaining glaze. Stir in the salt, pepper, and 2 teaspoons of the thyme. Cook until sauce is thickened slightly, about 1 minute.

3. Place the scallops back in the skillet and cook just until heated through. Stir in the minced tomato and remove from heat. Divide among 4 plates. Sprinkle with the remaining teaspoon thyme and serve immediately.

Serves 4 as a main course

FENNEL FROM BULB TO SEED

Like Persephone, fennel traffics between the darkness and the light. The pale green bulbous vegetable with its fibrous stalks and feathery fronds bespeaks the sun, as does its sweet, faintly herbaceous anise flavor when raw. When fennel is cooked, its flavor becomes more elusive yet somehow more intensely licorice, and hence tastes dark and mysterious.

In the concentric composition of its curving layers, the fennel bulb can be likened to a white onion. Its stalks can be compared to celery, mostly due to their crunch. Like both onions and celery, fennel is a lending ingredient. It gives a subtle shading to almost any dish, particularly fish and lamb. Fennel is an unobtrusive escort, familiar with myriad conflicting worlds, escorting appetite through a rich and heavy season by providing unexpected sweet notes.

Eaten raw as they do in Italy, where the baby bulbs are relished as a crudité, fennel is indisputably a vegetable. But its seeds—a component of Chinese five-spice powder as well the fiery Ethiopian *berberé* mix—are a spice. Its leaves and flowers are an herb, at least in Provence where they are used to season pickled green olives, cucumbers, and capers. Fed to rabbits or baby lamb, or dried and used on a fire for smoking or grilling, fennel is more distinct in what it does than for what it is.

Its subtle, pervading power and inherent multiplicity caused fennel to be widely used in witchcraft. "Thyme and Fennel, a pair great in power," reads the eleventh-century Nine-Herbs Charm. "The Wise Lord . . . put them in the seven worlds to aid all, poor and rich."

Fennel was one of the four medieval hot seeds as well as one of the nine holy herbs of the Anglo-Saxons. Fennel has been around. The plant probably originated in the Mediterranean basin: the Greeks used the young stalks and leaves of the plant; the Romans sprinkled fennel seeds on breads and used the leaves in raw greens.

Pliny lists twenty-two remedies that include fennel. Modern herbalists still employ the seeds for slimming, as well as to stimulate appetite. Fennel goes both ways. Perhaps its potency is in the mind of the consumer.

Certainly, on the palate of the taster, fennel is bewitching. In the traditional Italian fennel sausage, the seeds distract from the fatty, intensely pork flavor, at once mitigating and refreshing the taste. Likewise, the vegetable's natural affinity for lamb seems to be as a fat-buster and mellower. In the bouillabaisse of southern France, fennel, along with onion and garlic, provides an aromatic backbone that emphasizes the nature of each different fish and helps keep those flavors distinct while melding them.

A dash of Pernod exaggerates the licorice notes of fennel; an understated or aging bulb can use such a boost. Despite its physical resemblance to celery and white onions, fennel doesn't keep well. After three days in the refrigerator, it will lose its opalescent sheen, turn yellow, and dry out. Orange, thyme, peppers, and garlic all make good seasoning companions to fennel. Sometimes, though, fennel alone—shaved to make a slaw with orange segments and chili peppers or braised in chicken stock—is fennel enough.

As with many mysteries, one wants just enough fennel to be titillated and perhaps, thereby, emboldened to approach other unknowns. Fennel is primarily grown in Italy, southern France, and California. When it appears in the early fall, fennel seems to extend summer; abiding through the winter months it seems to promise spring. Those who acquire a taste for fennel seem to be those willing to entertain simultaneous opposites, particularly little patches of sun in the season of the bleak.

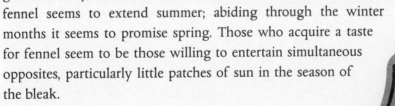

Fennel Slaw with Orange, Cumin, and Chilies

3 medium fennel bulbs, trimmed with green tops reserved, and julienned
2 tablespoons fennel seeds, crushed
¾ teaspoon ground cumin
¼ teaspoon crushed red pepper
1 teaspoon grated orange zest
1 small clove garlic, minced
3 tablespoons fresh lemon juice
3 tablespoons fresh orange juice
1½ teaspoons extra-virgin olive oil
2 teaspoons kosher salt
Freshly ground pepper to taste

Place the fennel in a large bowl. Combine the fennel seeds, cumin, and red pepper in a small bowl. Add to the fennel and toss to coat. Whisk together the orange zest, garlic, lemon juice, orange juice, olive oil, salt, and pepper. Pour over the fennel and toss well. Let stand at room temperature for 1 hour. Chop ¼ cup of the fennel tops and toss them into the salad. Divide among 4 plates and serve.

Serves 4 as a first course

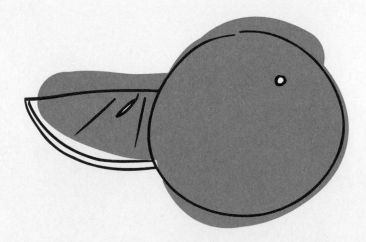

Braised Fennel with Parmesan

4 medium fennel bulbs, trimmed and halved lengthwise
2 cups chicken broth, homemade, or low-sodium canned broth
1 teaspoon olive oil
Freshly ground pepper to taste
4 tablespoons freshly grated Parmesan cheese

1. Preheat the oven to 325° F. Place the fennel in a large shallow baking dish and pour in the broth. Cover the dish with foil and bake until the fennel is very tender, about 2 hours.

2. Preheat the broiler. Drain the liquid from the fennel into a small saucepan. Cook over medium heat until reduced to a syrup consistency, about 5 minutes. Whisk in the olive oil. Season the fennel with pepper and brush with the broth mixture. Sprinkle with the Parmesan and broil until browned, about 2 minutes. Divide among 4 plates and serve.

Serves 4 as a side dish

Fennel and Potato Bisque with Crumbed Salt Cod and Green Olives

6 ounces salt cod
4 medium fennel bulbs, trimmed and cut into 1-inch chunks
2 small baking potatoes, peeled and cut into 1-inch chunks
4 cups chicken broth, homemade or low-sodium canned broth
8 cloves roasted garlic, peeled (page 175)
1 teaspoon kosher salt, plus more to taste
Freshly ground pepper to taste
¼ cup bread crumbs
2 teaspoons olive oil
4 teaspoons chopped pitted green olives

1. Soak the salt cod in water overnight, changing the water several times.

2. Combine the fennel, potatoes, and broth in a large saucepan and bring to a boil. Reduce the heat and simmer, uncovered, until the vegetables are tender, about 25 minutes. Transfer to a food processor, add the roasted garlic, and process until smooth. Return to the saucepan and season with the salt and pepper. Keep warm over low heat.

3. Drain the salt cod and shred with a knife. Place in a bowl and toss with the bread crumbs. Heat the olive oil in a medium nonstick skillet over medium heat. Add the cod and sauté until the crumbs are browned, about 5 minutes. Divide the soup among 4 bowls and top with the salt cod and olives. Serve immediately.

Serves 4 as a main course

THE ROSE BENEATH THE THORNS

What modern can't relate to the artichoke's armor, to its leathery facade and thistle? With the imperatives of a flashing digital clock more pressing than the beating of a human heart, who doesn't toughen eventually? Propelled by purpose, most people tend to grow prickly in what should be life's softest spots.

The artichoke, of course, has centuries more experience than man, at least in the departments of bristle and frustrated desire. A relative of the daisy, the artichoke is actually a giant bud, whose sole purpose on earth is to strain against its own bonds and burst open into a violet-blue bloom that can be up to seven inches in diameter, on a par with the sunflower, to which the artichoke is also related.

Instead, the green globes are harvested throughout the Mediterranean, in Monterey County, California, and other temperate climates. Throughout the world, only the rare artichoke realizes its botanical destiny; most meet their fate in a steaming pot. The choke around its heart is actually flowers, and, in the end, an artichoke's revenge.

In addition, when opened by human hands rather than a warming sun, artichokes deliver a flavor that confounds the sense of taste. The fleshy petals and heart contain cynarin, an organic acid that seems to stimulate the sweet receptors in one's taste buds, while simultaneously causing a pucker. Even a glass of water can taste sugary for up to ten minutes after eating an artichoke, leaving the eater as baffled as a suitor with an earful of mixed messages.

The artichoke is, therefore, anathema to wine and suspect in matters of highly refined cuisine. Too rough, too unpredictable, too much itself. Perhaps this, along with the vegetable's reputation as an aphrodisiac, was what shocked Le Tout Paris about Catherine de Médicis' voracious appetite for artichokes.

The fourteen-year-old bride is credited with carrying artichokes to France from her native Tuscany and scandalizing *tout le monde* with her penchant for the thistly globes. Observing her relish, according to Waverley Root, one matron sniffed, "Today young women are more forward than pages at the court."

Ah, those were the days. With the current lack of household help, one needs more perseverance than audacity to contend with an artichoke. One also needs patience for the difficult, as well as a certain sympathy for the bittersweet renderings of a tightly held, not fully realized life.

Artichokes can range from the two-ounce, bite-size buds so prized in Rome—where, in the Jewish quarter, they are fried and eaten whole, so young that their hearts are not yet thistled—to the ten-ounce, bristly monsters that can make a meal. But all are the same variety, "green globe," and none are simple to eat.

The process of paring the stem and pruning the leaves until the artichoke resembles a crew-cut pine cone is laborious, even if one does entertain the notion that truth reveals itself layer by layer. Removing the aptly named choke to unfetter the artichoke heart is tantamount to surgery. And when the entire artichoke is steamed and served, the eating isn't exactly easy.

After all that, the flavor of an artichoke is not for those who prefer a predictable life. Gnawing the fleshy base of the bracts or leaves or nibbling the heart changes one's taste and makes one doubt for a moment the primal sensor that determines one of the most basic human decisions: Is a substance nutritious or poison? This can lead to a fleeting suspension of all belief, which, depending on the kind of person you are, is either terrifying or exhilarating. In either case, it doesn't linger. The flavor of an artichoke, whether it's steamed, fried, pureed, or sliced into confetti and served raw, immediately fazes and just as quickly fades.

Perhaps this is why I think of artichokes in the fall. Artichoke season actually peaks in the spring. But there is a small second crop in September, celebrated by the annual Castroville Artichoke Festival in Monterey County, California. Castroville is the self-proclaimed artichoke capital of the world, and the later harvest, mounded along the city blocks and cooked in hundreds of guises, seems to me sturdier, denser than the slightly mealy spring version. Yet fall artichokes are still fragile, their taste summoning up impetuous youth.

Abandoned by summer, not yet claimed by winter, who doesn't hunger for a substantial vegetable with a young, unreconciled heart?

Basic Steamed Artichoke

1 artichoke
½ lemon

1. Snap off the artichoke stem. With a stainless steel knife, slice off the top, about 1 inch from the pointed end. Use scissors to cut off the tips of the outer leaves. Rub all cut surfaces with lemon juice. Bring water to boil in a pot with a steamer insert. Place the artichoke in the insert and cover the pot tightly. Steam until the base is tender and the leaves pull out easily, about 40 minutes.

2. If serving whole, pull out the cone of leaves in the center of the artichoke. Use a small spoon to scoop out the choke. If using the heart only, pull away all of the leaves and then scoop out the choke.

Makes 1 artichoke

Raw Artichoke Salad

2 tablespoons plus 2 teaspoons fresh lemon juice
8 fresh artichoke hearts
4 teaspoons olive oil
Salt and freshly ground pepper to taste
4 large radicchio leaves
¼ cup thinly sliced Parmesan cheese
½ scallion, green part only, thinly sliced

1. Fill a medium bowl with water and add 2 tablespoons of the lemon juice. Thinly slice the artichoke hearts and drop into the water. Whisk together the remaining 2 teaspoons lemon juice and the olive oil. Season with salt and pepper.

2. Place 1 radicchio leaf on each of 4 plates. Drain the sliced artichoke hearts and place in a bowl. Add the dressing and toss. Divide the salad evenly among the plates, arranging it so that it spills out of the radicchio leaves. Sprinkle each salad with the Parmesan and sliced scallion. Serve immediately.

Serves 4 as a first course

Fall Artichoke Salad with Roasted Peppers and Shiitakes

2 teaspoons plus 2 tablespoons olive oil

4 cups stemmed and quartered shiitake mushrooms

2 red bell peppers, roasted, peeled, seeded, and julienned

1 can (13¾ ounces) artichoke hearts, well drained, or 8 steamed artichoke hearts
    (page 287) cut into 1-inch pieces

8 cloves roasted garlic, peeled (page 175)

¼ teaspoon grated lemon zest

1 tablespoon fresh lemon juice

½ teaspoon kosher salt, plus more to taste

Freshly ground pepper to taste

1 tablespoon freshly grated Parmesan cheese

1. Heat 2 teaspoons of the olive oil in a large nonstick skillet over medium heat. Add the mushrooms and cook until tender, about 10 minutes. Transfer to a medium bowl and let cool to room temperature. Add the roasted peppers and artichoke hearts and toss.

2. Combine the roasted garlic and lemon zest in a small bowl. Whisk in the lemon juice and the remaining 2 tablespoons of the olive oil. Season with salt and pepper. Pour over the salad and toss to combine. Taste and season with additional salt and pepper, if needed. Divide the salad among 4 plates. Sprinkle with Parmesan and serve immediately.

Serves 4 as a first course

Roast Chicken with Artichokes, Tomatoes, and Peppers

1 can (13¾ ounces) artichoke hearts, well drained

2 cloves garlic

1 tablespoon olive oil

½ teaspoon kosher salt, plus more to taste

Freshly ground pepper to taste

1 chicken, 3½ pounds

½ lemon, quartered

3 branches fresh rosemary

1 can (14½ ounces) peeled tomatoes, well drained and coarsely chopped

1 green bell pepper, roasted, peeled, seeded, and julienned

⅛ teaspoon cayenne

1. Preheat the oven to 450° F.

2. Combine about two-thirds of the artichokes in a food processor with the garlic, 2 teaspoons of the olive oil, ½ teaspoon salt, and pepper and process until smooth, stopping as necessary to scrape the sides of the bowl.

3. Carefully loosen the skin over the breast from the meat of the chicken, forming 2 pockets. Stuff with the artichoke mixture. Rub the skin with the remaining teaspoon of the olive oil and season with salt and pepper. Fill the cavity with the lemon, the rosemary, and the remaining artichoke hearts. Place in a roasting pan and roast for 35 minutes, running a spatula under the chicken once or twice to prevent it from sticking to the pan.

4. Combine the tomatoes, roasted pepper, and cayenne and spoon the mixture over the chicken. Continue roasting until juices run clear when pricked in the thickest part of the thigh, about 35 minutes longer, basting every 10 minutes. Remove from the oven and let stand for 10 minutes before carving. Carve and divide among 4 plates, serving a little of the artichoke puree with each serving.

Serves 4 as a main course

HEAVY ON THE VINE

You must woo autumn squash. The eight major varieties of edible gourds that are picked hard and fully mature are constitutionally incapable of surrendering to anything less than a cook's fierce pursuit. Their leathery skin is resolutely protective, capable of defying sharp knives and the best intentions. Their flesh is dense. Don't dream of underlying suppleness. Winter squash is a world bent only on containing itself.

The cook reconciles herself to the determination it takes—the thwack of a heavy knife and then lots of heat—to coax the sweet, nutty nature out of these tough numbers. She can't help herself. Squash is the sweetness of cool weather, a vegetable that can act like itself or a root or a fruit.

Winter squash can become a soup; it can be boiled or baked and served as a counterpoint to rich, meaty winter meals. But in the fall, when the annual challenge of thick-skinned squash is young, the versatility of squash is recalled with the intensity due only to something once adored and then forgotten with the passage of time. Invariably, at least for a while, squash stands alone.

I understood this phenomenon initially with butternut squash, the elongated pear-shaped one with a perpetual tan, whose orange flesh is fine, moist, and sweet and whose anatomy and hide are less daunting to the knife. For a few years, I sweetened the passage from fall to winter by simmering a soup of softened onions, orange zest, cream, and butternut squash. Once the squash relented to slow, moist heat, it was easily pureed or, if I was in a poky mood, to being passed through a food mill, which preserves some of its texture. After a while, I used less cream and substituted chicken broth and herbs—particularly rosemary—which made a soigné bisque of herbaceous veneer.

The butternut lends itself to being diced and tossed with pasta and sage, or to make an autumn succotash with dried corn, chilies, and beans. Squash was an original member of the native American triumvirate, which also included corn and beans. The affinity of the three has not waned. Like most winter squash, butternut will cozy up to apples, pears, or nuts and responds as well to meat and intense spices such as curry and ancho chili paste.

At the risk of sounding like a squash Philistine, winter squash are, with the exception of spaghetti squash, interchangeable. Their individual flavors vary from sweet to nutty, their textures diverge, somewhat, but one pound of any winter squash will yield about two cups of cooked squash. And once conquered, winter squash subsides, becoming a backdrop for spices and other aromatics.

Butternut and buttercup, the drum-shaped, dark green squash that is topped with an undersized derby hat and is often pin-striped with gray, as well as turban squash, which comes in all colors and is best recognized by its squat shape, tend to have a fine, dense texture. Stringier and looser of flesh are the acorns, the melon-shaped green deeply ridged variety; the hubbard squash which has blue-gray skin and is so huge it is often sold by the wedge; and the pumpkin-shaped golden nugget squash.

My second realization about squash had to do with acorns, how one could stuff them with apples—or later, in winter, kumquats—drizzle them with butter, season them lightly with sugar or honey along with a touch of cinnamon, and bake them covered in a bath of apple cider or a mixture of water and wine to make dessert. The ability of these squash to retain their shape while holding any number of stuffings is a testament to their durability. As in the case of my butternut creations, I've moved from the obvious realm of the sweet to the darker world of the savory in terms of acorn squash. I tend now to stuff it with spiced meat or grains and exploit its container nature.

Spaghetti squash is the weirdest winter squash of all. Those obsessed by weight control like to concentrate on the spaghetti part of its name. They vent the squash with several triangles, steam it whole in a microwave oven or bake it in a conventional oven, fork out its stringy flesh, and call it pasta. Weight control is rife with potential cognitive dissonance.

Spaghetti squash is not spaghetti, it is squash, but it can be good tossed with a ragout of wild mushrooms, even a sauce made of sun- or oven-dried tomatoes, or with butter, black pepper, and savory herbs. But the tendrils are so dry that they are best baked with cream, nutmeg, and Parmesan cheese in a gratin or used as garnish and counterpoint to other, silkier winter squash.

Of course, spaghetti squash may be squash in its most basic form, a squash not yet melded elegantly to itself. Nevertheless, like any winter squash, it requires a certain effort but promises an amiable reward.

Rosemary Butternut Bisque

2 medium butternut squash, peeled, seeds and fibers scooped out, cut into
    ½-inch dice
6 cups chicken broth, homemade, or low-sodium canned broth
1 tablespoon chopped fresh rosemary
2 teaspoons grated orange zest
1 teaspoon kosher salt
Freshly ground pepper to taste
2 tablespoons heavy cream (optional)

1. Preheat the oven to 375° F.

2. Place the squash on a baking sheet and roast until tender, about 25 minutes. Transfer to a large saucepan and add the broth, rosemary, and orange zest. Bring to a boil over medium-high heat. Reduce the heat and simmer for 30 minutes.

3. Transfer the mixture to a food processor and process until smooth. Stir in the salt and pepper. Ladle the soup into bowls and swirl a little of the cream into each bowl, if desired. Serve immediately.

Serves 6 as a first course or 4 as a main course

Pasta with Butternut Squash and Sage

2 medium butternut squash, peeled, seeds and fibers scooped out, cut into
    ½-inch dice
1 pound farfalle (also called bowtie pasta)
4 teaspoons unsalted butter, melted
½ cup chicken broth, homemade, or low-sodium canned broth
2 tablespoons plus 2 teaspoons chopped fresh sage
2½ teaspoons kosher salt
½ teaspoon freshly ground pepper, plus more to taste
3 tablespoons freshly grated Parmesan cheese
½ cup dry bread crumbs

1. Preheat the oven to 375° F.

2. Place the squash on a baking sheet and roast until tender, about 25 minutes. Meanwhile, bring a large ovenproof pot of lightly salted water to a boil. Add the pasta and cook until al dente. Drain, rinse, and drain again.

3. Lower the oven temperature to 350° F. Place the pasta back in the pot and add the squash, butter, broth, 2 tablespoons of the sage, 2 teaspoons of the salt, pepper, and 2 tablespoons of the Parmesan. Toss to mix well. Combine the bread crumbs, remaining 2 teaspoons sage, ½ teaspoon salt, 1 tablespoon Parmesan, and pepper in a small bowl. Sprinkle the mixture over the top of the pasta. Bake for 15 minutes. Divide among 4 plates and serve immediately.

Serves 4 as a main course

Squash Baked with Apples and Cider

2 acorn squash, halved crosswise, seeds and fibers scooped out

2 small McIntosh apples, halved, cored, and cut into ¼-inch slices

4 teaspoons unsalted butter

3 cups apple cider

Slice off the bottom of each squash half so that it stands flat, being careful not to cut all the way through the squash. Place squash in a medium roasting pan. Fan half of an apple in the cavity of each squash half. Add 1 teaspoon butter and ¼ cup of the cider to each. Pour the remaining 2 cups cider into the roasting pan. Cover the squash loosely with aluminum foil. Roast until the squash is tender, about 1½ hours. Place 1 squash half on each of 4 plates and serve immediately.

Serves 4

Blue Hubbard and Maple Pie

CRUST

1¼ cups all-purpose flour

1 teaspoon kosher salt

1 teaspoon sugar

4 tablespoons cold unsalted butter, cut into small pieces

3 tablespoons cold vegetable shortening

3 tablespoons ice water

FILLING

1½ cups blue hubbard squash puree (see Note)

4 large eggs, lightly beaten

¾ cup pure maple syrup

½ cup half-and-half

½ teaspoon kosher salt

1 teaspoon ground cinnamon

½ teaspoon grated nutmeg

TOPPING

    1 cup heavy cream
    2 tablespoons pure maple syrup
    2 teaspoons vanilla extract

1. To make the crust, combine the flour, salt, and sugar in a medium bowl. Rub in the butter and shortening until the mixture resembles coarse meal. Gradually stir in the ice water, being careful not to overwork the dough. Form into a ball, flatten into a disk, and wrap in plastic. Refrigerate for 1 hour.

2. Preheat the oven to 400° F.

3. Roll out the dough and fit it into a 9-inch pie plate.

4. To make the filling, whisk all the filling ingredients together until smooth. Scrape into the pie shell and bake for 10 minutes. Reduce the heat to 325° F. and continue baking until the filling is set, about 50 minutes.

5. Just before serving, make the topping. Whip the cream to very soft peaks. Add the maple syrup and the vanilla and whip to soft peaks. Cut the pie into wedges and top each portion with a dollop of the cream.

Makes one 9-inch pie

Note: To make squash puree, halve the squash, scoop out the seeds and fibers, and cut into 5- to 6-inch pieces. Place on baking sheets and roast at 400° F. until soft, about 1 hour. Scoop the flesh from the skin with a spoon, drain off as much liquid as possible, and pulse briefly in a food processor. One 10-pound squash will yield about 8 cups of puree. The puree can be stored in an airtight container for up to 3 days in the refrigerator or several months in the freezer.

WITCHES, WARLOCKS, AND THE GREAT PUMPKIN

For anyone who grew up near Circleville, Ohio, the possibilities of pumpkin are a measure of one's maturity, one's level of sophistication, the depth of one's world view. For there, since 1903, in a town that would otherwise be unknown, is the Circleville Pumpkin Show, four days of unabashed Americana that features seven parades and an Olympian range of pumpkin contests. The orange globes are accorded such serious respect that the farmer who produces the largest pumpkin is looked at as agriculture's own Einstein. The premier pumpkin carver is accorded a Michelangelo awe.

And Miss Pumpkin. The real mystery about Marilyn Monroe is how she became an American icon without ever being crowned with pumpkin vines and riding astride the float that looks like Cinderella's carriage, far above the rest of us. There we were: hundreds of June-and-Ward-Cleaver couples, holding the hands of little boys, who harbored schemes of planting firecrackers inside jack-o'-lanterns, and little girls like me, who were worried about slipping knee socks and the possible consequences of the brisk fall wind under their pleated skirts. We all cheered Miss Pumpkin.

Of course, there was pie-eating, egg-tossing, tractor-pulling, and hog-calling at the Circleville Pumpkin Show. But the main events were growing pumpkins, carving pumpkins, and cooking pumpkins. When we were still too young to know which of us would grow up to be Miss Pumpkin contenders, my friends and I were mesmerized by The World's Largest Pumpkin, which was about the size of a VW Beetle, definite horse-drawn carriage material. We were in awe, also, of the World's Largest Pumpkin Pie, which was five feet in diameter and looked like a muddy pond that someone had smoothed over and varnished. Nothing like the big and obvious to capture small hearts.

As we grew, we were drawn to the jack-o'-lanterns, reassured, perhaps, by facing down the leery and the eerie. By then, we must have had inklings of the future

Miss Pumpkins in our midst, as well as presentiments of the pain of one day being among the unchosen. And so, as in Girl Scouts and jump-rope cliques, we circled like rings around the saturns of the prettiest girls and formed tight little universes of shared bias and taste.

Like all vulnerable creatures, we didn't dare to vary: We ate pumpkin pie. Pumpkin fudge, we all agreed, wasn't as good as chocolate. The very idea of pumpkin bread and pumpkin butter, deep-fried pumpkin chips, or "pumpkin Joes," the pumpkin version of sloppy Joes, revolted us. And the cooking contestants who dared to be gourmet reduced us to gales of laughter. So weird!

We remained staunch in pumpkin preference even after the exciting but disconcerting switch from saggy knee socks to nylon stockings. Or maybe that change, and the tumultuous cheerleading try-outs, football games, and dances in the junior high school gym kept our tastes fixed. Since we lived in a city, half an hour away from Circleville, we'd forgotten about Miss Pumpkin per se. Though really, the aspirations toward Prince Charming had just changed. A cute guy in a Mustang convertible would be fine, thanks. And when, as a lark, we drove south from Columbus to Circleville, we remained loyal to pumpkin pie. Conformity, it seems, can be sustained long after the original reason for it disappears.

I might never have known pumpkin as anything other than a pie if I'd made the varsity cheerleading squad. But I didn't, and soon after became convinced that life was elsewhere than the Buckeye State. In Vienna, Austria, I was served the Belgian *carbonnade,* a beef and beer stew that was braised inside a pumpkin. In Massachusetts, someone showed me how to make an Armenian pumpkin stew as well as pumpkin succotash. In Italy, I formed a deep attachment to pumpkin-filled ravioli tossed with brown butter and fried fresh sage. In Mexico, I fell for pumpkin flan, *pepitas,* the roasted and salted pumpkin seeds, and the brittle that is made from them. Pumpkin possibility, in other words, eclipsed pumpkin predictability.

Circlevillians are not alone in their pumpkin preference. Libby, the largest producer of canned pumpkin puree, estimates that 88 million pies are made for Thanksgiving Day alone. It's a national symbol. But that doesn't mean the pumpkin, which is thought to be native to the Americas, has to be limited to symbolic appearances.

The pumpkin can be sweetened with honey or molasses or by a dash of rum, bourbon, or cognac; its fine, dense, sweet flesh can also be flattered by savory herbs, spices, and chilies. It's a mutable medium.

The pumpkin, of course, is limited by a short season. But unsweetened canned purees can be used to make soups and pies; yams and sweet potatoes (which require a slightly longer cooking time) can be substituted if fresh pumpkin can't be found. Pumpkin's only insurmountable limitation is the sense of possibility in the heart of the cook.

Pumpkin Succotash with Dried Beans, Tomatoes, and Spicy Shrimp

¼ cup dried black beans, soaked overnight and drained
¼ cup dried kidney beans, soaked overnight and drained
¼ cup dried pinto beans, soaked overnight and drained
½ cup dried lima beans, soaked overnight and drained
½ cup pureed tomatoes
1 small pumpkin, peeled, seeded, and diced
3 cups chicken broth, homemade, or low-
  sodium canned broth
2 tablespoons chopped fresh marjoram
½ teaspoon kosher salt, plus more to taste
1 teaspoon freshly ground pepper
¼ teaspoon crushed red pepper
1 teaspoon canola oil
1 pound shrimp, peeled and deveined
2 tablespoons chopped fresh cilantro

1. Combine the beans, tomatoes, pumpkin, broth, and marjoram in a large saucepan. Cook, uncovered, over medium heat, stirring frequently, until the beans are tender, about 1 hour. Season with the salt and pepper.

2. Meanwhile, combine the red pepper and oil in a large cast-iron skillet. Heat

until almost smoking. Add the shrimp. Sauté until cooked through, about 5 minutes. Stir the shrimp into the stew. Divide among 4 bowls. Garnish with the cilantro and serve immediately.

Serves 4 as a main course

Pan-Seared Duck Breast with Pumpkin Polenta

¼ cup grated fresh ginger
1 clove
1 vanilla bean, halved lengthwise
½ cup red wine
4 shallots, minced
2 duck *magrets* (or 1 whole breast), about 12 ounces each
1 tablespoon plus 1 teaspoon canola oil
2 cups chicken broth, homemade, or low-sodium canned broth
½ cup stone-ground cornmeal
1 cup pumpkin puree
¼ cup minced sage leaves

1. Combine the ginger, clove, vanilla bean, and wine in a saucepan. Bring to a boil over high heat. Add half of the shallots. Set aside until cool.

2. Place the duck breasts in a large bowl and pour the marinade over. Cover and refrigerate for 2 hours, turning once. Remove the duck from the marinade, pat dry, and bring to room temperature. Strain the marinade and reserve. Set aside.

3. Preheat the oven to 200° F. Brush a pie plate with 1 teaspoon of oil. Set aside.

4. Pour 1 cup of broth into a large saucepan. Bring to a boil. Reduce the heat to medium-low. Gradually whisk in the cornmeal. Add the pumpkin puree. Whisk constantly until smooth, about 5 minutes. Spread the cornmeal mixture in the pie plate and place in the warm oven.

5. Heat the remaining oil in a heavy skillet over medium-high heat. Add the

duck, fat side down, and cook until golden brown, about 5 minutes. Turn the duck over, lower the heat to medium and cook until medium-rare, about 3 minutes more. Remove the duck from the pan and set aside. Pour in the marinade and add the remaining shallots. Simmer over high heat until reduced to ¼ cup, about 5 minutes. Add the remaining broth and simmer until reduced to 1 cup, 5 to 10 minutes. Strain and set aside.

6. Remove the polenta from the oven. Cut into 8 wedges. Place 2 pieces on each of 4 plates. Cut the duck across into thin strips and arrange around the polenta. Drizzle each plate with 2 tablespoons of sauce. Garnish with sage. Serve immediately.

Serves 4 as a main course

BEFORE THE BREAKWATER IS SUBMERGED

Clamped tight over its soft, plump, secret world, the mussel is nevertheless a canary of the sea. Tufted to rocks, pier pilings, or the hull of a boat, the mollusk inhales the ocean steadily whenever it can, at a rate of up to eighteen gallons a day. It filters nutrients with high tides and then lives off the past when the tide rolls out.

Like someone too trusting to discern the difference between good intentions and a slight, the mussel welcomes nourishment and toxicity indiscriminately. Nature didn't decree the bivalve sturdy enough to assimilate noxious flotsam and jetsam and continue to thrive. Rather, once tethered by the dozens of threads that it spins to make its beard, the mussel is loath to leave. Primordial but not stupid, the mussel makes the best of an often compromised situation.

It becomes an unpaid sensor for red tide and other pollution, which pleases marine biologists and health department officials. But given the state of the sea, and given the fact that the best mussel is steamed until just opened and is therefore moist and not thoroughly cooked, mussel lovers have begun to approach the wild bivalve with some trepidation.

Farmed mussels—both the blue-black Atlantic variety and the green-lipped Pacific variety that are farmed in New Zealand—now dominate the commercial market; most are safe and clean and very good. At the same time, they are technological mussels: sand-free, never a mudder, and generally of uniform size and taste. They lack some quotient of mussel mystique, namely the unknown. Threat of a mud-filled shell, annoyance at the inevitable and unavoidable grains of sand, give mussels the macho allure of a well-earned dinner.

Still, farmed mussels, like wild mussels, are tight little parcels of the mysterious deep. Given enough heat they release their briny liquor with reckless abandon. Their juice is an elixir of the sea, a distillation of the ever-changing that can change everything.

In the early fall, mussels from the North Atlantic are particularly juicy, their brininess most pronounced. Perhaps it is the cooler water temperature, or perhaps it is because summer is spawning season and by autumn the bivalves are recovered and self-satisfied. In either case, the cooler weather is also one of the safer times to gather wild mussels.

In the years when local fishermen were still experimenting with offshore mussel patches, dangling be-musseled ropes from floats and vying with the winds for three years until the farmed mollusks reached maturity, the breakwater in the west end of Provincetown was a prime mussel patch in the fall. The fence of piled rocks juts twenty yards into tidal flats and only in the cooler months are the waters high enough to give mussels the easy life. Pail in hand, I'd slip and slide, pick and pull until the water numbed my hands. The wind gusted across the water and made white caps that looked like sneering smiles. Winter was gaining on summer, again.

I'd be shivering before my pail was full, shoes and jeans soaked before I'd harvested even half the length of the breakwater. But there was an imperative to the ritual. Most years offer just a few weeks between summer's spent mussels and the thicker-shelled mussels of winter that tend to be less plump and juicy. And there was also a satisfying symmetry between those days and their dinner. A sink full of mussels in a warm kitchen is a buffer against early dusks and rusty leaves and the smoky smell of fall.

Like most cleaning, scrubbing and debearding mussels is boring work, although the rote pulling and twisting and scraping can also become a Zen. One sifts between the living, shell-clenched mussels and those that are beginning to sputter, open, and die. Saving and discarding accordingly, tedium can give way to tenderness. It's difficult not to savor survivors.

Steamed Mussels

2 tablespoons olive oil

¼ cup fresh lemon juice

¼ cup water

2 cloves garlic, minced

Up to 50 mussels, scrubbed and debearded

Combine the olive oil, lemon juice, water, and garlic in a large pot and place over medium-high heat. Bring to a boil. Add the mussels, in batches if necessary, and cover the pot. Cook, shaking the pot occasionally, until all the mussels open, about 4 minutes. Remove the mussels, letting any liquid in the shells drip back into the pot.

Makes up to 50 mussels

Mussels with Orecchiette and White Beans

¾ pound orecchiette pasta

50 Steamed Mussels (see above)

2 cups cooked white beans

4 teaspoons olive oil

2 teaspoons kosher salt

Freshly ground pepper to taste

3 tablespoons chopped Italian parsley

1. Bring a large pot of lightly salted water to a boil. Add the orecchiette and cook until al dente.

2. When the mussels are cool enough to handle, remove from the shells.

3. Drain the pasta and transfer to a large bowl. Add the mussels, beans, olive oil, salt, pepper, and parsley. Toss to combine well. Divide among 4 pasta bowls and serve immediately.

Serves 4 as a main course

Fettuccine with Mussels

2 tablespoons olive oil
½ cup water
½ cup white wine
4 cloves garlic, minced
32 mussels, scrubbed and debearded
6 tablespoons heavy cream
Kosher salt and freshly ground pepper to taste
1 pound dried fettuccine
¼ cup chopped Italian parsley

1. Combine the olive oil, water, wine, and garlic in a large pot over medium heat. Add the mussels and steam according to the directions on page 303. Remove the mussels from their shells and set aside. Strain the cooking liquid and place in a medium saucepan. Boil over medium heat until reduced to 1 cup. Add the cream and the mussels to the reduced cooking liquid and cook for 1 minute. Season to taste with salt and pepper.

2. Meanwhile, bring a large pot of lightly salted water to a boil. Add the fettuccine and cook just until al dente. Drain the pasta and transfer to a large bowl. Add the sauce and parsley and toss to coat well. Divide among 4 pasta bowls and serve immediately.

Serves 4 as a main course

Saffron Rice with Mussels, Chorizo, and Sweet Potatoes

40 Steamed Mussels (page 303)
2 teaspoons olive oil
1 large onion, chopped
3 cloves garlic, minced
½ pound chorizo, cut across into ¼-inch slices
3 cups long-grain white rice
1 cup white wine
2¼ cups water
¼ teaspoon saffron threads
2 teaspoons kosher salt, plus more to taste
½ teaspoon grated lemon zest
4 medium sweet potatoes, roasted until just tender,
    peeled, and cut into ½-inch pieces

1. Measure the broth from the steamed mussels and add enough water to make 2 cups. Set aside the mussels and the broth.

2. Heat the olive oil in a large pot over medium heat. Add the onion and garlic and cook until soft, about 5 minutes. Add the chorizo and cook until browned, about 5 minutes. Stir in the rice and cook, stirring, for 2 minutes. Add the reserved mussel liquid, wine, 2¼ cups of water, saffron, and 2 teaspoons salt and bring to a boil. Reduce to a simmer, cover, and cook until the liquid has absorbed and rice is tender, about 17 minutes.

3. Gently stir in the lemon zest, sweet potatoes, and additional salt to taste. Divide among 8 plates. Top with mussels and serve immediately.

Serves 8 as a main course

SWEET MUSCLE IN A COLD BAY

Terrible things happen to scallops in this world.

The calicoes, sea scallops found in southern waters, are so tiny that it is more cost-effective for fishermen to steam them open rather than open them by hand, as most scallopers do. Unfortunately, the meat of the calico arrives on the market with the consistency of rubber pellets. Sea scallops dragged from beds up to nine hundred feet beneath the sea and up to 150 miles offshore are sometimes shucked and piled on ice in the hulls of boats for the duration of the journey (which can take up to ten days). When unloaded, unscrupulous fishmongers sometimes soak the scallop meat in water and phosphate solutions so it arrives at the market whiter than snow, heavier than when the scallops were captured—and tasting like baking soda.

The tender bay scallops that lurk in the eelgrass around Long Island and Nantucket in the fall are so difficult to harvest that their price per ounce inches toward caviar territory. And that has given rise to stories of scurrilous scallop counterfeiters who, presumably under cover of night, stamp scallop shapes out of monkfish or skate steaks and peddle them to those who are none the wiser.

What slings and arrows the scallop has suffered!

Nevertheless, it remains the only bivalve that is mobile. Of the four hundred species of scallops found throughout the world, only about a dozen of the most abundant reach the market. They range from fingernail size to orbs on the scale of goose eggs. Their shells can be smooth or, more frequently, fluted, ranging in color from deep blue-black to rust, rose, and petal-pink. But all of them can roam freely. They move not at a lobster's creep nor in the straight-ahead-till-morning line of a school of bass. By sucking in and shooting out a jet of water, scallops leap and dance in yard-long spurts.

In a scalloper's wheelhouse in New Bedford, Massachusetts, I once read this description of the scallop's gait: "Deporting themselves most gaily, skipping about and snapping their valves in great glee." The scallop, of course, has much to celebrate. Most are hermaphroditic.

Attractive as the unfettered life of a scallop is, it is not without pathos. The large and well-developed adductor muscle that provides the bivalve its jet propulsion is the very thing that is so sweet to eat. And unlike mussels, clams, or oysters, scallops cannot snap their shells tight against predators. It takes practice to open an oyster or a clam, but any knave with a knife can open a scallop. They are the most vulnerable bivalves.

As soon as a breeze courses across scallop meat, it begins to lose its sweet, wet charm. All parts of the scallop's interior—adductor muscle, coral male parts, and the lesser muscles—are edible. But all deteriorate quickly. Fleeting, despite its dense substance, the scallop is like a love that won't be denied: You can't mistake it for anything else, at least for as long as it lasts. A cynical detachment, whether fostered by association with scalloped potatoes or by the memory of mistreated scallops, could ruin the moment of sublime pleasure.

I didn't understand this until the first time I ate a scallop raw, from its shell. Then I understood why the smartest chefs and fish buyers would stand at the end of the Provincetown pier, waiting for the boats to arrive, ready to buy the "top of the trip," the 40-pound muslin bags of scallops fished most recently and therefore at the top of the pile. Later, I understood why the inveterate bay scallopers I met in Nantucket carried knives, lemon slices, and sometimes small bottles of Tabasco when they went out to rake the eelgrass. A true scallop aficionado knows to seize the moment.

In the city, without the chance of returning boats, I've learned to look for scallops that are opalescent rather than milky and to sniff them for the smell of the sea. I dry them completely before cooking them, as a whiff of steam interrupts the crisping that is so essential in a cooked scallop. The idea is to sear or blanch the pearly muscle and to let the heat drift through the scallop and warm its center. Such deftness preserves a taste of the sweet freedom that is the essence of the bivalve, the very thing that scallop icons keep trying to evoke.

Faux Fried Scallops with Faux Ketchup

3 pounds tomatoes
½ cup canola oil
1½ pounds sea scallops
Olive oil spray
2 cups bread crumbs seasoned with kosher salt and pepper

1. Use a juicer to extract the juice from the tomatoes or puree them in a food processor and strain through a fine-mesh strainer. Pour the juice into a nonreactive pan and place over low heat. Simmer until reduced to ½ cup, about 20 minutes. Set aside to cool. When cool, whisk the oil into the juice, spoon into an airtight container, and place in the refrigerator overnight.

2. The next morning, put the scallops in a shallow nonaluminum container, add half the tomato oil, and toss gently to coat well. Marinate in the refrigerator for at least 8 hours, turning occasionally.

3. Preheat the oven to 400° F. Lightly coat a baking sheet with olive oil spray.

4. Remove the scallops from the tomato oil, dust them evenly with seasoned bread crumbs, and place on the baking sheet. Spray lightly with additional olive oil spray and bake, turning frequently, until the bread crumbs are golden and the scallops are firm to the touch, 5 to 7 minutes. Serve heaped on plates with the remaining tomato oil for dipping.

Serves 4 as a main course

Mediterranean Scallops (Adapted from Robert Kinkead)

2 teaspoons olive oil

6 shallots, minced

2 cloves garlic, minced

1 cup dry white wine

1 teaspoon saffron threads

12 ripe plum tomatoes, peeled, cored, seeded, and cut into ¼-inch dice

1 pint yellow cherry tomatoes

1 cup niçoise olives, pitted

2 tablespoons grated orange zest

1 teaspoon minced fresh rosemary

½ teaspoon kosher salt, plus more to taste

1 teaspoon freshly ground pepper, plus more to taste

½ cup minced fresh basil

1 teaspoon balsamic or sherry vinegar

1½ pounds bay scallops

1. Combine the olive oil, shallots, and garlic in a large skillet. Cook over medium-low heat until tender, about 5 minutes. Add the wine and saffron. Increase the heat to medium-high and simmer until reduced to ¼ cup, about 10 minutes.

2. Add three quarters of the diced tomatoes, the yellow cherry tomatoes, olives, orange zest, rosemary, salt, and pepper. Lower the heat to medium-low and cook, stirring frequently, until the sauce thickens, about 10 minutes. Meanwhile, combine the remaining diced tomatoes, basil, vinegar, and salt and pepper to taste in a glass or ceramic bowl and set aside.

3. Add the scallops to the tomato sauce on the stove and cook, stirring frequently, until cooked through, about 3 to 5 minutes. Divide among 4 plates. Top with the tomato and basil mixture. Serve immediately.

Serves 4 as a main course

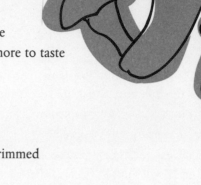

Scallops with Chanterelles

1 large baking potato, peeled and diced

1 large celery root, peeled and diced

1 cup milk

½ teaspoon kosher salt, plus more to taste

1 teaspoon freshly ground pepper, plus more to taste

1 ounce dried porcini mushrooms

2 cups water

1 teaspoon olive oil

6 shallots, peeled and minced

2 pounds fresh chanterelle mushrooms, trimmed

½ cup white wine

1½ pounds bay scallops, cleaned

1. Combine the potato, celery root, and milk in a small saucepan. Bring to a boil, reduce the heat, and simmer until tender, about 20 minutes. Puree in a food processor or blender until smooth. Season with salt and pepper. Set aside in a warm place.

2. Put the dried mushrooms in a small saucepan. Add the water and bring to a boil, reduce the heat, and simmer until reduced to 1 cup, about 20 minutes. Strain and reserve mushrooms and broth separately. Set aside.

3. Combine the olive oil, shallots, and chanterelles in a heavy saucepan. Cook over medium-low heat until soft, about 5 minutes. Add the dried mushrooms, mushroom broth, and wine. Simmer until the sauce has reduced to ½ cup, about 20 minutes. Add the scallops and continue simmering, stirring frequently, until the scallops are cooked through, about 5 minutes. Divide the potato and celery root puree among 4 plates. Top with the scallop and mushroom ragout. Serve immediately.

Serves 4 as a main course

AIMING TOWARD THE SKY

Life isn't frozen on the unforgiving late autumn mornings when coveys of quail hide near marshes and the occasional pheasant fans an earth-toned rainbow wing skyward, but eventual fate is apparent. The leaves are parched, dry and umber, old news. The cold obliterates all olfactory evidence of change. There is no regenerative slosh of leaves, twigs, and bark, grass and mud. There is no herbaceousness, haunting or hopeful, in the air. Every sniff gives the illusion of an unchanging evermore.

Hunters count on the steely stillness of a clinically depressed world. It isn't that they want to obliterate even the most fragile motion. It's that, like everyone, they're eager to snag any evidence of flux—be it quail or pheasant, grouse or squab—desperate to banish the bitterness that comes from not being able to affect the world.

Gaming is a cognitive sport. Game birds are points scored against the ultimate foe: the dreaded, immovable abyss.

A reluctant anthropologist, I've traipsed behind hunters a few times in the last ten years. I've nursed cold feet and then revulsion in the cabs of pickup trucks at the sight of otherwise civilized men, vainly attempting to warm the earth as they creep along on their flannel-shirted bellies or vainly tiptoe through crunchy underbrush. But against all preconception, the smell of trucks and wet flannel, utility, and comfort, endured.

A game bird is a talisman that signifies the possibility of a fluid and realized life, a life interrupted by skill and wit, not by fate. The dichotomy is reassuring, wrapped like the bacon around a quail, stuffed like cornbread in a pheasant. I take an additional, if wimpish, solace in the fact that most game birds are farm raised now.

Still, it's impossible to deny the satisfaction that comes from taming a sliver of something wild on the white Formica counter of a city kitchen.

Cooks, like hunters, must conform to the habits and character of each game bird. All work for a living and are sinewy, hence the sine qua non of game bird cookery is basting, larding, and otherwise moistening the cooking bird.

In the matter of quail, one bird makes an appetizer and two are necessary for a main course, unless the bird has hefty accompaniments. Since they are dry, small birds are best wrapped in bacon, larded, or basted with herb butter or olive oil. They should be roasted in a 425° F. oven for ten minutes and rested an additional five minutes prior to serving.

Any game bird appreciates an aromatic stuffing or inner-slathering—sage is wondrous in the quail cavity. The same herb, along with onion and bay, rosemary, or thyme works magic for squab, one of which can make a meal. A squab requires 20 minutes in a 425° F. oven, lends itself to a basting of soy and ginger, Indian spices, or an Italian mélange of garlic and olive oil, and should be rested ten minutes before serving so that the flavors can marry.

Likewise, a pheasant, which will serve two as a main course, is equally flattered by exotic seasoning or by stuffing the cavity with onions and rosemary, sage, or thyme—or with orange, lemon, and onion wedges—and requires 30 minutes in a 400° F. oven and a ten minute rest before serving.

Serving any game bird has a primal, ritualistic aura. A game bird is a reason to celebrate, evidence of freedom and incalculable luck plucked from the staid morning sky, transformed for dinner.

Quails with Rosemary on Soft Polenta

QUAILS

    8 quails, wing tips removed

    12 branches fresh rosemary

    Kosher salt and freshly ground pepper to taste

    16 thin slices pancetta

POLENTA

    2½ cups water

    2 teaspoons kosher salt

    ½ cup yellow cornmeal

1. Preheat the oven to 425° F.

2. Put 1 branch of rosemary in the cavity of each quail, cutting the rosemary as needed to fit. Wrap 2 pieces of pancetta around each quail and tie securely with string. Set aside.

3. Combine the water and salt in a medium saucepan. Bring to a boil over medium heat. Whisking constantly, add the cornmeal very gradually, pouring it in a light, steady stream. Change from a whisk to a wooden spoon and reduce the heat so that the mixture is at a slow simmer. Stir constantly until the polenta thickens, about 10 minutes.

4. When the polenta is almost done, place the quails in the oven and roast for 10 minutes. Remove the string. Divide the polenta among 4 plates and top each serving with 2 of the quails. Garnish with a sprig of rosemary and serve immediately.

Serves 4 as a main course

Squab Salad with Bacon and Chestnuts

2 shallots, minced
2 teaspoons Dijon mustard
4 teaspoons apple-cider vinegar
¼ cup olive oil
1 teaspoon kosher salt, plus more to taste
Freshly ground pepper to taste
6 slices bacon, cut into ½-inch squares
6 squab breasts
4 cups torn spinach leaves
1 cup roasted and peeled chestnuts

1. Put the shallots in a small bowl and whisk in the mustard and the vinegar. Whisking constantly, slowly drizzle in the olive oil. Season with salt and pepper. Set aside.

2. Place the bacon in a large skillet over medium heat. Cook until browned and slightly crisp. Remove with a slotted spoon and wrap in paper towels to drain and keep warm. Set aside. Pour off most of the fat. Add the squab breasts and sear until browned on the outside and medium-rare in the center, about 1½ minutes per side. Season with salt and pepper. Set aside.

3. Put the spinach leaves in a large bowl. Pour the vinaigrette into a small saucepan and place over low heat. Whisk constantly until the mixture is warmed. Pour the vinaigrette over the spinach and toss to coat well. Season lightly with salt and pepper.

4. Place a clean medium skillet over medium heat until hot. Add the chestnuts and cook, tossing from time to time, until hot.

5. Slice the squab breasts on the diagonal into thin slices. Divide the spinach among 4 plates. Fan the squab breasts over the spinach. Arrange the bacon and chestnuts around the squab and serve.

Serves 4 as a main course

Roast Pheasant with Wild Mushroom Duxelles and Roasted Vegetables

1½ teaspoons olive oil

2 cloves garlic, peeled and minced

2½ cups mixed wild mushrooms, such as shiitake, cremini, and portobello, stemmed and finely chopped

1 tablespoon chopped Italian parsley

½ teaspoon kosher salt, plus more to taste

Freshly ground pepper to taste

2 pheasants, wing tips removed

2 heads Roast Garlic (page 175)

8 medium carrots, peeled, halved crosswise, and quartered lengthwise

4 small baking potatoes, peeled and cut into 6 pieces

6 small onions, peeled and quartered

1. Preheat the oven to 450° F.

2. Put ½ teaspoon of the olive oil in a large nonstick skillet and place over medium-high heat. Add the garlic and cook for about 15 seconds. Add the mushrooms and cook, stirring frequently, until the mushrooms have given off their liquid and most of the liquid has evaporated, about 10 minutes. Stir in the parsley, ½ teaspoon of salt, and pepper.

3. Carefully loosen the skin over the breast of each pheasant. Slip some of the mushroom mixture under the skin of each bird. Place 1 head of roasted garlic into the cavity of each bird. Rub the remaining teaspoon of the olive oil over the skin of the pheasants. Season with salt and pepper. Tie the legs together. Place in a large roasting pan and surround with the carrots, potatoes, and onions.

4. Roast for 15 minutes, stopping to run a spatula under the pheasants to prevent sticking. Lower the oven temperature to 350° F. Roast until the juices run slightly pink when pricked with a fork in the thickest part of the leg, about 30 minutes longer. Let stand for 10 minutes. Remove the string. Season the vegetables with salt and pepper. Cut the pheasants in half and serve with the roasted vegetables.

Serves 4 as a main course

Roast Pheasant with Ancho Chili Pesto and Cornbread Stuffing

STUFFING

    1 teaspoon olive oil

    1 medium onion, chopped

    2 stalks celery

    2 cups coarse dried cornbread crumbs

    ½ teaspoon ground cumin

    1 teaspoon kosher salt

    Freshly ground pepper to taste

    ½ cup chicken broth, homemade, or low-sodium canned broth

    1 large egg, lightly beaten

PESTO AND PHEASANT

    3 ancho chilies

    2 cloves garlic, minced

    ¼ teaspoon kosher salt, plus more to taste

    2 pheasants, wing tips removed

    1 teaspoon olive oil

    Freshly ground pepper to taste

1. Preheat the oven to 450° F.

2. Heat 1 teaspoon of the olive oil in a large skillet over medium heat. Add the onion and celery and sauté until softened, about 5 minutes. Transfer to a medium bowl. Add the cornbread crumbs and toss to combine. Add the cumin, salt, pepper, broth, and egg and stir well. Set aside.

3. Place the chilies in a small saucepan and cover with water. Simmer over medium heat until softened, about 10 minutes. Drain. Stem and seed the peppers. Chop the peppers with the garlic and ¼ teaspoon of salt until they form a paste.

4. Carefully loosen the skin over the breast of each pheasant. Place some of the ancho paste under the skin of each bird. Fill the cavity of each bird with the

stuffing. If extra stuffing remains, place it in a small dish, cover, and bake with the pheasant. Rub 1 teaspoon of the olive oil over the skin of the pheasants and season them with salt and pepper. Tie the legs together to close the cavity. Place the birds in a large roasting pan.

5. Roast for 15 minutes, stopping to run a spatula under the pheasants to prevent sticking. Lower the oven temperature to 350° F. Roast until the juices run slightly pink when pricked with a fork in the thickest part of the leg, about 30 minutes longer. Let stand for 10 minutes. Remove the string. Cut the pheasants in half and serve with the stuffing.

Serves 4 as a main course

THE UNFASHIONABLE CLOVEN HOOF

I learned most of what I know about pork from a little black pig named Bart. I raised him with visions of prosciutto, smoked ribs, and fresh hams, but Bart had different plans. He ended up raising my consciousness about pork while positioning himself for a long and happy life as a six-hundred-pound house pet.

For a young woman who ate mostly vegetables, I'm not so sure why pigs had become a crucible for me. Perhaps it's because I grew up in Columbus, Ohio, where polite society saw itself as superior to pork, eating only the occasional crown roast or stuffed loin, while our neighbor to the south, Cincinnati, was known as "porkopolis" even before it was found that corn (Cincinnati is at the tip of the Corn Belt) was the ideal feed for hogs.

In any case, I'd been a vegetarian for several years before I started cooking meat in a restaurant. And, with the absolutism that is part and parcel of early adulthood, I became convinced that if I could only raise and slaughter a pig I could then ethically pursue my profession.

I hatched this nutty notion while living and working in Provincetown, Massachusetts, a town said to have had a public piggery whose roving inhabitants were fed from the public trough. All taxpayers were then entitled to a portion of the slaughter to tide them over for the winter.

By buying half a dozen piglets and feeding them leftovers from the restaurant, two fellow kitchen workers and I thought we could revive this tradition. Of course, it was not as easy as it seemed. And whether from travel, salt air, or a diet of day-old pasta and chef's salad, five piglets died within weeks, leaving Bart an only child.

After a night of cooking, I would gather the restaurant's leftovers in two five-gallon plastic buckets, balance the pails on the handlebars of my bike and pedal up to Bart's pen. In the dark, two hundred yards away, I'd hear snorts and squeals of delight. When I arrived, Bart would be panting like a puppy for dinner.

He learned to jump, roll, and beg. He nuzzled and was partial to sitting in laps. It is fair to say that Bart complicated my already ambivalent relationship to meat. His singularity significantly handicapped my experiment.

When the town's restaurants closed in the fall it was slaughter time. By then, my partners in piggery and I had assiduously researched preserving and smoking techniques. But before the auspicious day arrived, one partner succumbed to sentiment and arranged for Bart to be kidnapped by a ménage à trois of vegetarians, who later modified their kitchen door so that Bart could come and go as he pleased.

Ultimately, I ended up eating pork, as well as other meat, never really grappling with the ethical questions. I did, however, arrive at a few piggy insights.

Bart, you see, was a presence. He didn't demand a set routine. He simply required that when he was part of the picture he be the entire picture. Likewise, pork, while an extraordinarily accommodating ingredient, is always the dominant one. The purpose of a B.L.T., after all, is neither the L nor the T but the B. The soul of stewed greens, French pâté, or Italian sausage is the binding unctuousness of the pork they contain.

When American hogs were bred fat, they were slaughtered in the late fall and left to cure until spring. Today, with pork as lean as any other meat, crown roasts or loins, hams and chops can be the centerpiece of a meal any time of year.

Still, whether fresh or cured, pork will be forever associated with feasts, because pork is endemic to the life of a settled community. Pigs don't roam far; they will forage if forced, but are happiest lolling in the shade, close to water, protected from predators. Pigs are bred neither for autonomy nor adventure. They flourish in one place, preferably the pen. To eat pork, therefore, is to toast a community that agrees on a geographic and by extension a philosophical boundary.

Caribbean Jerk Pork Tenderloins

3 tablespoons allspice berries
1 teaspoon ground cinnamon
½ teaspoon ground nutmeg
4 teaspoons ground coriander
6 scallions, finely chopped
3 cloves garlic, chopped
1 Scotch Bonnet chili, with seeds
2 tablespoons dark rum
6 tablespoons water
1½ teaspoons kosher salt
Freshly ground pepper to taste
2 pork tenderloins

1. Grind the allspice berries in a spice grinder and transfer to a blender. Add the cinnamon, nutmeg, coriander, scallions, garlic, chili, rum, water, salt, and pepper and blend until a smooth paste forms, scraping down the sides of the jar as needed. Place the pork tenderloins in a shallow baking dish. Wearing rubber gloves, rub the paste all over the pork. Refrigerate several hours or overnight.

2. Preheat the broiler. Place the pork 4 inches under the broiler and broil, turning once, until pork is only slightly pink in the center, about 12 to 15 minutes. Let stand for 5 minutes. Cut into ¼-inch slices and serve.

Serves 4 as a main course

Pork Chops Baked with Apples and Onions

1 teaspoon vegetable oil
4 pork chops, ½ inch thick
1 medium onion, peeled and thinly sliced
¼ cup sherry
¼ cup apple cider
3 large McIntosh apples, peeled, cored, and cut into ¼-inch slices
½ teaspoon kosher salt, plus more to taste
Freshly ground pepper to taste

1. Preheat the oven to 350° F.

2. Heat the vegetable oil in a large ovenproof skillet over medium-high heat. Add the pork chops and sear until golden brown, about 1½ minutes per side. Remove the pork chops to a plate and set aside.

3. Add the onion to the skillet and cook, stirring often, for 2 minutes. Add the sherry and the cider and cook, stirring constantly, scraping up any browned bits stuck to the bottom of the pan. Add the apples, ½ teaspoon salt, and pepper. Reduce the heat and cook for 5 minutes.

4. Push the pork chops down into the apple mixture and pour any juices accumulated on the plate over them. Cover with foil and bake until the pork chops are tender and cooked through, about 15 minutes. Season with additional salt and pepper. Divide among 4 plates and serve immediately.

Serves 4 as a main course

Pork Loin with Mustard Seed Crust

8 ounces plain nonfat yogurt
2 cloves garlic, minced
1½ teaspoons kosher salt
½ teaspoon freshly ground pepper
1 boneless pork loin, 3 pounds
2 tablespoons sugar
2 tablespoons mustard seed

1. Combine the yogurt, garlic, 1 teaspoon of salt, and pepper in a small bowl. Place the pork loin in a shallow baking dish and coat well with the yogurt mixture. Cover with plastic wrap and refrigerate for several hours or overnight. Let the pork stand at room temperature for 1 hour before roasting.

2. Preheat the oven to 350° F.

3. Wipe the marinade off of the pork and place it in a roasting pan. Combine the sugar and mustard seeds and coat the pork with the mixture. Sprinkle with the remaining ½ teaspoon salt. Roast for 1 hour 20 minutes. Raise the oven temperature to 450° F. and continue roasting until the pork reaches 150° to 160° F. on a meat thermometer and the top is crisp, about 10 minutes longer. Let stand for 15 minutes, cut into slices, and serve with the pan juices.

Serves 6 as a main course

EVE WAS A LIBRA

Apples remain forever female—beautiful, bright, forbidden, and often big trouble. It doesn't seem to matter that Adam actually ate the apple from the tree of knowledge, that Hercules stole the apples of Hesperides as one of his twelve labors, that William Tell risked the thing he loved most when he shot an apple off his son's head or even that Isaac Newton watched an apple fall and understood, for the first time, gravity.

Adam may have done the eating, but Eve did the picking. Paris, on the other hand, proffered an apple, but it was by accepting the gift that Aphrodite instigated the Trojan War. There is no way a woman can be innocent if there is an apple involved.

Snow White's stepmother poisoned her with an apple. As recently as the nineteenth century, Brillat-Savarin, the French epicure, insisted that apples "gently provoke sleep." But crunching into a crisp, cool apple is more enlivening than it is relaxing. The fruit is so freighted with mythological danger that the first bite summons a deep-seated fear.

Along with the myth, there is the reality that the bright and shining apple is nature's last hurrah before the frost. Along with scarlet maple and oak leaves, apples are the bright spots in the rust, ochre, and orange landscape of the fall; likewise, the sweet scent of an orchard is a counterpoint in a world smelling of smoke and decay.

Maybe the insistence of life in a dying world renders the apple feminine. Or perhaps it is the simplicity of an apple in a complex world that makes the fruit somewhat suspect. An apple is skin and flesh wrapped around a compartmentalized core, a "delightfully uncomplicated" fruit, writes Ruth Ward in *A Harvest of Apples*. "Unlike fruits which must be peeled or stoned, or which leave the fingers sticky, the ripe apple can be picked and enjoyed straight from the tree."

But while the individual apple is simple, the apple family is complicated and wildly diverse. There are over seven thousand varieties of apples, ranging from the sweet and mealy to the firm and spicy and tart, most of which were developed in the eighteenth and nineteenth centuries. Today apples are bred for shipping and storing and not many more than a hundred varieties are grown commercially. The apple's robust and adaptable nature makes it one of America's favorite fruits, rivaled only by bananas. More than ten billion pounds of apples are harvested each year.

We say that we are attempting to transcend the tyranny of the supermarket's bland apples when we go apple picking in the fall. But really, it is a ritual of remembering. Our stated purpose is to find crisp red Baldwins, tart green Newtown Pippins, sweet winy Winesaps and spicy Northern Spies. But inevitably, the drive to western Massachusetts or upstate New York is about remembering the past in relation to apples picked and apples eaten and apples cooked.

Apples are an emblem of beginnings and endings. And, like the red spiral from a carefully peeled apple, the beginnings and endings add up to a concentric continuum. We can't help realizing these things in the fall. I can't help feeling like Eve when I pick the first apple; he can't help mentioning Johnny Appleseed every year. His and hers mythologies push life forward. Basically, that's what apples are all about.

Back home, with too many apples, we always seem to become very quiet as we pare and peel. Of course, by then it is dusk; our faces are windburned. It is warm in the kitchen, but it is cold outside. We will bake apples and make applesauce, apple cakes, apple pies, and apple crisps. We will dry apples in the oven, grate apples for pancakes and bread.

We will discuss the different characters a cook can pull from an apple: the pungent mysteriousness that an apple assumes when combined with cinnamon, the gentle forgiveness it seems to offer when combined with vanilla bean, the bright hopefulness a little bit of minced lemon rind seems to draw from it. But first we will pare, steadily and quietly, together.

In "Paring the Apple," the English poet Charles Tomlinson writes, "There are portraits and still lifes. And there is paring the apple." A portrait or still life is idealized reality, captured and stagnant. To pare an apple, on the other hand, is to peel away a veneer and, as the stripped flesh begins to brown, to witness the fact that the living is constantly changing.

"The cool blade," writes Tomlinson, "severs between coolness, apple-rind, / Compelling a recognition."

Apple Sauce

10 pounds sweet-tart cooking apples like Macoun, cored
½ cup apple cider
2 vanilla beans, split
Zest of ½ lemon, removed in long strips

Combine all the ingredients in a large pot. Place over low heat, cover, and cook until the apples are tender, about 2 hours. Remove the vanilla beans and pass the mixture through a food mill. Store refrigerated in airtight containers for up to 1 week or in the freezer for several months.

Makes 10 cups

Ginger-Roasted Apples with Vanilla Ice Cream

½ cup water
1 cup sugar
2 tablespoons grated fresh ginger
4 large sweet-tart cooking apples like Macoun,
    peeled, cored, and cut into ½-inch slices
1 pint vanilla ice cream

1. Preheat the oven to 400° F.
2. Combine the water, sugar, and ginger in a medium saucepan and bring to a boil over medium heat. Reduce the heat and simmer for 5 minutes. Let stand for 10 minutes. Strain through a fine-mesh sieve.
3. Lightly butter a baking sheet and place the apple slices on it in a single layer. Drizzle the apples with ¼ cup of the ginger syrup. Roast the apples until tender, turning once, about 20 minutes. Ladle some of the syrup onto each of 4 plates. Scoop the ice cream into 4 neat rounds and place on the plates. Fan the apple slices around the ice cream and serve immediately.

Serves 4

Maple Poached Apples with Cinnamon-Glazed Pecans and Cider Granita

2 cups apple cider
⅓ cup sugar
¾ teaspoon ground cinnamon
2 egg whites
2 tablespoons water
2 cups pecans
1½ cups maple syrup
3 cups water
¾ cup rum
4 large sweet-tart cooking apples like Macoun, peeled and cored

1. To make the granita, pour the cider into a large shallow pan and place it in the freezer. Stir every 30 minutes until firm throughout but not frozen solid, about 2 hours.

2. Preheat the oven to 250° F. Combine the sugar and cinnamon in a medium bowl. In another bowl, whisk together the egg whites and water until frothy. Stir the pecans into the egg white mixture to coat. Drain well. Place the pecans in the cinnamon sugar and toss to coat well. Spread the nuts on a baking sheet in a single layer. Bake, stirring twice, until the pecans begin to dry out, about 45 minutes. Set aside.

3. Combine the maple syrup, water, and rum in a medium nonreactive saucepan and bring to a simmer. Add the apples, cover and poach until the apples are tender, about 15 minutes. Remove the apples from the liquid and set aside. Bring the poaching liquid to a boil, reduce the heat slightly, and simmer until reduced to 1 cup, about 30 minutes.

4. To serve, coat the bottom of 4 plates with the syrup. Place 1 apple and a scoop of the granita on each plate. Scatter some pecans over the plate and serve immediately. You will not need all of the pecans. Store the rest at room temperature in an airtight container.

Serves 4

Apple Walnut Upside-down Cake

TOPPING

3 tablespoons plus 1 teaspoon unsalted butter

8 small sweet-tart cooking apples like Macoun, peeled, cored, and cut into eighths

½ cup (packed) light brown sugar

CAKE

¼ pound (1 stick) unsalted butter, softened

1 cup sugar

2 large eggs

1½ teaspoons vanilla extract

1¾ cups all-purpose flour

2 teaspoons baking powder

½ teaspoon kosher salt

½ cup ground walnuts

½ cup milk

1. For the topping, melt 1 teaspoon of the butter in a medium cast-iron skillet over medium-high heat. Add the apples and sauté until caramelized, about 10 minutes. Combine the remaining 3 tablespoons butter and the brown sugar in a small saucepan and stir over low heat until melted and well blended. Butter a 10-inch pan with 3-inch sides and spread the brown sugar mixture in the bottom. Arrange the apple slices in the pan in concentric circles. Set aside.

2. Preheat the oven to 350° F.

3. Cream the butter and sugar with an electric mixer until light and fluffy. Add the eggs, one at a time, and beat until light. Mix in the vanilla. Combine the flour, baking powder, salt, and ground walnuts. Add the dry ingredients to the egg mixture alternately with the milk, mixing just to combine. Spread the batter evenly over the apples. Bake until the cake springs back when touched in the center, about 1 hour. Let stand for 10 minutes. Invert onto a cake plate and let cool. Serve slightly warm or at room temperature.

Serves 8 to 10

A LEXICON OF PEARS

The fact that I first knew pears out of a can probably stamped an indelible limit on my appreciation for the fruit. Canned pears turned me against pears early. Nevertheless, when I attempt to enjoy pears, it is inevitably in the cooked, and potentially tin-reminiscent, form.

Intellectually, I grant the round green Comice pear its charms. It is sweet and juicy and, when ripe, almost buttery, and I sliced and ate one with smears of a ripe brie, ever so languidly or so I imagined, on a terrace overlooking a vineyard in Bordeaux one day. It was a good afternoon and an excellent pear. Later, I understood the sweet wine flavor of the Anjou, the tall russet, egg-shaped pear, and came to appreciate the long-necked Bosc as well as the bell-shaped Bartlett, which can be either red or gold but in either hue tastes sweet and mildly musky.

I've tasted the large, dark green Winter Nelis and admired its spice. Aesthetically, I appreciate the yellow, bell-shaped Forelle pear, more for its rosy flesh than its sweet, flat flavor. The tiny, russet-skinned Seckel pear, however spicy and sweet, reinforces my prejudice against raw pears. The grittiness of raw pear in the mouth revolts me, and Seckel pears are grit incarnate. And no pear will give the satisfying crunch of peel against teeth that an apple offers. A pear is more of a piece, softer and more fickle; a slight bruise can ruin the entity.

By experience I would tend to agree with François de la Varenne, the legendary French chef, who wrote: "The pear is the grandfather of the apple, its poor relation, a fallen aristocrat, the man-at-arms of our domains, which once, in our humid land, lived lonely and lordly, preserving the memory of its prestige by its haughty comportment."

Of course, styles have changed since 1650 when La Varenne made his decree. Today, the possibility of a pear-shaped figure is a not symbol of aristocracy but a sentence to a less glamorous caste, one to be avoided at all costs. I add fear of pear physique to my case against the fruit. This is as irrational as my preference for cooked pears. But I'm only human.

A pear is by nature contrarian. "The aloof, aristocratic pear, harder to grow, fussier about its surroundings, resists efforts to reduce it to uniformity," writes Waverley Root. The best eating pears—Comice, Bartletts, and Anjous—tend to fall apart when cooked. The cook is left with the less alluring flavor and more accommodating physique of the Bosc, Nelis, and Seckel pears.

The cook must move gently. Even the pear equivalent to apple sauce must be cooked slowly and carefully. Roasting pears requires less heat and more butter and sugar than apples. Poaching pears, whether for the classic *poires Hélenè* with chocolate sauce or to top with a granita, is more of a coddle than a poach.

I find it difficult to forgive a raw pear for not being an apple. At the same time, I never cease to be amazed by the versatility of a pear, its ability to conjure different faces in the face of different spices, its predilection for bridging the cold weather by assimilating warm, sweet, and vaguely mysterious tastes, its way of softening and giving, which I find so unforgivable, but only because I found pears first in a can.

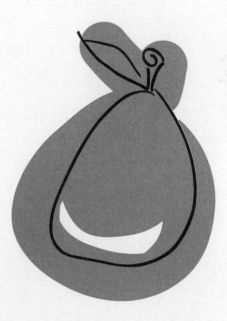

Pan-Roasted Pears with Honey, Hazelnuts, and Stilton

½ cup hazelnuts
2 teaspoons unsalted butter
2 large firm cooking pears like Bosc or Nelis, peeled, halved, and cored
⅓ cup honey
4-ounce wedge Stilton cheese, quartered

1. Preheat the oven to 350° F.

2. Spread the hazelnuts on a baking sheet and bake until toasted, about 10 minutes. Put the nuts between 2 kitchen towels and rub to remove as much skin as possible. Coarsely chop the nuts and set aside.

3. Melt the butter in a medium cast-iron skillet over medium-high heat. Add the pears and cook until caramelized on both sides, about 3 to 5 minutes. Reduce the heat and add the honey to the skillet. When the honey melts, turn the pears to coat them on both sides. Cover and cook until the pears are tender but not too soft, about 5 minutes.

4. Cut each pear half across into ¼-inch slices, keeping the shape intact. Place each half pear onto a plate and fan it forward. Place a piece of Stilton beside the pear and scatter some hazelnuts on the plate. Serve immediately.

Serves 4

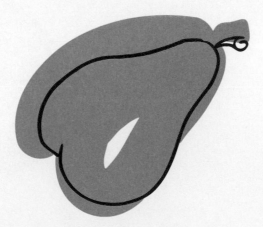

Pork Tenderloin with Pears and Ginger Beer Sauce

1 teaspoon vegetable oil
2 pork tenderloins
2 teaspoons kosher salt
Freshly ground pepper to taste
8 medium red potatoes, quartered
16 Seckel pears, peeled, stemmed, and cored through the bottom
2 cups ginger beer

1. Preheat the oven to 375° F.

2. Heat the oil over medium-high heat in a flameproof and ovenproof roasting pan. Season the pork with 1 teaspoon of the salt and pepper and place in the pan. Cook until browned on all sides, about 6 minutes. Remove the pork from the pan and set aside. Add the potatoes to the pan and season with the remaining teaspoon salt and pepper. Roast for 15 minutes.

3. Add the pears to the pan and roast for 5 minutes longer. Push the potatoes and pears to the side of the pan and place the pork tenderloins in the center. Roast until the pork is only slightly pink in the center, about 15 minutes. Remove the pork, potatoes, and pears from the pan and place the pan over medium heat. Add the ginger beer and cook, stirring and scraping the bottom of the pan. Reduce to ½ cup, about 5 minutes.

4. Cut the pork into 1-inch slices. Divide the pork, potatoes, and pears among 4 plates and spoon the sauce over. Serve immediately.

Serves 4 as a main course

Roasted Pear Cake with Chocolate Sauce

CAKE

> 4 large firm pears like Bartletts, peeled, halved, cored, and cut across into ¼-inch slices
>
> ½ pound (2 sticks) unsalted butter, softened
>
> 2½ cups sugar
>
> 4 large eggs
>
> 1½ teaspoons vanilla extract
>
> 4 cups all-purpose flour
>
> 1 teaspoon kosher salt
>
> 3 teaspoons baking powder

SAUCE

> 6 ounces bittersweet chocolate, coarsely chopped
>
> 1 cup heavy cream
>
> 2 tablespoons brandy

1. Preheat the oven to 400° F. Butter and flour a 10-inch tube pan.

2. Spread the pear slices on a baking sheet and roast until tender, about 10 minutes. Transfer the pears to a food processor and puree until smooth. Set aside. Reduce the oven temperature to 350° F.

3. Cream the butter and sugar with an electric mixer until light and fluffy. Add the eggs, one at a time, mixing until very light; batter may appear curdled at this point. Mix in the vanilla and the pear puree. Sift together the flour, salt, and baking powder. Mix the dry ingredients into the batter just until combined. Scrape the batter into the prepared pan and bake until the top springs back when touched in the center, about 1 hour. Place on a rack to cool. Turn the cake out of the pan and re-invert onto a cake plate.

4. Put the chocolate in a double boiler over barely simmering water. Stir occasionally until melted. Whisk in the cream and brandy. If the sauce was made ahead, rewarm before serving. To serve, place a slice of cake on a plate and spoon the chocolate sauce beside it.

Serves 8 to 10

THERE ARE NUTS EVERYWHERE

Nuts, at least the botanical sort, were probably more prevalent and certainly more prominent at the table when humans were hunters and gatherers. Nuts have been found in middens as far back as the middle Paleolithic period, when cave dwellers in northern Iraq ate chestnuts, walnuts, pine nuts, and acorns. The foodstuff may predate grains since, as Harold McGee notes in *On Food and Cooking*, the transcontinental distribution of many nut trees suggests that the trees existed before America and Europe slipped apart, over 60 million years ago.

Nut trees need little more than time to bear their edible seeds, but time in the case of nuts means decades. Nuts were serendipitous to gatherers and therefore a boon, but as a crop for commercial growers, nuts are less than efficient. In addition, nuts offer a decent cache of protein and a dense source of fat, up to 60 percent by weight, a nutritional profile that was presumably more attractive to cavemen than svelte-minded modern urban dwellers.

In the past, nuts were ground into flour and meal that were used to make bread or thicken porridges. Today, nuts are an adjunct. Spiced and sugared to make a sweet, baked in desserts or used to enrich poultry, vegetables, or salads, nuts bear witness to the past.

The long-standing attachment to nuts is reflected in how often their flavor is used to describe other foods: nutty brown butter, a ripe cheese with nut tones, the nuttiness of a baked squash, the nut flavors in the aftertaste of certain big red wines, the hint of nut in meaty mushrooms. Nutty means a sweet earthiness. The industrious squirrel is not far from mind.

At the same time, a lost mind is called a "nut." Several food historians say that the Romans saw the walnut as a paradigm of the human brain. The green husk was the scalp, the hard shell was the skull, the parchment within that housed the two halves of the nut was membrane. The Romans, according to Waverley Root, concluded that nuts had a homeopathic ability to cure headaches. Of course, the resemblance can be interpreted both ways. In 1393, the anonymous *Le Ménagier de Paris* claimed that nuts caused headaches.

Botanists are stricter than psychiatrists in defining a nut. For the botanist, a nut refers only to a one-seeded fruit with a hard shell rather than a fleshy epidermis. By this definition only acorns, hazelnuts, beechnuts, and chestnuts are real nuts. Almonds and walnuts, as well as the American pecan, are oversized seeds of a drupe, or fleshy fruit, like a peach, in which the nut is a stone.

The kitchen is more expansive than the laboratory. Cooking-wise, a nut is a nut. The almond is by far the most popular nut in the United States, though I find its flavor more sympathetic to spring and prefer in the winter to cook with walnuts, pecans, and hazelnuts.

Also known as the filbert, the hazelnut is an ancient nut of temperate regions that was used in China five thousand years ago and is grown today in Europe and the Pacific Northwest. The hazelnut tastes sweet. Its oil is prized in France, where it is used to dress winter salads. The nut itself is dense and abiding and lends itself to being ground for cakes or to encrust poultry or fish for frying.

Perhaps because the hazelnut is only recently gaining wide popularity in the American kitchen, it has the allure of an effete, high-class nut. Walnuts, on the other hand, which are second only to almonds in American consumption, are more proletarian. Native to Asia, Europe, and North America, walnuts, which despite their botanical drupiness are easily shelled, are mild and versatile. They are sweet when augmented with sugar, spicy when glazed in the Cantonese fashion. Walnuts are willing to go either way.

Pecans, on the other hand, remain inseparable from the American South. The nut is actually a kind of hickory nut indigenous to the Mississippi River valley. Southerners, particularly Texans, presumably had a jump on employing the nut in bourbon-laced pies and sticky buns, spicing and sugaring them, grinding them into cakes, and using them to stud pralines.

Nuts, like people, never completely escape their past. A walnut can be used with Stilton cheese as a counterpoint to a winter salad, but it remains essentially a common nut. Hazelnuts can be used in pies or breads, yet the nut remains an aristocrat. Pecans can be combined with mustard to coat chicken breasts, but the dish will evoke the languor of the South despite the fact that it was created by David Leiderman, a New York restaurateur.

The persistent nature of a nut is responsible for part of its charm and much of the comfort it brings to the winter kitchen. And then there is the sweetness. In the past few years, pushcarts selling honey-roasted nuts have begun to appear on street corners in Manhattan, a sweet nutty smell unfurling above the carts and drifting along some of the city's most beleaguered sidewalks like wisps of well-being.

Nuts are tied to winter holiday cooking, but that undeniable element of nostalgia doesn't fully explain the swoon their smell triggers. There is something also about the way a tough nut can be heated without softening, unlike onions or other cold weather vegetables. Nuts don't relent; they remain stalwart. The smell of roasting nuts—and with very few exceptions, nuts should always be lightly toasted before use—is hopeful, head turning, an irresistible talisman to surviving and thriving.

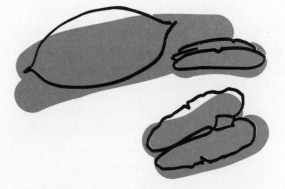

Roasted Capon with Pecan Stuffing

½ pound hot Italian sausage

2 small onions, chopped

Capon liver, chopped

3 cups crumbled stale cornbread

4 cups stale white bread, cut into ½-inch cubes

2 cups pecans, toasted and coarsely chopped

¾ cup dried cranberries, plumped in hot water and drained

1½ cups chicken broth, homemade, or low-sodium canned broth

1 tablespoon chopped fresh sage

¼ cup chopped Italian parsley

1 teaspoon kosher salt, plus more to taste

Freshly ground pepper to taste

1 capon, about 8 pounds, trimmed of excess fat and wing tips removed

1. Preheat the oven to 425° F.

2. Cook the sausage in a large skillet over medium heat, breaking it up with the back of a spoon, until browned, about 5 minutes. Add the onions and cook until softened, about 5 minutes. Add the liver and cook until brown, about 2 minutes. Transfer to a large bowl and add the cornbread, white bread, pecans, and cranberries. Add the broth and mix well. Stir in the sage, parsley, 1 teaspoon of salt, and pepper.

3. Fill the cavity with about half the stuffing and tie the legs together. Place the remaining stuffing in a baking dish and set aside. Place the capon on a rack in a large roasting pan. Season the capon skin with salt and pepper. Roast for 30 minutes, basting twice. Lower the oven temperature to 350° F. Continue roasting, basting every 20 minutes, until the juices run clear when pricked in the thickest part of the thigh, about 2 hours longer. Let stand for 10 minutes before carving.

4. About 40 minutes before the capon is done, put the extra stuffing in the oven and bake for 30 minutes. Carve the capon and serve with stuffing.

Serves 8 as a main course

Rich Hazelnut Chocolate Cake

½ pound (2 sticks) unsalted butter, cut into 1-inch pieces
8 ounces Callebaut bittersweet chocolate, coarsely chopped
8 large eggs, separated
1¼ cups granulated sugar
¾ cup hazelnuts, toasted, skinned, and ground
1 tablespoon hazelnut liqueur
Confectioners' sugar

1. Preheat the oven to 325° F. Butter and flour a 10-inch springform pan.

2. Combine the butter and chocolate in a double boiler over barely simmering water. Stir frequently until melted. Whisk the egg yolks with ¾ cup of the sugar. Whisk in the chocolate mixture, hazelnuts, and liqueur.

3. Using an electric mixer, beat the egg whites until soft peaks form. Gradually add the remaining sugar and beat to firm peaks. Stir a third of the whites into the chocolate mixture. Fold in the remaining whites. Scrape the batter into the pan and bake until a tester inserted into the center of the cake comes out slightly moist, about 55 minutes. Let cool. The cake will fall. Remove the sides of the pan and sift confectioners' sugar over the top of the cake. Cut into wedges and serve.

Serves 10

Pecan Indulgence

CRUST

1 cup all-purpose flour

½ teaspoon kosher salt

¼ pound (1 stick) cold unsalted butter, cut into 1-inch pieces

1 large egg yolk beaten with 1 tablespoon water

SUGARED PECANS

⅓ cup sugar

¼ teaspoon kosher salt

2 large egg whites

2 tablespoons water

2 cups pecan halves

FILLING

3 large eggs

¾ cup light corn syrup

¾ cup (packed) dark brown sugar

4 tablespoons (½ stick) unsalted butter, melted

1 tablespoon bourbon

1 teaspoon vanilla extract

¼ teaspoon kosher salt

1 cup chopped pecans

1. Combine the flour, salt, and butter in a food processor and pulse until mixture resembles coarse meal. Add the yolk mixture and process just until dough comes together. Wrap in plastic and refrigerate.

2. Preheat the oven to 225° F.

3. Combine the sugar and salt in a bowl. In another bowl, whisk together the egg whites and water until frothy. Toss the pecans in the egg white mixture. Drain, place in the sugar, and toss until well coated. Spread on a baking sheet and bake, stirring every 15 minutes, until dry, about 1 hour.

4. Whisk together the eggs, corn syrup, and brown sugar. Whisk in the melted butter, bourbon, vanilla, and salt. Stir in the chopped pecans.

5. Increase the oven temperature to 400° F. Roll out the dough to fit a 10-inch quiche dish and line the dish with the dough. Pour in the filling. Top with the sugared pecans. Bake for 15 minutes. Lower the oven temperature to 350° F. and bake just until the filling is set, about 20 minutes longer. Place on a rack to cool. Cut into wedges and serve.

Serves 8 to 10

Walnut Steamed Pudding with Vanilla-Orange Sauce

PUDDING

¼ pound (1 stick) unsalted butter, melted

½ cup granulated sugar

½ cup (packed) dark brown sugar

2 large eggs

½ cup milk

¼ cup brandy

2 cups all-purpose flour

1 tablespoon baking powder

1 teaspoon kosher salt

1 cup walnuts, toasted and ground

SAUCE

1 cup milk

½ vanilla bean, split and seeds scraped from pod

2 teaspoons grated orange zest

3 large egg yolks

2 tablespoons sugar

2 tablespoons fresh orange juice

1. Butter a 2-quart soufflé dish with a tight-fitting lid. Have ready a lidded pot, large enough to hold the covered soufflé dish with a rack that fits in the bottom of the pot. Bring a large kettle of water to a boil.

2. Whisk the butter, granulated sugar, and brown sugar together in a large bowl. Whisk in the eggs, milk, and brandy. In another bowl, combine the flour, baking powder, salt, and walnuts. Add to the liquid mixture and stir just until smooth. Scrape the mixture into the soufflé dish.

3. Cover the soufflé dish and place it on the rack in the pot. Pour in enough of the boiling water to come halfway up the sides of the dish. Cover the pot. Steam the pudding until a skewer inserted into the center barely comes out clean, about 1½ hours. Check occasionally to make sure there is enough water and that it is simmering; add boiling water to the pot if necessary.

4. Meanwhile, make the sauce. Combine the milk, vanilla bean pod and seeds, and the orange zest in a saucepan. Whisk the egg yolks and sugar together in a bowl. Bring the milk mixture just to a boil. Whisking rapidly, slowly pour the milk into the egg yolk mixture. Pour the mixture back into the pan and place over very low heat. Cook, stirring constantly, until the sauce thickens enough to coat the back of a spoon. Do not let it come to a boil. Remove from the heat and strain through a fine sieve. Whisk in the orange juice. Refrigerate until cold.

5. Carefully remove the soufflé dish from the pot, uncover, and let cool for 10 minutes. Unmold. Cut into wedges, place each wedge on a plate, and surround with orange sauce. The pudding can also be served at room temperature.

Serves 8

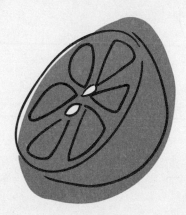

ALMOST
WINTER

AS THE WIND BLOWS

A bittersweet autumn doesn't plunge dramatically into the chilly vortex of winter; it evolves imperceptibly, weather, mood, and menu, while simultaneously the appetite for comfort rises.

On the cusp between autumn and winter, appetite becomes more and more the conservative curmudgeon as the world gets cold. But in late October and early November, the codgerly leanings can still be abated with unexpected variations on familiar themes. There is a solace in old-fashioned dishes, a reassurance in the aroma of baking bread or simmering stews. There is also a particular kind of sustenance in starchy meals at this time of year, one that is neither cerebral nor demanding, merely satisfying.

The homely and the elegant commingle in the late days of fall. I start thinking of roasting in a black iron skillet, braising or stewing beef or lamb shanks, making cassoulet. At the same time there are bacchanalian underpinnings to the homely yearnings of early winter. A hint of luxury defies an imminent winter, an indulgent sense of relish transcends pangs of foreboding. It's not winter really, no, not yet.

TO BAKE WITHOUT REMORSE

Some talk about the first time they slurped an oyster, or their introduction to béarnaise, but pizza was my first epicurean experience. I don't remember the precise moment of encounter. I know that from the beginning, pizza was extracurricular eating, consumed for its taste and texture and for what it represented rather than as a regularly scheduled meal. Pizza was, therefore, an excellent medium on which to cut connoisseur's teeth.

Pizza is ancient. The earliest prototypes were probably dough cooked over an open fire; modern pizzas are still an antidote to the civilizing forces you railed against in early adolescence. By sixth grade, pizza was firmly established as freedom food among my friends. The oil-drenched delivery box thrilled us. The smell of oregano was the very essence of self-determination. Pulling apart the pieces of the pie was one of life's early roulettes. You apologized profusely if the piece you pulled happened to bring along the cheese and pepperoni of a neighboring slice. But full restitution was as rare as a lottery winner's returning the prize.

We didn't know that the pizzas of our slumber parties and, later, of our college dorms were products of what Evelyne Slomon, in *The Pizza Book*, calls "the golden age of pizza in America." In retrospect, I see her point.

The halcyon years, according to Slomon, were from the early 1920s to the early 1950s, "before pizzas reached large-scale popularity and became doomed to mass production." During this time, the pies were typically cooked in coal-fired ovens, which blistered their crusts and gave them an irresistibly smoky flavor. Two distinct pizza styles emerged in the United States: first, the thin-crusted New York pizza and then, in the 1940s, the deep-dish Chicago pie. If you consider the map of the United States as a pizza today, the thickest crust is still in the middle; it grows thinner and thinner toward either coast.

Along with millions of other baby boomers, I acquired my personal taste in pizza toward the end of Slomon's golden age. As a population we are, therefore, outspoken about the particulars of pizza, the proper crust-to-topping ratio, for instance, the flavor of the sauce, the quality of the cheese. When mass production threatened the integrity of *our* pizza, we created the boutique form—individual pizzas with wafer-thin crusts topped with fanciful ingredients like chèvre, sundried tomatoes and fresh herbs.

Some disdain these as ersatz pizzas. They see the individual pies as a fitting emblem of "the me generation," as almost antithetical to the spirit of pizza. These people are, of course, overlooking the tradition of individual pizzas. In southern France, parts of which remained under Italian rule until the late nineteenth century, individual pies, called *pizzettes*—typically topped with caramelized onions, anchovies, and black olives, or simply with olive oil, roasted garlic, and rosemary—are still cooked in wood-burning ovens and served in small restaurants as a first course, snack, or light meal. The small California-style pizzas that began appearing in the last decade borrow more from Provence than they do from the baby boom. It is true that the rarefying of pizza can go too far. Caviar-and-crème fraîche pizza, for example, and wasabi-and-sushi pizza have left me deeply unsettled. But little pies topped with earthier combinations, like a roasted eggplant puree, a pungent tomato jam, or even a sprightly chiffonnade of artichokes, mint, and Parmesan, satisfy the primal pizza hunger. They are evolving emblems of individuality and freedom, which is, after all, where my taste for pizza began.

Pizza dough can be made ahead of time, divided into individual portions and either frozen (for up to a month) or stored in the refrigerator (for up to eight hours) before a party. Rolling the dough to make wafer-thin disks, improvising different toppings, and baking the pies are best done communally, after guests arrive. It breaks the ice, in a *Big Chill* kind of way.

The following topping recipes are suggestions; the varieties of pizza experience have yet to be definitively charted. "Your home oven, a bowl, a pan, and a good pair of hands are all that you really need to make pizza," says Slomon. Imagination doesn't hurt either. The recipe for basic dough that follows will bake crisp with a faintly tart taste on a cookie sheet in a hot oven. For an even crisper crust with a faintly smoky flavor, line the center of the oven floor with unglazed quarry tiles made of red clay, which are available at a ceramic tile supplier. In either case the baking pizza sends out a cozy, welcoming aroma.

There is something unspeakably soothing about nibbling at small pizzas with cocktails or as a first course. The way you have to cup the individual pies recalls every greasy slice that was ever folded and chomped. The singularity of designer pizza avoids the messy issues of who gets the largest slice. The pristine flavors and dietary correctness of these whole wheat pies, with their lean but unctuous toppings, deliver an updated promise of remaining, at least in appetite, forever young.

Basic Pizza Dough

1 cup warm water
3 packages active dry yeast
¾ cup whole wheat flour
2¼ cups unbleached all-purpose flour, plus up to 2 cups for kneading
1 tablespoon kosher salt
½ cup plain lowfat yogurt
2 teaspoons olive oil
2 tablespoons cornmeal
Toppings (pages 349–51)

1. Pour the warm water into a large mixing bowl, add the yeast, and gently stir with a fork until the yeast dissolves. Combine both flours and the salt and slowly add the flour mixture, 1 cup at a time, to the dissolved yeast. Add the yogurt and continue to mix the ingredients until the dough becomes soft and sticky, about 2 minutes.

2. Sprinkle a small handful of flour on a work surface. Knead the dough until it is smooth, about 5 minutes, adding flour as needed to prevent sticking. Brush the inside of a large bowl with the olive oil. Put the dough in the bowl and cover tightly with plastic wrap. Put the bowl in a warm place and let rise until doubled in volume, about 45 minutes to 1 hour. Punch down the dough, re-form it into a ball, cover the bowl with the plastic wrap, and let it rise for 1 hour.

3. Divide the dough into 8 balls. If you don't plan to use the dough within 2 hours, wrap each individually and refrigerate for up

to 8 hours or freeze. (Let frozen dough thaw in the refrigerator overnight before shaping.)

4. Preheat the oven to 425° F. To shape the dough, sprinkle a handful of flour onto a work surface. Using a rolling pin, roll each ball into a thin disk, about ⅛ inch thick and 6 to 8 inches in diameter, adding more flour as necessary to prevent sticking. Lightly dust 2 baking sheets with the cornmeal. Put 4 rounds of dough on each baking sheet and top with one of the toppings. Bake the pizzas until the crust turns golden brown, 15 to 20 minutes.

Makes 8 individual pizzas

Roasted Tomato Pizzettes

20 medium-size ripe tomatoes
2 large oil-packed sundried tomatoes, finely chopped
1 teaspoon crushed red pepper
¼ teaspoon sugar
½ teaspoon kosher salt
1 teaspoon freshly ground pepper
1 tablespoon olive oil
Basic Pizza Dough (page 348)
1 teaspoon *each* finely minced fresh thyme, savory, parsley, and basil

1. Preheat the oven to 425° F.

2. Put 16 tomatoes on a baking sheet and roast them until the skin begins to split, about 15 to 20 minutes. Set aside. When cool, remove the skin, core, and seeds and drain in a colander for 30 minutes. Puree in a food processor or blender until smooth.

3. Transfer the pureed tomatoes to a nonstick skillet. Add the sundried tomatoes, red pepper, sugar, salt, and pepper. Cover and simmer over medium-low heat until the mixture thickens, about 20 to 30 minutes.

4. Meanwhile, lower the oven temperature to 250° F. Core the remaining 4 tomatoes and cut them crosswise into twenty-four ¼-inch slices. Brush a baking sheet

with the olive oil, spread the tomato slices on the sheet, and bake until almost dry, about 2 hours.

5. Raise the oven temperature to 425° F. Shape the pizza dough as in Step 4 of the recipe. Spread a thin layer of the tomato sauce on top. Arrange the tomato slices in a circle on each pizza and sprinkle the herb mixture over the tomato slices. Bake until the crust turns golden brown, 15 to 20 minutes.

Yield: Eight individual pizzas

Onion Marmalade Pizzettes

2 tablespoons olive oil
4 pounds yellow onions, halved and cut crosswise into thin slices
1 teaspoon kosher salt
2 teaspoons freshly ground pepper
1 cup red wine
¼ cup red wine vinegar
2¼ cups chicken broth, homemade, or low-sodium canned broth
2 tablespoons sugar
Basic Pizza Dough (page 348)
½ cup oil-cured olives, pitted and halved

1. Preheat the oven to 425° F.

2. Warm the olive oil in a large cast-iron skillet over medium heat. Add the onions, salt, and pepper and cook, stirring constantly, until the onions begin to wilt, about 5 to 10 minutes. Mix the wine, vinegar, and broth in a nonreactive bowl. Pour the liquid over the onions. Sprinkle with sugar and bake until golden brown, about 1 hour. After 45 minutes have elapsed, stir the onions every 5 minutes. Set aside to cool.

3. Shape the pizza dough as in Step 4 of the recipe. Spread a thick layer of onion marmalade on each pizza and garnish with the olives. Bake until the crust turns golden brown, 15 to 20 minutes.

Makes 8 individual pizzas

Artichoke Pizzas

12 large fresh artichoke hearts, cooked and coarsely chopped
¼ cup plus 1 tablespoon fresh lemon juice
2 tablespoons olive oil
8 large raw artichoke hearts rubbed with lemon
¼ cup minced fresh mint
½ teaspoon kosher salt
1 teaspoon freshly ground pepper
Basic Pizza Dough (page 348)
¼ cup freshly grated Parmesan cheese

1. Preheat the oven to 425° F.

2. Put the cooked artichoke hearts in a food processor. Add 2 tablespoons of the lemon juice and 1 tablespoon of the olive oil and puree until smooth. Set aside. Cut the raw artichokes into very thin matchsticks and put them in a glass or ceramic bowl. Add the remaining lemon juice and olive oil, the mint, salt, and pepper and toss to combine.

3. Shape the pizza dough as in Step 4 of the recipe. Spread a layer of artichoke puree over the dough and lightly dust with Parmesan cheese. Bake until the crust turns golden brown, 15 to 20 minutes. Top the pizzas with the artichoke salad and serve.

Makes 8 individual pizzas

TO COOK A FINE SHANK

Like many things that live close to the earth, the shank is underrated and sometimes scorned. Traditional manuals of haute cuisine relegated the meat—beef, veal, or lamb—from the lower hind- and foreleg to the stockpot. Because it is so dense, and the bone it clings to so rich with marrow, shank meat yields a hearty broth, often so thick that it doesn't require much additional gelatin to turn it into aspic or additional thickening to make a sauce.

When shanks were served for dinner, it was a peasant meal. The Italians fashioned osso buco. The French braised the shank with Provençal herbs or used it to make headcheese or other terrines. The Germans marinated shanks in vinegar or roasted, broiled, or braised them—a dish, according to Horst Scharfenberg's *Cuisines of Germany*, that "you'd be willing to sell your birthright for."

There is a neat correspondence between the peasant nature of these dishes and the nature of a shank. The leg is the hardest-working part of a ruminant animal and, therefore, has the toughest meat. Shanks, like the people who traditionally called them dinner, can take a lot of heat.

Unlike more delicate and temperamental cuts of meat, a shank is hard to mistreat. In fact, the meat gets better as part of a slow-simmered mélange, taking on perfume and tenderness, giving body and heart. Shanks make a meal as hopeful as it is hearty. No wonder that long, cold days can hatch a hunger for shanks. No wonder the cut has suddenly been resurrected and gentrified.

In recent years, lamb and veal shanks have become stars on restaurant menus. At Alison on Dominick Street in lower Manhattan, the chef prepares a slow-stewed lamb shank that is faintly perfumed with anchovy and served with a soul-warming white bean puree. The seekers of romance who swarm to that restaurant are fierce about the dish. It seems to satisfy the yen for cozy intimacy. Long to simmer, slow to unfold, a shank is no flash in the pan.

For cooking, shanks are most frequently cut crosswise so that the meat encircles a cross-section of marrow bone, like a doughnut around its hole. Unlike the doughnut, however, the shank's raison d'être is the hole: The satiny marrow in the center of the bone makes meat eaters greedy. A friend who has everything (including a passion for marrow) used to bemoan his paucity of marrow spoons. Since shanks were low on the social ladder, the small, sterling shovels used to excavate the marrow were difficult to find.

My friend had scoured European antique stores for years and finally resigned himself to setting his table with the two mismatched strays he'd found. Since he had everything but the spoons, I kept up the search. But my resolve was unsuccessful in the face of food fashion: It wasn't until several years ago, when shanks were becoming chic, that a panoply of marrow spoons suddenly appeared at Au Bain Marie in Paris. I've since noticed them at other stores. Just as I've noticed shanks, neatly cut and tied, more often in the fresh meat counter lately than the deep freeze.

Butchers advise buying the hind shank, which is meatier; the less meaty foreshank remains the province of stocks. A good hind shank should be sawed into 1½-inch disks, which will have about five parts meat to one part bone. I suppose this makes a case for healthfulness. Though the shank is not particularly lean, its thick bone imparts a rich, meaty flavor. And because the broth in which it is simmered becomes as rich as the meat itself, a shank needs rice, a root vegetable puree, or noodles to act as an edible sponge. One eats more carbohydrate, less meat.

Shanks deliver a primordial, trophy-from-the-hunt kind of eating satisfaction. Even if you use a sterling marrow spoon.

Lamb Shanks   (Adapted from Alison on Dominick Street, Manhattan)

1 tablespoon vegetable oil
4 lamb shanks
1 onion, chopped
2 cloves garlic, minced
1 cup red wine
3 stalks celery, cut into large dice
3 carrots, cut into large dice
2 anchovy fillets
2 cups tomato puree
2 cups chicken broth, homemade, or low-sodium canned broth
1 bay leaf
1 tablespoon fresh thyme leaves
½ teaspoon whole black peppercorns
½ teaspoon kosher salt, plus more to taste
Freshly ground pepper to taste
1 cup Italian parsley leaves, chopped
White Bean Puree (page 357)

1. Heat the oil in a large heavy pot over medium heat. Add the shanks and sear until golden brown, about 5 minutes per side. Remove and set aside. Add the onion and the garlic. Sauté until the onion is translucent, about 5 minutes. Add the wine, increase the heat to high, and simmer until reduced to ½ cup, about 5 minutes.

2. Add the celery, carrots, anchovies, tomato puree, broth, bay leaf, thyme, peppercorns, and salt. Stir to combine. Return the shanks to the pot. Cover partially and simmer over medium-low heat until the meat falls off the bone, about 2 hours. Remove and discard the bay leaf. Season to taste with salt and pepper. Divide the shanks among 4 plates. Ladle the sauce over each shank. Garnish with parsley and serve immediately with the bean puree.

Serves 4 as a main course

Mediterranean Lamb Shanks

1 tablespoon olive oil

4 lamb shanks

1 large onion, peeled and minced

1 clove garlic, peeled and minced

1 large celery root, peeled and cut into ½-inch dice

3 carrots, peeled and cut into ½-inch dice

2 cups cracked green olives, pitted

2 tablespoons grated fresh ginger

1 cup red wine

3 cups chicken broth, homemade, or low-sodium canned broth

4 plum tomatoes, peeled, cored, seeded, and diced

2 tablespoons grated lemon zest

¼ teaspoon ground cumin

¼ teaspoon ground coriander

¼ teaspoon ground cinnamon

2 cardamom seeds, cracked

½ teaspoon crushed red pepper

1 bay leaf

½ teaspoon kosher salt, plus more to taste

1 teaspoon freshly ground black pepper, plus more to taste

½ cup fresh cilantro leaves, chopped

½ cup Italian parsley leaves, chopped

White Bean Puree (page 357)

1. Heat the olive oil in a large heavy pot over medium heat. Add the shanks and sear until golden brown, about 5 minutes per side. Remove and set aside.

2. Add the onion, garlic, celery root, carrots, olives, and ginger. Reduce the heat to medium and cook, stirring frequently, until the onion is translucent, about 5 minutes. Remove the vegetables from the pot and set aside. Add the wine, increase the heat to high and simmer until reduced to ½ cup, about 5 minutes. Add the broth, tomatoes, lemon zest, cumin, coriander, cinnamon, cardamom, red pepper, bay leaf, salt, and pepper. Stir to combine. Return the shanks and vegeta-

bles to the pot. Cover partially and simmer until the meat begins to fall off the bone, about 2 hours.

3. Combine the cilantro and parsley in a bowl. Set aside. Remove and discard the bay leaf. Season to taste with salt and pepper. Divide the shanks among 4 plates. Ladle the sauce over each shank. Garnish with the herb mixture and serve immediately with the bean puree.

Serves 4 as a main course

Veal Shanks with Preserved Lemon

2 lemons, thinly sliced

1½ teaspoons kosher salt

1 tablespoon sugar

2 cups water

½ pound double-smoked bacon, rind removed and cut into large dice (see Note)

4 pieces veal shank

1 large onion, peeled and minced

1 small clove garlic, peeled and minced

1 cup dry white wine

3 cups chicken broth, homemade, or low-sodium canned broth

2 carrots, peeled and cut into large dice

4 turnips, peeled and cut into large dice

¼ cup fresh thyme leaves

1 teaspoon freshly ground pepper

1 cup Italian parsley leaves, chopped

White Bean Puree (page 357)

1. Combine the lemons, 1 teaspoon of the salt, and the sugar in a small sauté pan. Cover with the water and simmer over medium heat until soft, about 15 minutes. Drain and set aside.

2. Cook the bacon in a large, heavy pot over medium-low heat until golden,

about 5 to 10 minutes. Remove and set aside. Increase the heat to medium-high, add the shanks, and sear until golden brown, about 5 minutes per side. Remove and set aside.

3. Add the onion and garlic. Reduce the heat to medium and cook until the onion is translucent, about 5 minutes. Add the wine. Increase the heat to high and simmer until reduced to ½ cup, about 5 minutes. Add the broth, lemons, carrots, turnips, thyme, the remaining salt, and pepper. Return the shanks and bacon to the pan. Cover partially and simmer until the meat falls off the bone, about 2 hours.

4. Divide the shanks among 4 plates. Ladle the sauce over each shank. Garnish with parsley and serve with the bean puree.

Serves 4 as a main course

> Note: Double-smoked bacon is available at some supermarkets and butcher shops. Slab bacon may be substituted.

White Bean Puree

1 pound Great Northern beans, soaked in water overnight and drained
2 bay leaves
3 cloves garlic, crushed
4 sprigs fresh thyme
4 cups chicken broth, homemade, or low-sodium canned broth
½ teaspoon kosher salt, plus more to taste
1 teaspoon freshly ground pepper, plus more to taste

Combine all the ingredients in a large saucepan over high heat. Bring to a boil, lower the heat to medium and simmer, uncovered, until the beans are soft, about 1½ to 2 hours. Remove the bay leaves and thyme sprigs. Transfer to a food processor and puree until smooth. Season to taste with salt and pepper.

Serves 4 to 6 as a side dish

WINTER

A SELFISH APPETITE

With the exception of the rare storm that might block the road to the local grocery, the man-over-nature mood of winter is no longer based on reality. But the winter appetite still harbors a fantasy of survivalism. At no other time of the year do we eat, or at least hunger for, big roasts and birds dripping with fat and juice. The urge alone would seem to force a confrontation with the fact that to sustain life, humans take life. Yet the harsh nature of the season protects us from embarrassment. The cold creates a closed-in life and a selfish appetite.

Early evenings and interminable nights fuel the same phenomenon. If the natural response to cold is to clutch and protect oneself, the response to living in more darkness than light is to turn inward and move with caution. Slow cooking—the long simmering of a winter stew or the baking of a casserole—embodies the cautious, self-occupied mood of winter.

Most cold-weather ingredients, dowdy root vegetables, cabbages and potatoes, connote hardship and are demanding. Like the winter soul, the season's produce cries me-me-me and requires slow, constant heat before relinquishing its bitterness and turning sweet. Paradoxically, slow cooking also makes one consider, at least briefly, something other than oneself. One must think about the ingredients, imagine and project the transformation that heat and seasoning will bring about. Slow cooking is a contemplative act that results in tenderness, even if only toward dinner.

A stew pot echoes a cauldron. And roasting, the other cooking technique particular to winter, summons the atavistic memory of the hunt and the subsequent orgiastic feeding. The constant flame mandated by both techniques seems, at least in a postdiluvian sense, capable of banishing the demons and doubts that thrive in the dark. The result of either cooking method is a communal meal. The winter appetite stretches foward from the selfish and singular to the social.

In the end, a satisfying winter meal is one that says "we're all in this together." Is it mere coincidence that the techniques the season's ingredients demand produce steam that soothes the senses and blankets the kitchen windows? Baby, it's cold outside. And when night begins at 5 P.M., the stirrings of dinner can seem like the only buffer between the vulnerable self and the mean, dark world.

THE LIFE AND TIMES OF A FINE PUREE

Squash and carrots, turnips and parsnips, celery and yams are too dowdy to be coy and too assertive to possess mystery. Their mealy texture and stalwart flavor render them incapable of teasing the senses. They are fated, instead, to offer solace and, when pureed, a mashed-potato kind of comfort.

Hence, the accord between winter's vegetables and the season's appetite. Pureed, the root vegetables of late fall and early winter are a soothing, sturdy panacea for the chilly emptiness brought on by wet winds and fallen leaves. Like a favorite sweater, a puree warms and comforts. It provides an uncomplicated pleasure, and one that's been underexplored.

Root-vegetable purees can make a light winter meal, thicken pan juices for gravy, or serve as condiments or foils for fish or roast meat. Thinned with cream, milk, or broth, a root-vegetable puree can also make a velvety soup.

Rather than push the creative limits of purees, however, cooks tend to take them for granted. Straight chestnut puree is for the holidays; plain potato or squash are standard most other times. The advent of the food processor has aided and abetted this diminished inspiration: As the act of making a puree was streamlined, so was the thought that went into it.

Pressing cooked vegetables through ricers, food mills, or fine-mesh strainers not only renders a puree more intriguing in texture but also gives the cook time to taste and smell it. Enveloped in a cloud of steam while pushing cooked vegetables through a sieve, you become quite intimate with your ingredients and begin to sense the subtler flavors lurking there, waiting to be complemented or enhanced.

Roasted beets with a dressing of allspice, cloves, and walnut oil suddenly become a wonderful accompaniment to smoked sausage or pork chops or, served with braised cabbage and rice, the centerpiece of a vegetarian meal. Butternut squash wants ancho chilies and then yearns to be a bed for sliced roasted chicken, barbecued shrimp, or, teamed up with black beans, the filling for a burrito.

A touch of spice—orange and ginger for butternut squash, for instance—can turn the mundane into the sublime. Something similar happens when the unexpected are paired: Apples pureed with sweet potatoes make an excellent accompaniment to roast pork or ham or a whole meal if served with a bitter green salad and Roquefort cheese.

Roasting, rather than boiling or steaming, lends a slightly caramelized note that mellows and softens the hard-scrabble nature of winter vegetables. With a little imagination and minor acts of alchemy, the dross of winter produce can be pushed and sieved into gold.

Orange-and-Ginger Butternut Squash Puree

1 medium butternut squash, peeled and cut into ½-inch cubes
1½ teaspoons grated fresh ginger
1 teaspoon grated orange zest
1 teaspoon kosher salt, plus more to taste
Freshly ground pepper to taste

Put the squash in a medium saucepan and cover with cold water. Place over medium-high heat and bring to a boil. Reduce the heat and simmer until tender, about 10 minutes. Drain well. Transfer the squash to a food processor. Add the ginger and orange zest and process until smooth. Add salt and pepper. Divide among 4 plates and serve.

Serves 4 as a side dish

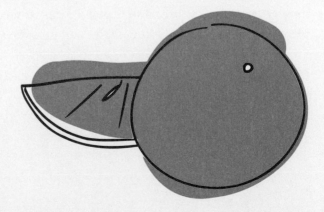

Winter Vegetable Puree

1 large celery root, trimmed, peeled, and cut into ½-inch cubes

2 medium baking potatoes, peeled and cut into 1-inch cubes

2 medium turnips, peeled and cut into ½-inch cubes

4 medium leeks, white parts only, washed well and cut across into 1-inch pieces

1 tablespoon kosher salt, plus more to taste

Freshly ground pepper to taste

Combine the celery root, potatoes, turnips, and leeks in a large saucepan and cover with cold water. Place over medium-high heat and bring to a boil. Reduce the heat and simmer until all of the vegetables are tender, about 30 minutes. Drain well and pass the vegetables through a ricer. Add salt and pepper to taste. Divide among 4 plates and serve immediately.

Serves 4 as a side dish

Roasted Apple and Sweet Potato Puree

2 large sweet potatoes, pricked several times with a fork

2 Granny Smith apples

⅛ teaspoon ground cardamom

Kosher salt and freshly ground pepper to taste

1. Preheat the oven to 450° F.

2. Place the sweet potatoes on a baking sheet and roast for 15 minutes. Place the whole apples on the baking sheet with the sweet potatoes. Roast until potatoes and apples are soft, about 25 minutes.

3. Peel the sweet potatoes. Pass the apples and the sweet potatoes through a food mill into a medium bowl. Stir in the cardamom and add salt and pepper. Divide among 4 plates and serve immediately.

Serves 4 as a side dish

Butternut Squash and Ancho Chili Puree

1 ancho chili
1 medium butternut squash, peeled and cut into ½-inch cubes
¼ teaspoon ground cumin
1 teaspoon kosher salt, plus more to taste
Pinch cayenne (optional)

1. Put the ancho chili in a small saucepan and cover with water. Bring to a boil. Reduce the heat and simmer until chili is soft, about 10 minutes. Remove the chili from the liquid. When cool enough to handle, stem the chili, split it open, and scrape out the seeds.

2. Meanwhile, put the squash in a saucepan and cover with water. Bring to a boil over medium-high heat. Reduce the heat and simmer until the squash is tender, about 10 minutes. Drain well and transfer the squash to a food processor. Add the chili and the cumin and process until smooth, stopping to scrape down the sides of the bowl. Season with the salt and cayenne, if desired. Divide among 4 plates and serve immediately.

Serves 4 as a side dish

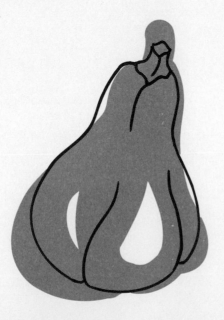

Spiced Beet Puree with Walnut Oil

6 medium beets, with 1-inch stem attached
2 large cloves garlic, unpeeled
2 bay leaves
4 cloves
4 allspice berries
1 teaspoon walnut oil
2 teaspoons kosher salt

1. Preheat the oven to 400° F.

2. Place the beets, garlic, bay leaves, cloves, and allspice on a large double sheet of aluminum foil. Wrap up into a package. Roast until the beets are tender, about 2 hours.

3. Discard the bay leaves, cloves, and allspice berries. Remove the stems from the beets and slip off the skins. Transfer the beets to a food processor and process until smooth. Stir in the walnut oil and the salt. Divide among 4 plates and serve immediately.

Serves 4 as a side dish

TAKING STOCK

Undeterred by current medical recommendations for temperance in the weight-loss department, undaunted by repeating the Sisyphean task of attempting, once again, to whittle away poundage during the months when damp cold winds send any sensible body rushing for something soulful, rib-sticking, and rich with fat, almost everyone I know greets January with firm resolutions to diet.

It's a national ritual and it usually lasts about a month. In the first seven days, determination is fierce and pounds tend to be sacrificed to the pagan god of thinness. In the weeks that follow, the reality of life and its social commitments, long-term eating habits and their comforts, and the improbability of cerebral resolve overwhelming biological pinings for any significant amount of time make their presence felt. Rather than acknowledging the difficulty of the weight-loss venture, dieters bow their heads in shame. They beat their breasts and beseech the pagan god of sloth to grant them release.

I've grown so accustomed to the ritual that, more than the ball dropping at Times Square or the pop of champagne corks across the land, it has come to symbolize a new beginning for me. I even look forward to the first week's victory stories. Of late, testimonies to the Lourdes-like effect of juice fasts have been particularly intriguing. But as real life impinges on steely self-discipline, a gray flannel cloud descends. As depressing as a tent dress when it's the only garment that fits, the weeks following firm and effective resolve are tedious and grim.

I've become obsessed with rewriting the second act of the annual shape-up drama. Rather than stocking up on chilly liquid cures, unsatisfying morsels of protein, and bushels of salad makings that are more appealing after a day at the beach than they are after a spin around the ice-skating rink, I've worked on developing a repertoire of intensely flavored vegetable broths that can be made ahead, frozen, and used to create soups, sauces and vinaigrettes or employed as a medium for poaching, braising, or steaming.

By using seasonal vegetables, the natural appetite of the cold gray months can be appeased, so the dieter is no longer battling at least one physiological urge. By using these broths inventively and generously, the hair-shirt mentality gives way to low-level sybaritic indulgence.

There are, of course, some potential culinary pitfalls. Unlike summer vegetables, winter vegetables can't be combined and simmered with abandon. If a rutabaga, parsnip, turnip, or cabbage is unregulated, it will do unfathomably terrible things to the flavor of a broth. The types of winter vegetables used and their proportion to each other are, therefore, rather exacting. Likewise, there is little flexibility in the length of simmering time as the broths from many winter vegetables and mushrooms can move from toothsome to acrid in a matter of minutes.

Like so many Jasons holding so many long-sought fleeces, chefs across the country have been raising beakers of tomato consommé toward the heavens and singing its praises.

"There is nothing like tomato consommé for poaching bass, other oily fish, or rich shellfish," says David Bouley, chef and co-owner of Bouley in Manhattan.

Charlie Trotter, the chef and co-owner of the Chicago restaurant that bears his name, seconds the refrain, adding that the tomato essence he makes from organic tomatoes at the end of the summer lends its sunny spell to rolled and stuffed chicken breasts, soups, and even pasta sauces throughout the winter.

Sounding vaguely reminiscent of the not-too-distant chorus for olive oil, these chefs and others extol the health benefits of the simple vegetable broth. They proclaim its versatility. They demonstrate how a vegetable that once had a mere supporting role can become the raison d'être of soulful dishes.

To distill that expansive tomato flavor with its clear, acidic underpinnings—and to use the resulting liquid as a medium for a soup, or as a glaze that marshals the mush of beans and the richness of scallops, or to poach a rather richly stuffed chicken breast—is to come quite close to the nectar of the gods. No wonder chefs partial to the medium get a little Olympian. Those who wish to burnish it like a prize use the traditional clarifying and straining methods to render a nearly clear substance. I suppose that if you have the time, the elegance of clarification isn't a bad thing. But the unclarified broth—even, *quelle horreur!* one made from canned plum tomatoes—does just fine.

I would say the same for the broth of the noble carrot, which, since it doesn't carry its own acid-notes, is less self-contained than the tomato. Still, when countered by a piece of fresh ginger, in the manner of Charlie Trotter, carrot broth becomes quite a respectable medium, for poaching or glazing shellfish, in particular. It also has enough backbone to stand up to boisterous root vegetables or even pork. Like tomato broth, carrot broth can be clarified. But, also like tomato broth, its natural hue is in itself remarkable.

I can't bring myself to advocate bleaching, er, clarifying. Rendering a substance visually unidentifiable is clever. But both the sunset burst of tomato broth and the Caribbean hue of carrot broth are friendly enough to do without another tiresome case of the clevers.

Vegetable broths can become the basis for stylish, appetizing dinners that don't break the fat and calorie bank. In fact, by making broths in large quantity and freezing them in pint containers for soup or in ice-cube trays so that smaller quantities can be used to make sauces or to poach single servings of meat or fish, the committed cook can pleasurably subvert the morality play of New Year's resolutions.

The broths acknowledge that desire, particularly the desire to eat everything in sight, isn't a sign of human frailty, a knell of dietary doom. It's a seasonal appetite, a predictable response to deprivation. Resisting and denying the appetite is useless. Cleverly appeasing that appetite honors reality in a way that's simple to sustain.

Wild Mushroom Broth

1 ounce dried porcini or other wild mushroom

2 pounds white mushrooms, wiped clean

½ pound fresh shiitake mushrooms, wiped clean

1 sprig fresh thyme

½ teaspoon black peppercorns

3 quarts cold water

Combine all the ingredients in a large pot over medium-low heat and simmer for 2 hours. Strain and discard the mushrooms. The broth will keep for up to 1 week in the refrigerator or up to 2 months in the freezer.

Makes 4 cups

Tomato Broth

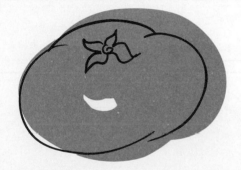

2 pounds ripe tomatoes, pureed to equal 5 cups
    (or drained unsalted, canned plum tomatoes)

1 tablespoon chopped fresh basil

1 tablespoon chopped Italian parsley

1 tablespoon chopped celery leaves

½ teaspoons kosher salt

¼ teaspoon freshly ground pepper

Combine all the ingredients in a saucepan over medium heat. Bring to a boil and remove from the heat immediately. Pass through a fine-mesh sieve, whisking occasionally to help the liquid pass through. The broth will keep for up to 1 week in the refrigerator. It will separate but needs only to be stirred. It can be frozen for up to 2 months.

Makes 3 cups

Carrot Consommé

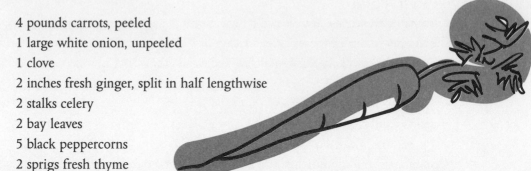

    4 pounds carrots, peeled
    1 large white onion, unpeeled
    1 clove
    2 inches fresh ginger, split in half lengthwise
    2 stalks celery
    2 bay leaves
    5 black peppercorns
    2 sprigs fresh thyme
    3 quarts cold water

Combine all the ingredients in a large pot over very low heat. Simmer for 3 hours. Remove from the heat and cool for 1 hour. Strain through a fine-mesh sieve. Discard the vegetables and reserve the broth. The broth will keep up to 1 week in the refrigerator. It can be frozen for up to 2 months.

Makes 8 cups

Roasted Vegetable Broth

    1 teaspoon vegetable oil
    8 large carrots, peeled and cut into large pieces
    2 large onions, peeled and quartered
    2 turnips, peeled and halved
    1 clove garlic, peeled
    3 quarts plus 1 cup cold water
    1 clove
    1 sprig fresh thyme
    1 teaspoon grated fresh ginger

1. Preheat the oven to 400° F.
2. Lightly oil a baking pan or cast-iron skillet and fill it with the carrots,

onions, turnips, and garlic. Roast, turning frequently, until well caramelized, about 45 minutes to 1 hour.

3. Transfer the vegetables to a soup pot. Place the roasting pan over medium-high heat, add 1 cup of water, and scrape the bottom with a wooden spoon to loosen any bits stuck to the pan. Pour into the soup pot. Add 3 quarts of water, the clove, and thyme and simmer for 2 hours.

4. Remove from heat. Add the ginger. Allow the broth to stand for 1 hour. Strain and discard the vegetables. The broth will keep in the refrigerator for up to 1 week. It can be frozen for up to 2 months.

Makes 2 cups

Wild Mushroom Broth with Buckwheat Noodles

1 teaspoon vegetable oil
½ pound shiitake mushrooms, stemmed and cut into 1-inch bands
8 cups Wild Mushroom Broth (page 371)
½ teaspoon soy sauce
1 pound soba (Japanese buckwheat noodles)
½ cup minced scallions

1. Heat the oil in a large sauté pan. Over high heat sauté the mushrooms until softened, about 3 to 5 minutes. Set aside.

2. Pour the mushroom broth into a saucepan and simmer over medium heat until reduced by half, about 30 minutes.

3. Add the soy and the noodles, stir well, and simmer until tender. Remove from heat. Stir in the mushrooms. Ladle into 4 bowls, garnish with scallions, and serve.

Serves 4 as a first course or 2 as a main course

Spiced Shrimp and Carrot Soup

8 cups Carrot Consommé (page 372)
½ pound orzo or pasta stars
1 pound cooked peeled tiny shrimp
2 tablespoons grated fresh ginger
1 cup finely diced carrots
½ cup grated fresh fennel
Kosher salt and freshly ground pepper to taste
2 tablespoons minced scallions
1 tablespoon minced Italian parsley or cilantro

Bring the consommé to a boil in a large pot. Add the orzo, reduce the heat to medium, and cook for 7 minutes. Add the shrimp, ginger, and carrots and cook for 2 minutes more. Add the fennel and cook for 1 minute. Season with salt and pepper. Ladle into bowls, garnish with minced scallions and parsley, and serve immediately.

Serves 4 as a main course

Warm White Bean and Scallop Salad with Spicy Tomato Glaze

2 cups dried white beans, soaked in water overnight and drained
10 sprigs fresh thyme
1 bay leaf
¼ teaspoon kosher salt, plus more to taste
2 cups Tomato Broth (page 371)
1 strip orange zest, 1 × 3 inches
¼ teaspoon freshly ground pepper
12 sea scallops, cleaned
2 bunches (about 6 ounces each) arugula or
    watercress, heavy stems removed
½ cup minced red onion

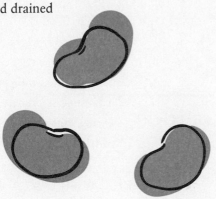

1. Combine the beans, thyme, and bay leaf in a pot over medium-low heat. Add enough cold water to cover and cook until almost tender, about 1 to 1½ hours. Add ¼ teaspoon of salt and continue cooking until tender, about 10 more minutes. Remove from heat and set aside.

2. Combine the broth and orange zest in a pot over low heat and simmer for 1 minute. Add the pepper and the scallops and poach until barely cooked, about 2 minutes. Remove the scallops and orange zest. Return the broth to the heat and boil until it has reduced to about 1 cup and is thick and syrupy, about 5 minutes. Season to taste with salt.

3. Arrange the arugula in the bottom of 4 large soup bowls. Spoon in the beans and put 3 scallops on top of each. Drizzle with tomato glaze, sprinkle with onion, and serve immediately.

Serves 4 as a main course

Salmon Braised in Winter Vegetable Essence

1 tablespoon olive oil

2 large leeks, white and light green parts only, washed and cut into 1-inch
    rounds

2 large heads Belgian endive, halved, cored, and cut into 1-inch strips

½ cup white wine

¾ cup Roasted Vegetable Broth (page 372)

2 tablespoons prepared horseradish

4 pieces salmon fillets, 4 ounces each, skinned

Kosher salt and freshly ground pepper to taste

1. Pour the olive oil into a pot that has a steamer insert and place over medium heat. Add the leeks and endive and cook until they begin to brown, about 5 minutes. Add the white wine and use a wooden spoon to scrape the pan well. Add the broth and the horseradish and bring to a boil.

2. Season the salmon lightly with salt and pepper and place it in the steamer over the vegetables. Cover and steam until salmon is cooked, about 5 minutes. Remove the steamer and divide the vegetables among 4 plates. Top each with a piece of salmon fillet. Ladle sauce over each and serve.

Serves 4 as a main course

Sweetbreads Braised in Wild Mushroom Broth

1 cup all-purpose flour

¼ teaspoon ground clove

¼ teaspoon kosher salt

¼ teaspoon freshly ground pepper

1 pound sweetbreads, cleaned and divided into 4 servings

¼ teaspoon vegetable oil or vegetable spray

4 large shiitake or cremini mushrooms, stemmed and thinly sliced

1 teaspoon soy sauce

2 cups Wild Mushroom Broth (page 371)

1 tablespoon fresh thyme leaves

¼ cup minced scallions

¼ cup minced fresh tomato

1. Preheat the oven to 350° F.

2. Combine the flour, ground clove, salt, and pepper and dredge the sweetbreads in the mixture. Warm a cast-iron skillet over high heat, coat with vegetable oil, and quickly sear the sweetbreads.

3. Place each sweetbread piece in a small ovenproof soup bowl and top with a sliced mushroom. Add the soy sauce to the mushroom broth and divide evenly among the 4 bowls. Sprinkle each with thyme, scallions, and minced tomato. Cover and bake for 15 minutes. Uncover and serve immediately.

Serves 4 as a main course

Roasted Vegetable Fagioli with Winter Pesto

SOUP

    1 white onion, peeled and minced

    2 cloves garlic, peeled and minced

    1 teaspoon olive oil

    1 cup white fagioli beans, soaked in water overnight and drained

    8 cups Roasted Vegetable Broth (page 372)

    1 teaspoon kosher salt, plus more to taste

    ¾ teaspoon freshly ground pepper, plus more to taste

    2 carrots, peeled and diced

    1 celery root, peeled and diced

    1 turnip, peeled and diced

    ½ pound dried fusilli

    1 tablespoon sherry vinegar

PESTO

    3 tablespoons minced fresh sage

    3 tablespoons minced fresh rosemary

    3 cloves roasted garlic, peeled (page 175)

    2 oil-packed sundried tomatoes

    ¼ teaspoon capers

    2 tablespoons freshly grated Parmesan cheese

1. Combine the onion, garlic, and olive oil in a large soup pot over medium-low heat and cook until tender, about 5 minutes. Add the beans and broth. Season with salt and pepper and simmer until the beans are almost tender, about 1 hour.

2. When the beans are tender, add the carrots, celery root, and turnip and continue simmering until vegetables are barely tender, about 10 minutes. Add the fusilli and simmer until pasta is tender. Stir in the vinegar and adjust the seasoning with additional salt and pepper.

3. While the soup is cooking, make the pesto. Combine the sage, rosemary,

garlic, tomatoes, and capers in a blender or use a mortar and pestle to make a paste. Set aside.

4. Ladle the soup into 4 large bowls. Swirl a spoonful of pesto into each bowl, sprinkle with Parmesan cheese, and serve immediately.

Serves 8 as a first course or 4 as a main course

SWEET ON YAMS

Everyone has a private dinner, at least everyone I know. A friend, whose husband is out of town, talks about her baked potato supper as if it were a secret rendezvous. Another confesses to solitary evenings with Spam. On his bachelor evenings, one of my brothers looks forward to a meal of Frosted Flakes. Most private dinners are of a regressive nature and are executed furtively. In her book *Serve It Forth,* M. F. K. Fisher calls such meals "secret eatings."

My mother's private dinner was a quart-size chocolate milk shake and when she'd "had it with cooking," she served one to each of us. This happened perhaps five times in my entire life, but I remember each meal as an orgy and I remember that she looked embarrassed and pleased. In the winter, her moments of despair or abandon, whichever they were, yielded hot chocolate and cinnamon toast. I adapted the menu during college: half a peck of popcorn, one tankard of instant hot chocolate. The meal endured for nearly a decade. But now I bake yams.

I am not sure how it started. I know that it had to do with their smell. That burnt sugary, husky perfume reminds me of the pushcarts in Mexico City that hawk the toasted tubers. It takes me back to a New England fireplace where yams once roasted after a day of cross-country skiing. It reminds me of the smell that billows from Bob the Chef restaurant in Boston, and from Sylvia's Restaurant in Harlem. The smell is Thanksgiving, winter in Chinatown, a summer morning in a North Carolina market where the aroma of sweet potato pie filled the air. Every few months, on an evening when it's me and my yam, I waft between each memory in the 40 minutes it takes to bake the sweet tuber, as the aroma slowly builds and detonates into one big blast of well-being in my kitchen.

Forgive the rhapsody. As Popeye would say "I yam what I yam." And I am, by the way, not alone. In the *Invisible Man,* Ralph Ellison writes that the smell of Carolina yams roasting on a pushcart in Harlem brought a "stab of swift nostalgia" that stopped him like a shot: "At home we'd bake them in the hot coals of the fireplace, had carried them cold to school for lunch, munched them secretly, squeezing the sweet pulp from the soft peel as we hid from the teacher behind the largest book," he wrote. "Yes, and we'd loved them candied, or baked in a cobbler, deep-fat fried in a pocket of dough, oven roasted with pork and glazed with the well-browned fat; had chewed them raw—yams years ago."

This kind of yam memory consistently overwhelms actual botanical facts in America. What Americans call "yam" is in fact a sweet potato, and the confusion is enduring and entrenched.

The true yam, *Dioscorea,* a vining plant that probably originated in Asia, grows in the tropics, and can reach a size of up to six hundred pounds. On the Pacific Island of Ponape, writes Elizabeth Schneider in *Uncommon Fruits & Vegetables*, yams are described as two-man, four-man, and six-man yams, depending on how many it takes to carry them. It's tough to find even a two-hand yam in local groceries today. Clearly, the vernacular went awry.

According to "Seeds of Change," a display at the Smithsonian that charted the interchange of Old and New World foods, Columbus may have started the confusion. On his first journey in 1492, he was served sweet potatoes in the West Indies and wrote that they looked like yams and tasted like chestnuts. African slaves called them "nyam" or "nyami" because the sweet potato reminded them of their native yams.

The sweet potato, or *Ipomoea batatas*, is a member of the morning glory family that probably originated in tropical America and is now produced primarily in China, though Africa and Latin America are no weaklings in the international sweet potato stakes. In *Why We Eat What We Eat*, Raymond Sokolov writes that the International Potato Center in Lima, Peru, has gathered over five thousand types of sweet potatoes.

The true yam has a neutral starchy flavor. Sweet potatoes, on the other hand, earn their name, even though the deeper their orange hue and the sweeter their taste, the greater the chance that the sweet potato will be called a yam. The terms are considered interchangeable, and so are some of the spiritual properties with which they are imbued. So sacred is the tuber to the Trobriand islanders of the South Pacific that they build ornate houses to display them; the Cubans reserve them for special occasions; the Japanese use them as a homeopathic fertility drug.

When Shakespeare was writing, sweet potatoes were luxuries that were imported to England from Spain and were thought to be a potent aphrodisiac. "It was a luxury only to be enjoyed by the wealthy," according to *The History and So-*

cial Influence of the Potato. That reputation waned as sweet potatoes grew to rank second only to regular potatoes among the root crops of the world. Yet the epicurean perversity to worship only the rare hasn't stripped the tuber of its primitive powers.

I have friends who now eat yams as they once consumed an apple a day. They speak of the tuber's high carbohydrate content and low calorie count, its dense concentration of beta-carotenes, its vitamin A. They speak of yams as economical and convenient. But I suspect this is all just a socially acceptable way of explaining an evening alone with a yam. I can't blame them for needing an excuse. I have yet to serve either family or friends a meal of only baked yams.

I've edged toward going public with my private dinner. I began by slipping sweet potato puree next to roast chicken and proceeded to scalloped versions, gratins, and panfried cakes. A well cooked yam can convert. Along the way I learned to buy medium-size yams that weigh about a third of a pound, that are neither nicked nor pocked, and to store them in a cool place but not the refrigerator. This keeps them sweeter.

The closest I've come to making yams the center of a meal was when I cooked them with risotto at a family reunion. And that may be as close as I get.

One of my brothers complimented the dish and then asked: "How come you look so weird? It's like you're just as embarrassed as you are pleased."

Yam Soup with Yogurt

6 medium yams, peeled and cut into 1-inch chunks

1 red onion, coarsely chopped

1 small clove garlic, finely chopped

3 carrots, coarsely chopped

1 stalk celery, coarsely chopped

1 bay leaf

1 tablespoon fresh thyme

6 cups chicken broth, homemade, or low-sodium canned broth

½ teaspoon kosher salt

1 teaspoon freshly ground pepper

6 tablespoons plain lowfat yogurt

6 sprigs Italian parsley, stemmed and finely chopped

Put the yams, onion, garlic, carrots, celery, bay leaf, thyme, and broth in a large pot and bring to a boil over medium-high heat. Reduce the heat and simmer until the yams are tender, about 30 minutes. Working in batches, place the vegetables and broth in a blender until smooth. Pass the soup through a sieve. Season with salt and pepper. Ladle the soup into bowls, garnish with dollops of yogurt, sprinkle with chopped parsley, and serve.

Serves 6 as a first course or 4 as a main course

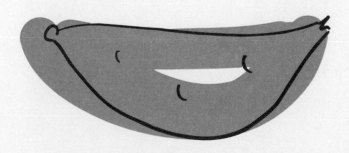

Baked Yams with Red Onions

3 medium red onions, cut into paper-thin round slices
3 medium yams, cut into thin round slices
2 cups apple cider
2 teaspoons brown sugar
½ teaspoon kosher salt
¼ teaspoon freshly ground pepper
1 tablespoon fresh thyme
1 tablespoon unsalted butter, cut into small pieces

1. Preheat the oven to 350° F.

2. Arrange the onion and yam slices in alternating layers in a 9-inch round or oval gratin dish. Pour the apple cider into a small saucepan, add the brown sugar, salt, and pepper, and stir over medium heat until the sugar dissolves. Pour the hot cider over the onions and yams and sprinkle with thyme. Dot with butter, cover the dish with foil, and bake for 1 hour.

3. Remove the foil and continue baking, basting often, until the onions and yams are tender, about 30 minutes. Divide among plates and serve.

Serves 4 to 6 as a side dish

Risotto with Yams and Sage

(Adapted from Union Square Café, Manhattan)

BROTH

  16 cups chicken broth, homemade, or low-sodium canned broth
  3 medium yams, peeled and cut in half
  1 carrot, peeled and cut into 1-inch pieces
  1 stalk celery, cut into 1-inch pieces

GARNISH

  ½ teaspoon olive oil
  1 teaspoon water
  ¼ teaspoon kosher salt
  ⅛ teaspoon cayenne
  1 cup slivered almonds

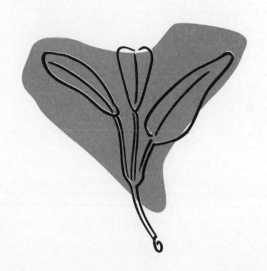

RISOTTO

  1 tablespoon unsalted butter
  1 white onion, peeled and minced
  3 cups Arborio rice
  ½ cup fresh sage leaves, minced
  1 tablespoon minced fresh chives
  1 tablespoon freshly grated Parmesan cheese
  ½ teaspoon kosher salt, plus more to taste
  1 teaspoon freshly ground pepper
  2 cups bitter greens, such as mustard or dandelion, rinsed and shredded
  1 cup fresh mozzarella, cut into ¼-inch dice

1. Combine the broth, yams, carrot, and celery in a large pot and bring to a boil. Reduce the heat and simmer until reduced to 10 cups, about 30 minutes. With a slotted spoon, remove 1 yam and cut it into ½-inch dice. Set aside. Remove the broth and remaining vegetables from the heat, puree in a blender, and set aside to cool.

2. Preheat the oven to 350° F.

3. Combine the olive oil, water, salt, and cayenne in a bowl. Add the almonds and toss to coat. Spread the almonds on a baking sheet and bake until golden, about 15 minutes. Remove from the sheet and set aside. The recipe can be prepared to this point up to 3 days before serving; refrigerate the broth and diced yam.

4. About 40 minutes before serving, warm the yam broth over low heat and bring the reserved yam to room temperature if necessary. Melt the butter in a heavy pot over low heat. Add the onion, cover, and cook until soft, about 5 minutes, stirring to avoid browning. Add the rice and stir well. Ladle in ½ cup of the reserved yam broth and stir. Increase the heat to medium-high and for the next half hour, continue ladling in the broth and stirring the rice. When 1 cup of yam broth remains, the rice should be tender. If it is not, add simmering water and continue stirring until it is. Remove from the heat immediately.

5. Vigorously stir in the remaining yam broth. This should make a very soupy porridge. Quickly stir in half the minced sage and chives, the Parmesan, and the diced yam. Season with salt and pepper. Stir in the greens. Carefully stir in the mozzarella. Divide among bowls. Garnish with a sprinkling of the spiced almonds and the remaining fresh sage and chives and serve immediately.

Serves 8 to 10 as a first course or 4 as a large main course

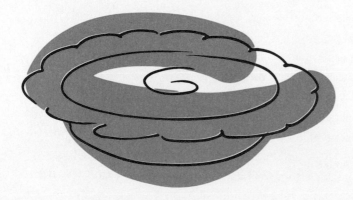

THE SQUARE ROOT

*I*t takes a lot to like a turnip. The squat little bulbs of bitterness are like a homely cousin or an old lover you'd rather not remember, unavoidable and inevitably embarrassing. The root is so persistent, so omnipresent from November to May, such a yeoman of the soup and stew pot that you accept it, grudgingly, in your kitchen. And then the turnip repays you by reeking of the hardscrabble, dirt-poor life.

A turnip's sulfurous aroma conjures difficult, unforgiving climes and the lives such environments dictate. As the Irish have shown, the only way to thrive on a turnip-heavy diet is through lyricism and poignancy. Some stout doesn't hurt either. Even as the mainstay of northern European diets for centuries, turnips conferred a kind of shame.

In the fifteenth century, one anonymous writer said that the Dutch turnip-eaters were like swine, "digging for roots." Rabelais called the people of France's Limousin region "turnip chewers." Even today, a real turkey of an artwork is deemed a *navet,* or turnip, in France. "One may suspect," writes Waverley Root, ". . . that one reason why the turnip was looked down upon was that it was so often a food of the poor."

Like cabbage, mustard greens, and brussels sprouts, to which it is related both botanically and aromatically, a turnip is definitely not an ingredient for a romantic dinner, a celebratory dinner, or for an evening when optimism is a desired guest. For, like a spiteful fairy, the turnip will infuse the meal with doubt and inexplicable sadness. A turnip belongs among friends and family. On evenings when the clan is bracing itself against cold winds, when each member is silently, sullenly, achingly aware of how fragile a thing contentment is, turn to the turnip.

On wet wool evenings, the turnip is actually upbeat. When one is tired and tentative, the turnip's unapologetic, I-am-what-I-am nature is reassuring.

In the first place, there is comfort in its longevity: most historians agree that turnips, which probably originated in Eurasia, are one of the oldest crops in existence. In his book *On Food and Cooking,* Harold McGee writes that turnips have been under cultivation for four thousand years. Before that they abounded in the wild, and he presents evidence that primitive Europeans relied on the stable, starchy food. The little round white turnip is the one most commonly available in the United States. It is better eating than the torpedo-shaped roots and, usually, also better than the yellow or so-called Swedish turnip, which is actually a rutabaga, and is best mashed.

In the second place, there is absolutely no way a cook can shoulder the blame for not transforming a turnip: Unlike onions or garlic, this contrarian root becomes *more*, not less, bitter the longer it cooks. Rather than teasing out a sweet inner nature, long baking or boiling simply draw from the turnip more of its sulfurous same. What a relief to have one thing in this life for which one is not accountable, one thing the cook can shrug off: It is what it is.

The cook must therefore take care not to overcook the turnip. At their freshest and youngest, white turnips, the small white bulbs with purple crowns which begin showing up in the early spring, can be shaved, like a radish, on salad. Later turnips, those that show up in the fall and winter and are as large as four inches in diameter, are more bitter. So are a lot of things this time of year; a modicum of misery does love company for a meal.

So the sympathetic cook makes a simple bisque, whose velvety texture softens the bitter edge of the turnip. He or she mashes the turnips, as the Horn & Hardart automat used to do. The same technique, with a lot more butter, was revived several years ago at the Union Square Café in Manhattan, where mashed turnips with a frizzle of caramelized shallots continues to be the main call of guests looking for solace in their vegetables.

Roasting a chicken with mashed turnips is a lesson in how the sweetness of the bird can mellow the taciturn root, without undermining the integrity of either party. James O'Shea, the owner of the West Street Grill in Litchfield, Connecticut, uses turnip pancakes to brace and flatter rich seafood.

But most turnip sorts of evenings seem to want something slowly simmered, something that fogs the kitchen windows, a meal that is perhaps more perfunctory and primitive than it is even vaguely effete.

Meals like this, when life is brittle as ice and just as prone to crack, seem to me a psychic hair-of-the-dog. Anyone inhaling the perfume of a cooking turnip knows that it smacks of just about everything there is to fear in this world. So a turnip-centric meal is cosmic relief, a culinary talisman that tastes surprisingly good.

Turnip Bisque

1 teaspoon olive oil

4 medium turnips, peeled and cut into 1-inch pieces

1 small baking potato, peeled and cut into 1-inch pieces

2½ cups chicken broth, homemade, or low-sodium canned broth

1¼ teaspoons kosher salt, plus more to taste

Freshly ground pepper to taste

3 tablespoons milk

1 teaspoon fresh thyme

1. Preheat the oven to 400° F. Brush a baking sheet very lightly with the olive oil.

2. Using a vegetable peeler, make long, very thin strips from 1 of the turnips. Place the strips on the baking sheet and bake until crisp and partly browned, about 6 minutes. Set aside.

3. Put the remaining turnips and the potato in a medium saucepan. Add 2 cups of the broth, and bring to a boil over medium-high heat. Reduce to a simmer and cook until vegetables are tender, about 15 minutes. Drain, reserving the liquid.

4. Transfer the vegetables and ¼ cup of the chicken broth to a food processor and puree until smooth. Add the reserved broth, salt, and pepper. Puree until smooth. Divide among 4 soup bowls. Drizzle some of the milk in a circle over the soup. Sprinkle some of the turnip crisps and thyme leaves in the center of each circle. Serve immediately.

Serves 4 as a first course.

Mashed Turnips with Crispy Shallots

(Adapted from Union Square Café, Manhattan)

1½ pounds turnips, peeled and coarsely diced
3 tablespoons unsalted butter, melted
1 cup shallots, peeled and thinly sliced
1 cup heavy cream
Kosher salt and freshly ground black pepper to taste
⅛ teaspoon freshly grated nutmeg
1 teaspoon minced Italian parsley

1. Put the turnips in a large pot of cold water and bring to a boil over medium-high heat. Cook until tender, about 15 minutes. Drain and puree in a food processor. Set aside.

2. Meanwhile, heat 2 tablespoons of the butter in a deep saucepan over medium heat. Add the shallots and sauté until they turn golden brown, about 15 minutes. Remove the shallots with a slotted spoon and drain on paper towels.

3. Set a heavy saucepan over medium heat. Add the cream and the remaining butter and bring to a simmer. Briskly stir in the pureed turnips. Season with salt, pepper, and nutmeg. Divide the puree among 8 serving plates. Garnish liberally with the shallots and lightly with parsley. Serve immediately.

Serves 8 as a side dish

Turnip Pancakes Topped with Cod and Smoked Salmon

8 medium turnips, peeled and cut into 1-inch cubes

4 nickel-size slices of fresh ginger, peeled and lightly smashed

2 teaspoons toasted sesame oil

2 teaspoons unsalted butter

¾ teaspoon kosher salt

Freshly ground pepper to taste

6 tablespoons all-purpose flour

Cornmeal

1 small cod fillet

Olive oil spray

1 thin slice smoked salmon, cut into 8 thin strips

3 tablespoons minced scallion, green parts only

1. Put the turnips and ginger in a large saucepan and cover with cold water. Add the sesame oil and bring to a boil over medium-high heat. Reduce the heat and simmer until the turnips are tender, about 20 minutes. Drain. Return the turnips to the pan and set over low heat until dry, 7 to 8 minutes, stirring often to prevent sticking.

2. Remove the turnips from the heat. Add the butter and mash with a hand masher until the turnips are slightly lumpy. Stir in the salt, pepper, and flour. Set aside to cool. Shape the turnip mixture into eight 3-inch patties. Dust with cornmeal. Cover with a towel and refrigerate for 1 hour. Let stand at room temperature for 30 minutes.

3. Meanwhile, steam the cod fillet until done, about 10 minutes. Cut into 1-inch pieces.

4. Lightly coat a large nonstick skillet with olive oil spray. Heat over medium heat until hot. Add as many of the pancakes as will fit without overcrowding. Cook until browned on both sides, about 3 minutes per side. Transfer to a heated serving platter and keep warm until all of the pancakes are cooked. Top each cake with a piece of cod. Coil the strips of smoked salmon and set 1 on each piece of cod. Sprinkle minced scallion over all. Serve immediately.

Serves 4 as a first course

Chicken Stuffed with Mashed Turnips

6 medium turnips, peeled and cut into ½-inch cubes
1 medium baking potato, peeled and cut into ½-inch cubes
2 teaspoons unsalted butter
1 teaspoon kosher salt, plus more to taste
Freshly ground pepper to taste
1 chicken, 3½ pounds

1. Put the turnips and potato in a saucepan and cover with water. Bring to a boil over medium-high heat. Reduce the heat and simmer until the vegetables are tender, about 12 minutes. Drain. Puree in a food processor. Stir in the butter, salt, and pepper.

2. Preheat the oven to 450° F. Stuff the cavity of the chicken with the mashed turnip mixture. Use a trussing needle and twine to sew the cavity closed. Place in a roasting pan. Roast until juices run clear when pricked in the thickest part of the leg, about 1 hour 10 minutes. Let stand for 10 minutes before carving. Carve and serve with the mashed turnip stuffing.

Serves 4 as a main course

TOUGH LETTUCE

The flavor of some winter vegetables, particularly most cabbages, bespeaks the bitter hardship of a frozen and unforgiving land. But other leafy things of winter are tough and irascible by reputation, not by nature.

Kale, for instance, though a member of the hardy *Brassica oleracea*, or cabbage family, is a mild-mannered and tender cousin, containing fewer of the mustard oils that blanket the winter kitchen with a skunky shroud. Nevertheless, because kale sprouts resolutely from poor soil and perseveres through (some say is improved by) frost, it has been seen as a hardship crop.

In her book *Uncommon Fruits & Vegetables*, Elizabeth Schneider writes that kale carries connotations of bitterness and hence "most immigrants who came to the United States from kale-growing countries have steered clear of the vegetable."

Likewise, escarole, Belgian endive's close cousin, which grows in broad, deep green leaves or in loose, pale frizzy heads, though a staple of Mediterranean country cooking, has, until recently, been suspect in fine homes and restaurants. Both broad-leaf and curly varieties are available deep into winter and like most survivors are probably blamed for what they do best.

It doesn't matter that escarole is only faintly bitter and slightly tough when used raw in salads, or even that, unlike cabbages, it becomes milder when cooked. What matters is that escarole has carried the multitudes through meager times and seems, therefore, too plebeian for good times.

It may be emblematic of a paradigm shift—a move from glorifying the effete to romanticizing the peasant—that both kale and escarole are beginning to climb the social ladder of winter vegetables. Baby kale is starting to appear, buttered and sautéed, in pricey restaurants, ditto escarole. On the other hand, the arms of America are opening wider and wider to all vegetables, particularly any with a Mediterranean lineage.

Kale probably originated in the dry heat of the Mediterranean seaboard; like all cabbages, it has thick, water-storing leaves. But Mediterranean countries largely dismissed the plant, and kale became a fixture of northern European kitchens.

In Scotland, according to Schneider, "to come to cail" was an invitation to dinner. The same was true in the homes of Portuguese fishermen in Provincetown when I lived there: Kale was the all-purpose green of the winter table, inseparable from spicy linguiça sausage and potatoes and a counterpoint to fatty winter fish.

Recent devotees extol the virtues of undercooked kale, particularly the small curly leaves that look like parsley, and crisp kale can be a fine thing. But five winters on the tip of Cape Cod left me partial to long-cooked kale, kale simmered in bacon or sausage fat or braised in chicken broth or wine long enough to become soft and sweet. Likewise, escarole, as the Italians have long known, benefits from long, slow cooking.

In what they require from the cook, both tough greens resonate with the mood of the cold-weather kitchen. Broad-leaf escarole, with its deep green tips and thick white ribbing, cooks better than the curly variety, which is best used in winter salads, particularly those with warm dressings that wilt the greens and mitigate their sharp flavor.

Like kale, broad-leaf escarole can be simmered or stewed for hours, but still remains a substantial, fibrous green. Escarole's mild bitterness is neither enhanced nor diminished by long, slow cooking, it simply abides and is, by its nature, a perfect counterpoint to rich duck, lamb, or beef dishes. Escarole braised in olive oil with garlic can be tossed with pasta and strong cheese, or even sardines and chili peppers, to make a soulful meal, or it can be baked under bread crumbs and shaved Parmesan cheese and served beside roasted meat.

Like kale, stewed escarole can be used as a bed for cod fillets or sea scallops. Any way that the greens are used, they will bespeak substance by what they are, perseverance by where they've been, and patience by the way that long unattended cooking brings out the best in them.

Braised Escarole with Garlic

2 teaspoons olive oil

18 cloves garlic, lightly crushed

2 large heads escarole, cut into 2-inch pieces, washed but not dried (about
    16 cups)

½ teaspoon kosher salt

Freshly ground pepper to taste

Heat the olive oil in a large, wide pot for 1 minute over high heat. Add the garlic and cook, stirring frequently, until fragrant, about 45 seconds. Add the escarole and cover immediately. Cook for 2 minutes. Stir, reduce the heat, cover, and cook for 1 hour. Season with salt and pepper and serve.

Serves 4 as a side dish

Kale Soup with Potatoes and Sausage

1 pound linguiça or chorizo, cut across into ⅛-inch slices

1 large onion, peeled and chopped

1 clove garlic, peeled and minced

2 large baking potatoes, peeled and cut into ¼-inch cubes

1½ heads kale, stemmed and coarsely chopped (about 6 cups)

4 cups chicken broth, homemade, or low-sodium canned broth

1 tablespoon balsamic vinegar

2 teaspoons kosher salt

Freshly ground pepper to taste

3 plum tomatoes, cored and cut into ½-inch dice

Put the sausage in a large pot over medium-low heat and cook until it begins to render its fat, about 2 minutes. Add the onion and cook for 2 minutes. Add the garlic and potatoes and cook for 2 minutes. Add the kale and cook, stirring constantly, for 2 minutes longer. Stir in the broth, vinegar, and salt. Bring to a boil, reduce the heat, cover, and simmer for 1 hour. Season with pepper. Stir in the toma-toes and cook, uncovered, for 15 minutes. Divide among 4 bowls and serve.

Serves 4 as a main course

Kale and Oven-Dried Tomato Lasagna

2 large baking potatoes, peeled and thinly sliced
1 teaspoon olive oil
2 cloves garlic, peeled and minced
5 teaspoons chopped fresh rosemary
6 heads kale, stemmed and coarsely chopped (about 24 cups)
2½ teaspoons kosher salt
¼ teaspoon crushed red pepper
Olive oil spray
2 cups skim-milk ricotta
1 large egg, beaten
Freshly ground pepper to taste
9 lasagna noodles, cooked and drained well
2 cups Basic Oven-Dried Tomatoes (page 242)
3 tablespoons grated hard ricotta salata cheese

1. Bring a large pot of lightly salted water to a boil. Add the potato slices and blanch for 7 minutes. Drain and set aside. Heat 1 teaspoon of the olive oil in a large pot over medium heat. Add the garlic and rosemary and cook for 30 seconds. Add the kale, stir once, and cover. Cook for 12 minutes. Stir in 1½ teaspoons of the salt and the red pepper.

2. Preheat the oven to 350° F. Lightly coat an 11 × 7-inch baking dish with olive oil spray.

3. Whisk together the ricotta, egg, remaining salt, and pepper. Line the bottom of the dish with 3 of the noodles, trimming them to fit if necessary. Spread the noodles with half of the ricotta mixture. Spread 3 cups of the kale mixture over the ricotta. Layer half of the potatoes over the kale and scatter with ¾ cup of the tomatoes. Repeat the layers, ending with noodles.

4. Spread the remaining kale mixture over the noodles. Sprinkle with the ricotta salata and the remaining tomatoes. Cover with aluminum foil. Bake for 30 minutes. Cut into 6 pieces and serve.

Serves 6 as a main course

Escarole Risotto with Duck

6½ cups chicken broth, homemade, or low-sodium canned broth
2 cups dry white wine
3 teaspoons olive oil
1 small onion, finely chopped
2 large cloves garlic, minced
1½ cups Arborio rice
1 large head escarole, chopped (about 8 cups)
1 teaspoon kosher salt, plus more to taste
Freshly ground pepper to taste
2 small boneless and skinless duck breasts, split

1. Pour the broth and wine into a medium saucepan and bring to a boil. Reduce the heat and keep at a simmer. Heat 2 teaspoons of the olive oil in a large wide pot over medium heat. Add the onion and garlic and cook, stirring, until soft, about 3 minutes. Add the rice and stir for 1 minute.

2. Ladle in ½ cup of the broth mixture and stir constantly with a wooden fork until most of the liquid is absorbed. Continue adding broth, ½ cup at a time, and stirring until the rice is tender, about 50 minutes. Stir in the escarole and cook for 2 minutes longer. Season with 1 teaspoon salt and pepper.

3. Heat the remaining teaspoon of olive oil in a large nonstick skillet over medium-high heat. Add the duck breasts and cook until medium-rare, about 3 minutes per side. Cut on the diagonal into thin slices and season with salt and pepper to taste. Divide the risotto among 4 shallow bowls and fan the duck slices over the top. Serve immediately.

Serves 4 as a main course

BRUSSELS SPROUTS

In flavor, a Brussels sprout is even more overwhelming and potentially as depressing as its cousin, head cabbage. The dreaded eau de sulfur that sprouts emit while cooking recalls privation and therefore bespeaks a vegetable that is sustenance in the meanest sense of the word: one accepted, not gladly chosen.

One can embrace this fact of Brussels sprout nature, confronting the bitter darkness of a winter evening with a taste of its own medicine. There is little produce as bitter as boiled Brussels sprouts and much is to be said for the fortifying, homeopathic approach of countering like with like.

One can cook around the Brussels sprout, tempering its mustardy character with butter, pine nuts, or chestnuts or countering its bitterness with rich ham or pungent cheeses. But one cannot deny that the significant difference between cabbage and Brussels sprouts is size. A cabbage goes on forever; a Brussels sprout can end in a bite.

Despite all this, its miniature cabbage physique, along with its inherent challenge to the cook, have made the Brussels sprout a darling of the winter kitchen. The flavor of the small green vegetable balls provides a perfect foil for rich roasts, particularly duck, lamb, and beef. And again, their size is a nice contrast to a lumbering roast.

But to bring the best from a Brussels sprout takes thought. First one thinks before buying just any old Brussels sprout. Tightly curled ones still clinging to their vertical stem are generally fresher than those packed in plastic and will taste delicately sharp and faintly nutty. Basically, the smaller the better, though one should also avoid any discoloration.

After purchase, one considers the nature of the bud, seeks to flatter or counter it, but has no illusion that a Brussels sprout will ever be anything but a Brussels sprout. Nothing emphasizes this point better than a sauté of Brussels sprouts and chestnuts: if the mouth momentarily mistakes the nut for the vegetable, it is not without a gasp of betrayal, at least initially. Afterward, there is the amusement of two similar shapes being, from a flavor standpoint, so dissimilar.

Brussels sprouts lose their serious sturdiness when they are shredded and baked, rather than boiled or steamed whole. They can also be shredded and tossed with sautéed chicken, duck or lamb chops. When cooked as tiny globes, they warm most evenly when the stem end is scored with a sharp knife prior to boiling.

A full-flavored pancetta or bacon doesn't faze the cabbage bud, though like garlic or ginger, the rich meat counters the vegetable's sharpness. Pine nuts enrich the mild nutty flavor of very fresh Brussels sprouts. A rich cheese such as Taleggio makes the intrinsically austere vegetable more unctuous, as do butter and cream or even rich chicken stock. Diced carrots sweeten the sprouts; sweet peppers do the same, in a sunnier way.

Still nothing really changes a Brussels sprout. Once picked, the lateral buds become so many self-contained worlds, sour winter suns that remain an implacably if delicately bitter axis around which other ingredients revolve.

Brussels Sprout and Potato Gratin with Taleggio

3 cups Brussels sprouts, trimmed

3 medium baking potatoes, peeled and cut across into ⅛-inch slices

1½ teaspoons kosher salt

Freshly ground pepper to taste

½ cup chicken broth, homemade, or low-sodium canned broth

¼ cup heavy cream

⅓ cup grated Taleggio

1. Preheat the oven to 350° F.

2. Bring a large pot of water to a boil. Add the Brussels sprouts and blanch for 8 minutes. Drain well and cut in half. Place half of the potatoes in an 8-inch round gratin pan, in slightly overlapping layers. Season with some of the salt and pepper. Spread half of the Brussels sprouts over the potatoes and season with salt and pepper. Repeat the layers, seasoning each one. Pour the chicken broth over the top and drizzle on the cream. Cover with aluminum foil. Bake until the potatoes are tender, about 45 minutes.

3. Preheat the broiler. Sprinkle the top of the gratin with the cheese. Place under the broiler until the cheese is melted and beginning to brown. Divide among 4 plates and serve immediately.

Serves 4 as a main course

The Best Brussels Sprouts   (Adapted from Arcadia, Manhattan)

6 slices bacon, cut across into ¼-inch pieces
½ cup pine nuts
2½ pounds Brussels sprouts, halved, cored, and each half cut into quarters
2 teaspoons minced garlic
1 cup very finely diced carrots
2 teaspoons kosher salt
Freshly ground pepper to taste
¼ cup chopped Italian parsley

Put the bacon in a large skillet over medium heat and cook until the fat is rendered. Add the pine nuts and cook until the bacon is crisp and the nuts are golden, about 1 minute. Add the Brussels sprouts and the garlic, cover, and cook, shaking the pan, until the Brussels sprouts are wilted but still bright green and crisp, about 1 minute. Add the carrots and cook for 1 minute longer. Stir in the salt, pepper, and chopped parsley. Serve warm.

Serves 10 to 12 as a side dish

Sautéed Brussels Sprouts with Pancetta and Chestnuts

4 cups Brussels sprouts, trimmed

1 cup chicken broth, homemade, or low-sodium canned broth

2 ounces pancetta, diced

4 cloves garlic, minced

2 cups frozen pearl onions, defrosted

1½ cups peeled roasted chestnuts, halved

Kosher salt and freshly ground pepper to taste

2 tablespoons chopped Italian parsley

1. Bring a large pot of water to a boil. Add the Brussels sprouts and blanch for 5 minutes. Drain well and cut in half. Set aside. Meanwhile, pour the chicken broth into a small saucepan over medium-high heat. Reduce to ¼ cup, about 8 minutes. Set aside.

2. Heat a large skillet over medium heat, add the pancetta and sauté until browned, about 5 minutes. Add the garlic and cook, stirring constantly, for 30 seconds. Add the onions and cook for 30 seconds. Stir in the Brussels sprouts and chestnuts and cook until sprouts are tender, about 3 minutes. Stir in the reduced broth, salt, pepper, and parsley. Divide among 4 plates and serve immediately.

Serves 4 as a first course

LET THE GAME BEGIN

Venison is suddenly a dietary darling. It contains about the same amount of fat and calories as skinless chicken and has a dense beeflike texture and mild gamy flavor, like that of lean lamb.

Chefs find that it sates the appetite stirred by northerly winds and the endless evenings of winter. Nutritionists hail it as if it were the cure for a massive societal beef withdrawal. In a number of restaurants, venison has actually supplanted beef on seasonal menus in the past several years.

Yet visions of Bambi hover. And it isn't clear whether health concerns can quiet the queasiness. Both dietary restrictions that promote venison consumption and the pause that could impede its digestion are products of a society removed from the hunt.

Prehistoric man hunted stag in China 500,000 years ago. According to Anne Willan, author of *La Varenne Pratique,* excavations in Dordogne in France indicate that deer was the third most important food 110,000 years ago. Only horse and wild boar were consumed more, she writes.

Initially, the New World was enthusiastically celebrated as "home of the deer." But somewhere between cattle drives and Hollywood cartoons, the succulence of deer meat and the Diana worship inherent in the quest for it became suspect.

"A redneck sport" is the way Romi Perkins, an owner of the Orvis Company (the sporting-goods retailer), an inveterate hunter and the author of *Game in Season,* describes it. "We don't shoot large game," she said. But after talking of the superior challenge of hitting the tiny, fleeting target of a quail in flight, she admitted to cooking (and relishing) the deer meat that others have shot for her.

"Deer have to be harvested," she said. "They overpopulate and starve to death. It's just such macho hunting."

I didn't know the word macho the first time I saw a deer swinging from the rafters of a neighbor's garage. But cigarette smoke and the smells of gas and oil, sweat and damp wool hunting jackets coalesced when my father took me to see what our neighbor had killed. I was six or seven years old, and a feeling of being even tinier, even more vulnerable than the dead deer mingled (and still does) with those smells. I've had flashbacks at hockey games and during Presidential campaigns.

But I've never had a problem cooking or eating venison. Semantics may have safely distanced me. Venison is meat in a pot; deer is a potential Bambi frozen in the headlights. Or perhaps, in the years that I gardened, the infuriating chain of heart-shaped footprints that inevitably led to the rows of my most prized and tender lettuces, early peas, and herbs hardened my soul to the deer. The mark a creature leaves on this earth might be the fragile heart shape of its hoof; nevertheless, it invariably treats your mâche, your Boston, your bibb lettuces as small villages to raze.

More likely, however, it was my father who mitigated the sight of the deer on display in the suburban garage. Somehow what he said got me thinking about brave Indian hunters and Greek goddesses who ran with the wind in their hair. The poetry carried me through my first glimpse behind the tidy, plastic-wrapped packages of meat that I helped my mother select at the grocery store, buoyed me through my first encounter with the sacrifice inherent in any meal.

Venison lends to the edge of appetite another layer of misgiving and demands that savoring resolve the past as well as celebrate the present. In other words, it isn't enough to appreciate the health benefits of venison. To enjoy it, you need to accept, at least for the duration of the meal, your place in the food chain, your time in history.

It doesn't hurt to know that most commercial venison is now farm raised in New Zealand and, increasingly, on former cattle farms in the American Midwest. The celebrations of the meat show its universal appeal. In Norway, venison loin is roasted with cranberries; in Finland and Sweden with lingonberries; in Great Britain, with cherries. In France, shoulder and rib meat are stewed with onions, mushrooms, and wine. The Germans favor juniper berries with their venison. The Italians use junipers as well as red wine, root vegetables, rosemary, and peppercorns. Cloves, tomatoes, garlic, cinnamon, and pancetta all stand up well to the full flavor of venison. The blends of pungent herbs and aromatics underscore the gamy flavor of venison, that is a trophy, an ode to a hunt, however long ago.

Venison Burgers

¼ cup dry bread crumbs

¼ cup milk

¾ pound ground venison

¼ pound ground pork

½ cup minced green bell pepper

½ cup minced onion

1 teaspoon kosher salt, plus more for skillet

2 teaspoons minced fresh sage

¼ teaspoon freshly ground pepper

1 teaspoon dried mustard

½ teaspoon red wine vinegar

1. Stir the bread crumbs and milk together. Let stand for 15 minutes. Using your hands and working quickly, combine the bread crumb mixture with the remaining ingredients in a large bowl. Form into 3-inch patties, using about ⅓ cup for each.

2. Heat a large heavy skillet over medium heat until very hot. Sprinkle the skillet lightly with salt. Fry the burgers, in batches if necessary, for 4 minutes on each side. Serve immediately.

Makes 10 burgers

Venison Cider Stew

1 tablespoon bacon fat

1 pound boneless leg of venison,
    cut into 1-inch cubes

2 tablespoons flour seasoned lightly
    with salt and pepper

1 onion, peeled and minced

2 small celery roots, trimmed, peeled,
    and cubed

½ cup apple cider

1 tablespoon apple-cider vinegar

2 cups beef broth, homemade, or low-sodium canned broth

1 teaspoon kosher salt, plus more to taste

½ teaspoon freshly ground pepper, plus more to taste

1 cinnamon stick

½ cup dried apples, diced

¼ cup calvados

¼ cup unsalted pistachios, coarsely chopped

1. Warm the bacon fat in a large heavy pot over medium heat. Dust the venison with the seasoned flour. Add to the pan and cook, stirring, until well browned. Remove the venison from the pan with a slotted spoon and set aside. Add the onion to the pan. Reduce the heat and cook until onion is soft, about 5 minutes. Add the celery roots and cook for 3 minutes. Add the apple cider, vinegar, broth, salt, pepper, and cinnamon stick. Simmer until the celery root is tender, about 1 hour. Taste and adjust the seasoning with salt and pepper. Remove and discard the cinnamon stick. Stir the venison into the stew.

3. Meanwhile, soak the dried apples in the calvados. Ladle the stew into large bowls. Garnish with the apple-calvados mixture and pistachios and serve.

Serves 4 as a main course

HOME ON THE RANGE

Riding the Montana range with George Kahrl, one of the rising generation of organic beef growers, you are conscious of the land, the way it rolls flat and dry as an abandoned river bottom, a big lonesomeness. The plains inch up to foothills; they are seamed occasionally by brush-lined creeks and straggly fences. But these demarcations, along with the grazing herd of 140 cows, and your two horses, are only passing through, not much different than the wind or the occasional spatter of rain. You adjust your world view accordingly. And for a moment you understand the taste for a big fat steak.

Despite its dietary devilishness—beef has an average of 22 percent fat and is cited by cardiac specialists as the leading dietary contributor to coronary heart disease.

Despite the embarrassing decadence of eating beef in a world where famine and hunger persist. (It takes about eight pounds of grain to yield one pound of beef, and economists estimate that the water and acreage required to raise beef for one person could feed up to twenty people if it were used instead for grains.)

Despite the fact that a rampant appetite for beef has fueled the destruction of some rain forests, the erosion of some topsoil, the pollution of some water tables.

Despite the fact that slabs of beef have gone the way of the Marlboro Man, déclassé.

Even knowing all this, a two-hour trot across Kahrl's ranch, which sprawls over five thousand acres 35 miles west of Bozeman, Montana, leaves you crazed for a steak.

What can explain this primal and, for now at least, politically incorrect and socially suspect appetite? Do lungfuls of fresh air trigger a craving for the trophy of a hunt? Our national carnivorousness has long been equated with bloodthirstiness, an explanation as feasible as it is revolting. And then there are football and ice hockey, whose seasons neatly coincide with an increased hankering for red meat.

"We see a switch toward bigger cuts of beef, pot roasts, and stewing meat as soon as it gets cold," said Mary Adolf, a vice president of the National Live Stock and Meat Board in Chicago. Perhaps then, it is the nip in the air, as much as the air itself, that pushes your thoughts fondly toward a thick porterhouse blackened on a grill; a sirloin rubbed with a mixture of one part confectioners' sugar, one part black pepper, two parts salt and broiled; a flank steak seared in a red-hot cast-iron skillet dusted with salt. Because your mother favored that technique for cube and flank steaks, your thoughts linger there, warmly, before proceeding to rump roast, meatloaf, a good beef stew.

Beef began resonating with family values in the past century. Despite startling statistics about diet-related mortality, America has retained the highest consumption of red meat per capita of any nation, about 66 pounds per person annually. A whiff of a hamburger imparts a sense of well-being. What began as a necessity—frontiersmen hunting and eating those few ruminant creatures that the scruffy plains would support—became a ritual. Consider the hamburger. Consider barbecue. Consider the steak.

The appetite for beef can be curbed but not quelled. Instead of frequent heavy steaks, you have infrequent heavy steaks, or you go lighter on the steak and heavier on the accoutrements, stir-frying, stewing, and side-dishing beef. But beef remains. As do the sticky underpinnings of yearning, the thrust and parry of violence and reassurance involved in any sacrificial slaying, the interplay of guilt and indulgence at eating so high on the food chain. Deeper than that, you realize as you shiver on the Montana range, is yet another two-sided coin of desire: the passion for freedom and self-determination, fighting loneliness and isolation. To eat meat is to know you are not alone.

This may have as much to do with communion as it has to do with domination. Meat, particularly beef in the past century, has been a conduit of camaraderie: What bread and wine are to the French, beef is to Americans. Leafing through community cookbooks from Montana, you note the frequency of the campfire image. Menus from the greasiest of spoons in Bozeman, to chic Southwestern restaurants in Washington, D.C., consistently pay homage to the beef-and-bean theme. What is barbecue, whether made of beef or pork, if not a celebration of place and clan? What is a burger if not a national symbol of good times and good fellowship?

And what is all of this but a variation on the "make hay while the sun is shining" theme? Anyone traveling through the western landscape knows the chill of insignificance that washes over you there.

"The land is bigger than me, older than me, it's going to be around a lot longer than me," said Kahrl, who is thirty-four years old and chose to be a modern cowboy when he and his wife Kathleen Crawford bought the Sarah Faith Ranch in 1987. He ranches, rather than farms, because soil erosion in this type of landscape can be controlled through prudent grazing. Generally, he grazes a given fifteen- to twenty-acre patch for one week, then he moves his herd and allows the grazed land to rest for at least 90 days. He's proud of the healthy grasses that cover his ranch, smug that the fall breeze carries little dust.

He's also proud that, due to careful husbandry, 50 percent of his herd never requires antibiotics and can therefore be sold as organic. "It's healthier for the land, healthier for the animals, healthy for people," he says.

By an odd twist, this style of ranching places Kahrl, and a few hundred other organic beef ranchers across America, back on a frontier. They are preservationists, but most preservationists scorn their methods. They are health-minded, but most health advocates disdain their product. They are cattlemen, but their slow, costly methods threaten conventional beef producers. They are modern cowboys.

Occasionally these growers form small cooperatives, such as O-M of Great Falls, Montana, which Kahrl and a handful of like-minded organic beef growers organized several years ago to sell and market their beef. Specialty butchers across the country are beginning to carry the well-marbled beef from O-M and others. Its clean, rich, distinct flavor delivers hints of lonesome cowboys and wide open plains. It's a balm to wind-chapped cheeks and achy, well-exercised limbs. Sure, the craving is archaic. But it is irrepressible.

Circle the wagons, let's eat.

Seared Steak with Caramelized Shallots

1 teaspoon whole green peppercorns
1 teaspoon whole black peppercorns
1 teaspoon whole pink peppercorns
4 juniper berries
1 1½- to 2-pound porterhouse steak,
    1½ inches thick
12 large shallots, peeled
3 teaspoons vegetable oil
4 baking potatoes, peeled and cut into
    2 × 1 × ¼-inch rectangles
1 cup red wine
2 cups beef broth, homemade,
    or low-sodium canned broth

1. Preheat the oven to 350° F.

2. Combine the green, black, and pink peppercorns and the juniper berries in a spice mill or coffee grinder. Grind until smooth. Dust the steak with the spice mixture. Refrigerate.

3. Brush the shallots with 1 teaspoon of the oil. Place them in a small roasting pan. Set aside. Using a sharp paring knife, shape the potatoes into rounded ovals. Brush with 1 teaspoon of the oil and add to the shallots. Roast until shallots and potatoes are tender and golden, about 45 minutes to 1 hour. Set aside.

4. Heat the remaining vegetable oil in a large cast-iron skillet over medium heat until hot. Add the steak and cook until medium rare, about 5 to 10 minutes per side. Transfer to a cutting board and set aside for 15 minutes. Pour the wine into the pan and bring to a boil over medium-high heat. Reduce the heat and simmer until reduced to ½ cup. Add the broth and continue simmering until reduced to 1 cup. Pour through a fine-mesh sieve. Set aside.

5. Cut the steak into thin slices. Spoon some shallots and roasted potatoes in the center of each of 4 plates. Drape slices of meat over the vegetables. Drizzle with ¼ cup of the sauce. Serve immediately.

Serves 4 as a main course

Bozeman Flank and Beans

6 plum tomatoes, halved lengthwise
4 frying peppers, halved lengthwise and seeded
1 hot red pepper, seeded and cut across into ¼-inch slices
1 teaspoon dry mustard
3 tablespoons molasses
4 teaspoons salt, plus more to taste
1 teaspoon freshly ground pepper
1 teaspoon olive oil or bacon fat
1 medium onion, minced
1 pound dry pinto beans, soaked in water overnight

STEAK

1 flank steak, about 1 pound
2 teaspoons kosher salt
1 teaspoon coarsely ground pepper

1. Preheat the oven to 400° F.

2. Spread out the tomatoes and peppers, skin side up, on a baking sheet. Roast for 25 minutes. Carefully transfer the vegetables, with their juices, to a food processor or blender. Add the hot red pepper. Puree until smooth. Set aside. Stir together the mustard, molasses, salt, and pepper in a small bowl. Set aside.

3. Pour the olive oil into a large heavy ovenproof pot and warm over medium heat. Add the onion and cook until soft, about 5 minutes. Drain the beans and add to the onion. Pour in enough water to barely cover the beans. Stir in the tomato-pepper puree and the molasses mixture. Cover. Bake until tender, about 1 hour and 45 minutes, adding water as needed to keep beans very moist but not soupy. Add salt to taste.

4. About 15 minutes before serving, season the steak with 1 teaspoon of the salt and pepper. Set aside. Ten minutes before serving, place a cast-iron skillet over high heat. Add the remaining salt to the skillet and heat until hot. Quickly sear the steak, allowing it to cook 2 to 3 minutes on each side, depending on how

thick it is and how you like it cooked. Remove from pan. Let stand for 5 minutes. Slice and serve around beans.

Serves 6 as a main course

Filet Mignon of Beef with Roghan Josh Spices

(Adapted from Raji's, Memphis)

MEAT

    2 teaspoons ground coriander

    ½ teaspoon ground cumin

    ½ teaspoon ground turmeric

    ¼ teaspoon ground fenugreek

    1 teaspoon red chili powder

    1 large clove garlic, peeled and smashed to a paste

    2 tablespoons grated fresh ginger

    2 tablespoons grape-seed oil

    4 tournedo steaks, 6 ounces each

    1 teaspoon vegetable oil

SALAD

    ½ cup fresh lime juice

    1 tablespoon apple cider vinegar

    ½ teaspoon kosher salt

    1 teaspoon minced jalapeño

    2 tablespoons olive oil

    1 medium celery root, peeled and grated

    1 large Red Delicious apple, peeled and grated

    1 small jícama, peeled and grated

    ½ cup minced fresh mint

    ½ cup minced fresh cilantro

VINAIGRETTE

 ¼ cup fresh lime juice

 1 teaspoon grated orange zest

 ¼ teaspoon kosher salt

 ½ teaspoon freshly ground pepper

 1 tablespoon olive oil

1. Combine the coriander, cumin, turmeric, fenugreek, chili powder, garlic, ginger, and grape-seed oil in a blender and puree until smooth. Scrape into a large glass or ceramic bowl, add the tournedos and turn to coat. Marinate in the refrigerator for 6 hours.

2. Combine the ½ cup lime juice, vinegar, salt, and jalapeño in a large glass or ceramic bowl. Whisk in the olive oil. Add the celery root, apple, and jícama and toss. Refrigerate for 4 hours.

3. To make the vinaigrette, combine the ¼ cup lime juice, orange zest, salt, and pepper in a small glass or ceramic bowl. Whisk in the olive oil. Set aside.

4. Heat the vegetable oil in a seasoned cast-iron skillet over medium-high heat. Add the tournedos and cook until medium-rare, about 5 minutes per side. Set aside to rest for 5 minutes.

5. Add the mint and cilantro to the salad and toss. Divide among 4 plates. Cut the meat into thin strips. Drape the meat around the salad. Drizzle with the vinaigrette. Serve immediately.

Serves 4 as a main course

RABBIT

T he dark days of winter, its steely dawns and gauzy afternoons and interminable evenings, seem to erode some of the conventions of modern civilization. It is, for instance, during the coldest months that the soft and fuzzy suddenly seem fair game. Deer becomes venison and then becomes dinner. Rabbit is served as *lapin à la moutarde* or *pappardelle con la lepre* or *conejo en mole*. In a world that grew up on *The Wind in the Willows*, Peter Rabbit, and Bugs Bunny, these phrasings seem somehow less upsetting than simply saying rabbit stew.

Deer and some wild game birds were once limited by weather to the colder months. Rabbits have been hutch raised year round for centuries, yet, in most cultures, rabbit remains a winter meat. This custom, like many of the ways that rabbit continues to be prepared, may be left over from the age of wild rabbits and hares, both of which have dark, gamy flesh that requires pungent marinades and long, slow cooking.

The dark flavors of cinnamon and clove, garlic and mustard, heady red wines and dried fruits are as aromatically in tune with the season as they are with the taste of rabbit meat. The gamier hare and wild rabbit are still bagged by hunters, though most rabbit sold in the United States today is the domestic variety. It has lightly colored flesh and a delicate flavor. It is most often compared to chicken, but then what isn't?

Rabbit actually contains about twice as much fat as chicken (but less than a third that of beef). Unlike chicken, however, and for obvious reasons, rabbit is not cooked with its skin and therefore tends to dry out easily. The most successful recipes are stews in which a full-flavored sauce imbues the meat as the meat melts into the sauce. It's an even exchange and both are better for it.

Traditional rabbit stews tend to be rather painstaking, which may point to an abiding ambivalence about eating the meat. A perfect Mexican mole sauce, I'm told by an octogenarian practitioner in Oaxaca, the capital of the sauce, is a full day's work of pounding and crushing and roasting and mixing and simmering. After all that, the addition of a quartered rabbit is probably a relief.

The years when I shied away from rabbit for dinner were those when I had a rabbit for a pet. B.W., short for Bunny Wabbit, which she'd been named by her previous owner, a six-year-old girl, hopped around the apartment freely, loved lettuce, and did tricks like dancing on her hind legs for Carr's water crackers, which she adored. But her best trick was jumping out of the soup pot.

Whenever I entertained, I put B.W. in a big pot with a lid on an unlit burner. Eventually, I'd ask a guest to check the soup. And they would take the lid off the soup pot. B.W. would jump up on her hind legs, throw her front paws over the rim of the pot and wiggle her ears. The guest would shriek. After a few minutes, B.W. would sit back down in the pot to wait for her mâche and cracker reward.

"Oh, it's not quite done," I would say, nonchalantly. I was young and stupid. But my relationship with rabbit had, for the duration, changed. When we spent a summer on Nantucket, an island of a zillion rabbits, B.W., who was a dwarf, was courted regularly by jack rabbits three times her size. They would hurl themselves against the screen door as B.W. regarded them curiously from the other side. We acted like we were defending her honor. "Get out of here!" we'd screech. It must have been then that I began to distinguish between pets and dinner.

When we left Nantucket late in the fall, B.W. stayed. She'd been adopted by a family with three little girls. They liked to lie like logs as B.W. hopped over them and back, over them and back. I don't remember exactly how, but B.W. made it clear that she liked this trick at least as well as jump-from-the-soup-pot. She also indicated that she preferred the sound of her wild suitors thumping in the tunnels beneath her house to the sound of the New York City subway.

Maybe I missed B.W., or maybe I had to remind myself of the difference between affection and appetite, or maybe it was a particularly cold winter in the city. I don't remember. I remember cooking a lot of rabbit.

It began innocuously, with rabbit sauce for wide fresh pappardelle noodles, but before long, I was simmering rabbit in mustard sauce, the classic bistro dish that can be mistaken for nothing else. Whether the recipes are European or Asian, they tend to give a fierce perfume that's like a note of forgetting after a day of living on the edge of never-quite-warm.

Rabbit and Wild Mushroom Ragout

2 teaspoons unsalted butter
1 rabbit, about 2½ pounds, boned and cut into ½-inch pieces
1 onion, thinly sliced
2 cups stemmed and coarsely chopped shiitake or porcini mushrooms
1 cup stemmed and sliced white mushrooms
¾ cup chicken broth, homemade, or low-sodium canned broth
½ cup dry white wine
1 teaspoon kosher salt, plus more to taste
½ teaspoon freshly ground pepper, plus more to taste
Pinch grated nutmeg
4 brioche rolls or 4 thick slices of another egg bread, like challah
1 tablespoon minced fresh thyme
1 tablespoon minced Italian parsley

1. Melt the butter in a large heavy skillet over medium-high heat. Add the rabbit and sauté for 2 minutes. Remove the rabbit from the pan and set aside. Add the onion to the pan. Sauté, stirring occasionally, until caramelized, about 10 minutes.

2. Add the mushrooms and cook, stirring frequently, for about 5 minutes. Add the broth, wine, salt, pepper, and nutmeg. Reduce the heat and simmer for 30 minutes. Stir in the rabbit and simmer for 5 minutes more.

3. If using brioche, cut in half crosswise. Toast brioche or bread and place each roll or bread slice on a plate. Cover with the ragout. Garnish with thyme and parsley. Serve immediately.

Serves 4 as a main course

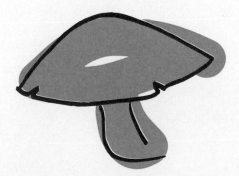

Dark Roasted Pomegranate Rabbit (Adapted from Biba, Boston)

MARINADE

½ cup pomegranate juice

½ cup olive oil

1 small onion, minced

3 small shallots, minced

1 teaspoon minced fresh thyme

½ teaspoon ground cumin

1 teaspoon honey

¼ teaspoon freshly ground pepper

RABBIT

1 fresh rabbit, about 3½ pounds, cut into 6 to 7 pieces

1 tablespoon olive oil

Kosher salt and freshly ground black pepper to taste

1. Whisk together all the marinade ingredients in a glass dish. Add the rabbit pieces and marinate overnight in the refrigerator, turning the rabbit several times.

2. Preheat the oven to 400° F.

3. Remove the rabbit from the marinade, reserving the marinade. Pat the rabbit dry. Heat the olive oil in a large skillet over medium heat. Working in batches, add the rabbit and sear until golden, about 8 minutes per batch. Place the rabbit on a baking sheet. Bake until tender, 8 to 15 minutes, removing smaller pieces as they are done.

4. Meanwhile, pour the marinade into the skillet. Simmer over medium heat for 5 minutes, scraping up browned bits from the bottom of the pan.

5. Pour juices that have accumulated on the baking sheet into the sauce. Strain through a fine sieve. Degrease. Season with salt and pepper. Place the rabbit on a serving platter, pour the sauce over, and serve.

Serves 4 as a main course

Rabbit with Pappardelle

(Adapted from Follonico, Manhattan)

>   2 tablespoons olive oil
>   1 fresh rabbit, about 3½ pounds, cut into 6 to 7 pieces
>   2½ teaspoons kosher salt, plus more to taste
>   Freshly ground black pepper to taste
>   4 carrots, finely chopped
>   8 stalks celery, finely chopped
>   3 cloves garlic, finely chopped
>   1 bay leaf
>   1 branch fresh rosemary
>   4 sprigs fresh thyme
>   1 cup white wine
>   4 cups water
>   1 medium onion, unpeeled, coarsely chopped
>   5 canned Italian plum tomatoes, coarsely chopped, with ¼ cup of their liquid
>   ¾ pound fresh pappardelle
>   2 tablespoons chopped Italian parsley
>   Freshly grated Parmesan cheese to taste

1. Heat the olive oil in a large sauté pan over medium heat. Season the rabbit with 1 teaspoon of the salt and pepper. Add to the pan and sear until golden brown, about 10 minutes. Add half of the carrots, half of the celery, and all of the garlic, bay leaf, rosemary, and thyme. Cook for 5 minutes. Pour in the wine. Lower the heat until the liquid barely simmers. Cover and cook until the rabbit is tender, about 30 minutes.

2. Remove the rabbit from the pan and let cool. Set aside the pan with the vegetables. Pull the meat off the bone and cut into bite-size pieces. Set aside. Place the bones in a large saucepan. Add the water, unpeeled onion, and the remaining carrots and celery. Simmer until liquid is reduced to about 2 cups, about 45 minutes. Strain.

3. Pour the strained broth into the pan with the vegetables. Bring to a simmer.

Stir in the tomatoes. Simmer slowly for 45 minutes. Stir in the rabbit meat. Add remaining salt and pepper. Remove and discard the herbs. (Sauce can be made 1 to 2 days ahead. When ready to serve, reheat with a little additional rabbit stock or cooking liquid from the pasta, to thin slightly.)

4. Bring a large pot of salted water to a boil. Add the pappardelle. Cook until tender, 1 to 2 minutes. Drain. Toss with the rabbit mixture. Divide among 4 plates. Sprinkle with parsley, pepper, and Parmesan. Serve immediately.

Serves 4 as a main course

Rabbit Mole

RABBIT

    1 tablespoon bacon fat

    1 rabbit, about 2½ pounds, cut into 7 pieces

    1 medium onion, peeled and minced

    4 cloves garlic, peeled and minced

    1 teaspoon dried thyme

    1 teaspoon kosher salt, plus more to taste

    ½ teaspoon black pepper, plus more to taste

    2 cups chicken broth, homemade, or low-sodium canned broth

SAUCE

    8 ancho chilies, soaked in 2 cups boiling water for 30 minutes

    1 cup drained stewed tomatoes

    ¼ cup sesame seeds, toasted

    1 tablespoon dried oregano

    2 cloves

    2 allspice berries

    ¼ teaspoon ground cinnamon

    9 cloves garlic, peeled

    ½ small ripe banana, peeled

    2 tablespoons dried bread crumbs

    ½ ounce unsweetened chocolate, melted

    1 teaspoon kosher salt, plus more to taste

1. Warm the bacon fat in a large heavy casserole over medium-high heat. Add the rabbit pieces and brown well. Add the onion, garlic, thyme, salt, and pepper. Cook, stirring frequently, until the onion is soft, about 5 minutes. Add the broth. Reduce the heat and simmer for 30 minutes.

2. Meanwhile, drain the chilies, reserving 1 tablespoon of the soaking liquid. Stem and seed the chilies. Transfer the chilies to a blender, add the tomatoes, sesame seeds, oregano, cloves, allspice, cinnamon, and garlic and puree until very

smooth. Add the reserved soaking liquid, the banana, bread crumbs, chocolate, and salt. Process until smooth, stopping to scrape down the sides of the jar.

3. Remove the rabbit pieces from the broth. Whisk in the sauce. Taste and adjust seasonings if needed. Return rabbit to pan. Simmer until thick, about 15 minutes. Serve with white rice or warm flour tortillas.

Serves 4 to 5 as a main course

EASY AS TARTE TATIN

C ooking can be guided more by smell and taste and feel than by precise measurements. Cooks with an inherent sense of direction tend to view recipes as a snapshot rather than a road map. Baking is a different matter. While cooking, like jazz, is improvisational, baking is all études and scales. Deviating from a pastry recipe is, for all but masters, about as advisable as trying to outriff Thelonious Monk.

This is the voice of experience speaking. I am constitutionally incapable of following recipes, even my own. Perhaps it is an innate character flaw or a vestige of adolescent rebellion. My mother is both a superb baker and an accomplished pianist. I am neither.

Even as a ten-year-old, with a sinfully rich fudge hanging in the balance, I bridled at the necessity of cooking sugar syrup to the soft-ball stage; grainy brown bricks were my reward. "Just too bullheaded to follow the darned recipe," my mother would offer.

Later, after I attended cooking school in Paris, my attempts at serendipity continued to produce pasty marjolaines and runny butter creams, though my mother was kind enough to rationalize: "It's probably the weather, so humid." But she couldn't resist adding: "Baking is very precise. Details matter." Baking, I decided, was for the birds.

"I don't like dessert," I announced one Christmas, possibly while my mother was unmolding another one of her perfect charlottes. "Since when?" she asked. Actually, this bit of denial enabled me to ignore my own culinary shortcomings until I tasted my first Tarte Tatin at age twenty-five. The fact that my mother never made a Tarte Tatin in her life may have figured in my undying affection for the dessert. Also, its apparent simplicity appealed to me, along with the fact that it is not overly sweet. But even more important, this delicious pastry—made famous, according to *Larousse Gastronomique*, by the Tatin sisters of France—accommodated my propensity to reinvent rather than simply duplicate a dish. No two Tartes Tatin are ever identical.

It took a few autumns and winters to come up with the basic technique, one that would produce deeply caramelized apples and a thick crust that would cradle the fruit and not become soggy. Soon I was operating in a fugue state, baking pear Tatin, pineapple Tatin, banana Tatin. They were the perfect dessert for cold-weather entertaining. The fruit can be caramelized in a skillet, covered with a pastry dough, and refrigerated until guests arrive; then it is baked in a hot oven perfuming the house, and served warm.

My mother tells me the plain apple is the best, which is her way of expressing approval and relief that her efforts at schooling me in the finer points of baking weren't all for naught. After all, I did master her perfect pie crust when I was still young enough to want to imitate, years before I developed my irascible case of baker's block.

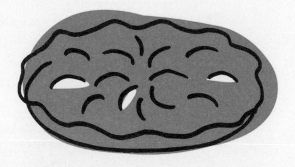

Tarte Tatin Pastry

2 cups all-purpose flour, plus additional for rolling dough
1 teaspoon kosher salt
½ pound (2 sticks) cold unsalted butter, cut into small pieces
1 egg yolk
2 tablespoons water

1. Combine the flour and salt in a large mixing bowl. Add the butter. Rub the flour and butter together between your fingers until most of the butter is incorporated and only pea-size pieces remain.

2. Whisk together the egg yolk and water. Add to the flour mixture and stir until dough begins to come together. Gently press the dough into a ball. Refrigerate until firm but not hard, about 30 minutes. (If made ahead, let dough stand at room temperature until pliable but still cold.) Do not roll out until just before the fruit is finished cooking.

3. To roll out the pastry, flour a work surface and a rolling pin well. Divide the dough in half. (Freeze the remaining dough if not needed.) Pat the dough into a flat disk then roll it out into a circle almost ¼ inch thick and at least 11 inches in diameter, flouring the surface and the rolling pin frequently to prevent sticking.

4. Carefully place the pastry over the fruit in the skillet. Trim the dough to ½ inch larger than the skillet. Tuck the overhanging dough in around the fruit.

Makes 2 Tartes Tatin pastry shells

Apple Tarte Tatin

For a Pear Tarte Tatin, substitute six large firm pears (Bosc or Anjou pears would be good) for the apples. Peel the pears, cut them in half lengthwise, and core them. Arrange them like spokes in the pan.

8 large Granny Smith apples
2 tablespoons fresh lemon juice
¾ cup sugar
4 tablespoons (½ stick) unsalted butter
Tarte Tatin Pastry (page 424)

1. Peel, quarter, and core the apples. Put in a large mixing bowl and toss with the lemon juice. Set aside.

2. Place the sugar in a 10-inch skillet or Tarte Tatin pan over low heat. When some of the sugar begins to melt, begin stirring with a wooden spoon until all of the sugar is melted and begins to turn a pale golden color. Remove the pan from the heat. Arrange the apple pieces in the skillet, rounded side down, in concentric circles, fitting them together as close as possible. Fill the center with 2 or 3 apple pieces, as needed. Arrange the remaining pieces, rounded side up, in concentric circles, filling in the gaps left in the first layer. Cut the butter into small pieces and scatter over the apples. Place the pan over medium heat. Cook until the sugar turns a deep caramel color and the juices released from the apples are nearly evaporated, about 15 to 20 minutes.

3. Preheat the oven to 375° F. Position the rack in the bottom third of the oven.

4. Roll out the dough and cover the apples according to the directions on page 424. Bake until the crust is golden brown, about 25 to 30 minutes. Remove from the oven and let cool for 10 minutes.

5. Run a knife around the edge of the tarte to loosen it. Place a large plate or platter over the skillet and carefully but quickly invert the tarte onto the plate. Let stand a few minutes to cool slightly. Cut into wedges and serve.

Serves 8

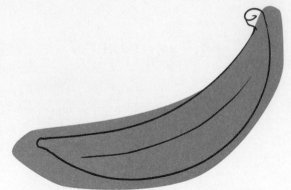

Banana-Walnut Tarte Tatin

1 cup coarsely chopped walnuts
¼ pound (1 stick) unsalted butter
1 cup (packed) brown sugar
8 large bananas
Tarte Tatin Pastry (page 424)
Vanilla ice cream, optional

1. Preheat the oven to 375° F.

2. Place a 10-inch skillet over medium heat until hot. Add the walnuts and cook, stirring constantly, until nuts are toasted, about 2 minutes. Remove walnuts from pan and set aside.

3. Place the butter in the skillet and heat until melted. Add the brown sugar and stir until combined with the butter. Remove from the heat. Peel the bananas. Cut them in half lengthwise and then crosswise. Arrange the banana pieces in the skillet in concentric circles, rounded side down, so that the curve of the banana fits into the curve of the pan. Make layers as necessary. Scatter the walnuts around the bananas.

4. Place the pan back on the heat and cook for 5 minutes. Roll out the dough and cover the bananas according to the directions on page 424. Bake until the crust is golden brown, about 25 to 30 minutes. Remove from oven and let cool for 10 minutes.

5. Run a knife around the edge of the tarte to loosen it. Place a large plate or platter over the skillet and carefully but quickly invert the tarte onto the plate. Let stand a few minutes to cool slightly. Cut into wedges and serve with vanilla ice cream if desired.

Serves 8

Pineapple-Coconut Tarte Tatin

¾ cup sugar
2 large pineapples, trimmed, peeled, cored, and cut into ¼-inch rings
4 tablespoons (½ stick) unsalted butter
Tarte Tatin Pastry (page 424)
½ cup shredded coconut, toasted

1. Preheat the oven to 375° F. Position the rack in the bottom third of the oven.

2. Place the sugar in a 10-inch skillet or Tarte Tatin pan over low heat. When some of the sugar begins to melt, begin stirring with a wooden spoon until all of the sugar is melted and begins to turn a pale golden color.

3. Remove the pan from the heat. Arrange the pineapple rings in layers, overlapping them slightly. Cut the butter into small pieces and scatter over the pineapple. Place the pan over medium heat. Cook until the sugar turns a deep caramel color and the juices released from the pineapple are nearly evaporated, about 20 minutes.

4. Roll out the dough and cover the pineapple according to the directions on page 424. Bake until the crust is golden brown, about 25 to 30 minutes. Remove from oven and let cool for 10 minutes.

5. Run a knife around the edge of the tarte to loosen it. Place a large plate or platter over the skillet and carefully but quickly invert the tarte onto the plate. Sprinkle the toasted coconut over the top. Let stand a few minutes to cool slightly. Cut into wedges and serve.

Serves 8

RENEWING VOWS

Like the batty old relative who predictably tries patience and politesse at holiday family gatherings, fruitcake elicits a snicker, a twinge of guilt, a sigh. Those who receive fruitcakes may, as the joke goes, store the sweet, moist bricks to give as gifts a year later. At the same time, fruitcake recipients are embarrassed by their own embarrassment.

The perennial distaste for fruitcakes stems not so much from the prototypical cake, which was made to be eaten on the road by errant knights during the Crusades, but from its twentieth-century descendant—the commercial fruitcake, with its cloying taste of candied fruit. Commercial fruitcakes are to traditional holiday dining what shopping malls are to the spirit of giving: mass market usurping soul. Each institution turns the season of remembering into something one would rather forget.

The distaste extends to candied and dried fruit in general. But savoring the classic Italian panforte, a prune tart from the Dordogne region of France, even a well-made steamed pudding with dried fruit undermines the widespread prejudice.

Leached of the juice from its younger incarnation, dried fruit has an intense sweetness balanced by spicy undercurrents that, along with a tougher hide, seem to come with age. The taste of fruit is therefore stronger and more substantial than it was in its youth, more adaptable and, at the same time, more demanding.

A prune is not a plum. Its charms aren't as apparent and accessible; they require coaxing. Gently macerated, steamed, or poached, given counterpoints of herbs or spices, turned into cakes, pies, or compotes, dried fruit is more complex than summer's fresh, and less mature, versions.

Paradoxically, dried fruit keeps puddings and cakes moist and succulent—perhaps explaining the earliest fruitcake and plum pudding confections, designed to gain flavor as they age.

The taste of dried fruit lingers. Its sweet complexity serves as a reminder that winter is a consequence of summer; the fruit links the seasons, as well as eras. Dried fruit is an ode to the weathered, to the carefully preserved and enduring, a memory that in turn stirs memory. To make a dessert of dried fruit is to experience the difference between renewal and something new.

Prunes Poached in Red Wine

Zest of 2 oranges, removed in long strips
3 tablespoons black peppercorns
½ cup fresh orange juice
1 bottle merlot wine
1 cup sugar
2 pounds pitted prunes

Tie the orange zest and peppercorns in a piece of cheesecloth and place in a large saucepan. Add the orange juice, wine, and sugar and stir to combine. Place over medium heat and simmer for 10 minutes. Remove from the heat and add the prunes. Refrigerate overnight. Serve at room temperature.

Serves 8

Fig Compote with Honey and Thyme

3 cups water
¾ cup honey
¾ cup sugar
2 teaspoons dried thyme
1 pound dried figs, stemmed

Combine the water, honey, sugar, and thyme in a large saucepan and bring to a boil. Reduce the heat to a simmer and add the figs. Cook until the figs are softened, about 10 minutes. Transfer the figs to a bowl using a slotted spoon. Increase the heat and reduce the liquid to 1 cup. Let cool slightly and pour the liquid over the figs. Serve at room temperature.

Serves 4

Cranberry-Pear Bread Pudding

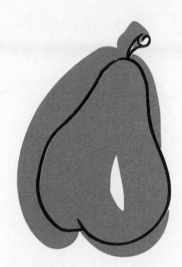

2 large loaves brioche, cut into 1-inch cubes
1 cup dried cranberries
1½ cups dried pears, cut into ½-inch pieces
1½ cups tawny port
1 cup pitted dried dates, coarsely chopped
1 cup walnuts, toasted and coarsely chopped
4 cups milk
½ cup sugar
1 teaspoon vanilla extract
6 large eggs, separated

1. Preheat the oven to 350° F.

2. Spread the brioche cubes on a baking sheet and bake, tossing from time to time, until toasted on all sides, about 10 minutes. Set aside.

3. Meanwhile, combine the cranberries, pears, and port in a saucepan and bring to a simmer. Simmer for 5 minutes, remove from the heat, and let stand for 15 minutes. Drain.

4. Toss together the brioche cubes, cranberries, pears, dates, and walnuts in a large bowl. In another bowl, whisk together the milk, sugar, vanilla, and egg yolks. Pour over the bread mixture. Beat the egg whites until stiff peaks form. Stir a third of the whites into the bread mixture. Fold in the remaining whites. Pour into a 13 × 9-inch baking dish.

5. Bake until set, about 45 minutes. Let cool slightly. Cut into wedges and serve warm.

Serves 8 to 10

SWEET DISSONANCE

Like anything exotic, tropical fruit in the winter shocks first and lures later. The soft, satiny flesh of a papaya, banana, or mango summons a world that is neither cold nor brittle. The flavors of these fruits, like those of pineapple, litchi, and grapefruit, are peregrines from a place in the sun.

Whether honeyed or musky, tart or exhaustingly sweet, tropical fruit commands a mood change, first in the palate, though it doesn't necessarily stop there. A piece of pineapple can provide comfort on a chilly evening. The fruit's thick, prickly skin isn't unlike the bundling that mere mortals assume, layer by layer, against the frost. But the fruit manages to maintain a certain sweet suppleness beneath the armor.

The pineapple is simultaneously sweet and tart in an unpredictable balance. Because of the enzymes in the fruit, unripe pineapple can leave the mouth feeling raw, while overly ripe pineapple can taste fermented. Pineapples must be picked ripe, since they won't sweeten further but just get mushy. The small Red Spanish pineapples tend to be sour, the larger Cayenne pineapples tend to be sweeter. But to gauge the precise flavor balance of any uncut pineapple is the province of soothsayers. All pineapples have hints of apple, peach, quince, or grapes; some taste like honey, some like vinegar. None tastes like winter. A sugar glaze is the best revenge, particularly a sugar macerated with vanilla, another denizen of the tropics. In addition to sweetening, the crackle of the glaze gives pineapples—as well as grapefruit and bananas—a contrasting texture.

Ripe mangoes are postcards from the sun, startling to the winter sensibility, generally as silky and custardlike under their glovelike leather-thick skin as pineapples are fibrous. Asian countries, led by India, grow most of the world's mangoes, but Mexico is the largest exporter to the United States. Thanks to varying climates and growing seasons, a selection of mangoes from Central and South America and even from Florida are available year round. In *Uncommon Fruits & Vegetables*, Elizabeth Schneider writes that there are probably more differences among mangoes than there are between some mangoes and apples; for desserts, the Haden and Tommy Atkins are generally the sweetest.

The aroma of a mango is a better indicator of ripeness than is the scent of an unpeeled pineapple. Still, the precise correlation between the piney, herbal aromas and the sweet, peachy flavors of the fruit is difficult to predict. Because of its texture, the mango can make a delicious granita or become a soft and gentle counterpoint to brittle sugar-glazed fruit in a dessert soup.

Papaya provides a similar note to such a soup. However, most of the papayas available in the Northeast come from Hawaii, Florida, and Mexico, where they are picked and shipped before they are ripe. Consequently, the fruit tastes like a bland squash. But allowed to ripen in a dark room or in a brown paper bag along with a banana, which traps the released gas, the papaya becomes unmitigatedly sweet, tasting alternatingly flowery and musky.

To eat a stout supper in winter is to accept one's circumstances; to end on a tropical note with something fresh is to go someplace else for dessert. Pineapples, bananas, grapefruits, papayas, and mangoes are slants of the sun, unpredictable and occasionally unruly, as life, unfrozen, can be.

Vanilla Sugar

1 vanilla bean, split in half lengthwise
2 cups sugar

Using the tip of a small knife, scrape the seeds from the vanilla bean. Rub the seeds into the sugar until incorporated. Place the sugar in an airtight container and push the vanilla bean down into the sugar. Cover and let stand for at least 3 days.

Makes 2 cups

Vanilla Roasted Bananas

6 medium bananas, peeled and halved crosswise
¼ cup fresh lemon juice
1 cup plus 4 teaspoons Vanilla Sugar (see above)

1. Preheat the oven to 450° F.
2. Line a baking sheet with foil. Rub each banana half in lemon juice and then coat in 1 cup of the sugar. Spread out on the baking sheet. Roast the bananas until the undersides caramelize, about 15 minutes. Turn the bananas over and roast until the other side browns, about 10 minutes longer.
3. Fan 3 banana halves on each of 4 plates and sprinkle with the remaining sugar. Serve immediately.

Serves 4

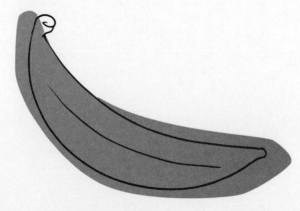

Glazed Pineapple

1 large pineapple
½ cup Vanilla Sugar (page 434)

Preheat the broiler. Remove the top from the pineapple and cut off the skin. Cut across into 8 slices, each about ¾ inch thick. Core each slice and coat with the vanilla sugar. Place on a foil-lined baking sheet. Broil until the sugar is browned, about 8 minutes. Place 2 pineapple slices on each of 4 plates and serve immediately.

Serves 4

Glazed Pink Grapefruit

3 large pink grapefruits
½ cup plus 4 teaspoons Vanilla Sugar (page 434)

Preheat the broiler. Peel the grapefruits. Cut between the flesh and the membranes to remove the grapefruit sections. Arrange the sections in a 9-inch pie plate and coat with ½ cup of the sugar. Broil until the sugar begins to brown, about 4 minutes. Sprinkle with 4 teaspoons sugar, divide among 4 plates, and serve immediately.

Serves 4

Pineapple Cinnamon Sorbet

2 cups pineapple juice
2 cups sparkling wine
½ cup light corn syrup
½ cup (packed) light brown sugar
5 cinnamon sticks
3 tablespoons fresh lime juice

Combine the pineapple juice, wine, corn syrup, and brown sugar in a nonreactive saucepan. Bring to a boil over medium heat. Add the cinnamon sticks and remove from the heat. Set aside to cool. Stir in the lime juice, strain the mixture, place in a container, and refrigerate several hours or overnight. Freeze in an ice cream machine according to the manufacturer's directions.

Serves 4

Exotic Fruit Soup

3 tablespoons unsalted pistachios, coarsely chopped

4 cups water

2 cups sugar

2 teaspoons grated fresh ginger

1 teaspoon grated lemon zest

3 tablespoons fresh lime juice

1 mango, peeled and cut into ½-inch dice

1 papaya, peeled, seeded, and cut into ½-inch dice

½ recipe Glazed Pineapple (page 435), cut into ½-inch chunks

½ recipe Glazed Pink Grapefruit (page 435)

1 recipe Pineapple Cinnamon Sorbet (page 436)

1. Preheat the oven to 350° F.

2. Roast the pistachios on a baking sheet until lightly toasted, about 3 minutes.

3. Combine the water, sugar, ginger, and lemon zest in a medium saucepan and bring to a boil over medium heat. Reduce the heat and simmer for 5 minutes. Remove from the heat and let stand until cool. Stir in the lime juice and strain. Stir the mango, papaya, pineapple, and grapefruit into the syrup. Ladle the soup among 4 bowls. Place a scoop of sorbet in each bowl and sprinkle with the pistachios. Serve immediately.

Serves 4

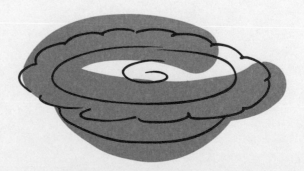

ALMOST
SPRING

NEVER MIND THE WIND

Maybe winter simply subsides, like dirty old snow eventually melting away. But I'd rather think that winter is conquered, that the gentler side of life can defeat the harsh, that the selfish survivalism of the winter appetite will eventually succumb to an atavistic craving for change, a hunger that is careful but alert, tentative but committed.

The rising of rice in the early warmth of southerly climates suggests this appetite, as its blades reach from the mud and all that's past toward the sun and presumably all that is still possible. Of course, the metaphor of rice may just be a way of saying that rice tastes good on the blustery nights when winter and spring tango. And the idea that winter succumbs may be the working of a hopelessly hopeful mind.

Hey, I can even align the stirring of crawfish in Louisiana bayous with a terrestrial awakening. I can see the eventual thrust of asparagus, unfurling of fiddlehead ferns, and rush of shad on the Hudson as emblematic of a refreshed world and hence a second chance for those of us who tread it. I can see the urge to recycle leftovers into fishcakes or meatloaf or warm composed salads as a way of breathing new life into old life. That's what happens this time of year.

Of course I think that earth-dwellers are profoundly affected by its cycles. That the further we are removed from nature, the more powerfully we miss its dictates. That cooking, in the end, is communion. Cooking acknowledges the world as we've found it. One's style of cooking mirrors one's past, one's ambitions, one's reactions to the present tense. But in the end, one can't cook without caring, particularly and universally, though the balance of these preoccupations shifts from cook to cook.

One sees this most as the winter world loosens its grip. The ambitious and congenitally optimistic will do anything to rush the warming. The contented or constitutionally depressed make another stew, wait, and watch. Regardless of personality type, regardless of fantasy or dream, we thaw and unfurl as winter loosens its hold.

It is the time of year that we are forced to realize the implication of standing on two feet, reaching with two hands. We seek. We choose. We cook dinner. Late winter winds, like trends and popular conceits, sway things. But the act of cooking connects one to something more fundamental and durable. We are alive.

THE RICE ALSO RISES

ice is undergoing a renaissance. Rather than a mere afterthought—a sad spoonful of white on a dinner plate—rice is now rivaling pasta as both backbone and canvas for a main dish.

It was actually the popularity of pasta that blazed a trail for other humble staples like rice. Risotto, the Italian dish made from Arborio rice, boosted the common kernel still further—its foreign, mellifluous-sounding name adding, even more than health, to what seems to be irresistible appeal.

And while rice is a staple for six out of every ten humans, it had a long way to climb in America. In her book *The Carolina Rice Kitchen; The African Connection*, Karen Hess details the culture that grew up around Carolina Gold, a long-grain rice that was planted in the swampy Carolina lowlands in the eighteenth century.

Carolina Gold was highly regarded, and for a long time South Carolina was to rice what New York was to strip steak. Nevertheless, within the United States the grain was associated more with the poor blacks who cultivated it and for whom it was a mainstay than with the privileged few usually evoked by the word "gourmet."

After the Civil War, rice-growing in South Carolina dwindled and was eventually surpassed, in cultivated acreage at least, by other southern and western states. Today Arkansas is the largest rice-producer. And though that state has its own hardscrabble image, rice has finally shrugged off the stigma of being strictly poverty food.

This has something to do, no doubt, with America's current infatuation with Mediterranean fare and that of many third world nations; as if, having sampled everybody else's humble offerings, we're now ready to take a belated look at our own. Also, of all the grains, rice is probably the most simple and direct. Generally stripped of its bran layers (when intact, the grain is brown) and often fortified with vitamins, it is less processed than wheat, barley, or oats, and, somehow, more easily turned into dinner.

There are about forty thousand varieties of rice, but only three main types:

long-grain, which grows in hot, humid climes, and medium- and short-grain, which thrive in cooler temperatures. Long-grain rice includes the aromatic varieties, like basmati. It is drier than short-grain, and unless severely mangled in the kitchen, it cooks up nice and fluffy.

The popcorn rice that Ellis Stansel grows in Gueydan, a small town in southwestern Louisiana, belongs in the long-grain category. Its wonderfully nutty aroma is as distinct as Ellis Stansel's way of speaking. When I ordered my first cloth bag of rice from him, he told me there was "no finer sight than a paddy of pale green grass rising on a spring morning," except "when the field turns gold." He added that there was "no finer feel than the mud. No finer smell than the rice." And no, he said, not skipping a beat: "I don't take credit cards. Just send me a check someday, young lady." After a decade of fussed-up food, the simplicity of rice is a refreshing change.

Diana Kennedy, the doyenne of Mexican cooking, has documented that country's technique for simmering one-pot meals from long-grain rice. Her recipe is a basic rice dish, endlessly amenable to different ingredients and moods. For example, I used duck and okra in one of my earliest variations as a kind of homage to Gueydan, which is not only the home of Ellis Stansel's rice but is also advertised as "the duck capital of the world." Later, I substituted beef cubes for the duck, and I've also used fish, vegetables, and various leftovers to make one-pot dishes that deliver the comforting ballast one longs for at the cusp of the season.

But despite the trimmings, the rice in these recipes is never far from its earthy origins. Simmering there in its pot, it invites you to experience what the poet Mary Oliver described at the end of "Rice":

I don't want you just to sit down at the table.
I don't want you just to eat, and be content.
I want you to walk out into the fields
where the water is shining, and the rice has risen.
I want you to stand there, far from the white tablecloth.
I want you to fill your hands with the mud, like a blessing.

Mexican Rice

(Inspired by Diana Kennedy)

1½ cups unconverted long-grain rice
1 cup finely chopped fresh or well-drained canned tomatoes
2 tablespoons peeled and finely chopped onion
1 clove garlic, peeled
3 tablespoons vegetable oil
3½ cups chicken broth, homemade, or low-sodium canned broth
1 teaspoon kosher salt, plus more to taste
⅓ cup peeled and thinly sliced carrot (optional)
½ cup peas or diced zucchini (optional)
½ cup chicken giblets (optional)

1. Soak the rice in hot water for 10 minutes. Drain. Rinse with cold water and drain well.

2. Place the tomatoes, onion, and garlic in a blender and puree until smooth. Set aside.

3. Heat the oil in a medium-large heavy pot over medium-high heat. Add the rice. Cook, stirring frequently, until the rice turns a light golden color, about 5 minutes. Stir in the tomato puree. Cook for 8 minutes, frequently scraping the bottom of the pan to prevent sticking.

4. Stir in the broth, salt, vegetables, and giblets, if using. Cook, uncovered, until all of the broth has been absorbed and air holes appear on the surface of the rice, about 20 minutes.

5. Turn the heat to very low. Cover the pot with a towel. Continue cooking for 5 minutes. Remove from the heat and let stand, covered, for 15 minutes. Adjust seasoning if needed and serve.

Serves 6 as a side dish

Rice with Andouille and Kale

1 recipe Mexican Rice, without optional ingredients (page 445)
1 clove garlic, peeled
2 teaspoons minced fresh rosemary
1 pound andouille sausage, cut across into ¼-inch slices
3 cups (firmly packed) stemmed kale, cut across into ½-inch strips

Follow the directions for Mexican Rice, pureeing the garlic and rosemary with the tomato mixture in Step 2. Add the sausage and kale with the chicken broth and salt in Step 4. Continue as directed. Serve hot.

Serves 6 as a main course

Indian Rice with Shrimp

1 recipe Mexican Rice, with carrots and peas (page 445)
½ teaspoon ground cumin
¼ teaspoon ground coriander
¼ teaspoon ground turmeric
⅛ teaspoon crushed red pepper
½ pound medium shrimp, peeled and deveined
¼ cup minced fresh cilantro

Follow the directions for Mexican Rice, pureeing the cumin, coriander, turmeric, and red pepper with the tomato mixture in Step 2. When the liquid has been absorbed in Step 4, bury the shrimp in the rice. Cover and continue as directed. Stir to distribute the shrimp and serve hot, garnishing each serving with cilantro.

Serves 6 as a main course

Spicy Rice with Pork and Tomatillos

2 ancho chilies
1 recipe Mexican Rice, without optional ingredients (page 445)
¾ teaspoon ground cumin
8 tomatillos, husked and cut into eighths
1 pound pork tenderloin
Salt to taste

1. Preheat the oven to 400° F.
2. Place the chilies in a small saucepan, cover with water, and bring to a simmer. Remove from the heat and let stand until soft, about 10 minutes. Drain. Stem and seed the peppers. Follow the directions for Mexican Rice, pureeing the cumin and chilies with the tomato mixture in Step 2. Add the tomatillos with the chicken broth and salt in Step 4.
3. Meanwhile, place the pork tenderloin on a baking sheet. Roast until the pork is tender and slightly pink inside, about 15 minutes. Cut into 1-inch cubes.
4. When liquid has been absorbed in Step 4, spread the pork over the rice. Cover and continue as directed. Stir to distribute the pork. Season with salt. Serve hot.

Serves 6 as a main course

SPRING THAW

Cabin fever is not just about the cabin, it is also about the self. Winter makes the eyes turn inward and, for a few months, the cold justifies a perpetual posture of self-hugging. But eventually, self-fatigue strikes. You find yourself looking for a slender skein of blue in the late February flannel sky. The nights are still long, the winds are irascible, but your arms itch to embrace something or someone else.

You take an inordinate interest in reports of the groundhog, become impatient with root vegetables and sturdy, slow-cooked meals, oppressed by the cloister that was, for months, a comfort. You rail against the cabin, but really you're straining against the limits of the familiar. The first stirrings of spring are in fact a longing for something new that will eclipse the old and well-known.

Ever since the spring break ritual in college, I haven't been able to resist rushing south to intercept the season. At first it was just the sun but lately subtler signs, like the crayfish stirring in the fresh water bayous in southern Louisiana, have cured my cabin fever. By late February, cars clog the sides of the 80-mile "airline highway" that stretches from Baton Rouge to New Orleans, while their drivers dip nets or bare hands into the brown water to capture the miniature lobster-like crustaceans.

There is something atavistic about the predators' determination. They turn rocks to wake the crustaceans, float fish heads or beef fat to lure them, and never capture enough to make an "honorable," which is the Cajun way of saying "an endless," crayfish boil.

Crayfish grow wild throughout the Mississippi River valley, as well as in shallow streams in the Pacific Northwest and from Wisconsin to Maine. In fact, according to A. J. McClane, crayfish run in fresh water on every continent except Africa, ranging from the barely visible in size to the inch-long dwarf crayfish of America to the eight-pound Tasmanian crayfish. Of the 250 species native to North America, only a handful grow to a tempting size. I still think the sweetest, most succulent ones are those between three and a half to five inches that come from the swamps and bayous of southern Louisiana.

The little shelled monsters are farmed in Louisiana, Missouri, Texas, Mississippi, Alabama, and Arkansas. But Breaux Bridge, Louisiana, in the heart of Cajun country, continues to insist that it alone is La Capitale Mondiale des Ecrevisses, the crayfish capital of the world. This title may no longer relate to the actual quantity of crayfish caught in the small town, but it continues to connote a place where life is lived around Red Swamp crayfish, one of the twenty-nine different types of the crustacean found in Louisiana alone.

In that state, crayfish are called crawfish, and while the actual crustacean is the same, the difference in name, the rolling "craw" of Louisianans, as opposed to the pert, quick "cray" pronounced elsewhere in the United States, bespeaks a profound difference in the regard, the understanding, and the cooking of the tough-shelled creature.

On cold days, the crustaceans are shelled and baked in pies, simmered in buttery brown sauce to make étouffée, floated in dense, wintry gumbos with bacon and duck. But the crustacean can cozy up to artichokes (as a stuffing) and asparagus or spring mushrooms (as part of a sauté dish) or add a sweet chewiness when used to stuff white-fleshed spring fish. Crayfish bridge the seasons. Most often, they are simply boiled in spiced water and served hot or cold, a dish that, like breaded and fried crayfish tails, summons the spirit of a hot summer day on a boardwalk.

The tails and claws are sweet and firm, a herald of warm-weather flavors. The rich fat, which true devotees suck from the creatures' head, is a final taste of winter. Taken together, the meat and fat of a crayfish signal the triumph of sweetness over the primordial miasma of, well, mud.

In Breaux Bridge, crayfish are not called crawfish but "mud bugs." And no time of the year is as charged as the time when the earth begins to warm and the mud bugs start to stir from their muddy winter holes to scavenge the floors of freshwater streams. The little dinosaurs are not without ambivalence in their stirrings: They swim backwards, face toward home, body toward the unknown.

There are rational reasons for this particular propulsion. But under a warm sun, on a not-yet-warm day, it is difficult to avoid the poetry of a mud bug in motion. It is as if the wet, warming mud has pushed the crustaceans forth as emissaries of hope, a sign that paradigms are shifting, that another season is being pushed to the surface.

It is unclear whether it is the cabin or the bugs that get a fever, but it is undeniable that, once expelled, the miniature lobsterlike beings violently snap their tails and churn the muddy water; the stagnant moves and so, finally, does the human spirit. "The world's alive again," shouted one Buddy Ray Lepeau several years ago, waving a fistful of thrashing and snapping mud bugs on a late February morning outside Breaux Bridge.

Later that night there would be a zydecko band in a bar whose wooden floor crackled with crayfish shells underfoot. The air would be steamy and spicy while the harbingers of spring were boiled as if in so many witches' cauldrons—orgiastically warming the air, thawing the soul, banishing the cabin fever, the ghosts of winter, and a whole lot more.

But for a moment that morning, there was simply Buddy Ray shaking his mud bugs triumphantly in his muddy hands, shaking them like a rattle to rouse the gods of blue skies.

Crayfish-Stuffed Avocados

½ pound cooked crayfish tails
1 medium carrot, shredded
½ small zucchini, shredded
6 tablespoons fresh lime juice
¼ teaspoon Tabasco
1 teaspoon kosher salt, plus more to taste
Freshly ground pepper to taste
2 large ripe avocados, halved and pitted
2 tablespoons chopped fresh cilantro

Combine the crayfish, carrot, and zucchini in a medium bowl. Add the lime juice, Tabasco, salt, and pepper and toss to combine. Sprinkle the avocado halves lightly with salt and divide the crayfish mixture among them. Sprinkle with the cilantro and serve immediately.

Serves 4 as a first course

Farfalle with Crayfish and Artichokes

1 pound farfalle (also called bowtie pasta)

2 teaspoons olive oil

4 cloves garlic, minced

4 teaspoons seeded and minced jalapeño

4 tablespoons plus 2 teaspoons chopped Italian parsley

4 raw artichoke hearts, very thinly sliced

1 pound cooked crayfish tails

4 plum tomatoes, seeded and finely diced

6 tablespoons plus 2 teaspoons chopped fresh mint

¼ cup fresh lemon juice

1 teaspoon kosher salt

Freshly ground pepper to taste

1. Bring a large pot of lightly salted water to a boil. Add the farfalle and cook until al dente.

2. Meanwhile, heat the olive oil in a large nonstick skillet over medium heat. Add the garlic and cook, stirring, for 30 seconds. Add the jalapeño, 4 tablespoons of the parsley, and the artichokes and cook for 3 minutes, stirring often. Stir in the crayfish tails, cover, and cook until heated through, about 4 minutes. Add in the tomatoes and 6 tablespoons of the mint and cook for 1 minute.

3. Drain the pasta and transfer to a large bowl. Add the crayfish mixture and toss to combine. Add the lemon juice, salt, and pepper and mix well. Divide among 4 plates and garnish with the remaining parsley and mint. Serve immediately.

Serves 4 as a main course

Crayfish with Asparagus and Morels

1 teaspoon unsalted butter

4 tablespoons minced shallots

1 cup fresh morels, rinsed if sandy, and dried well

32 medium-thin asparagus spears, trimmed, tips cut off, halved lengthwise, and reserved

48 crayfish, steamed and shelled

4 teaspoons fresh lemon juice

¼ teaspoon kosher salt, plus more to taste

Freshly ground pepper to taste

1. Melt the butter in a large nonstick skillet. Add the shallots and sauté until soft, about 3 minutes. Add the morels and the asparagus tips and sauté until tender, about 5 minutes. Add the crayfish and cook for 2 minutes. Stir in the lemon juice, salt, and pepper.

2. Steam the asparagus spears until crisp-tender, about 4 minutes. Mound in the center of 4 plates and top with the crayfish mixture. Serve immediately.

Serves 4 as a main course

INDEX

Acorn Squash, 291
Almond:
Lemon Curd Tart with Candied, Topping,
84–85
Turnovers, Peach-, 228–29
Ancho Chili:
-Garlic Butter, 187
Pesto and Cornbread Stuffing, Roast Pheasant
with, 316–17
Puree, Butternut Squash and, 366
Apples, 323–24
Ginger-Roasted, with Vanilla Ice Cream, 325
Maple Poached, with Cinnamon-Glazed
Pecans and Cider Granita, 326
Pork Chops Baked with Onions and, 321
Puree, Roast Sweet Potato and, 365
Sauce, 325
Squash Baked with Cider and, 294
Tarte Tatin, 425
Walnut Upside-down Cake, 327
Artichoke(s), 285–86
Chicken with Tomatoes, Peppers, and, Roast,
289
Farfalle with Crayfish and, 451
Greek Lamb and Stew, 78
Pizzas, 351
Salad, see Salad, Artichoke
Steamed, Basic, 287
Arugula, Fava Bean Pudding with Shiitakes,
Bacon, and Wilted, 182
Asparagus, 27–28
Crayfish and Morels and, 452
and Farfalle with Lemon and Pepper, 29
Flounder Sauté with, and Crab Vinaigrette,
16
and Mint Flan with Poached Scallops and
Shrimp, 30–31
Sole with Ramps, and Roasted Potatoes,
67–68
Steamed, 29

Autumn:
almost, recipes for, 237–57
recipes for, 261–341
Avocados, Crayfish-Stuffed, 450

Banana, 432
Vanilla Roasted, 434
-Walnut Tarte Tatin, 426
Barbecuing and grilling, 112–13, 238
Korean Barbecue, 116
salsas, see Salsas
see also Herb mashes; Marinade(s); Seasoned
salts; Spice blends
Barley, Corn, and Lobster Salad, 154
Basil:
Cucumber Vinaigrette with Garlic and, 142
Oil, see Oils, infused, Basil
Tomato(es):
Lobster with, and Gnocchi, 211
and Mint Vinaigrette, 142
Oven-Dried, Penne with, 246
Sauce with Olives and, Fresh, 161
Bass, 197–98
with Mustard Mayonnaise, Broiled, 198
with Roasted Shallot and Garlic Puree and
Carmelized Leeks, Seared, 200–1
with Tomato and Black Olives, Steaks, 199
Beans:
Fava Beans, see Fava Beans
Flank and, Bozeman, 411–12
Lima Beans, see Lima Beans
Pumpkin Succotash with Dried, Tomatoes, and
Spicy Shrimp, 298–99
White Beans, see White Beans
Beef, 407–9
Filet Mignon of, with Roghan Josh Spices,
412–13
Flank and Beans, Bozeman, 411–12
Glaze, see Glazes, Beef
Salad, Thai, 107

Beef (*cont.*)
   Seared Steak with Caramelized Shallots, 410
   Stew:
      Goulash, 265
      Old-Fashioned, 264
   with Watercress and Cucumber, Peppered, 21
Beet Puree with Walnut Oil, Spiced, 367
Bisque:
   Butternut, Rosemary, 292
   Fennel and Potato, with Crumbed Salt Cod and Green Olives, 284
   Red Pepper, with Zucchini-Shrimp Salsa, 194–95
   Tomato, 162
   Turnip, 389
Blueberries, 219–21
   Muffins, 222
   Pie, Lattice, 224
   Sorbet, Ginger-, 221
   Soup with Orange-Herb Sorbet, Cold, 223
Bluefish, 202–3
   Chili-Lime, Grilled with Red Peppers and Corn, 204
   Coconut and Curry Marinated, with Lime Bean Dal, 205
   Soy, Ginger, and Mustard-Coated, with Grilled Scallions, 203–4
Bread:
   Pudding, Cranberry-Pear, 431
   Salad:
      Roast Chicken with, 73–74
      Tomato, 105
Broccoli Rabe, Halibut Topped with Oven-Dried Tomatoes, Shiitakes, and, 248
Broth, 368–70
   Carrot Consommé, 372
   Garlic:
      Custard with Shrimp and Tomato Broth, 177–78
      with Lobster or Chicken, 176–77
   Mushroom, Wild, 371
      with Buckwheat Noodles, 373
      Sweetbreads Braised in, 377
   Tomato, 371
   Vegetable, Roasted, 372–73
Brussels Sprouts, 398–99
   the Best, 401
   with Pancetta and Chestnuts, Sautéed, 402
   with Potato Gratin and Taleggio, 400

Buckwheat Noodles, Wild Mushroom Broth with, 373
Bulgur, 152
   Salad, Parsley and, 153
Butter:
   Ancho Chili-Garlic, 187
   Lime, 187
   Peach, 227
   Soft-Shell Crabs Sautéed in, 50
Butternut Squash, 290–91
   Bisque, Rosemary, 292
   Pasta with Sage and, 293
   Puree:
      Ancho Chili and, 366
      Orange-and-Ginger, 364

Cake:
   Apple Walnut Upside-down, 327
   Cream Cheese-Cherry Pound Cake with Sour Cherry Sauce, 90–91
   Hazelnut Chocolate, Rich, 337
   Pear, with Chocolate Sauce, Roasted, 332
Capon with Pecan Stuffing, Roasted, 336
Carrot(s):
   Consommé, 372
   Sesame-Crusted Tofu with Spinach and, 18
   Soup, Spiced Shrimp and, 374
Chanterelles, Scallops with, 310
Cherry(ies), 86–88
   Crumble, Sour, 88
   Fruit Soup with Shortbread Croutons, Mostly Cherry, 89–90
   Pound Cake with Sour Cherry Sauce, Cream Cheese-, 90–91
Chestnuts:
   Brussels Sprouts Sautéed with Pancetta and, 402
   Squab Salad with Bacon and, 314
Chicken, 69–70
   Artichokes, Tomatoes, and Peppers, Roast, 289
   with Bread Salad, Roast, 73–74
   with Couscous and Green Olives, Rolls, 11
   Garlic Broth with, 176–77
   Glaze, *See* Glazes, Chicken
   Herb-Crumbed Roasted, with Watercress, 72–73
   Lemon Roasted, 83
   Lime-Marinated, over Creamed Corn, 188
   with Morels, Fava Beans, and Spring Potatoes, 71–72

Paillards, Pepper and Onion-Topped, 19
Salad with Red Pepper Vinaigrette and Wilted
    Spinach, 146
Smoked Breasts of, 176–77
    Tomato and Pasta, 253
Stuffed with Mashed Turnips, 392
Chickpea(s):
    Orecchiette with Spinach and, 274
    Pie, Spinach and, 44–45
    Salad, Provençale, 103
Chili:
    Ancho Chili, *see* Ancho Chili
    Bluefish Grilled with Red Peppers and Corn,
        Lime-, 204
    Peppers Stuffed with Chilies and Corn, Sweet,
        196
    -Polenta Crust, Corn and Lobster Pie in a,
        189–90
    Squid, Tomato, and Roasted Poblano Stew,
        216
Chocolate:
    Cake, Rich Hazelnut, 337
    Sauce, Roasted Pear Cake with, 332
    Sorbet, Bittersweet, 232
Chorizo:
    Kale Soup with Potatoes and Sausage, 395–96
    Saffron Rice with Mussels, Sweet Potatoes,
        and, 305
Chowder:
    Corn, Cold Red Pepper and, 137
    Lobster, 210
Chutney, Tomato-Lemon, 160
Cilantro-Soy Paste, 121
Coconut:
    Bluefish with Lima Bean Dal, Coconut and
        Curry-Marinated, 205
    Soup, Indian-Spiced Zucchini-, 172
    Tarte Tatin, Pineapple-, 427
Cod and Smoked Salmon, Turnip Pancakes
    Topped with, 391
Consommé, Carrot, 372
Corn, 184–86, 238
    Barley, and Lobster Salad, 154
    Bluefish Grilled with Red Peppers and, Chili-
        Lime, 204
    Chowder, Cold Red Pepper and, 137
    on the Cob, Basic, 186
    Creamed, Lime-Marinated Chicken over, 188
    and Lobster Pie in a Chili-Polenta Crust,
        189–90

Peppers Stuffed with Chilies and, Sweet, 196
and Rice Stuffing, Spiced, 61
Salsa, Roasted, 126
Couscous:
    Chicken Rolls with Green Olives and, 11
    and Crab Salad with Cucumber Juice and
        Mint, 145
    Vegetables with Spiced Beef Glaze and,
        Roasted, 278
Crab(s):
    Salad with Cucumber Juice and Mint,
        Couscous and, 145
    Soft-shell, *see* Soft-shell Crabs
    Vinaigrette, Flounder Sauté with Asparagus
        and, 16
Cranberry beans, 179, 180
    with Garlic and Rosemary, 181
Cranberry-Pear Bread Pudding, 431
Crayfish, 448–50
    with Asparagus and Morels, 452
    Farfalle with, Artichokes and, 451
    -Stuffed Avocados, 450
Cucumber:
    Beef with Watercress and, Peppered, 21
    Ices, Tomato, Lobster, and Pepper Soup with
        Tomato-Cumin and Cucumber-Coriander,
        150–51
    Juice, 136
        Couscous and Crab Salad with, and Mint,
        145
    Salsa, Thai Mint and, 124
    Vinaigrette:
        with Basil and Garlic, 142
        Dill, 141
Custard Garlic with Shrimp and Tomato Broth,
    177–78

Dried fruit, 428–29
    Cranberry-Pear Bread Pudding, 431
    Fig Compote with Honey and Thyme, 430
    Prunes Poached in Red Wine, 430
Drying foods in the oven, *see* Oven-drying
Duck:
    Escarole Risotto with, 397
    Pumpkin Polenta with Pan-Seared Breast of,
        299–300
Dumplings, Curried Root Vegetable Stew with
    Mace-Currant, 266–67

Eggplant, 164–65, 237
    Arabic, 167

Eggplant (*cont.*)
    Grilled and Chilled Japanese, 102
    Grilled Summer Vegetables, Tuscan, 115
    Rissa's, 166
    Soup, Roast White, 168
    Steaks with Chinese Black Bean Sauce, 276
Escarole, 393, 394
    with Garlic, Braised, 395
    Risotto with Duck, 397
Espresso Granita, 233

Farfalle:
    Asparagus and, with Lemon and Pepper, 27
    with Butternut Squash and Sage, 293
    with Crayfish and Artichokes, 451
    Salad, Arugula, Tomato, and, 104
    Smoked Tomato and Chicken Pasta, 253
Fava Beans, 179, 180
    Chicken with Morels, and Spring Potatoes,
      71–72
    Pudding with Shiitakes, Bacon, and Wilted
      Arugula, 182
Fennel, 280–81
    with Parmesan, Braised, 283
    and Potato Bisque with Crumbed Salt Cod and
      Green Olives, 284
    Slaw with Orange Cumin, and Chilies, 282
Fettuccine:
    with Fresh Morels, 25
    with Mussels, 204
Fiddlehead Ferns, 32–33
    in Lemon Oil, Steamed in, 34
    with Pancetta, Sautéed, 34
    Veal with, and Shiitake Sauce, 35
Fish:
    Smoked, Brandade, 106
    see also specific types of fish
Flan with Poached Scallops and Shrimp,
    Asparagus and Mint, 30–31
Flounder, 63–64
    Meunière, A Fisherman's Perfect, 65
    with Mushrooms, Scallions, and Parsley, 66
    with Ramps, Asparagus, and Roasted Potatoes,
      67–68
    Sauté with Asparagus and Crab Vinaigrette, 16
Fruit:
    dried, *See* Dried Fruit
    Soup, Exotic, 437
    see also specific types of fruit

Game birds, 311–17
Garlic, 173–75

Bass with Roasted Shallot and Garlic Puree
    and Carmelized Leeks, Seared, 200–1
Broth:
    Custard with Shrimp and Tomato, 177–78
    with Lobster or Chicken, 176–77
Butter, Ancho Chili-, 187
Cranberry Beans with Rosemary and, 181
Cucumber Vinaigrette with Basil and, 142
Escarole with, Braised, 395
Lamb with Feta-Garlic Crust, Rack of, 77
Linguine with Lemon and, 176
Roast, 175
Spinach with Lemon and, 42
Vapor, Roasted Lemon and, 10
Ginger:
    Bluefish with Grilled Scallions, Soy and
      Mustard-Coated, 203–4
    -Roasted Apples with Vanilla Ice Cream, 325
    Shad, Potted, 56
    Sorbet, Blueberry-, 221
    -Soy Beef Glaze, Salmon Fillet with, 277
Glazes, 268–70
    Beef, 268–69, 272
      Salmon Fillet with Ginger-Soy, 277
      Scallops and Mushrooms and, 279
      Vegetables Roasted with Spiced, and
        Couscous, 278
    Chicken, 269
      Egg Noodles with Paprikás Sauce, 275
      Eggplant Steaks with Chinese Black Bean
        Sauce, 276
      Orecchiette with Chickpeas and Spinach,
        274
      Rich, 271
      Vegetables Steamed in, 273
    Tomato, Warm White Bean and Scallop Salad
      with Spicy, 375
Gnocchi, Lobster with Tomatoes, Basil, and,
    211
Goulash, 265
Grains, 152–53
Granita, 230–31
    Cider, Maple Poached Apples with Cinnamon-
      Glazed Pecans and, 326
    Espresso, 233
    Watermelon, 232
Grapefruit:
    Glazed Pink, 435
    Sorbet, 231
Grapes:
    Oven-Dried, 244

Linguine with Oven-Dried Tomatoes, Mushrooms, and Anchovies, 247

Vegetable Salad with Oven-Dried Tomatoes, Squash, Mushrooms and, Fall, 245–46

Grilling, see Barbecuing and grilling

Halibut Topped with Oven-Dried Tomatoes, Shiitakes, and Broccoli Rabe, 248

Hawayej, Zvia's, 119

Hazelnut(s), 334
Chocolate Cake, Rich, 337
Pears Pan-Roasted with Honey, Stilton, and, 330

Herb mashes, 118–19

Herb Soup, Lettuce and, 148

Hubbard Squash and Maple Pie, Blue, 294–95

Ice Cream:
Ginger-Roasted Apples with, 325
Honey Peach, 228

Jalapeño:
Lemon Grass and Mint Steam, Fiery, 8
Orange, Chili, and Rosemary Vapor, 12

Juices:
Tomato, see Tomato(es), Juice
Vegetable, 134–38

Kale, 393–94
and Oven-Dried Tomato Lasagna, 396–97
Rice with Andouille and, 446
Soup with Potatoes and Sausage, 395–96

Lamb, 75–76
and Artichoke Stew, Greek, 78
Chops, Artichoke-Mint Salad over, 20
with Feta-Garlic Crust, Rack of, 77
Middle Eastern Tomato, Split Pea, and Lamb Stew over Rice, 79
Shanks, 254, 352–53
Mediterranean, 355–56

Lasagna, Kale and Oven-Dried Tomato, 396–97

Leeks:
Bass with Roasted Shallot and Garlic Puree and Carmelized, Seared, 200–1
with Lemon and Parsley Oil, Poached, 132
Potato and Morel Salad with Truffle Oil Vinaigrette, 26

Lemon Grass Steam, Mint and Fiery, 8

Lemon(s), 80–81
Chicken, Roasted, 83
Chutney, Tomato-, 160

Fiddleheads Steamed in, Oil, 34
and Garlic Vapor, Roasted, 10
Linguine with Garlic and, 176
Oil, see Oils, infused, Lemon and Parsley
Preserved:
with Cardamom and Black Pepper, 82
Veal Shanks with, 356–57
Spinach with Garlic and, 42
Tart with Candied Almond Topping, Curd, 84–85
Vinaigrette, Mediterranean Lentil Salad with Thyme-, 155

Lentil Salad with Lemon-Thyme Vinaigrette, Mediterranean, 155

Lettuce, 139–40
Soup, Herb and, 148

Lima Beans, 179–80
Dal, Coconut and Curry-Marinated Bluefish with, 205
Ragout with Grilled Shrimp, 183
and Romaine Lettuce Slaw with Orecchiette, Fresh, 104–5

Lime:
Bluefish Grilled with Red Peppers and Corn, Chili-, 204
Butter, 187
-Marinated Chicken over Creamed Corn, 188

Linguine:
with Garlic and Lemon, 176
with Oven-Dried Tomatoes, Mushrooms, Grapes, and Anchovies, 247
with Pea Greens and Shrimp, 39
with Smoked Mussels and Tomatoes, 256

Lobster, 206–8
Chowder, 210
Garlic Broth with, 176–77
Pie in a Chili-Polenta Crust, Corn and, 189–90
Salad, Barley, Corn, and, 154
Smoked, 254
with Corn and Peppers over Soft Polenta, 254–55
Soup with Tomato-Cumin and Cucumber-Coriander Ices, Tomato, Pepper, and, 150–51
Steamed, Basic, 208
with Tomatoes, Basil, and Gnocchi, 211
and Wild Mushroom Salad, 209

Mango, 432–33
Marinade(s), 113

Marinade(s) (*cont.*)
  Cilantro-Soy Paste, 121
  Korean Barbecue, 116
  Spice Island, 117
  Tuscan, 114
Mayonnaise, Bass Broiled with Mustard, 198
Melon Salsa, Fiery Peanut and, 125
Mint:
  Basil Oil and, Zucchini with, 131
  Couscous and Crab Salad with Cucumber Juice
    and, 145
  Flan with Poached Scallops and Shrimp,
    Asparagus and, 30–31
  Salad over Lamb Chops, Artichoke-, 20
  Salsa, Thai Cucumber and, 124
  Steam, Fiery Lemon Grass and, 8
  Vinaigrette Tomato, Basil, and, 142
Morels, 22–24
  Chicken with, Fava Beans, and Spring
    Potatoes, 71–72
  Crayfish with Asparagus and, 452
  Fettuccine with Fresh, 25
  Gratin, 24
  Salad with Truffle Oil Vinaigrette, Potato,
    Leek, and, 26
Muffins, Blueberry, 222
Mushrooms:
  Broth, Wild, *see* Broth, Mushroom, Wild
  Chantereles, Scallops with, 310
  Morels, *see* Morels
  Oven-Dried, 243
    Linguine with Oven-Dried Tomatoes,
      Grapes, and Anchovies, 247
    Spinach Salad with Bacon and, 43
    Vegetable Salad with Oven-Dried Tomatoes,
      Squash, Grapes and, Fall, 245–46
  Parsley Pickled, 101
  Pheasant with Wild Mushroom Duxelles and
    Roasted Vegetables, 315
  Porcini, *see* Porcini Mushrooms
  Rabbit with Wild, Ragout, 416
  Shad Fillets Braised with Wild, and Tomatoes,
    55–56
  Shiitakes, *see* Shiitake Mushrooms
  Sole with, Scallions, and Parsley, 66
  Spinach Salad with Bacon and Oven-Dried, 43
Mussels, 301–2
  Fettuccine with, 304
  with Orecchiette and White Beans, 303
  Saffron Rice with, Chorizo, and Sweet
    Potatoes, 305

  Smoked, and Tomatoes with Pasta, 256
  Steamed, 303
Mustard:
  Bluefish with Grilled Scallions, Soy, Ginger,
    and Mustard-Coated, 203–4
  Mayonnaise, Bass Broiled with, 198
  Pork Loin with, Seed Crust, 322

Noodles:
  Buckwheat, Wild Mushroom Broth with, 373
  Egg Noodles with Paprikás Sauce, 275
Nuts, 333–35
  see also specific types of nuts

Oils, infused, 128–29
  Basil, 130
    and Mint, Zucchini with, 131
    Potato and Shrimp Salad with Peas and,
      132
  Lemon and Parsley, 130–31
    Leeks with, Poached, 132
    Squid, Salad with, 133
Olives:
  Bass Steaks with Tomato and Black, 199
  Chicken Rolls with Couscous and Green, 11
  Salsa, Moroccan Orange, Red Onion, and
    Black, 127
  Tomato Sauce with Basil and, Fresh, 161
Onion(s):
  Pizzettes, Marmalade, 350
  Pork Chops Baked with Apples and, 321
  Salad, My Mother's Tomato and Red, 159
  Salsa, Moroccan Orange, Red Onion, and
    Black Olive, 127
  Sorbet, Cold Blueberry Soup with Herb-,
    223
  Stuffing, Roasted Potato-, 62
  Yams with Red, Baked, 384
Orange(s):
  Oven-Dried Tomatoes, Rosemary-, 242
  Salsa, Moroccan Red Onion, Black Olive, and,
    127
  Vapor, Chili, Rosemary, and, 12
Orecchiette:
  with Chickpeas and Spinach, 274
  Lima Bean and Romaine Lettuce Slaw with,
    Fresh, 104–5
  Mussels with White Beans and, 303
Orzo Salad, Scallops Poached in Tomato Juice
    and, 138
Oven-drying, 238–48

Oysters and Watercress Ragout, Spaghetti Squash Topped with Smoked, 257

Pancetta:
Brussels Sprouts Sautéed with Chestnuts and, 402
Fiddleheads with, Sautéed, 34
Papaya, 432, 433
Parsley:
and Bulgur Salad, 153
Mushrooms, Pickled, 101
Oil, *see* Oils, infused, Lemon and Parsley Oil
Sole with Mushrooms, Scallions, and, 66
Zucchini Gratin with Thyme and, 170
Pasta:
Farfalle, *see* Farfalle
Fettuccine, *see* Fettuccine
Lasagna, Kale, and Oven Dried Tomato, 396–97
Linguine, *see* Linguine
Orecchiette, *see* Orecchiette
Penne with Oven-Dried Tomatoes and Basil, 246
Peach(es), 225–26
Butter, 227
Ice Cream, Honey, 228
Turnovers, Almond-, 222–29
Pea Greens, 36–37
Linguine with Shrimp and, 39
Salad with Sesame Dressing, Wilted, 38
and Snow Pea Soup, 38
Peanut Salsa, Fiery Melon and, 125
Pears, 328–29
Cake with Chocolate Sauce, Roasted, 332
Cranberry-, Bread Pudding, 431
Pan-Roasted, with Honey, Hazelnuts, and Stilton, 330
Pork Tenderloin with and Ginger Beer Sauce, 331
Peas:
Greens, *see* Pea Greens
Potato and Shrimp Salad with, and Basil Oil, 132
Snap Peas, *see* Snap Peas
Split Peas, Middle Eastern Lamb Stew over Rice with Tomatoes and, 79
Pecan(s), 334
Indulgence, 338–39
Maple Poached Apples with Cinnamon-Glazed, and Cider Granita, 326
Stuffing, Roasted Capon with, 336

Penne with Oven-Dried Tomatoes and Basil, 246
Pepper, Preserved Lemons with Cardamom and Black, 82
Pepper(s), 191–92, 238
Bisque with Zucchini-Shrimp Salsa, Roasted, 194–95
Chicken:
with Artichokes, Tomatoes, and Peppers, Roast, 289
Paillards, Pepper and Onion-Topped, 19
Grilled Summer Vegetables, Tuscan, 115
Red Peppers, *see* Red Pepper(s)
Roasted, 193
Soup with Tomato-Cumin and Cucumber-Coriander Ices, Tomato, Lobster, and, 150–51
Stuffed with Chilies and Corn, Sweet, 196
Pesto:
Oven-Dried Tomato, 244
Pheasant with Ancho Chili and Cornbread Stuffing, 316–17
Potato Watercress Soup with Watercress-Walnut, 149
Winter, Roasted Vegetable Fagioli with, 378–79
Pheasant, 311, 312
with Ancho Chili Pesto and Cornbread Stuffing, 316–17
with Wild Mushroom Duxelles and Roasted Vegetables, Roast, 315
Pie:
Blueberry Lattice, 224
Blue Hubbard Squash and Maple, 294–95
Corn and Lobster, in a Chili-Polenta Crust, 189–90
Windfall, 163
Pineapple, 432
Glazed, 435
Sorbet, Cinnamon, 436
Tarte Tatin, Coconut-, 427
Pizza, 346–48
Artichoke, 351
Dough, Basic, 348–49
Onion Marmalade Pizzettes, 350
Tomato Pizzettes, Roasted, 349–50
Polenta:
Pumpkin, Pan-Seared Duck Breast with, 299–300
Quail with Rosemary on Soft, 313

Porcini Mushrooms:
  Broth, Wild Mushroom, *see* Broth, Mushroom, Wild
  Rabbit with Wild Mushroom Ragout, 416
Pork, 318–19
  Chops Baked with Apples and Onions, 321
  Loin with Mustard Seed Crust, 322
  Rice with Tomatillos and, Spicy, 447
  Sausage, *see* Sausage
  Tenderloins:
    Caribbean Jack, 320
    with Pears and Ginger Beer Sauce, 331
Potato(es):
  Bisque with Crumbed Salt Cod and Greek Olives, Fennel and, 284
  Brussels Sprout and, Gratin with Taleggio, 400
  Chicken with Morels, Fava Beans, and, Spring, 71–72
  Kale Soup with Sausage and, 395–96
  -Onion Stuffing, Roasted, 62
  Salad, *see* Salad, Potato
  Salmon:
    Seared Scallops with Warm, and Snap Pea Salad, 17
    with Sugar Snaps in Shrimp Broth, 59–60
  Smoked Fish Brandade, 106
  Sole with Ramps, Asparagus, and Roasted, 67–68
  Watercress Soup with Watercress-Walnut Pesto, 149
Pudding:
  Bread, Cranberry-Pear, 431
  Fava Bean, with Shiitakes, Bacon, and Wilted Arugula, 182
  Walnut Steamed, with Vanilla-Orange Sauce, 340–41
Pumpkin, 296–98
  Polenta, Pan-Seared Duck Breast with, 299–300
  Succotash with Dried Beans, Tomatoes, and Spicy Shrimp, 298–99
Puree, 363–64
  Apple and Sweet Potato, Roasted, 365
  Beet, with Walnut Oil, Spiced, 367
  Butternut Squash:
    Ancho Chili and, 366
    Orange and Ginger, 364
  Winter Vegetable, 365

Quail, 311, 312
  with Rosemary on Soft Polenta, 313

Rabbit, 414–15
  Mole, 420–21
  with Pappardelle, 418–19
  Pomegranate, Dark Roasted, 417
  and Wild Mushroom Ragout, 416
Raspberries, 92–93
  -Champagne Soup with Rosemary-Raspberry Sorbet, 95
  Sorbet, 94
  Vinegar, Tarragon-, 93
Red Pepper(s), 191–92
  Artichoke Salad with Roasted Peppers and Shiitakes, Fall, 288
  Bisque with Zucchini-Shrimp Salsa, Roasted, 194–95
  Bluefish Grilled with Corn and Chili-Lime, 204
  Juice, Sweet, 136
    and Corn Chowder, Cold, 137
  Roasted, 193
  Stuffed with Chilies and Corn, Sweet, 196
  Tapenade, Sweet, 194
  Vinaigrette:
    Balsamic, 143
    Chicken Salad with Wilted Spinach and, 146
    Cumin, 144
Rice, 441, 443–44
  with Andouille and Kale, 446
  Indian, with Shrimp, 446
  Lamb Stew over, Middle Eastern Tomato, Split Pea, and, 79
  Mexican, 445
  Saffron Rice with Mussels, Chorizo, and Sweet Potatoes, 305
  Spicy, with Pork and Tomatillos, 447
  Stuffing, Spiced Corn and, 61
  Trout with Sticky, Zucchini, and Pine Nuts, 13
  see also Risotto
Risotto, 443
  and Duck, Escarole, 397
  with Yams and Sage, 385–86
Rosemary:
  Butternut Bisque, 292
  Cranberry Beans with Garlic and, 181
  Oven-Dried Tomatoes, Orange-, 242
  Quails with, on Soft Polenta, 313
  -Raspberry Sorbet, Raspberry-Champagne Soup with, 95
  Vapor, Orange, Chili, and, 12

Salad, 139–41
  Artichoke:
    -Mint, over Lamb Chops, 20
    Raw, 287
    with Roasted Peppers and Shiitakes, Fall,
      288
  Barley, Corn, and Lobster, 154
  Beef, Thai, 107
  Bread:
    Roast Chicken with, 73–74
    Tomato, 105
  Bulgur and Parsley, 153
  Chicken:
    with Bread, Roast, 73–74
    with Red Pepper Vinaigrette and Wilted
      Spinach, 146
  Chickpea, Provençale, 103
  Couscous and Crab, with Cucumber Juice and
    Mint, 145
  Fall Vegetable, with Oven-Dried Tomatoes,
    Squash, Mushrooms, and Grapes, 245–
    246
  Lentil, with Lemon-Thyme Vinaigrette,
    Mediterranean, 155
  Lobster and Wild Mushroom, 209
  Orzo, Scallops Poached in Tomato Juice and,
    138
  Pea Green, with Sesame Dressing, 38
  Potato:
    Leek, Morel, and, with Truffle Oil Vinai-
      grette, 26
    Shrimp and, with Peas and Basil Oil, 132
    and Snap Pea, Seared Salmon Scallops with
      Warm, 17
  Shrimp:
    with Peas and Basil Oil, Potato and, 132
    with Tarragon Vinaigrette, White Bean and,
      156
  Smoked Vegetable, 252
  Spinach, with Bacon and Oven-Dried Mush-
    rooms, 43
  Squab, with Bacon and Chestnuts, 314
  Squid, with Lemon and Parsley Oil, 133
  Tomato, see Tomato(es), Salad
  White Bean and Scallop, with Spicy Tomato
    Glaze, Warm, 375
Salad dressing, 140
  Vinaigrette, see Vinaigrette
Salmon, 57–59
  Braised in Winter Vegetable Essence, 376
  Ginger-Soy Beef Glaze, Fillet with, 277

Potato and Snap Pea Salad, Seared Salmon
    Scallops and Warm, 17
  and Shiitakes Wrapped in Lettuce Leaves, 9
  Smoked, Turnip Pancakes Topped with Cod
    and, 391
  Snap Peas:
    and Potatoes in Shrimp Broth, 59–60
    Salad, Seared Salmon Scallops with Warm
      Potato and, 17
  Steaks, Teriyaki, 60
  Whole, Stuffed and Roasted, 61
Salsa, 123–24
  Corn, Roasted, 126
  Melon and Peanut, Fiery, 125
  Moroccan Orange, Red Onion, and Black
    Olive, 127
  Thai Cucumber and Mint, 124
Sausage:
  Kale Soup with Potatoes and, 395–96
  Rice with Andouille and Kale, 446
  Saffron Rice with Mussels, Sweet Potatoes, and
    Chorizo, 305
Scallops, 306–7
  Asparagus and Mint Flan with Poached, and
    Shrimp, 30–31
  with Beef Glaze and Mushrooms, 279
  with Chanterelles, 310
  Faux Fried, with Faux Ketchup, 308
  Mediterranean, 309
  Salad with Spicy Tomato Glaze, Warm White
    Bean and, 375
  Tomato Juice Poached, with Orzo Salad, 138
Seafod, see specific types of seafood
Seasoned salts, 118–19
  Spiced Salt, 120
Sesame-Crusted Tofu with Carrots and Spinach,
  18
Shad, 53–54
  Ginger Potted, 56
  with Wild Mushrooms and Tomatoes, Fillets
    Braised with, 55–56
Shiitake Mushrooms:
  Artichoke Salad with Roasted Peppers and,
    Fall, 288
  Broth, Wild Mushroom, see Broth, Mushroom,
    Wild
  Fava Bean Pudding with, Bacon and Wilted
    Arugula, 182
  Halibut Topped with Oven-Dried Tomatoes,
    and Broccoli Rabe, 248
  Lobster and Wild Mushroom Salad, 209

Shiitake Mushrooms (*cont.*)
  Rabbit with Wild Mushroom Ragout, 416
  Salmon and, Wrapped in Lettuce Leaves, 9
  Scallops with Beef Glaze and, 279
  Veal with Fiddlehead and, Sauce, 35
Shrimp:
  Asparagus and Mint Flan with Poached
      Scallops, 30–31
  and Carrot Soup, Spiced, 374
  Garlic Custard with, and Tomato Broth,
      177–78
  Indian Rice with, 446
  Lima Bean Ragout with Grilled, 183
  Pea, Greens and, Linguine with, 39
  Pumpkin Succotash with Dried Beans,
      Tomatoes, and Spicy, 298–99
  Salad:
    with Peas and Basil Oil, Potato and, 132
    with Tarragon Vinaigrette, White Bean and,
        156
  Salmon with Sugar Snaps and Potatoes in,
      Broth, 59–60
  Salsa, Roasted Pepper Bisque with Zucchini-,
      194–95
Smoked foods, 249–50
  Chicken Breasts, 252
    Tomato and Pasta, 253
  Lobsters, 254
    with Corn and Peppers over Soft Polenta,
        254–55
  Mussels and Tomatoes, Pasta with, 256
  Oyster and Watercress Ragout, Spaghetti
      Squash Topped with, 257
  Trout in Carmelized Apple and Onion Broth,
      255–56
  Vegetables:
    Autumn, 251
    Salad, 252
Snap Peas:
  Salad, Seared Salmon Scallops with Warm
      Potato and, 17
  Salmon with, and Potatoes in Shrimp Broth,
      59–60
Snow Pea Soup, Pea Green and, 38
Soft-shell Crabs, 46–49
  with Black Bean Sauce, 51
  Sautéed in Brown Butter, 50
  Thai, 52
Sole:
  Meunière, A Fisherman's Perfect, 65
  with Mushrooms, Scallions, and Parsley, 66

  with Ramps, Asparagus, and Roasted Potatoes,
      67–68
Sorbet, 230–31
  Blueberry Soup with Orange-Herb, Cold, 223
  Chocolate, Bittersweet, 232
  Grapefruit, 231
  Pineapple Cinnamon, 436
  Raspberry, 94
    Raspberry-Champagne Soup with
        Rosemary-, 95
Soup:
  Bisque, *see* Bisque
  Broth, *see* Broth
  Carrot, Spiced Shrimp and, 374
  Cherry Fruit, with Shortbread Croutons, 89–90
  Chowder, *see* Chowder
  Cold, 89–90, 95, 147–51, 223, 437
  Exotic Fruit, 437
  Kale, with Potatoes and Sausage, 395–96
  Lettuce and Herb, 148
  Potato Watercress, with Watercress-Walnut
      Pesto, 149
  Raspberry-Champagne, with Rosemary-
      Raspberry Sorbet, 95
  Snow Pea, Pea Green and, 38
  Tomato:
    Bisque, 162
    Lobster, and Pepper Soup, with Tomato-
        Cumin and Cucumber-Coriander Ices,
        150–51
  Yam, with Yogurt, 383
  Zucchini-Coconut, Indian-Spiced, 172
Spaghetti Squash Topped with Smoked Oyster
    and Watercress Ragout, 257
Spice blends, 118–19
  Hawayej, Zvia's, 119
  Spice Paste for the Thrill of the Grill, 122
Spinach, 40–41
  Chicken Salad with Red Pepper Vinaigrette
      and Wilted, 146
  and Chickpea Pie, 44–45
  with Garlic and Lemon, 42
  Orecchiette with Chickpeas and, 274
  Salad with Bacon and Oven-Dried Mush-
      rooms, 43
  Sesame-Crusted Tofu with Carrots and, 18
Spring:
  almost, recipes, 441–52
  recipes for, 3–95
Squab, 212
  Salad with Bacon and Chestnuts, 314

Squash, 290–91
  Acorn, 291
    with Apples and Cider, Baked, 294
  Blue Hubbard, and Maple Pie, 294–95
  Butternut Squash, *see* Butternut Squash
  Oven-Dried Summer, 243
    Vegetable Salad with Oven-Dried Tomatoes,
      Mushrooms, Grapes, and, Fall, 245–46
  Spaghetti Squash Topped with Smoked Oyster
    and Watercress Ragout, 257
Squid, 212–14
  Marinated, 215
  Paillard of, 217–18
  Salad with Lemon and Parsley Oil, 133
  Tomato, and Roasted Poblano Stew, 216
Stew, 263
  Beef:
    Curried Root Vegetable, with Mace-Currant
      Dumplings, 266–67
    Goulash, 265
    Old-Fashioned, 264
Stock, 268, 269
Stuffing:
  Corn and Rice, Spiced, 6
  Cornbread, Roast Pheasant with Ancho Chili
    Pesto and, 316–17
  Pecan, Roasted Capon with, 336
  Potato-Onion, Roasted, 62
Summer:
  almost, recipes for, 99–107
  recipes for, 111–233
Sweet Potatoes:
  Puree, Roasted Apple and, 365
  Saffron Rice with Mussels, Chorizo, and,
    305

Tapenade, Sweet Pepper, 194
Tarragon Vinaigrette:
  Tomato, 143
  White Bean and Shrimp Salad with, 156
Tarte Tatin, 422–23
  Apple, 425
  Banana-Walnut, 426
  Pastry, 424
  Pineapple-Coconut, 427
Tart with Candied Almond Topping, Lemon
  Curd, 84–85
Thyme:
  Lemon-Thyme Vinaigrette, Mediterranean
    Lentil Salad with, 155
  Zucchini Gratin with Parsley and, 170

Tofu with Carrots and Spinach, Sesame-Crusted,
  18
Tomato(es), 157–58, 238
  Basil:
    and Mint Vinaigrette, 142
    Sauce with Olives and Fresh, 161
  Bass Steaks with Black Olives and, 199
  Bisque, 162
  Broth, 371
    Garlic Custard with Shrimp and, 177–
      178
  Chicken with Artichokes, Peppers, and, Roast,
    289
  Chutney, Lemon-, 160
  Juice, 136
    Scallops Poached in, with Orzo Salad,
      138
    Strained, 245
  Lamb Stew over Rice, Middle Eastern Split Pea
    and, 79
  Lobster with, Basil, and Gnocchi, 211
  Oven-Dried:
    Basic, 240, 242
    Halibut Topped with, Shiitakes, and
      Broccoli Rabe, 248
    Lasagna, Kale and, 396–97
    Linguine with, Mushrooms, Grapes, and
      Anchovies, 247
    Penne with Basil and, 246
    Pesto, 244
    Rosemary-Orange, 242
    Vegetable Salad with, Squash, Mushrooms,
      and Grapes, Fall, 245–46
  Pie, Windfall, 163
  Pizzettes, Roasted, 349–50
  Pumpkin, Succotash with Dried Beans, and
    Spicy Shrimp, 298–99
  Salad:
    Bread, 105
    Farfalle, Arugula, and, 104
    and Red Onion, My Mother's, 159
  Sauce:
    with Olives and Basil, Fresh, 161
    Zucchini Pasta with Fresh, 171
  Scallops, Mediterranean, 309
  Smoked, and Chicken Pasta, 253
  Soup:
    Bisque, 162
    Lobster, and Pepper, with Tomato-Cumin
      and Cucumber-Coriander Ices, 150–51
  Squid, and Roasted Poblano Stew, 216

Tomato(es) (*cont.*)
    Vinaigrette:
        Basil, and Mint, 142
        Tarragon, 143
Trout:
    Smoked, in Carmelized Apple and Onion
        Broth, 255–56
    with Sticky Rice, Zucchini, and Pine Nuts, 13
Turnips, 387–89
    Bisque, 389
    Chicken Stuffed with Mashed, 392
    with Crispy Shallots, Mashed, 390
    Pancakes Topped with Cod and Smoked
        Salmon, 391

Vanilla:
    Roasted Bananas, 43
    Sugar, 434
Veal:
    with Fiddlehead and Shiitake Sauce, 35
    Shanks, 352–53
        with Preserved Lemon, 356–57
Vegetable juices, 134–38
Vegetables:
    Beef Glaze and Couscous, Vegetables Roasted
        with Spiced, 278
    Broth, Roasted, 372–73
    Chicken Glaze, Steamed in, 273
    Fagioli with Winter Pesto, Roasted, 378–79
    Grilled Summer, Tuscan, 115
    Pheasant with Wild Mushroom Duxelles and
        Roasted, 315
    Puree, Winter, 365
    Smoked:
        Autumn, 251
        Salad, 252
    Stew with Mace-Currant Dumplings, Curried
        Root, 266–67
    see also specific vegetables
Venison, 403–4
    Burgers, 405
    Cider Stew, 406
Vinaigrette:
    Cucumber:
        with Basil and Garlic, 142
        Dill, 141
    Lemon-Thyme, Mediterranean Lentil Salad
        with, 155
    Red Pepper, *see* Red Pepper(s), Vinaigrette
    Tarragon, *see* Tarragon Vinaigrette

Tomato:
    Basil, and Mint, 142
    Tarragon, 143
Vinegar, Raspberry-Tarragon, 93

Walnuts, 334
    Pudding with Vanilla-Orange Sauce, Steamed,
        340–41
    Tarte Tatin, Banana-, 426
    Upside-down Cake, Apple, 327
Watercress:
    Beef with Cucumber and, Peppered, 21
    Chicken with, Herb-Crumbed Roasted, 72–
        73
    Ragout, Spaghetti Squash with Smoked Oyster
        and, 257
    Soup with Watercress-Walnut Pesto Potato,
        149
Watermelon Granita, 232
White Beans:
    Mussels with Orecchiette and, 303
    Puree, 357
    and Scallop Salad with Spicy Glaze, Warm,
        375
    and Shrimp Salad with Tarragon Vinaigrette,
        156
    Vegetable Fagioli with Winter Pesto, Roasted,
        378–79
Winter:
    almost, recipes for, 345–57
    recipes for, 361–437

Yams, 380–82
    with Red Onions, Baked, 384
    Risotto with, and Sage, 385–86
    Soup with Yogurt, 383
Yogurt:
    Cheese, making, 31
    Yam Soup with, 383

Zucchini, 169–70, 237
    with Basil Oil and Mint, 131
    -Coconut Soup, Indian-Spiced, 172
    Gratin with Parsley and Thyme, 170
    Grilled Summer Vegetables, Tuscan, 115
    Oven-Dried Summer Squash, 243
    Pasta with Fresh Tomato Sauce, 171
    -Shrimp Salsa, Roasted Pepper Bisque with,
        194–95
    Trout with Sticky Rice, Pine Nuts, and, 13